MOTIVATION, CAREER STRIVING, AND AGING

Joel O. Raynor
State University of New York
at Buffalo

Elliot E. Entin
Ohio University

With contributions by
Eileen T. Brown
Louis D. English
Norman T. Feather
Hillary S. Liber
Howard B. Pearlson
Robin J. Ridley
Richard C. Teitelbaum

● HEMISPHERE PUBLISHING CORPORATION
Washington   New York   London

DISTRIBUTION OUTSIDE THE UNITED STATES
McGRAW-HILL INTERNATIONAL BOOK COMPANY
Auckland   Bogotá   Guatemala   Hamburg
Johannesburg   Lisbon   London   Madrid   Mexico
Montreal   New Delhi   Panama   Paris   San Juan
São Paulo   Singapore   Sydney   Tokyo   Toronto

To John W. Atkinson
Recipient of the Distinguished Scientific Contribution Award,
American Psychological Association, 1979
and "captain of the team"

Table 6 on page 28 is redrawn after Tables 42 and 43 in Harvey C. Lehman, Age and Achievement, *published by Princeton University Press (copyright 1953 by the American Philosophical Society), pp. 250–251. Reprinted by permission of Princeton University Press.*

MOTIVATION, CAREER STRIVING, AND AGING

1 2 3 4 5 6 7 8 9 0   B C B C   8 9 8 7 6 5 4 3 2 1

This book was set in Press Roman by Hemisphere Publishing Corporation. The editors were Karen Zauber and Edward Millman; the production supervisor was Miriam Gonzalez; and the typesetter was Linda Holder.
Bookcrafters, Inc., was printer and binder.

Library of Congress Cataloging in Publication Data

Raynor, Joel O
    Motivation, career striving, and aging.

    Bibliography: p.
    Includes indexes.
    1. Achievement motivation. 2. Occupations—
Psychological aspects. 3. Time perspective.
4. Aging—Psychological aspects. I. Entin,
Elliot E., date, joint author. II. Brown,
Eileen T., joint author. III. Title.
BF503.R39   153.8   80-27082
ISBN 0-89116-189-9 (Hemisphere)
ISBN 0-07-051274-4 (McGraw-Hill)

Contents

Preface

The beginning of our collaborative effort can be traced back to the mid-1960s when we were graduate students at the University of Michigan. We were both excited by the work of the people at the university on relating individual differences in personality to motivation in particular situations. By that time the groundwork had been laid for systematic research on achievement motivation. At the university we had the benefit of continuing interaction with others who were working on various aspects of achievement motivation, such as Marvin Brown, Matina Horner, Norman Feather, Stuart Karabenick, and Robert Moulton. To us the guiding light of this informal group was Jack Atkinson, to whom we have dedicated this volume. We were able to develop a sense of what had gone before and what it was like to work on the frontier of a field, to contribute to an ongoing research program. We both came to believe in the tradition that combines the experimental analysis of human behavior with the use of mathematical models to represent theory and yet accounts for individual differences in personality. We believed this tradition offered a framework for building a psychology of personality and motivation and a framework for further research and theorizing.

It now seems inevitable that our collaboration in data collection and analysis on our dissertation projects would continue with our respective colleagues and students as we took up our university careers at SUNY/Buffalo and Ohio University. In 1974 we realized that a reasonable goal would be to collate our efforts and those of our collaborators to extend, elaborate, refute, and/or alter the initial elaboration of expectancy X value theory of achievement motivation. This position, now referred to as a more general expectancy X value theory of achievement motivation, guided our early research in the 1970s. Soon our efforts extended to other areas as our students and colleagues began to point out inadequacies, weaknesses, and implications that had not been considered previously. Our own experience in learning more about the implications of the theory and how to test them continued to suggest new directions for further work. Also, as some of the data disconfirmed expectations, and we began to determine what that data meant, new research was suggested to test out the emerging means of modifying theory to fit the data. We soon found that we had moved sufficiently beyond the initial guiding ideas. As a result, the present volume would not only provide evidence concerning the validity of the more general theory of achievement motivation (Chapter 2) but would also suggest means of accounting for data not consistent with it and, in doing so, extend our conceptual framework (Chapters 11 and 13).

Programmatic research over time on the same general topic and using the same general research tools has been an exciting experience for us. There are several distinct advantages to this approach over a more piecemeal approach, not the least of which is being able to correct one's own mistakes. Changes in theory, in interpretation of research findings, and in extension of past empirical work have come about so rapidly that there has been little time to tire of the project. Thus while we have examined the previous research on achievement motivation concerning choice (Chapter 2), performance level (Chapter 7 and the summary in Chapter 2), persistence (Chapter 3), the Zeigarnik effect (Chapter 9), the use of the *n* Achievement score as a dependent rather than an independent variable (Chapter 14), and the relationship between achievement motivation and learning (Chapter 8), we have also been able to explore some new areas, such as in the distinction between success as a personal standard and as a criterion for moving on to subsequent activity (Chapter 4), the motivational analysis of future plans (Chapter 5), the effects of psychological distance as both time and task hierarchies (Chapter 6), the relationships between self-importance, future importance, and self-possession of attributes (Chapters 10 and 11), achievement motivation and causal attribution in contingent and noncontingent paths (Chapter 12), and the major extension of theory to the relationship between motivation and aging (Part IV, Chapters 13 to 18).

We have used some general guidelines, which have worked reasonably well over time: (1) state the existing theory explicitly so that it can be tested and so that we can know when its implications are disconfirmed by data; (2) generate evidence in support of the theory so that the theory can be taken more seriously; (3) remember that contradictory data provide the basis for change in theory, and determine what the data mean when they do not confirm initial expectations; (4) revise the theory when we believe that disconfirming evidence should be taken seriously (usually after several replications of the disconfirming finding) and (5) figure out the implications of the revised theoretical statement. We have tried to take this last step, but we recognize that our latest extension of theory introduces so many new variables that it will take some time before precise specifications, particularly in a mathematical model, will allow explicit derivation.

We find that our work is best understood as a very personal experience—in terms of our newer ideas—from the internal rather than from the external viewpoint. It is not easy to be one's own critic. We have not liked being wrong when the data have come in. Being wrong is difficult to deal with, but a scientist must keep a firm grasp on the ultimate goals of science. Otherwise, there is the temptation to (1) change rather than continue in the same area, to turn to some currently popular research area where so little is known that it is hard to be wrong or (2) defend the status quo by hiding, disregarding, or explaining away disconfirming evidence so that there seems to be no need to change theory. In fact, the theoretical perspective presented in Part IV of this book is concerned with predicting the conditions under which scientists and others in psychological careers might take one of the two options above, or other options. Our one constant goal has been to provide an explicit and testable theory that will explain the behavior of the individual(s) developing that theory! We suggest that this should be a legitimate criterion for evaluation of a theory about human behavior in life situations. We hope that this continuing self-corrective process of science can offer the reader some better ideas and some research findings of interest, and we hope that we are moving closer to explaining our own behavior as scientists. Our treatment of the relationship between motivation, aging, and stages of striving makes an explicit attempt to do so. We also recognize the inadequacy of such theory at this stage in the development of the field of psychology and that eventually this theory will give way to better ideas based on more adequate research.

In preparing this volume we have had the help of several individuals in addition to those acknowledged throughout the text. We owe a special thanks to Richard Teitelbaum, who carried out many of the computer simulations and data analyses that appear in the book. We thank Marilyn Freedman and Ellen Konor-Goldband, who assisted in this work, Dianne Workman, who provided valuable help and assistance in carrying out several research projects, and Linda Hereth and Katherine Baird, who typed the manuscript, which was no small task given the continual revisions that were made as additional data analyses and theoretical modifications required changes.

We would like to acknowledge and thank the following publishers for kindly granting permission to reprint or adapt materials from books and journals: Academic Press, American Psychological Association, Hemisphere Publishing Corporation, and Princeton University Press.

Joel O. Raynor
Elliot E. Entin

1

Introduction and Overview

Joel O. Raynor and Elliot E. Entin

HISTORICAL PERSPECTIVE

The present volume represents a continuation and extension of theory and research on human motivation whose contemporary antecedents can be traced back more than 30 years to the development and validation of the *n* Achievement measure of the achievement motive (1947) and the test anxiety measure of the motive to avoid failure (1952), and whose historical roots lie in the work begun more than 50 years ago by Kurt Lewin and his students. The initial theoretical analysis of behavior using what is now called an expectancy X value theory of action was stated by Lewin, Dembo, Festinger, and Sears (1944) in their resultant valuence theory of level of aspiration and was expanded by Atkinson (1957) to include both relatively stable individual differences in personality and a more precise statement of the inverse relationship between expectancy and value found for achievement-oriented activity. Periodic progress reports of the contemporary program have dealt with the development and validation of the *n* Achievement measure of the achievement motive (McClelland, Atkinson, Clark, & Lowell, 1953), and the effects of individual differences in the achievement motive on (1) fantasy and action (Atkinson, 1958), (2) entrepreneurial activity in society (McClelland, 1961) and (3) choice, performance level, and persistence in both laboratory and life situations (Atkinson & Feather, 1966). The latest precursors of the present volume (Atkinson & Raynor, 1974, 1978) ended by extending the conceptual analysis to motivation for achievement in important life situations, whether that be a critical test of some intellective ability or of some important life goal.

The newer theoretical efforts presented in this volume, which end by stating a general theory of personality functioning and change based on an expectancy X value approach to the study of motivation and personality, must also be seen in the context of basic revisions concerning the definition of the problem of motivation—as the study of change of (immediate) activity or of the recurring patterns of activity over time—as suggested by the theory of the dynamics of action (Atkinson & Birch, 1970, 1974, 1978a, 1978b) and analysis of motivation and career striving (Raynor, 1974a, 1974b).

In the present volume we continue the systematic use of a general expectancy X value approach to the study of motivation. Our work can be taken as an elaboration, extension, and specification of the approaches of Lewin (1938), McClelland (1951, 1961), and Atkinson (1957, 1964) as carried out through the study of achievement-oriented action—activity where there is some standard of good performance against which immediate performance can be evaluated, there is some uncertainty as to the outcome (success or failure), and the person feels responsible for these outcomes. Or, it can be taken as a general approach to the study of the individual in a particular situation where individuals believe that the outcomes of their actions may define their self-identity. From our perspective, immediate behavior is conceived of as a series of steps in a path whose motivational impetus comes from outcomes of that behavior in the anticipated future, the retrospected past, and/or the immediately evaluated present, and whose outcomes can be used by the individual as a means of self-identity and self-esteem. Individual differences in personality dispositions (e.g., motives) are assumed to interact with these time-linked sources of value and their subjective probability of attainment (expectancy) to determine motivation of immediate activity. The newer theory integrates the study of motivation and personality from the perspective of Maslow (1957) and Rogers (1959) with the more research-oriented and experimentally based theory of achievement motivation (Atkinson & Feather, 1966; Atkinson & Raynor, 1974, 1978) to yield a general theory of personality, motivation, and action. The present volume presents the work that led from the earlier ideas to the current ones.

It is important that the work included here be viewed in the context of the previous research and theory, of which it is but the latest version. The issues and problems we are concerned with in part owe their importance to what has gone before. Previous theory and research defined the boundary between what we believed we knew at the outset and what we needed to find out. Our work is certainly not a "new beginning." We are committed to the idea and practice of programmatic research over time—the continued investigation of a topic with common research methods and from a particular theoretical perspective that evolves through attempts to account for those research findings that emerge. In this way theory is initially based on data, comes to have an increasingly more adequate empirical foundation, becomes increasingly more sophisticated as it changes to fit the newer data, and (ultimately) can be abandoned in favor of a more adequate theoretical perspective when that is demanded by the discrepancies between existing theory and newer data. Good theory in science is explicit enough so that its implications can be disconfirmed; the better the theory, the longer it takes to be eventually disconfirmed, but sooner or later it will be. In fact, the theory (presented in chapter 13) spells out those psychological factors that are the determinants of such "open path" striving. An adequate theory of personality and motivation should be good enough to (at least) explain the behavior of the individual(s) constructing it. In the meantime, the theory serves as an organizer of existing data, as a bridge between data and circumstances not explicitly represented in the research, and as a guide for generating newer ideas and hypotheses that can be tested in subsequent research. Our goal has been to separate those ideas that continue to be supported by data from those that are not, and to suggest newer ideas when the evidence indicates that they are needed.

CONTENTS

In this book we present in detail theory and research that is concerned with "important" life situations, as seen by the individuals engaged in behavior in these situations. We evaluate previous theory in light of the data, modifying it to fit the most recent findings when necessary, and eventually we substantially extend and generalize it to provide a much more general approach to the study of personality functioning and change from the perspective of an expectancy X value theory of motivation.

In Parts I and II we deal with the more general theory of achievement motivation and evidence bearing on its validity. This elaboration of the initial theory of achievement motivation served as the guide for our research efforts. We begin by reviewing its assumptions, derivations, and relevant empirical evidence (chapter 2). This theory is concerned with the effects of striving for some number of future goals whose attainment is contingent upon earning the opportunity to strive for them through more immediate successful performance. Thus, immediate behavior is seen by the individual as important because its outcome (success or failure) determines whether or not future goal striving will be possible. The mathematical model from which all hypotheses are derived is presented in detail, with illustrative examples of how hypotheses follow from the use of numerical computations, so that the reader is able to use the theory as well as see its functional significance for the prediction of immediate activity. The basic hypothesis of the theory is that when doing well *now* is seen by the person as a necessary prerequisite for earning the opportunity to try for later success (termed a *contingent path*), individual differences in achievement-related motives (the motives to achieve success and to avoid failure, M_S and M_{AF}, respectively) are accentuated and become apparent in action, so that success-oriented individuals ($M_S > M_{AF}$) are more motivated to do well but failure-threatened individuals ($M_{AF} > M_S$) are more inhibited by the prospect of failure, as compared to when immediate activity has no such future implications (termed a *noncontingent path*). Hypotheses concerning immediate behavior in (1) contingent versus noncontingent paths (which are analogous to those for situations where immediate action is rated as important or not for achieving future goals) (2) length of a contingent path and (3) perceived difficulty (expectancy or subjective probability of success) of tasks along the anticipated contingent path, among others, are derived and presented with illustrative examples of their implications for both the experimental analysis of human motivation and the analysis of career striving in important life situations. Research is reviewed so that consistencies and inconsistencies in data become apparent. This prepares the reader for later chapters in which research and theory suggest necessary changes in the original guide to our work. The theory and research of Parts I and II provide the basis for an understanding and analysis of motivation and career striving in society from an expectancy X value perspective, and serve as the basis for the extension of this approach later in the volume to understanding behavior in important tests of competence and in psychological careers not necessarily involving educational-occupational goals.

Part I includes research concerned with the investigation of persistence in the face of continued success on an ability test constructed as a contingent or a non-contingent path (chapter 3), the distinction between success as a personal standard of performance and as a criterion for moving on to later tasks of a contingent path (chapter 4), and how the rated importance of a future goal per se and individual differences in achievement-related motives are jointly related to the imagery used to describe future plans and goals (chapter 5).

Part II presents various empirical extensions of work on future orientation and achievement motivation, all of which share the common characteristic of use of a direct measure of achievement motivation—the Mehrabian (1968, 1969) Scale of Resultant Achievement Motivation (RAM)—as a means of assessing individual differences in achievement-related motivation. The search for such a direct measure of individual differences has a long, and until recently, unsuccessful history (see Atkinson & Feather, 1966, and Atkinson & Raynor, 1974, for discussions of this issue). Yet the practical need for a relatively simple method to substitute for the use and scoring of the projective TAT thought-sample measure of the achievement motive (the *n* Achievement score) has motivated us to assess the construct validity of the Mehrabian measure under well-controlled experimental conditions: Does this measure function the way it is supposed to, according to theory, and/or is it related to behavior in a consistent and meaningful way? The evidence is mixed. Thus chapter 6 includes both distance in time in a contingent path and the number of tasks in the contingent path in an attempt to disentangle effects due to time versus tasks. Support is found for expectations using the Mehrabian measure that make sense from the point of view of the more general theory of achievement motivation. Chapter 7 returns to the original problem that led to the eventual consideration of future orientation as a determinant of aroused achievement motivation—the distinction between so-called relaxed versus achievement-oriented conditions. The study systematically varies both the degree of achievement arousal (low vs. high) as well as the nature of the future-oriented path (contingent vs. noncontingent) while attempting to hold subjective probability of success constant. Results provide evidence that both the degree of achievement arousal and the nature of the path influence immediate performance level, but, unfortunately, the Mehrabian measure by itself does not predict performance at all. (Data presented in chapter 4, study I, also show no relationship between scores on the Mehrabian measure and behavior). However, in chapter 8, study II, results for learning in programmed instruction show the predicted interaction between subjects high and low on the Mehrabian score and contingent versus noncontingent path learning conditions. In addition, results for recall of incompleted and completed tasks under relaxed, achievement, and contingent path conditions (chapter 9) show results for differences on the Mehrabian score that are similar to those obtained in this study when differences on the test anxiety score are viewed. Therefore we can cite three studies (plus an additional one [Weinberg, 1975] discussed in chapter 11) in which meaningful results are obtained using the Mehrabian measure of resultant achievement motivation, and two studies (plus two additional ones [Weitzenkorn, 1974] discussed in chapter 2) in which this measure is not at all related by itself to behavior. The box score of 4 and 4 by itself is hard to interpret. Certainly the measure cannot be dismissed as totally lacking in validity. Yet we are unsure as to whether or not to recommend its use by itself. We have used a *resultant measure* of Mehrabian score and test anxiety score with enough success to suggest that it may provide a substitute for the resultant measure employing the n Achievement score and test anxiety score.

In part III we extend the study of achievement motivation from the expectancy X value perspective to include the role of perceived ability (competence), as well as attributions as to the causes of success and failure that may include ability (as well as effort, task difficulty, and luck); the latter is based on the earlier work of Weiner (1972, 1974) and his associates. In chapter 10 we replicate and extend the finding of a positive relationship between the future importance and self-importance of immediate activity (Raynor, Atkinson, & Brown, 1974, based on data first reported by Atkinson, 1966) to include the degree of self-possession of personality attributes. The results show that if people tend to see doing well now as important to achieving future success, they tend also to see doing well now as important for their own self-evaluation, and, in terms of personality attributes, if, for example, individuals believe they possess a great deal of competence (self-possession), they also believe that possession of competence is necessary for achieving their future goals (future importance) and for feeling good about themselves (self-importance). In chapter 10 we begin to conceptualize how such relationships can be accounted for in terms of an expectancy value theory of achievement motivation, and what changes need to be made in the theory to do so. Chapter 11 presents the first experimental study of attributions of the causes of success and failure in immediate activity of contingent versus noncontingent paths. Thus, theory and research in this section extend earlier work to embrace concern about the evaluation of competence in skill-demanding activity, and the perceived responsibility of such competence (as well as other factors) in causing success or failure in future-oriented (contingent vs. noncontingent) performance situations.

Part IV begins by presenting a major new theoretical effort (chapter 13) in which the expectancy X value theory of achievement motivation is extended and integrated with a new view of an expectancy X value theory of self-esteem and self-evaluation to produce a theory of personality functioning and change that can stand by itself as an attempt to account for the motivational determinants of adult development and aging. Several variables entirely new to the theory of achievement motivation are included so that the more recent theory, when applied to the study of achievement motivation, is able to account for research findings that are inadequately dealt with using the more limited perspective of previous theory. The newer theory is then used to reconsider the n Achievement score (chapter 14) and to view the differences in psychological careers between teachers and students in the context of a discussion of music-related activity (chapter 15). It is also used, along with other personality and sociological approaches to adult personality development, to view midlife transitions in women (chapter 16). The theory is also applied to motivational crises in self-identity faced by the elderly through review of the literature (chapter 17) and through use of personal experiences in dealing with personal adjustments made by the elderly (chapter 18). The latter chapters anticipate the application of the new theory to research on aging aimed at validation of its implications for changes over time in psychological careers in substantive activities represented by occupational, familial, and sexual paths in a culture.

I

FUTURE ORIENTATION AND ACHIEVEMENT MOTIVATION

In the first part we present in more detail than ever before the assumptions and derivations of the theory concerning future orientation and achievement motivation (Raynor, 1968a, 1969, 1974a) that has guided our work, as well as some research that employed the traditional (*n* Achievement and test anxiety) methods of assessing individual differences in achievement-related motives that have been associated with it. This work sets the stage for later sections of the book that deal with empirical extensions using the newer Mehrabian (1968, 1969) measure of resultant achievement motivation (Part II), and with theoretical extensions to deal explicitly with assessment of ability and the arousal of achievement motivation (Part III), and motivation and aging (Part IV).

In chapter 2 we set out to accomplish two goals: (1) to present in detail the mathematical derivation of hypotheses that have guided our research, and (2) to summarize the data bearing on the validity of the theory. We go far beyond earlier efforts in presenting the details of the assumptions and of the derivations (including computational examples) from the so-called elaborated or more general theory of achievement motivation, which is really *an* elaboration of the initial work of Atkinson (1957) and Atkinson and Feather (1966) using the logic of a general expectancy × value theory within the context of Lewin's (1938) conceptions of steps in a path to a goal.

The substance of the more general theory concerns how differences in the nature and extent of contingent future orientation influences motivation of immediate activity. Our method of presentation involves a step-by-step application of the more general theory to particular predictions in such a way that the reader is able

7

to see how we move from the theory to the predictions by use of algebraic manipulation of the equations of the theory, given particular numerical substitutions in these equations.

We feel strongly that such use of theory in psychology *should* and *will* become a routine matter—in fact, the only acceptable way to derive implications from a theory. At present it is not, particularly in the fields of personality and social psychology, where at best statements of theory and its assumptions rely heavily on interpreting the meaning and implication of words and their grammatical function and meaning. All too often these words are far too imprecise to allow independent users of such theory to derive unambiguously the same implication from the same starting point.

We wish to encourage others to begin the routine use of this particular mathematical statement of theory to derive implications and thereby generate hypothesis testing on their part, and whatever changes in theory that might result from their efforts, now that we have some confidence based on our own empirical findings that such an enterprise is worth pursuing.

There can be little doubt that extensive (eventually, exclusive) use of mathematical and computer statements of theory in psychology will become not only routine, but the only acceptable, state of affairs, as is already the case with our work and the more general theory of the dynamics of action in which it is embedded (cf. Atkinson & Birch, 1970, 1974, 1978). The fact of the matter is that the mathematical model—the equations that represent it—must be taken as the theory itself, whether implications are derived by hand calculation or by writing a computer program that then does these calculations. Computer simulation of the implications of the theory becomes a routine matter of substituting values for the various terms of the equations. The psychologist's job then becomes (1) stating the assumptions of the theory precisely enough so that such computations can be carried out, (2) interpreting the psychological meaning of the derivations of the equations/computer program, (3) refining the statements of assumptions represented by the equations through successive tests against empirical data and logical analysis, (4) replacing, when necessary, statements of assumptions with others that take a quite different view of the problem if and when theory becomes incompatible with the data, and (5) where appropriate, discovering the experiential and phenomonological correlates and/or representations of variables of the theory and/or its implications. This last task may or may not be perceived as necessary, depending upon whether or not variables of the theory are assumed to have or not to have such experiential or phenomonological representations. Although we are sure that we have not become either precise enough or accurate enough in terms of our mathematical representations to completely achieve these goals at present, and our later efforts await precise statement after initial research studies aid in specifying the exact form of these assumptions, such programmatic objectives over time define the basic tasks of the psychologist as scientist. Our inevitable failure to attain these goals so that further improvement is not possible merely defines the task for the future, and we are confident that subsequent work will surpass our own in this regard. To coin a phrase based on professional football: "Monday morning quarterbacks are always better than Sunday afternoon quarterbacks—and they had better be!"

Throughout chapter 2 we have used algebraic representations of the assumptions of the more general theory of achievement motivation, and derivations based on substitutions of numbers that represent some reasonable range of these variables. It is not that we necessarily believe in the interval or ratio scale qualities of these numbers as representations of psychological phenomena but merely that this is the only precise way to derive what the equations imply—what they are trying to tell us. Nor does the use of extensive tables showing the results of these derivations imply that we can achieve such precision in the statement of operational hypotheses and operational definitions that seek to test the theory—although we can try. In fact, many of the derivations are first tested as qualitative rather than quantitative hypotheses, and we have moved to more precise testing only after the more crude but simple qualitative hypotheses have received some initial empirical support. Nor do we believe that all initial statements of theory demand precise mathematical representation in the absence of relevant data. In our work, we have had the benefit of 20 years of accumulated research using common methods and guiding ideas prior to mathematical elaboration (cf. Atkinson, 1958; Atkinson, 1964; Atkinson & Feather, 1966; McClelland, 1961).

And finally, such precision in statements of assumptions does not necessarily imply that research can or should test these assumptions directly. Often the implications of assumptions, when supported but not derivable from some alternative set of assumptions, are as convincing as such direct tests might be if they were psychologically possible and meaningful. Our testing of the "multiplicative assumption" concerning probabilities along a contingent path (discussed in chapter 2) illustrates our preference for testing the implications of an assumption through construct validation rather than directly. An example of this would be asking subjects to report how they compute joint probabilities. This would probably tell us as much (if not more) about their knowledge of the laws of combining probabilities, taught in a mathematics class, as about how psychologically they view a sequence of probabilities.

We are always more interested in functional significance than in structural arrangements—how variables influence action rather than in how they are to be represented in a structural model. In fact, we have in this instance resisted change in this multiplicative assumption in the face of some contradictory evidence obtained from verbal reports because no other assumption appears to derive hypotheses that have been confirmed in our experimental work. If and when data suggest an alternative assumption that better fits direct tests of how probabilities are seen to combine along a path, and that assumption is also able to derive the results of replicable research findings, then, of course, we will substitute the alternative for the original. In fact, attempts at directly testing the multiplicative assumption had led to changes in the relationship between the theory and its possible operational definitions, rather than to the change in assumptions per se.

This should not be taken to mean that the theory cannot be disproved. The functional significance of an assumption is challenged when data are inconsistent with initial expectations, and any such changes in theory, operational definitions, or operational hypotheses require a new batch of data for validation.

Our commitment to quantitative and illustrative derivation is made in this volume to help "demystify" the link between the equations and their implications, with the hope that others will be encouraged to pursue this area of research. We suspect that previous publications (e.g., Raynor, 1969, 1974a) have not produced more research by others in part because our readers feel uncertain of how we do, and how they could, arrive at the implications of the theory that we have subjected to empirical test. While it is always possible to give some meaning to a theory when it is stated in words, even if that meaning is at variance with what was intended—as when a musician interprets a composer's score—mathematical statements leave the reader cold unless those mathematical statements can be used to derive implications in an understandable and straightforward way. And since many research psychologists are not as yet accustomed to use of such mathematical statements, and distrust them without the "interpretive" element so common in personality and social psychological research, they remain on the sidelines as skeptical observers of a "premature attempt at precision in the behavioral sciences." We have found that use of computational examples for our students has been very successful in allowing their direct involvement in the program of research, particularly when they have subsequently been able to (correctly) point to our inadequate interpretation of the implications of theory because we failed to heed our own advice to work out "what the equations are trying to tell us," although the students had done so. At that point they did not have to ask our opinion about what the theory implied. They could merely *tell us*, based on their working it out for themselves.

We hope that the presentation in chapter 2, though somewhat more involved and complicated than would have been the case if we had omitted computations and merely asked the reader to "take our word for it," will help bridge the gap between those who are spectators and those who would become participants. The reader should be able to use the equations of the theory along with our examples of how those equations are intended to be used to explore the psychological meaning of the theory, independently of our efforts. Our summary of research findings embedded in the derivations of various hypotheses gives further indication of what these "psychological meanings" were for us, as seen by the studies they have generated. And in viewing the correspondence between theory and data, we do not make claims for construct validation, but rather note consistencies and discrepancies between theory and findings, and between various replications of a similar study. This points the way toward later refinements of theory that bring it more closely in line with findings, or, in some instances, toward more appropriate research designs that are required before the theory is adequately tested.

The research evidence summarized in chapter 2 consists of both "field" and "laboratory" data collections involving both "assessment" and "manipulation" of theoretically relevant variables. We have consistently tried to obtain both kinds of data so that we can be as convincing as possible at any point in time both in terms of the degree of validity that might be claimed for the theory, and in terms of the relevance of the theory for prediction of behavior in life situations. Above all, theory used here is meant to account for *life behaviors*. Most of the continued extension, refinement, and revision of theory to fit data have been concerned with bridging the gap between an experimental-laboratory-oriented theory and one that can claim increased validity in dealing with complex life activity. But it remains a "fact of methodological life" that the more convincing arguments concerning validity of a theory can be made only by use of experimental-laboratory designs, and that assessment studies involving life behavior are often unable to deal effectively with issues concerning directionality of effect and possible alternative explanations of empirical relationships.

We have tried to maintain a dialogue between research findings in both kinds of studies, and have often become more convinced of an "increment in construct validity" when similar patterns of results have emerged from an experiment and an assessment study concerning the same theoretical hypothesis. We have also tried to be on the lookout for existing data that could be interpreted as consistent with theory, for while such postdiction does not necessarily add to construct validity, it does indicate the utility of the theory and the possible range of its applicability. There is no one foolproof method for guaranteeing valid theory. We have tried to be sensitive to various approaches to the question of validity, and, in particular, we have tried to insist that whatever current version of theory we are working with be stated explicitly so that we can find out if it does not conform to any particular empirical finding. Much of our later work reported in this volume has been concerned with changing theory to fit newer data as discrepancies between them become apparent.

The remaining chapters of Part I give more detailed treatment to several research problems. In chapter 3 (Raynor and Entin) we present research on persistence in contingent and noncontingent paths. Though not readily apparent from our presentation, this study was especially important for later theoretical developments for several reasons: (1) it first challenged us to devise a method of studying persistence in the face of success rather than failure, since failure in a contingent path rules out further striving, but then made us face the question of the possible meaning of "failure" within a contingent path that did not rule out further striving, which ultimately lead to (2) the distinction between "success" in terms of some personal standard of good performance and "success" in terms of moving on in a contingent path (chapter 4); (3) trying to interpret the meaning of the results for persistence in the male sample made us begin to think in terms of a distinction between success per se as "doing well" and success as finding out about one's degree of possession of abilities by using outcomes on such a "test of competence" and (4) possible differences between men and women in the extent to which they might value a particular kind of ability, in this case mathematical ability, and how such a difference might be conceptualized within existing theory, independent of subjective probability of success.

While none of these ideas is directly required by the manipulations and/or the findings, the results of our study of persistence moved us toward these various new directions, all of which were eventually dealt with more completely in other research. For example, in chapter 4 (Entin and Raynor), we present our experimental investigation of the distinction between "success" as a personal standard versus "success" as earning the opportunity to move on in a contingent path. Here we recognize that success/failure with regard to some personal standard of good performance need not be synonomous with success/failure as moving on in a contingent path, and that, in fact, failure to meet a personal standard might occur without loss of the opportunity to move on, or success in meeting a personal standard might still result in failure to meet a moving-on criterion of a contingent path.

This distinction between meanings of success came relatively late in our research work, and its implications concerning theory have not as yet been fully explored. In experimental tests of theory, we have always set "success" as meeting the moving-on criterion, so that research in contingent and noncontingent paths bears on the issue of the functional significance of the "moving-on" meaning of success/failure. However, in field tests of the "multiplicative assumption" concerning how probabilities combine along a contingent path we failed to emphasize success as "moving on" so that we now believe such data are inadequate for a fair test (as discussed in chapter 2). In any event, the research reported in chapter 4 points out that such a distinction is necessary, and while we are sure that more needs to be learned before adequate revision of theory is made, the initial findings suggest that an individual's preference for attaining one or another of these two meanings of success is an important determinant of performance in the next immediate step of a contingent path. We have not as yet explored what might be the determinants of such preferences; we find that when assessed, such preferences significantly interact with other relevant theoretical variables to influence performance scores.

In chapter 5 (Pearlson and Raynor) we explore a definition of "importance" of future goals that is independent of the meaning of "importance" as "earning the opportunity to move on (and eventually succeed) in a contingent path." We are here interested in how importance ratings of the future goal per se interact with achievement-related motives to influence how individuals describe their future plans and goals. The results provided a challenge to us to start to think in terms of determinants of "achievement value" that might be independent of subjective probability of success, which in Part IV (chapter 13) results in the systematic use of the concept of "individual cultural value" that in the achievement context might interact with achievement-related motives to further accentuate motivational differences. While no such variable is assessed in chapter 5, the results imply that important future goals influence aroused achievement motivation in a way analogous to that of contingent future orientation, and while other evidence implies that differences in subjective probability of success—which is reported to be higher for important than for less important future goals—might mediate such an accentuation without recourse to a new variable, other arguments and evidence that were stimulated in viewing these findings convinced us that cultural value as "individual achievement value" is worth conceptualizing as determined by factors other than perceived task difficulty.

2

Theory and Research on Future Orientation and Achievement Motivation

Joel O. Raynor and Elliot E. Entin

The earlier work in our research was guided by an elaboration of the expectancy X value theory of achievement motivation (Raynor, 1969, 1974a, 1978a). The elaboration built upon and extended an earlier statement of a theory of achievement motivation (Atkinson, 1957, 1964; Atkinson & Feather, 1966). This in turn can be seen as a refinement of the resultant valence theory of level of aspiration (Lewin, Dembo, Festinger, & Sears, 1944) to include the role of individual differences in achievement-related motives in determining the valence (attractiveness) of success and failure to the individual and to specify the precise relationship between the expectancy (subjective probability) of success and failure and the incentive value of success and failure.

Specifically, in the earlier statement of a theory of achievement motivation (e.g., Atkinson & Feather, 1966), the tendency to achieve success Ts is assumed to be a multiplicative function of the motive to achieve success M_S, the subjective probability of success Ps, and the incentive value of success Is; that is, $Ts = M_S \times Ps \times Is$, where the incentive value of success is inversely proportional to the subjective probability of success, or $Is = 1 - Ps$. The tendency to avoid failure Tf is assumed a multiplicative function of the motive to avoid failure M_{AF}, the subjective probability of failure Pf, and the (negative) incentive value of failure $-If$, where $If = 1 - Pf$. The resultant tendency to achieve Tr is assumed equal to the algebraic sum of the tendency to achieve success and the tendency to avoid failure $(Ts + Tf)$. Since Tf is always negative, the resultant tendency to achieve is best represented as $Ts - Tf = Tr$. Achievement-oriented activity is therefore seen as determined by the resolution of a conflict between the tendency to engage in achievement-related activity Ts so as to succeed and the tendency not to engage in achievement-related activity Tf so as not to fail. Algebraic manipulation of the basic assumptions of this theory has been shown to lead to a most useful summary statement, namely, $Tr = (M_S - M_{AF}) [Ps (1 - Ps)]$. This indicates that resultant achievement motivation Tr is determined by two kinds of components: a person component $M_S - M_{AF}$, represented by the difference in strength of achievement-related motives, the motive to achieve success M_S, and the motive to avoid failure M_{AF}, and a situation component $Ps (1 - Ps)$, a product determined entirely by the value of the subjective probability of success Ps.

13

Other positive "extrinsic" sources of motivation are also assumed to determine the final strength of tendency to act in a certain way: $Ta = Tr + T_{ext}$. The implications of this theory and its supportive evidence have been presented in detail in successive research monographs (cf. Atkinson & Feather, 1966; Atkinson & Raynor, 1974).

The earlier theory of achievement motivation (e.g., Atkinson & Feather, 1966) is now referred to as an initial theory, and its elaboration, which guided our research, is now referred to as a more general theory (cf. Raynor, 1978a) because the earlier statement can be shown to be the simplest case of the more general one (Raynor, 1974a, 1978a; Atkinson & Birch, 1978). The more general theory assumes the logic of a general expectancy-value theory of motivation, where strength of tendency to act is a multiplicative function of the strength of expectancy that the act will result in a consequence (success or failure in the achievement domain of activity) and the value of that consequence to the individual, summed over all expected consequences of the activity. In the more general theory, a particular activity is considered the immediate next step in a path. A path consists of a series of steps. Each step represents an activity (task) and its expected outcome(s) or consequence(s). A step is achievement related if skill activity can result in success or failure. Any achievement-related step may have, as expected outcomes, one or more extrinsic rewards (positive incentives) or threats (negative incentives). A consequence is called a *goal* when it has positive incentive value. Steps in the path are identified by their anticipated order of occurrence and by the kind of consequence that is expected. The individual's knowledge of what activities will lead on to what outcomes within a class of incentives determines the length of path.

The tendency to achieve success in immediate activity Ts is determine by the sum of the component tendencies to achieve Ts_n, each a multiplicative function of motive M, subjective probability P, and incentive value I:

$$Ts_n = M_S \times P_1 s_n \times Is_n \tag{1}$$

and

$$Ts = Ts_1 + Ts_2 + \cdots + Ts_n + \cdots + Ts_N \tag{2}$$

where the subscripts $1, 2, \ldots, n, \ldots, N$ represent the anticipated order of steps (activities and outcomes) in a path, from the first (1) to the last (N), and n represents a general term for any particular position in this anticipated sequence. In a similar manner the tendency to avoid failure (i.e., not to engage in achievement-related activity) is assumed to be additively determined by component inhibitory tendencies:

$$Tf_n = M_{AF} \times P_1 f_n \times If_n \tag{3}$$

and

$$Tf = Tf_1 + Tf_2 + \cdots + Tf_n + \cdots + Tf_N \tag{4}$$

The resultant achievement-oriented tendency (also referred to as resultant achievement *motivation*) is obtained by the summation of the tendencies to achieve success and to avoid failure and is written symbolically as *Tr*. The most useful algebraic statement of the determinants of resultant achievement motivation is

$$Tr = Ts - Tf = (M_S - M_{AF}) \sum_{n=1}^{N} (P_1 s_n \times I s_n) \qquad (5)$$

which indicates that it is determined by the resultant strength of an individual's characteristic achievement motivation $M_S - M_{AF}$ and a summed situational component that, given certain assumptions relating subjective probabilities and incentive values of success and failure in a contingent path (see below), can be determined by knowledge of an individual's perception of the difficulty of each activity (step) in the path.

If an individual believes that immediate success is necessary to guarantee the opportunity to strive for some number of future successes, while immediate failure means future failure by guaranteeing loss of the opportunity to continue in that path, as in what is called a *contingent path,* the strength of expectancy that immediate activity will result in future success (i.e., $P_1 s_2$) is represented by the product of the subjective probability of immediate success $P_1 s_1$ and the subjective probability of future success, given the opportunity to strive for it $P_2 s_2$. In other words, the combined difficulty of immediate success and future success, given the opportunity to strive for future success, determines the probability that immediate activity will lead on to future success. More generally, the strength of expectancy that immediate activity will result in some future success $P_1 s_n$ is assumed a multiplicative function of the subjective probabilities of success in each step of the path:

$$P_1 s_n = P_1 s_1 \times P_2 s_2 \times P_3 s_3 \times \cdots \times P_n s_n \qquad (6)$$

This can be written in shorthand in terms of sequential multiplication:

$$P_1 s_n = \prod_{i=1}^{n} P_i s_i \qquad (7)$$

Consequently, component tendencies to achieve success (and to avoid failure) will be aroused in a contingent path to influence strength of motivation sustaining immediate activity, their particular strength being determined by $P_1 s_n$ and $I s_n$ for each anticipated success s_n and failure f_n, respectively. The special assumption relating P and I will be introduced and discussed shortly.

Consistent with earlier analyses (see Festinger, 1942; Atkinson, 1957), in the more general theory it was assumed that the incentive value of some anticipated success s_n in a contingent path is inversely related to the (total) subjective probability that immediate activity will (eventually) result in that success,

$$I s_n = 1 - P_1 s_n \qquad (8)$$

and that the incentive value of some anticipated failure f_n is represented by the negative value of (total) subjective probability of success,

$$If_n = -P_1 s_n \tag{9}$$

Subjective probabilities of success and failure are assumed to vary between 0 and 1 and sum to 1 for computational purposes to determine the implications of algebraic manipulation of Equations 1–9.

We begin our understanding of the assumptions of the more general theory as stated above by referring to Figure 1, where a series of steps in a path to a goal are represented. Each line represents a step. Each step consists of some substantive activity to be engaged in and the relevant outcomes of that activity, namely, success and failure. Since the steps intervene between the person and the goal, each step must be taken to reach the goal of the path.

There are two ways to view the situation depicted in Figure 1, from the external viewpoint and from the internal viewpoint. From the external viewpoint, a student faced with the goal of graduating from college could be represented as having to take four steps, each consisting of a year's worth of college courses, to graduate from college. From this external viewpoint, Figure 1 is not at all concerned with how the student views steps in the path to graduation from college, but rather with the description found in the college catalogue. Minimum grade requirements for both continuation into the next year and being dropped from college might define the sequence as a contingent path from this external viewpoint, or it may be a non-contingent path. The equations of the more general theory of achievement motivation do not apply to the external viewpoint. However, the external viewpoint can be a useful one to take in trying to relate the determinants of an individual's behavior (i.e., the internal viewpoint) to the structural arrangements of society as they are evaluated by some "objective" observer or student of that society.

The second way of viewing the situation depicted in Figure 1 is to assume that the steps in the path and the goal of the path are those believed by the student to be faced prior to engaging in activity along that path. This is the participant's viewpoint, the internal viewpoint, the student's understanding of the course sequence and requirements that the student believes himself or herself about to undertake to "graduate from college." Note, however, that the goal of the student might be to "graduate with honors" or some other goal that bears little correspondence

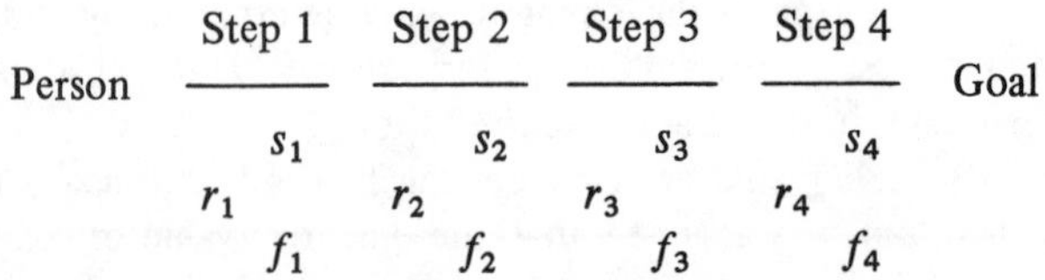

Figure 1   Schematic representation of the steps in a path to a goal. Here the person is faced with the first step of the path. Each step consists of an activity *r* and its possible achievement-related outcomes, success *s* and failure *f*.

with the objective one as seen from the external viewpoint. From the internal viewpoint, Figure 1 refers to anticipated steps and possible outcomes, namely "success" and "failure" as defined by the student and/or by the student's understanding of the necessary prerequisite course grades needed to continue on in college (if the path is believed by the student to be a contingent one). Additional (extrinsic) outcomes of each step might also be anticipated by the student, such as receiving a cash bonus from parents for a certain grade-point average after the first year, or a European vacation upon graduation from college. The equations of the more general theory apply exclusively to the internal viewpoint, the psychological representation of the anticipated future as construed by the person whose immediate behavior we are interested in predicting. In this way the theory consistently pursues a Lewinian (1943) analysis of the life-space of the individual, here termed the internal viewpoint, as opposed to an analysis of the objective determinants of behavior, here termed the external viewpoint.

The fact that it is possible to assess both an internal viewpoint and an external viewpoint for a particular step-path situation allows for a great deal of integrative understanding of the determinants of individual behavior in the context of society. However, it is important to apply equations of the theory only from the internal viewpoint, and to be consistent in taking that viewpoint in attempting to predict the individual's life behavior. We have referred to this internal viewpoint as requiring the assessment of the cognitive structure of the individual (Raynor, 1974a). We have referred to the external viewpoint as requiring the assessment of the functional significance of contingent and noncontingent career paths offered in a society (Raynor, 1974b). An integrative understanding of the motivation of an individual within society comes from an attempt to compare the "normative" functional significance of a path in society with its particular functional significance for a given individual, as mediated by the individual's perceptions of that societal path.

In Figure 2 we represent steps in a path to a goal, but now with the person at some midpoint of the path. We can view Figure 2 from the external or internal point of view. It can represent the objective description of the progress of the participant along some career path of society (external view). Or it can represent the (internal) participant's anticipation of steps remaining to be taken to attain the goal (steps 3 and 4 in Figure 2a) and retrospection of steps having been taken along the path so far (steps 1 and 2 in Figure 2a), which brought the participant to now be faced with the immediate next step (step 3 in Figure 2a). Note that if we compare Figures 1 and 2a, we see that the "immediate next step in the path" is numbered 1 in Figure 1 and 3 in Figure 2a. It is convenient always to refer to the immediate next step in the path as step 1. This is shown in Figure 2b, where both future steps are represented by positive numbers, and both past steps are represented by negative numbers.

The internal point of view represented by Figure 2b can be used as a means of describing the evolution of theory and research to be presented in the present volume. Parts I and II deal with the anticipated future. More general theory of achievement motivation is concerned with how the internal view of this future—

	Past		Present	Future		
	Step 1	Step 2		Step 3	Step 4	
(a)	——	——	Person	——	——	Goal
	s_1	s_2		s_3	s_4	
	r_1	r_2		r_3	r_4	
	f_1	f_2		f_3	f_4	
	Step -2	Step -1		Step $+1$	Step $+2$	
(b)	——	——	Person	——	——	Goal
	s_{-2}	s_{-1}		s_{+1}	s_{+2}	
	r_{-2}	r_{-1}		r_{+1}	r_{+2}	
	f_{-2}	f_{-1}		f_{+1}	f_{+2}	

Figure 2   Two different representations of the steps in a path to a goal. (*a*) The external view-point; (*b*) the internal viewpoint. Here the person is faced with some middle step of the path after having taken several steps in that path.

the participant's anticipated future—influences motivation in the immediate next step of the path. Part III deals with the present. The emphasis here is on the person's attributes, competences, and information seeking to evaluate one's competences, as the person is faced with possible future steps to a goal. Part IV deals with the past, present, and future, including how the retrospection of past steps in a path, along with anticipated future steps in the path and assessment of present prerequisite abilities, influences the motivation of the participant at different stages (early, middle, and late) in a career path.

We use Figure 3 to represent the strictly internal point of view of steps in a path to a goal. Here we refer to the person's *anticipated* future steps (+1 and +2 in Figure 3), *retrospected* past steps (−1 and −2), and the evaluated present prerequisite abilities and competences O_i, O_j, O_k the person believes himself or herself to possess (and the extent of possession of each), which are believed necessary for activity in the future anticipated steps of the path, and which were necessary for success in past steps of the path, all as perceived by the person faced with the immediate next step (step +1) of the path to the goal.

More general theory of achievement motivation as originally formulated (Raynor, 1969, 1974a) referred only to the anticipated future and how it influences motivation of immediate activity. In terms of Figure 3, only the anticipated future is presented in the equations of the general theory. We reserve for parts III and IV of this book the consideration of evaluated present and retrospected past.

Another distinction must be made with regard to the anticipated future. It became apparent during our early research work that it is possible to reapply the general theory of achievement motivation to each successive first step of a path as viewed by the individual as that person moves through the path from step to step. Such an analysis, while neglecting the present and retrospected past, became the link between theory of motivation and our analysis of aging (see part IV). Figure 4

Retrospected past		Evaluated present	Anticipated future		
Step − 2	Step − 1		Step + 1	Step + 2	
		Person			Goal
s_{-2}	s_{-1}	o_i	s_{+1}	s_{+2}	
r_{-2}	r_{-1}	o_j	r_{+1}	r_{+2}	
f_{-2}	f_{-1}	o_k	f_{+1}	f_{+2}	

Figure 3 **Representation of the individual's anticipated future, evaluated present, and retrospected past for a particular path, from the internal viewpoint.**

illustrates how the anticipated future is used in the more general theory. In Figure 4*a* we see the individual faced with four anticipated (future) steps to a goal. Each of the four anticipated steps is assumed to contribute a component of motivation sustaining activity in the immediate next step (step 1). In Figure 4*b* we see the individual after having moved from step 1 to step 2. Old step 2 is now the new anticipated step 1–the immediate next step–and there are only three anticipated steps to the goal.

The first application of the more general theory of achievement motivation will be restricted to the use of equations to derive components of motivation and then the total motivation for the immediate next step of a path of a given length. Later we shall be concerned with the derivation of the total motivation for each (new) successive step of a path as the person moves from one step to another.

CONTINGENT VERSUS NONCONTINGENT PATHS

In our theory and research we have focused attention upon what is called a contingent path. A contingent path is defined as a series of steps to a goal in which success in a more immediate step is necessary to earn the opportunity to move on

Anticipated future

(*a*)	Person	Step + 1	Step + 2	Step + 3	Step + 4	Goal
(*b*)		Person	Step + 1	Step + 2	Step + 3	Goal
(*c*)			Person	Step + 1	Step + 2	Goal
(*d*)				Person	Step + 1	Goal

Figure 4 **Representation of the same anticipated future steps of a path to a goal as the person moves from the first step (*a*) to the last step (*d*) of the path, from the internal viewpoint.**

to the next step of the path, and immediate failure in a more immediate step means loss of the opportunity to move in the path and hence guarantees future failure, through loss of the opportunity to continue. The theory holds that when individuals believe themselves faced with the immediate next step of a contingent path, each anticipated step of the path contributes a component of motivation for activity in the immediate next step, or step 1 in Figure 4. To obtain the total amount of motivation for activity in step 1, it is necessary to calculate the component motivation aroused by the first step itself, that aroused by the second step for action in the first step, that aroused by the third step for action in the first step, etc. After these component values are obtained, they are summed to determine the total motivation for activity in the first step of this contingent path.

We have also viewed activity in the immediate next step of a noncontingent path, defined as a series of steps in which immediate success or failure has no bearing on the opportunity to move on the next step of the path. Here the theory assumes that motivation sustaining activity in the first step is due to motivation aroused by that step itself, and is not influenced at all by anticipated future steps of the path.

It follows from the above that, for paths of equal numbers of steps, motivation for the first step of a contingent path will always be greater than motivation for the first step of a noncontingent path, other things equal. This is because in the contingent path we add components of motivation aroused by each of the anticipated future steps of the path to the component of motivation aroused by the first step itself to determine the total motivation sustaining immediate activity in the first step. However, for the noncontingent path we use only the motivation aroused by the first step itself to determine total motivation. In other words, total motivation for the immediate next (first) step of a contingent path is equal to the summation of component tendencies contributed by each anticipated step of the path, while total motivation in a noncontingent path equals motivation aroused by the first step alone.

MOTIVATION FOR THE FIRST STEP OF A ONE-STEP OR NONCONTINGENT PATH

Early statements of a theory of achievement motivation (Atkinson & Feather, 1966) dealt with deriving the amount of motivation aroused by the first step of a path. Note that the earlier theory did not refer to steps in a path, but in hindsight we can see that if it did, it would apply to calculation of motivation aroused by the first step. Thus the earlier theory is assumed to be a special case of the more general theory. We assume it applies in situations where a task is perceived to stand by itself, which we call a *one-step* path. We have also assumed that the earlier theory applies when a task is perceived as part of a noncontingent path, but the evidence (see chapter 7) suggests that this assumption is incorrect. Rather, achievement motivation seems not aroused at all for immediate activity in noncontingent paths, where immediate success or failure is explicitly seen as unrelated to moving on in the path. At the beginning of our research we did not believe that explicit noncontingent situations, in which the person knows or is told that immediate success or failure has no bearing on the opportunity for taking future steps, would be different from a situation where a single activity stands by itself. We therefore assumed that one-step and noncontingent path situations would be equivalent in terms of the amount of motivation aroused for the first step of the noncontingent path and the activity of the one-step path. In fact, our interest in noncontingent paths came only from their required use in experimental studies in which contingent paths were induced. We wanted to show that motivation in the first step of contingent paths was greater, as predicted, not merely because the person perceived additional steps per se to be later engaged in, but because earning the opportunity to engage in later steps was contingent upon success or failure in the more immediate (first) step of the path. Because of our assumption of the equivalence of one-step and noncontingent paths, we have in general not compared noncontingent path behavior with that in a single activity.

DERIVATION OF HYPOTHESES

Throughout our work we have used the mathematical model of the more general theory of achievement motivation (Equations 1–9 above) (Raynor, 1969, 1974a) to derive hypotheses. However, it is clear that research comparing contingent and noncontingent path behavior does not test the full set of assumptions of the model (Atkinson & Birch, 1978). As a consequence, for this volume we derive hypotheses using only those assumptions that are necessary to lead to predictions that are tested. This allows for evaluation of the various parts of the theoretical position, rather than forcing a global evaluation without the ability to point to particular assumptions for which research evidence may be much stronger than for others.

Contingent versus Noncontingent Paths of Equal Length

For the derivation of hypotheses comparing behavior in the first step of contingent and noncontingent paths of equivalent numbers of steps (e.g., of equivalent length), we assume that the resultant tendency to achieve in performing activity in the first step of a contingent path Tr_C is equal to the sum of the component resultant tendencies to achieve, where each step of the contingent path contributes one such component:

$$Tr_C = \sum_{n=1}^{N} (Ts - Tf)_n = (Ts_1 - Tf_1) + (Ts_2 - Tf_2) + \cdots + (Ts_n - Tf_n)$$

$$+ \cdots + (Ts_N - Tf_N) \tag{10}$$

For a noncontingent path, only the component resultant tendency to achieve aroused by the first step of the path is assumed to determine total resultant achievement motivation, so that the first component and the total are equivalent:

$$Tr_{NC} = Ts_1 - Tf_1. \tag{11}$$

It follows from the above that for all paths having more than one step,

$$Tr_C > Tr_{NC}. \tag{12}$$

Other things equal, the number of components for the contingent path will always be greater than the number of components for the noncontingent path. For the noncontingent path, the number of components always equal one, that contributed by the first step. The number of components for the contingent path will always be greater than one, and will be greater the larger the number of anticipated future steps of the contingent path.

Figure 5 is the schematic representation of the design of research comparing behavior in the immediate activity in a contingent and a noncontingent path. The person is led to believe that he or she faces either (for example, as shown here) a four-step contingent path or a four-step noncontingent path. Ideally, all other factors are held constant in the situation, so that any differences obtained from a measure that is supposed to reflect motivation in step 1 of the path are due to the difference between the contingent and noncontingent linkages between steps of the two paths. In Figure 5 the difference in paths is represented by C for the contingent links between steps, and by NC for the noncontingent links between steps. Note that in Figure 5 the goal at the end of the path is bracketed. In this research no explicit statement concerning a final goal is made, to prevent the arousal of

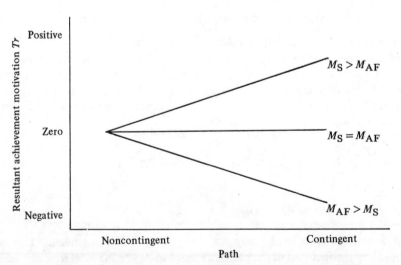

Figure 5   Representation of (a) a contingent (C) path and (b) a noncontingent (NC) path of equivalent lengths (four steps); and (c) the predicted strength of resultant achievement motivation Tr for immediate activity (step 1) in each path.

sources of motivation other than that concerned with doing well and moving on per se. For the situation depicted in Figure 5, when $M_S > M_{AF}$ (a success-oriented individual), Tr_C is more positive than Tr_{NC}; but when $M_{AF} > M_S$ (a failure-threatened individual), Tr_C is more negative than Tr_{NC}; and when $M_S = M_{AF}$ (an achievement-indifferent individual), $Tr_C = Tr_{NC}$. If Tr is directly related to performance level, then a particular pattern of results is derived for performance level in immediate activity in contingent and noncontingent paths, shown at the bottom of Figure 5. Note that as we move from the noncontingent to the contingent path, we predict an increment for the success-oriented subjects, a decrement for the failure-threatened subjects, and no change for the achievement-indifferent subjects, so that the expected higher performance of the success-oriented over the failure-threatened group is greater in immediate activity in the contingent path than in the noncontingent path.

Academic Motivation in Presumed Contingent and Noncontingent Paths

The above predictions (see Figure 5) summarize the pattern of results of one study in which measures of achievement-related motives (n Achievement and test anxiety) were related to academic performance in a college introductory psychology course. The students rated as high or low the helpfulness/importance of a good grade in the course for their future career success (Raynor, 1970, study I). In our research as well as earlier work (e.g., Atkinson & Feather, 1966; Atkinson & Raynor, 1974) on achievement motivation, the usual assessment of motives involves use of the n Achievement score (cf. McClelland, Atkinson, Clark, & Lowell, 1953; Atkinson, 1958, chap. 12 and app. III) to infer the strength of the motive to achieve success M_S and the first third of the Test Anxiety Questionnaire (TAQ) (Mandler & Sarason, 1952) to infer the strength of the motive to avoid failure M_{AF}. Those high in n Achievement and low in test anxiety (based on median breaks of the obtained distributions of scores) are assumed to have $M_S > M_{AF}$ and are termed success-oriented; those low in n Achievement and high in test anxiety are assumed to have $M_{AF} > M_S$ and are termed failure-threatened; those high-high and low-low on both measures are assumed to have $M_S \approx M_{AF}$ and are considered to be achievement-indifferent, neutrally motivated, or the intermediate motive group. It is assumed that students who score high on rating good grades as helpful/important/necessary for future career success face a contingent path to their future goal, while those who score low face a noncontingent path to their future goal. Members of the high n Achievement-low test-anxiety group who rated the course grade as high in importance (termed *high perceived instrumentality* in these studies) received higher grades than those rating it as low in importance, but the low n Achievement-high test-anxiety group that rated the course grade as high in importance received lower grades than that rating it as low in importance, with the high-high and low-low motive groups also high in importance having grades intermediate between these extremes. The increment for the success-oriented group coupled with the decrement for the failure-threatened group, with less change for the middle groups, is the pattern of accentuation predicted by theory. This pattern of results was found for men and women separately, and for n Achievement and test anxiety separately (see Table 1). The elaborated theory of achievement motivation had first been constructed so as to derive this particular pattern of results, based on an earlier study (Isaacson & Raynor, 1966).

An early followup to the Isaacson and Raynor (1966) study was first reported by Atkinson (1966) and later in greater detail by Raynor, Atkinson, and Brown (1974). The n Achievement and test anxiety were assessed at the beginning of the semester, and ratings of perceived instrumentality at the end of the semester, just before the course final examination, along with subjective reactions of students about to take the final. Concern about doing well and reported anxiety were coded from the subjective reactions. A compositive measure of resultant motivation reaction was obtained by classifying students simultaneously as to whether or not they reported concern about doing well and/or anxiety in the testing situation. The data are shown in Table 2. The more positive the resultant reaction score shown here, the greater the concern over doing well relative to anxiety for that group. Note that there is an accentuation from low (presumed NC path) to high importance (presumed C path), such that the high n Achievement-low test anxiety group shows a more positive reaction (more concern about doing well relative to anxiety), while the low-high group shows a more negative reaction (increase in anxiety relative to concern about doing well). This pattern is similar to that reported in the Isaacson and Raynor (1966) and Raynor (1970, study I) studies, and is consistent with the accentuation now predicted by theory (as shown in Figure 5) when extrinsic sources of motivation are relatively small.

Note, however, that a second pattern of results was also obtained by Raynor (1970, study II). Here all subjects tended to receive higher grades when grades were seen as helpful/important (perceived instrumentality) to attain future goals. These

Table 1 Mean Grades in Introductory Psychology as a Function of Motive Groups, Perceived Instrumentality (PI), and Sex

	Males				Females			
	Low PI		High PI		Low PI		High PI	
Motive group	N	Mean	N	Mean	N	Mean	N	Mean
n Achievement								
High	15	3.07	20	3.25	15	3.20	16	3.31
Low	14	3.00	18	2.72	6	3.33	15	3.00
Test anxiety								
Low	13	3.07	18	3.17	11	3.00	17	3.35
High	16	3.00	20	2.85	10	3.50	14	2.93
n Achievement−test anxiety								
High−low	7	2.86	10	3.30	8	3.00	9	3.44
High−high	8	3.25	10	3.23	7	3.43	7	3.14
Low−low	6	3.33	8	3.00	3	3.00	8	3.25
Low−high	8	2.75	10	2.50	3	3.67	7	2.71

Note. From Raynor (1968a, study I) with permission.

Table 2 Mean Composite Scores Indicating Concern about Doing Well and/or Getting a Good Grade Relative to Unqualified or Elaborated Anxiety.

| | Perceived instrumentality of exam | | | | | |
| | Low | | Intermediate | | High | |
Motive group	N	Mean	N	Mean	N	Mean
n Achievement						
High	24	.21	29	.17	31	.29
Low	27	.22	17	.12	24	-.08
Test anxiety						
Low	31	.23	18	.33	21	.48
High	20	.20	28	.04	34	-.09
n Achievement-test anxiety						
High-low	15	.20	9	.33	16	.56
High-high	9	.22	20	.10	15	.00
Low-low	16	.25	9	.33	5	.21
Low-high	11	.18	8	-.13	19	-.16

Notes. From Raynor, Atkinson, and Brown (1974) with permission.
The more positive the score, the greater the concern about doing well relative to anxiety; the more negative the score, the greater the anxiety relative to concern about doing well.

data are show in Table 3. In these data, motive measures do not predict grades, but importance does, with higher grades for high importance than for low importance.

Two additional follow-up studies have again yielded the two differing patterns of results first reported by Raynor (1968a, 1970). In the first, Raynor (1968b) included n Achievement, test anxiety, and a measure of perceived instrumentality in

Table 3 Mean Grades in Introductory Psychology as a Function of Motive Groups and Perceived Instrumentality, for Male College Students

| | Perceived instrumentality | | | |
| | Low | | High | |
Motive group	N	Mean	N	Mean
n Achievement				
High	38	3.18	37	3.51
Low	29	3.31	44	3.43
Test anxiety				
Low	34	3.06	40	3.48
High	33	3.42	41	3.46
n Achievement-test anxiety				
High-low	21	2.95	20	3.50
High-high	17	3.47	17	3.53
Low-low	13	3.23	20	3.45
Low-high	16	3.38	24	3.42

Note. From Raynor (1968a, study II) with permission.

the Bachman, Kahn, Mednick, Davidson, and Johnson (1967) nationwide study of 10th-grade boys. The n Achievement measure was adapted to the survey research technique following the procedures for doing so first used by Veroff, Atkinson, Feld, and Gurin (1960). A test anxiety scale that closely parallels the Mandler-Sarason (1952) Test Anxiety Questionnaire was also included. Verbal reports of each student's grade-point average in the previous year were obtained. In addition, perceived instrumentality of grades for future success was measured by asking each student to rate the importance of his high-school grades for making his future plans work out. Five statements describing various degrees of importance were provided. Almost three-quarters of the sample chose the most extreme statement, indicating that grades are "very important" in making future plans work out. These students were called high in perceived instrumentality (PI); the remainder were called low. The results indicate both a main effect due to achievement-related motives and a main effect due to perceived instrumentality, with little interaction between these factors. Reported grades were significantly higher for students classified high n Achievement-low test anxiety than for low n Achievement-high test anxiety students, and students high in perceived instrumentality reported significantly higher grades than those low in PI.

Atkinson, Lens, and O'Malley (1976) report on the follow-up of these students that took place 3 years later to determine which students had pursued some form of post-high-school education. This can be taken as a measure of persistence in pursuit of an education. The results were very similar to those obtained by reported grades 3 years earlier; there are both a main effect of motives and a main effect of perceived instrumentality on enrollment in school after high school, with little interaction between the two factors. The direction of results is also similar: the high-low group on n Achievement-test anxiety was more likely to pursue post-high-school education than the low-high group, and the group of students high in PI were more likely than those low in PI to continue on in their education.

We now expect that this main effect of perceived instrumentality (importance) will occur when non-achievement-related (positive extrinsic) sources of motivation are stronger than sources of achievement-related motivation, but this was not an a priori expectation for this study.

Data collected by Mitchell (1974) and reported by Raynor (1974c) allowed for a replication of Raynor's (1968a, 1968b, 1970) research. The study was designed to investigate the joint effects of both future importance and self-importance on grades obtained in an introductory psychology course. Need achievement, test anxiety, and questions regarding (1) the necessity of getting a B or better grade for future plans to work out, and (2) the necessity of getting a B in the course for self-esteem (feeling good about yourself)[1] were obtained at the beginning of the semester (Fall, 1973) at SUNY/AB. Final course grades were obtained at the end of the semester, 4 months after the initial assessment. The results (see Table 4) for men were first reported by Raynor (1974c). The male data again show the predicted accentuation of motive differences within high as opposed to low importance

---

[1] Data concerning the effects of self-importance in this study are discussed in Chapter 11.

Table 4 Proportion of B or Better Grades in Introductory Psychology as a Function of Motive Group, Rated Necessity of a B or Better Grade for Future Career Plans to Work out, and Sex of Student

Motive group*	Men				Women			
	N	Loc Nec	N	High Nec	N	Low Nec	N	High Nec
High-low	11	.18^a	11	.64^b	13	.31^c	8	.50^f
High-high	14	.43	8	.38	9	.89	18	.39
Low-low	28	.25	14	.43	13	.38	11	.27
Low-high	20	.45^c	11	.09^d	11	.55^g	16	.56^h

Note. Based on Raynor (1974c) analysis.

b–d: $t = 2.75, p < .005$; a–b: $t = 2.30, p < .025$; c–d: $t = 2.00, p < .025$; e–f: $t < 1$, n.s. (b–d) − (a–c); $t = 3.07, p < .001$.

*n Achievement-test anxiety, based on median breaks.

(necessity) for future goals, while the female data fail to show the predicted decrement from low to high importance of the low-high motive group.

Experimental Manipulation of Contingent and and Noncontingent Paths

While the various follow-up studies to the Isaacson and Raynor (1966) and Raynor (1968a, 1968b, 1970) research relating achievement-related motives to grades as a function of high and low perceived instrumentality were being conducted, we began to experimentally induce contingent and noncontingent paths of equivalent length in laboratory situations. Our goal was to demonstrate that the predicted interaction effect obtained in the grade studies would be found in immediate activity in contingent versus noncontingent paths, particularly since we did not expect large sources of extrinsic motivation aroused in the laboratory situation to produce a main effect of higher performance in the contingent path.

Two studies were initially conducted. Both employed the same performance task, complex three-step arithmetic (Wendt, 1955) that was known to be sensitive to individual differences in achievement motivation. However, different university subject samples were used, different procedures were used to create paths, and different probabilities of success were employed. The second study (Entin & Raynor, 1973) employed procedures that tended to rule out possible problems of interpretation subsequently found in the first study (Raynor & Rubin, 1971).[2] None of the differences between the two studies were expected to produce different results. In fact, both studies supported all but one of the predictions of the elaborated theory, as shown in Figure 5. Tables 5 and 6 present the appropriate data for the complex arithmetic task used in these studies. Note in Table 5 (the Raynor and Rubin study) that the high n Achievement-low test anxiety group performed better, while the low n Achievement-high test anxiety group performed worse, in the first step of the contingent as opposed to the noncontingent condi-

---

[2] See chapter 7 for detailed instructions used to induce contingent and noncontingent paths based on those used by Raynor and Rubin (1971).

Table 5 Mean Number of Three-Step Arithmetic Problems Attempted and Solved (for Males) as a Function of Motive Groups and Experimental Conditions

	Condition					
	Noncontingent			Contingent		
Motive group*	N	Attempted	Solved	N	Attempted	Solved
High-low	8	15.63^a	13.00^b	7	18.43^e	17.43^f
High-high	6	11.67	8.83	6	14.17	12.00
Low-low	10	14.40	12.70	6	12.67	11.33
Low-high	7	14.14^c	11.86^d	8	8.38^g	7.00^h

Note. After Raynor and Rubin (1971) with permission of the authors and of the publisher, the American Psychological Association.

a—e: $t = 1.35, p < .10$; b—f: $t = 1.91, p < .05$; c—g: $t = 2.77, p < .005$; d—h: $t = 2.10, p < .025$; b—d: $t = 5.98; p < .001$; f—h: $t = 5.01, p < .001$.

*n Achievement-test anxiety, based on median breaks.

tion. Within the contingent condition the high-low group outperformed the low-high group, and the high-high and low-low groups fell intermediate between these extremes. All hypotheses concerning the pattern of results described so far were supported. However, it was expected but not found that within the noncontingent condition the high-low group would outperform the low-high group. This difference is negligible (in the predicted direction) and not statistically reliable. All other effects are present at acceptable levels of statistical reliability. In Table 6 we find three rather than four motivation groups were used, based on the theoretically justified assumption that the difference score between Z n Achievement and Z test anxiety yields a meaningful index of resultant achievement motive strength. This index was then broken into thirds so that those high on resultant achievement motivation were assumed to have $M_S > M_{AF}$, those low on resultant achievement motivation were assumed to have $M_{AF} > M_S$, while those moderate were assumed to have $M_S = M_{AF}$. Note that we find an increment in performance for the high group coupled with a decrement in performance for the low group, from noncon-

Table 6 Mean Number of Problems Solved Correctly (for Males) on the Simple (Addition) and Complex (three-step) Arithmetic Tasks as a Function of Motive Groups and Experimental Conditions

	Condition					
Resultant achievement motivation*	Noncontingent			Contingent		
	N	Simple	Complex	N	Simple	Complex
High	18	135.83^{ae}	31.78^b	17	143.29^e	36.41^f
Moderate	19	131.26	31.53	15	146.73	32.28
Low	22	123.68^c	29.64^d	12	116.50^g	26.41^h

Note. From Entin and Raynor (1973) with permission. Results were almost identical for problems attempted and therefore were not reported.

a—c: $t < 1$, n.s.; b—d: $t < 1$, n.s.; e—g: $t = 2.04, p < .025$; f—h: $t = 2.53, p < .01$.

*Obtained by subtracting the standard on test anxiety from the standard score on n Achievement.

tingent to contingent conditions. Within the contingent condition, we find the high group highest, the low group lowest, and the moderate group intermediate on performance scores. The direction of these results is consistent with hypotheses, and the interaction effect is statistically reliable. Again, only within the noncontingent condition do we find lack of support of expectations in that the performance for the high group is not reliably higher than that for the low group, although the result is in the expected direction.

A subsequent study on persistence (see chapter 3) also included a measure of performance level obtained in the first activity in contingent and noncontingent paths. The predicted pattern of interaction was again obtained, this time for both male and female college students. However, one difference in the pattern of results emerged; the results in the noncontingent condition show a reverse of the predicted superiority of the high-low over the low-high n Achievement-test anxiety groups. A similar pattern of results is reported in Chapter 12.

In related research, Weitzenkorn (1974) used the same performance task in an attempt to replicate the Raynor and Rubin (1971) results. He used high-school male and female subjects. The Raynor-Rubin procedure was used to create contingent and noncontingent conditions, termed the *norm* condition to indicate that a specific performance norm (a certain number of problems solved correctly) defined the criterion for moving on in the contingent path. However, Weitzenkorn substituted the Mehrabian (1968, 1969) measure of resultant achievement motivation for the n Achievement measure to obtain a resultant motive classification (Z Mehrabian $- Z\ TAQ$) in an attempt to validate the Mehrabian score as a substitute for the n Achievement score. He then split the resultant distribution into high, moderate, and low groups. The predicted pattern of results was obtained for the male subjects but not for the female subjects, but careful inspection suggests that differences in test anxiety rather than Mehrabian score accounted for his results. In addition, Weitzenkorn created several new operational ways to induce contingent and noncontingent paths. In one, called the *competition contingent* condition, subjects were told that "the criterion for subsequent opportunity to work on the (next) test was scoring higher than their partners," rather than scoring above the norm (Weitzenkorn, 1974, p. 364). Results for the competitive contingent condition fail to yield the predicted pattern of results. In fact, the trends from noncontingent to contingent for the two extreme motive groups are in the opposite directions from those predicted. Also, within the competitive contingent condition, there are no differences between motive groups. For this study, at least, the data suggest that competition against another person to earn the opportunity to move on functions differently from competition against a performance norm to earn the opportunity to move on. The reversal of results for men in "competition against another person" as compared to "competition against a normative standard of good performance" resembles the reversal reported by Horner (1974) for performance of males for competition against others in a one-step performance situation.

Weitzenkorn (1974) also attempted to replicate the Raynor-Rubin (1971) pattern of results comparing noncontingent and contingent performance of high-school females. However, the pattern of results fails to show the predicted changes in performance for the extreme motive groups, comparing the norm-noncontingent to the norm-contingent conditions. In addition, both noncontingent-competitive and contingent-competitive conditions were included in the female study. Again, predicted noncontingent-contingent effects were not obtained. Overall, for the female sample, Weitzenkorn again notes that motive groups constructed with the Mehrabian measure by itself failed to yield any significant results, while differences between extreme motive groups on test anxiety were significant.

Weitzenkorn (1974) presents a third set of data collected from college female students where three different contingent conditions are created: norm, competition, and team, the latter created by informing subjects "that the contingency for being able to qualify for subsequent tests was for their team, as a whole, to score above the norm." While these data do not bear directly on the noncontingent-contingent comparison, since only versions of contingent conditions were created, the results show resultant motive groups (Z Mehrabian $- Z\ TAQ$) ordered correctly from high, moderate, and low on performance in both the norm contingent and competition contingent conditions, but not the team contingent condition, with separate analyses for the two motive measures suggesting that the extreme groups on the Mehrabian measure by itself were significantly different ($p < .05$) but differences in TAQ were not.

The tentative conclusion to be drawn from experimental studies that were conducted as the initial part of the research is that when competition against a clear-cut standard of good performance defines the "moving on" criterion of a contingent path (see chapter 4 for research separating "success" and "moving on" criteria), (1) for individuals with $M_S > M_{AF}$ (high n Achievement-low test anxiety), contingent future orientation consistently produces a higher performance level and greater positive subjective reaction, as obtained in the field studies on academic motivation; (2) for individuals with $M_{AF} > M_S$ (low n Achievement-high test anxiety), contingent future orientation sometimes produces a lower performance level and greater negative subjective reactions of the field studies on academic motivation; (3) for individuals with $M_S = M_{AF}$ (either high-high) or low-low on n Achievement-test anxiety, or in a "moderate" group on n Achievement alone or test anxiety alone when thirds are used for one motive measure only), contingent future orientation has little (certainly less) effect on performance level and subjective reactions. This link between the initial field studies (Isaacson & Raynor, 1966; Raynor, 1968a, 1968b, 1970; Raynor, Atkinson, & Brown, 1974) and well controlled manipulation studies seems a plausible one. However, some of the Weitzenkorn (1974) findings, and the Sorrentino data to be reviewed now, suggest some caution in making this inference.

PERFORMANCE LEVEL IN IMMEDIATE ACTIVITY OF CONTINGENT AND NONCONTINGENT PATHS: AN UNEXPECTED OVERMOTIVATION EFFECT?

A doctoral dissertation conducted by Sorrentino (1971, 1973, 1974) studied the effects of both achievement-related and affiliative motives (an explicit "extrinsic" motivating factor) on the level of individual and group performance. The performance task used and the group circumstances of the study most probably created a much higher level of total (positive) motivation than is usually obtained in studies where subjects work individually on an achievement-related task. Groups of four subjects who were preselected to represent appropriate motive groups were given three-step contingent and three-step noncontingent instructions. Subjects then worked individually for five "practice trials" of the task. The results (see Figure 6) were startling and surprising, but subsequent analysis seems to provide a firm basis for understanding them. The performance results (see Figure 6a) for subjects *low* in *n* affiliation show the predicted pattern of interaction found in experimental studies cited earlier (e.g., Raynor & Rubin, 1971; Entin & Raynor, 1973; chapters 4 and 12). The high *n* Achievement-low test anxiety group had higher performance scores in the contingent than the noncontingent condition. The low-high group did worse in the contingent than the noncontingent condition. Within the contingent condition the high-low group outperformed the low-high group. These results are as found in the other experimental studies and were the results that were predicted for the entire sample. Thus the Sorrentino results apparently replicate earlier findings, but only for subjects low in *n* affiliation. On the other hand, when results for subjects high in *n* Affiliation are viewed, there is a striking reversal of the predicted pattern of interaction, and of the results found in the research just cited. That is, contrary to predictions and previous findings, there is a substantial *decrement* for the high *n* Achievement-low test anxiety group in performance level under contingent versus noncontingent conditions. This is coupled with a substantial *increment* for the low *n* Achievement-high test anxiety group in performance level under contingent versus noncontingent conditions. This produced superior performance of the low-high over the high-low group within the contingent condition! Apparently the elaborated theory is disconfirmed for subjects high in *n* affiliation, particularly

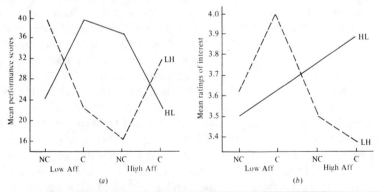

Figure 6 Scores on two dependent measures for high *n* Achievement-low test anxiety (LH) and low *n* Achievement-high test anxiety (HL) subjects in the noncontingent (NC) and contingent (C) conditions who are also classified high and low in *n* affiliation (Aff). (*a*) Performance on practice trials; (*b*) self-rating of interest. (From Sorrentino, 1974, with permission.)

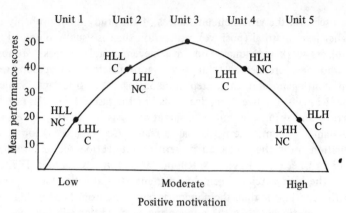

Figure 7   Schematic representation of the dominant pattern of
interaction using data from performance on the practice trials
of the Sorentino (1974) study. Here it is assumed that *n*
affiliation was the major contributor of positive motivation
to all groups (+3 to groups high in comparison to low in *n*
affiliation), while contingent future orientation changed the
resultant tendency to achieve by only 1 unit (+1 added to
the high-low group and —1 to the low-high group in the
contingent in comparison to the noncontingent condition.
(From Sorrentino, 1974, with permission.)

since these reversals are statistically reliable using conservative tests of significance.

A further consideration of recent arguments by Atkinson (1967, 1974a) and
their apparent consistency with several well controlled studies (Entin, 1968; Horner,
1968; Atkinson & O'Connor, 1966), as well as other independent evidence available
in the Sorrentino study (see Figure 6*b*), suggests a plausible explanation for this
reversal of effects, given the following assumptions: (1) contingent future orientation accentuated characteristic achievement motivation as predicted by the elaborated theory; (2) contingent future orientation and/or high affiliation motivation
in this group setting produced so much positive motivation that performance efficiency dropped substantially for the high *n* Achievement-low test anxiety group;
(3) contingent future orientation produced greater inhibition for the high *n* affiliation contingent groups, but this greater inhibition led, for high *n* affiliation subjects,
to a paradoxical performance increment (rather than a further decrement) because
it dampened too much positive motivation (caused by high *n* affiliation in the
group setting) to a more optimal level for maximum performance efficiency (cf.
Atkinson, 1974a, for a detailed treatment of these arguments, which are summarized graphically in Figure 7). Independent measurement of total aroused motivation
through a question concerning "anticipated interest" in the task, which was obtained
prior to work on the performance trials, is consistent with the above argument:
total positive motivation (interest) increased for the high *n* Achievement-low test
anxiety group from noncontingent to contingent conditions among those high in *n*
affiliation (see Figure 6*b*). This independent measure of interest also shows a
decreased interest that is consistent with the notion that there was great inhibition

for the low *n* Achievement-high test anxiety group in the contingent as opposed to the noncontingent condition for this motive group, also high in *n* affiliation. Thus this explanation is not unreasonable. What was needed to make it plausible was some evidence that the low *n* Achievement-high test anxiety group was sufficiently positively motivated so that inhibition could dampen too much motivation. The finding in the low *n* affiliation noncontingent groups that the low-high subjects outperformed the high-low subjects provided a basis for such an assumption, coupled with the added reasoning that *n* affiliation influenced positive motivation about three times as much as did contingent future orientation (see Sorrentino, 1974, for the detailed argument, shown graphically in Figure 7 here).

Sorrentino (1974) has carefully considered the extent to which such an explanation fits the data. He has also proposed an alternative explanation that may also turn out to be correct. His program of research represents an important additional fund of knowledge in the continuing program of research on future orientation and achievement motivation. Whatever the ultimate theoretical explanation that is found to be superior, the findings obtained are of great importance. It is now obvious that the other studies in this program of research failed to provide large affiliative (and other extrinsic) positive incentives (*intentionally,* so that achievement motivation would predominate and expected effects would be determined by achievement motivation and not some other kind of motivation). Therefore, the total motivation aroused failed to reach levels sufficiently strong (on laboratory tasks) to produce the presumed overmotivation effects that have been obtained in other studies where affiliative incentives were apparent (Atkinson & O'Connor, 1966; Entin, 1968; Horner, 1968, 1974; Smith, 1961, 1966; Atkinson & Reitman, 1956). The results obtained by Sorrentino suggest that an important oversight in planning studies was the failure to take seriously the possibility that too much positive motivation might be produced by a combination of contingent future orientation and some other source of positive (extrinsic) motivation, which would result in a performance decrement in success-oriented individuals, owing to either their "trying too hard" or their attempts to engage in incompatible behaviors (e.g., trying to please others while tyring to succeed in competition against them). Similarly, we failed to consider the possibility that failure-threatened individuals might become too positively motivated by extrinsic reasons and that any subsequent inhibition produced by contingent future orientation might serve to dampen motivation to a more optimal level. This solution to the explanation of the Sorrentino (1971) data assumes that the problem does not concern the elaborated theory nor the otherwise demonstrated effects of contingent future orientation (as illustrated by Raynor and Rubin 1971, Entin and Raynor, 1973, and chapters 3 and 12, among others, and observed for those low in *n* affiliation in the Sorrentino study), but rather the failure to consider the possibility that the relationship between total motivation and performance level may not be linear, but is rather curvilinear for certain kinds of relatively complex tasks. The Sorrentino study forces a reconsideration of previous hypotheses of elaborated theory concerning the impact of contingent future orientation on *actual performance* rather than *aroused achievement motivation* and suggests a more cautious stance in future research when trying to relate motivation to actual performance under contingent conditions where levels of extrinsic motivation are unknown. Frankly, we did not think that such intense levels of motivation would be created in a laboratory situation. But, on the other hand, we find no evidence for an overmotivation effect on the studies of academic motivation reviewed earlier. These remain unresolved issues for future research.

MOTIVATION IN THE FIRST STEP OF CONTINGENT PATHS THAT DIFFER IN LENGTH

The theory as thus far used for comparison of motivation in immediate activity of contingent and noncontingent paths can be used with only slight modification to make predictions concerning motivation in the first step of contingent paths that differ in the *number* of anticipated future steps. In Figure 8 we represent two contingent paths, one of four steps, the other of two steps. Since both are contingent paths, all steps in each path are assumed to contribute components of motivation for activity in the first step. However, the greater the number of steps (e.g., the greater the length of the contingent path), the more components of resultant achievement motivation are summed to determine the total resultant achievement motivation for the first step. Using Equation 10, with $N = 4$ and $N = 2$, respectively for two contingent paths differing in length, we derive that $Tr_{C4} > Tr_{C2}$. We therefore expect resultant achievement motivation to be greater in the first step of the four-step path than in the first step of the two-step path, other things being equal. Note again that in Figure 8 the final "goal" is in brackets to indicate that no explicit statement concerning a final goal is made, to prevent arousal of additional components of motivation besides that assumed to be aroused by concern over doing well and moving on at each step in the path.

Research using junior-high-school students partially confirmed predictions for length of contingent path (Raynor, Entin, & Raynor, 1972). When differences in

Anticipated future

		Step + 1	Step + 2	Step + 3	Step + 4	
(a)	Person	——— C	——— C	——— C	———	[Goal]
			Step + 1	Step + 2		
(b)			Person	——— C	———	[Goal]

or

		Step + 1	Step + 2	Step + 3	Step + 4	
(a)	Person	——— C	——— C	——— C	———	[Goal]
		Step + 1	Step + 2			
(b)	Person	——— C	———	[Goal]		

Figure 8   Representations of two contingent paths that differ in number of steps (i.e., in length of path), one (a) having four steps, and the other (b) having two steps.

test anxiety were used to infer the motive strength of subjects, data were consistent with hypotheses. However, no support for expectations was found when n Achievement scores were used. The difficulties encountered in using the n Achievement measure perhaps account for its failure to predict according to theory. In any event, the data provide only partial confirmation of the hypothesis that persons with $M_S > M_{AF}$ should be more motivated to do well, and attain a higher performance level (if motivation is directly related to performance efficiency) as the length of a contingent path increases, but persons with $M_{AF} > M_S$ should be more inhibited (resistant), and attain a lower level of performance, as the length of a contingent path increases. Subjects low in test anxiety in fact did significantly better on a (simple) arithmetic performance task involving addition or subtraction when it was the first of a four-task contingent path in comparison to a two-task contingent path. Also, there was a nonsignificant trend for lower performance in the four-step than in the two-step contingent path for the high test-anxiety subjects. But there were no differences between conditions for those high and low in n Achievement. The fact that n Achievement did not relate to performance at all in this study suggests that the methodological changes made to control for verbal fluency in the sample produced invalid motive scores. An interesting secondary finding of this study was that the word count obtained from the TAT protocols (used to score for n Achievement), when used as a measure of time spent in this story-writing task (and hence as a measure of achievement motivation), suggested that it might serve as a valid indicator of motivation differences in contingent and noncontingent paths: those who wrote longer stories did better in the four-step than in the two-step path, suggesting some construct validity for the word-count measure. Of course, this is highly speculative and would warrant additional research before being taken seriously.

The Confounded Effects of Time and Task Variables in Paths Differing in Length

The original conception of the effects of anticipated future consequences on motivation of immediate activity (Raynor, 1968a, 1969) explicitly ignored the possible effects of *distance in time* from a goal. This was done for several reasons. First and most important, previous research had systematically neglected the possible effects of psychological distance in terms of the number of tasks intervening between the person and the future goal. Work on "time orientation" seemed to be misleading in its suggesting that the "closer" to a goal a person is, the greater the amount of aroused motivation, insofar as the so-called "task hierarchy" was concerned. Our decision to give attention to the number of steps in a path (task hierarchy) rather than to the elapsed time to goal attainment (time hierarchy) seems to have been a good one, as judged by the increment in knowledge our research program has produced. However, we suspected, along with others, that "time" per se, or the effects that time mediates, were also important. But we ignored time as a variable because it would have greatly complicated our experimental designs. Also, we did not expect that the traditional ideas about goal gradients, particularly that for all people the gradient of avoidance is steeper than the gradient of approach as one moves closer to a (one-step) goal, would apply, and we were unaware of any research data bearing on the issue.

In the time between the initial statement of the theory (Raynor, 1968a) and our research on length of path, Gjesme (1974) reported results that not only helped to conceptualize the possible effects of time, but suggested a solution to a problem that our research had encountered. The problem was that, in general, the predicted effects of length of contingent path were not obtained in two large attempted replications of the Raynor, Entin, and Raynor (1972) study (cf. Brecher, 1972, 1975). The results reported by Gjesme indicated that closeness in time to a real examination increased aroused resultant achievement motivation. The two taken together suggested that time and task hierarchies are systematically confounded, that they work in opposite directions, and that research on length of contingent paths would not yield consistently positive results, even if the theory were correct, unless the effects of time were systematically taken into account (see chapter 6).

Since the research evidence suggested that both time and task hierarchies influence motivation and performance level in achievement-oriented situations, and that individual differences in achievement-related motives interact with the extent of both the time hierarchy (Gjesme, 1974) and the task hierarchy (Raynor & Rubin, 1971; Entin & Raynor, 1973; among others), it became of both theoretical and practical importance to begin the investigation of the joint effects of time and task hierarchies on the motivation of immediate skill activity.

Psychological distance as time suggests that the closer a goal event the greater its motivating properties, so that movement in time that brings the person closer to the anticipated outcome(s) should function to increase the strength of aroused achievement motivation (both positive and negative). On the other hand, psychological distance as tasks along a path has here been shown to predict that, other things equal, the greater the number of tasks between the person and the future goal, the greater the aroused achievement motivation to attain the future goal through immediate action in the contingent path in which that goal belongs. The fact is that time and the number of tasks to be worked along a path are always correlated in nature; the greater the number of tasks seen as part of a path, the greater the time that is expected to be needed to successfully complete the tasks whose positive outcomes are necessary to attain the final goal of the contingent path and to move through the entire path. Thus, time and task hierarchies should work in opposite directions with regard to the arousal of achievement-related motivation: (1) when few tasks are involved, time is seen as relatively short so that greater achievement motivation is aroused, just as when many tasks are involved, as compared to a situation in which time is seen as relatively long; (2) according to theory, when few tasks are involved in a contingent path, relatively little achievement motivation is aroused for performance of the immediate tasks, just as where time is relatively long, in comparison to when many tasks are involved. Thus Pearlson (1979; also chapter 6) predicted a "tradeoff" between the time and task contributions to motivation of immediate activity of "confounded" contingent paths: short paths arouse more motivation due to time but less motivation due to task; long paths arouse less motivation due to time but more due to task.

Pearlson's (1979) doctoral research (presented in detail in chapter 6) clearly confirmed expectations for both time and task effects so that we can have substantially greater confidence in our conception of achievement motivation as influenced by number of steps in a contingent path. However, the real-world problem of the systematic confounding of time and task hierarchies remains and poses a substantial complication for applying theory to prediction in life situations. Future research will be needed to identify those units of psychological time that are used by individuals in different situations, and to determine the relative strengths of effect of the time and task variables in determining arousal of achievement motivation.

The resolution of the confounding between time and task hierarchies clears the way for the investigation of the implications of the more general theory of achievement motivation concerning increasingly longer contingent paths, rather than the comparison of short and long paths. The theory predicts that as length of contingent path increases, motivation sustaining immediate achievement-oriented activity increases (positive or negative, dependent upon whether M_S dominates M_{AF} or the opposite), but the increments are expected to become smaller and smaller. One such derivation is shown later (see Figure 10) for the particular values of $P_n s_n$ indicated in that example. In general, the theory predicts such an effect for a wide variety of contingent paths. Future research will be addressed to evaluating this hypothesis as derived for particular varlues of $P_n s_n$ and particular lengths of path N. We expect that use of the "short" time intervals of Pearlson's research will allow us to both hold time "constant" as he did in his design and to allow the effects of different lengths of contingent paths to emerge without the complications introduced when longer time periods are used.

MOTIVATION IN THE FIRST STEP OF CONTINGENT PATHS OF EQUIVALENT LENGTH BUT DIFFERING IN SUBJECTIVE PROBABILITY OF SUCCESS AT EACH STEP OF THE PATH

Up to this point the hypotheses that have been derived did not require any assumptions about the values of subjective probability or incentive value of success, either at a particular step or along the entire path from the person to a particular distant goal of the path. Therefore the positive evidence thus far reported can be taken as consistent with the general assumption that anticipated future steps influence motivation of immediate activity when immediate activity is seen as the first step of (1) a contingent as opposed to a noncontingent path, and (2) a longer contingent path than a shorter contingent path, holding time to complete the path constant.

The more general theory of achievement motivation, from the start, included a particular set of assumptions concerning subjective probability and incentive value of success along a contingent path (see Equations 6 through 9). These assumptions were based upon what seemed reasonable at the time, rather than upon any existing empirical evidence. As already noted, it was assumed that the subjective probability that the activity of a person in the first step of a contingent path would (eventually) result in success in, for example, the fourth step of the path, was equal to the product of the subjective probabilities of success at each step intervening between the person and that success; that is $P_1 s_4 = P_1 s_1 \times P_2 s_2 \times P_3 s_3 \times P_4 s_4$, where $P_1 s_1$ represents the subjective probability that immediate activity (in step 1) will result in success in the first step, and each of the values $P_2 s_2$, $P_3 s_3$, etc. represents the subjective probability that activity in that respective step will result in its immediate success, as seen by the person faced with the first step of the path. It was further assumed that the incentive value of a success as seen at the first step of the contingent path was equal to 1 minus the subjective probability that immediate activity would (eventually) result in that success.

Figure 9 represents schematically the way in which these assumptions are used to calculate the particular quantitative values of component tendency contributed to motivation of immediate activity in the first step of the contingent path by each of the anticipated future steps of the contingent path. First, we assume some arbitrary values for Ps at each step along the path, as seen by the person faced with the path (see Figure 9d). For example, here we assume that the person believes the subjective probability of success in the first step is .9; that right now if the person were to work at the second activity of the path (step 2), the subjective probability of success would be .6; that right now if the person were to work at the third activity of the path, the subjective probability of success is .4; and that right now if the person were to work at the fourth activity of the path the subjective probability of success is .1.[3] To apply the theory, we either have to assess what these values are for a particular individual faced with a particular path at a particular time, or induce them experimentally through appropriate instructions or manipulations. Given that we know the values of Ps, we can proceed as indicated in Figure 9 to calculate the component tendency contributed by each step to the total aroused resultant achievement motivation in the first step (step 1) of the four-step contingent path. We first calculate the subjective probability that immediate activity will result in the success in question. For the component tendency contributed by the first step (Figure 9a), subjective probability of success in that step is equivalent to the subjective probability that the activity will eventually lead on to the first success in question, that is $P_n s_n = P_1 s_1$. In this case its value is .9. Therefore, the incentive value of the first success, as seen by the person faced with this contingent

---

[3] Note that at the outset we considered the idea that these subjective probabilities should be represented as conditional probabilities (e.g., Ps_2/s_1), since in a contingent path the psychological situation faced by the person corresponds to the notion that "my chance of success in step 2 is .6, given I get the opportunity to work at step 2 through success in step 1." It did not seem that anything would be gained by stating the theory in terms of conditional probabilities (success at step 2, given success at step 1), but we may be in error. It is possible that such a representation is either better logically or more correct empirically. Thus far we have not had reason to move in this direction.

	Calculation of resultant achievement motivation Tr in the first step
Path	

(a) One-step path ($N = 1$)

$$P_1 s_1 = .9$$

Person ——

$P_1 s_1 = .9$
$Is_1 = 1 - .9 = .1$
$Tr = Tr_1 = .9 \times .1 = .09$

(b) Two-step contingent path ($N = 2$)

$$P_1 s_1 = .9 \quad P_2 s_2 = .6$$

Person —— ——

$P_1 s_2 = .9 \times .6 = .54$
$Is_2 = 1 - .54 = .46$
$Tr_2 = .54 \times .46 = .25$
$Tr = Tr_1 + Tr_2 = .09$
$+ .25 = .34$

(c) Three-step contingent path ($N = 3$)

$$P_1 s_1 = .9 \quad P_2 s_2 = .6 \quad P_3 s_3 = .4$$

Person —— —— ——

$P_1 s_3 = .9 \times .6 \times .4 = .22$
$Is_3 = 1 - .22 = .78$
$Tr_3 = .22 \times .78 = .17$
$Tr = Tr_1 + Tr_2 + Tr_3$
$= .09 + .25 + .17 = .51$

(d) Four-step contingent path ($N = 4$)

$$P_1 s_1 = .9 \quad P_2 s_2 = .6 \quad P_3 s_3 = .4 \quad P_4 s_4 = .1$$

Person —— —— —— ——

$P_1 s_4 = .9 \times .6 \times .4 \times .1 = .02$
$Is_4 = 1 = .02 = .98$
$Tr_4 = .02 \times .98 = .02$
$Tr = Tr_1 + Tr_2 + Tr_3 + Tr_4$
$= .09 + .25 + .17 + .02$
$= .53$

Figure 9 Representation of (a) one-, (b) two-, (c) three-, and (d) four-step contingent paths, and the calculation of component tendencies contributing to motivation of immediate activity of the particular contingent paths shown here, using Equations 5, 7, and 8 of the more general theory of achievement motivation. When $M_S > M_{AF}$, the difference $M_S - M_{AF}$ is arbitrarily assumed for this example to equal +1. When $M_{AF} > M_S$, the difference $M_S - M_{AF}$ is arbitrarily assumed for this example to equal −1. When $M_S = M_{AF}$, the difference $M_S - M_{AF}$ is 0.

path, is .1. Then the product of subjective probability and incentive value of success gives us the magnitude of the absolute value of the component tendency contributed by the first step, assuming use of the most useful algebraic statement of the theory, as indicated in the description of Figure 9.

Thus far, the component tendency for step 1 is equivalent to what the total resultant achievement motivation would be if the first step stood by itself (as in

Figure 9a), and application of the general equations is equivalent to use of the equations for the simplest case, a one-step path. However, when we come to calculation of the component tendency contributed by the anticipated second step (see Figure 9b), $P_1 s_2$ is assumed equal to the product of the subjective probabilities of success in step 1 and in step 2, or .9 × .6 = .54. The incentive value of success in step 2, as seen by the individual when faced with the first step of the contingent path, is equal to $1 - P_1 s_2 = 1 - .54 = .46$, and the component tendency contri- .buted by step 2 is the product of .54 and .46, or .25, rounded to the nearest 100th. In Figure 9c and d the component tendencies contributed by steps 3 and 4 are also calculated, and the components are added to give the absolute value of total resultant achievement motivation for the first step of this four-step contingent path (Figure 9d). When resultant motive differences are taken into account, the value of Tr for the success-oriented individual ($M_S > M_{AF}$) faced with this particular path with these values of Ps would be + .53, but it would be − .53 for the failure-threatened individual ($M_{AF} > M_S$), and would be 0.00 for the achievement-indifferent individual ($M_S = M_{AF}$). If only two steps were faced by the person with values of $P_n s_n$ (as indicated in Figure 9b) of .9 and .6, then to obtain the absolute value of Tr we would sum only over the first two components, which are obtained from the calculations in parts a and b of Figure 9. Note that the absolute value for a contingent path of length 2 would be .09 + .25 = .34. If the person faced three steps (as shown in Figure 9c) then the absolute value of Tr would be .09 + .25 + .17 = .51. With achievement-related motive differences taken into account, we can see the predicted pattern of resultant achievement motivation as calculated in Figure 9 by referring to the graph in Figure 10. This represents the predicted differences in performance in immediate activity in contingent paths differing in length, with the particular Ps values of Figure 9, assuming performance level directly reflects resultant achievement motivation. Note that differences in immediate performance between motive groups are expected to become larger as the length of contingent path increases, although the increments do not form a linear trend.

In principle, any possible combination of subjective probabilities along the path might be perceived by a person faced with a path to a goal. We had to decide on which of the infinite variety of possibilities were of theoretical and empirical interest. Several cases were considered. First, we worked out the implications of the theory for situations in which the values of subjective probability of success were the same at each anticipated step along the path. This we termed the *constant probability* contingent path, and it is represented by a constant value of $P_n s_n$ in our notation. The results for high, moderate, and low values of constant $P_n s_n$ (.9, .5, and .1, respectively) are calculated and shown in Table 7.

The implications were very surprising to us, when first viewed. For example, they are contrary to expectations for a single activity, which are that resultant achievement motivation will be greatest for a subjective probability of intermediate value (.5). The equations imply that, for long contingent paths, a sequence consisting of an anticipated series of easy steps will arouse greatest resultant achievement motivation ($Tr = \pm 3.07$ in Table 7), whereas the theory for the one-step case led us

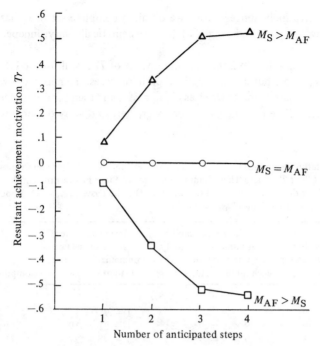

Figure 10 Graphic representation of resultant achievement
motivation *Tr* for contingent paths of different
lengths as shown in Figure 9, given the particular
values of subjective probabilities of success at each
step of the respective paths of Figure 9.

to expect equal and smaller amounts of motivation aroused for both easy and difficult tasks. Here we were faced with the first of a series of nonobvious predictions,
as seen from the theoretical perspective at that time, which consisted only of a
theory about behavior in isolated activities or one-step paths, as we later called
them. Our first derivations concerning length of path merely suggest an accentuation of predictions made from the initial theory (see Figure 10). However, here we
are faced with a clear-cut difference in predictions. Or are we? A closer look at
Table 7 clearly suggests that as the length of contingent path decreases, the predictions for the contingent-path situation and the isolated-activity or one-step situation become increasingly similar. This is seen most clear in Table 8, in which the
values of *Tr* are presented based on the calculation of Table 7 for various lengths of
contingent paths differing in constant value of subjective probability of success.
These values were obtained as follows: If we assume only one step for each of the
three kinds of paths, then only the first step contributes a component of motivation to total tendency. If, however, we assume a contingent path of two steps, then
both step 1 and step 2 contribute a component tendency, and total tendency in the
first step equals the sum of the components contributed by steps 1 and 2. So we
sum these values from Table 7 for each of the three kinds of paths, and enter these
total values in the new Table 8 opposite *Tr* for path length 2. By repeating this pro-

cedure for increasingly longer paths, we obtain a complete set of values in which both Ps along the path and length of path systematically vary, independently of each other.

Note that for path length 2 the maximum value of Tr is still for the intermediate-Ps series ($P_n s_n = .5$), but as the length of path increases, the maximum value shifts from the intermediate to the easy series ($P_n s_n = .9$), and then the difference between easy and intermediate becomes increasingly greater, so that by the time we have 15

Table 7   Computation of the Strength of Component Tendencies to Achieve Success or to Avoid Failure (*Ts* or *T—f*) and Their Summation over All Steps in a Contingent Path Where Each Step Along the Path is Perceived (at the Outset) to be Easy ($P_n s_n = .9$), Moderately Difficult ($P_n s_n = .5$), or Difficult ($P_n s_n = .1$)

Each step along the path perceived as	Subjective probability of success at each step[a]	Subjective probability of immediate activity (the first step) leading to each more distant success[b]	Incentive value (at the outset) of immediate and more distant successes[c]	Component tendency[d]
Easy[e]				
Step 1	.9	.9	$1 - .9 = .1$	$.9 \times .1 = .09$
2	.9	$.9 \times .9 = .9^2 = .81$	$1 - .81 = .19$	$.81 \times .19 = .15$
3	.9	$.9 \times .9 \times .9 = .9^3 = .73$	$1 - .73 = .27$	$.73 \times .27 = .20$
4	.9	$.9^4 = .66$	$1 - .66 = .34$	$.66 \times .34 = .22$
5	.9	$.9^5 = .59$	$1 - .59 = .41$	$.59 \times .41 = .24$
6	.9	$.9^6 = .53$	$1 - .53 = .47$	$.53 \times .47 = .25$
7	.9	$.9^7 = .48$	$1 - .48 = .52$	$.48 \times .52 = .25$
8	.9	$.9^8 = .43$	$1 - .43 = .57$	$.43 \times .57 = .25$
9	.9	$.9^9 = .39$	$1 - .39 = .61$	$.39 \times .61 = .24$
10	.9	$.9^{10} = .35$	$1 - .35 = .65$	$.35 \times .65 = .23$
11	.9	$.9^{11} = .31$	$1 - .31 = .69$	$.31 \times .69 = .21$
12	.9	$.9^{12} = .28$	$1 - .28 = .72$	$.28 \times .72 = .20$
13	.9	$.9^{13} = .25$	$1 - .25 = .75$	$.25 \times .75 = .19$
14	.9	$.9^{14} = .23$	$1 - .23 = .77$	$.23 \times .77 = .18$
15	.9	$.9^{15} = .21$	$1 - .21 = .79$	$.21 \times .79 = .17$
				Ts or *T—f* = 3.07
Moderately difficult[f]				
Step 1	.5	.5	$1 - .5 = .5$	$.5 \times .5 = .25$
2	.5	$.5 \times .5 = .5^2 = .25$	$1 - .25 = .75$	$.25 \times .75 = .19$
3	.5	$.5 \times .5 \times .5 = .5^3 = .13$	$1 - .13 = .87$	$.13 \times .87 = .11$
4	.5	$.5^4 = .06$	$1 - .06 = .94$	$.06 \times .94 = .06$
5	.5	$.5^5 = .03$	$1 - .03 = .97$	$.03 \times .97 = .03$
6	.5	$.5^6 = .02$	$1 - .02 = .98$	$.02 \times .98 = .02$
7	.5	$.5^7 = .01$	$1 - .01 = .99$	$.01 \times .99 = .01$
8	.5	$.5^8 = < .01^g$	$1 - < .01 = > .99$[h]	$< .01 \times > .99 = < .01^i$
9	.5			*Ts* or *T—f* = .67
10	.5			
11	.5			
12	.5			
13	.5			
14	.5			
15	.5			

Table 7 Computation of the Strength of Component Tendencies to Achieve Success or to Avoid Failure (Ts or $T-f$) and Their Summation over All Steps in a Contingent Path Where Each Step Along the Path is Perceived (at the Outset) to be Easy ($P_n s_n = .9$), Moderately Difficult ($P_n s_n = .5$), or Difficult ($P_n s_n = .1$) *Continued*

Each step along the path perceived as	Subjective probability of success at each step[a]	Subjective probability of immediate activity (the first setp) leading to each more distant success[b]	Incentive value (at the outset) of immediate and more distant successes[c]	Component tendency[d]
Difficult[j]				
Step 1	.1	.1	$1 - .1 = .9$	$.1 \times .9 = .09$
2	.1	$.1 \times .1 = .1^2 = .01$	$1 - .01 = .99$	$.01 \times .99 = .01$
3	.1	$.1 \times .1 \times .1 = .1^3 = <.01^g$	$1 - <.01 => .99^h$	$<.01 \times >.99 = <.01^i$
4	.1			
5	.1			
6	.1			
7	.1			
8	.1			
9	.1			
10	.1			
11	.1			
12	.1			
13	.1			
14	.1			
15	.1			
				Ts or $T-f = .10$

Note. From Raynor (1978a) with permission.

[a]$P_n s_n$.

[b]$P_1 s_n = \prod\limits_{i=1}^{n} (P_i s_i)$.

[c]$Is_n = 1 - \prod\limits_{i=1}^{n} (P_i s_i)$.

[d]$Ts_n = M_S \times P_1 s_n \times Is_n$; $T-f = M_{AF} \times P_1 f_n \times If_n$; $Ts_n + T-f_n = (M_S - M_{AF})(P_1 s_n \times Is_n)$.

[e]$P_n s_n = .9$.

[f]$P_n s_n = .5$.

[g]Values less than .01 are not calculated.

[h]Values greater than .99 are not calculated.

[i]Values less than .01 are not calculated.

[j]$P_n s_n = .1$.

steps, the differences are quite substantial. In this way we see how the more general theory recaptures, as a special case, the simplest one, the earlier statement of the theory, when $N = 1$.

The research now to be summarized required the complete set of theoretical assumptions as stated in Equations 1-9, to derive specific hypotheses.

PERSISTENCE IN IMMEDIATE ACTIVITY OF CONTINGENT AND NONCONTINGENT PATHS IN THE FACE OF CONTINUED SUCCESS

Our early research did not emphasize the use of behavioral persistence to test the elaborated theory because of problems involved in measuring persistence (in the

Table 8   Values of Resultant Achievement Motivation T_r for Easy ($P_n s_n = .9$), Moderately Difficult ($P_n s_n = .5$), and Difficult ($P_n s_n = .1$) Constant Subjective Probability Contingent Paths that Differ in Length of Path N, as Calculated in Table 7

Length of contingent path	Value of constant $P_n s_n$		
	.1	.5	.9
1	.09	.25	.09
2	.10	.44	.24
3	.10	.55	.44
4	.10	.61	.66
5	.10	.64	.90
6	.10	.66	1.15
7	.10	.67	1.40
8	.10	.67	1.65
9	.10	.67	1.89
10	.10	.67	2.12
11	.10	.67	2.33
12	.10	.67	2.53
13	.10	.67	2.72
14	.10	.67	2.90
15	.10	.67	3.07

Note. For $M_S > M_{AF}$, values of T_r are positive. For $M_{AF} > M_S$, values of T_r are negative. For $M_S = M_{AF}$, all values of $T_r = 0$.

face of failure) in a contingent path. Since by definition a failure in such a situation rules out further striving, how could a measure of additional "tries" be obtained? The problem was first solved by recognizing that persistence in the face of continued *success* is also a legitimate means of measuring motivational effects on behavior (cf. Brown, 1967; Weiner, 1965). A situation was devised (cf. chapter 3) where "pages" of problems that were attempted in the first of three tasks was taken as a measure of persistence. Three "tests" were presented as relatively difficult items of an ability test. The subjective probability of success in the first test was induced as .5, with the additional tests described as of increasingly greater difficulty. Performance criteria were set for each page of the first test. Success feedback was given after each page. Contingent and noncontingent groups were created. In the contingent condition, failure to reach criterion performance on any page ruled out working on subsequent pages and thereby defined the subject's level of ability. In the noncontingent condition subjects were told that the usual means of administering the ability test would be changed so that even if they failed to make the criterion for a page, they would be allowed to work on additional pages in the first test. Finally, all subjects were told that as long as they succeeded on each page they were free to move on to the second test when they thought they were good enough to do well on it.

For these particular circumstances, it was predicted that individuals with $M_S > M_{AF}$ would persist to a greater extent in the first test of the contingent condition than in the first test of the noncontingent condition. It was also predicted

Value of resultant achievement motivation Tr

	Noncontingent $(N = 1)$	Contingent $(N = 5)$

Before success

Initial activity (Booklet 1)

Person

$P_1s_1 = .50$	$P_2s_2 = .45$	$P_3s_3 = .40$	$P_4s_4 = .35$	$P_5s_5 = .30$
$Is_1 = 1 - .50 = .50$	$P_1s_2 = .50 \times .45 = .23$	$P_1s_3 = .23 \times .40 = .09$	$P_1s_4 = .09 \times .35 = .03$	$P_1s_5 = .03 \times .30 = .01$
$T_1 = .50 \times .50 = .25$	$Is_2 = 1 - .23 = .77$	$Is_3 = 1 - .09 = .91$	$Is_4 = 1 - .03 = .97$	$Is_5 = 1 - .01 = .99$
$Tr = .25 + .18 + .09 + .01 = .56$	$Tr_2 = .23 \times .77 = .18$	$Tr_3 = .09 \times .91 = .09$	$Tr_4 = .03 \times .97 = .03$	$Tr_5 = .01 \times .99 = .01$

Value: Noncontingent .25 Contingent .56

Alternative activity (Booklet 2)

Person

$P_1s_1 = .25$	$P_2s_2 = .20$	$P_3s_3 = .15$	$P_4s_4 = .10$	$P_5s_5 = .05$
$Is_1 = 1 - .25 = .75$	$P_1s_2 = .25 \times .20 = .05$	$P_1s_3 = .05 \times .15 = .01$	$P_1s_4 = .01 \times .10 = <.01$	$Tr_5 = <.01$
$T_1 = .25 \times .75 = .19$	$Is_2 = 1 - .05 = .95$	$Is_3 = 1 - .01 = .99$	$Is_4 = 1 - <.01 = >.99$	
$Tr = .19 + .05 + .01 = .25$	$Tr_2 = .05 \times .95 = .05$	$Tr_3 = .01 \times .99 = .01$	$Tr_4 = <.01 \times >.99 = <.01$	

Value: Noncontingent .19 Contingent .25

After success (P_ns_n is assumed to increase by .20 due to prior success in each case.)

Initial activity (Booklet 1)

Person

$P_1s_1 = .70$	$P_2s_2 = .65$	$P_3s_3 = .60$	$P_4s_4 = .55$	$P_5s_5 = .50$
$Is_1 = 1 - .70 = .30$	$P_1s_2 = .70 \times .65 = .46$	$P_1s_3 = .46 \times .60 = .28$	$P_1s_4 = .28 \times .55 = .15$	$P_1s_5 = .15 \times .50 = .08$
$T_1 = .70 \times .30 = .21$	$Is_2 = 1 - .46 = .54$	$Is_3 = 1 - .28 = .72$	$Is_4 = 1 - .15 = .85$	$Is_5 = 1 - .08 = .92$
$Tr = .21 + .25 + .20 + .13 + .07 = .86$	$Tr_2 = .46 \times .54 = .25$	$Tr_3 = .28 \times .72 = .20$	$Tr_4 = .15 \times .85 = .13$	$Tr_5 = .08 \times .92 = .07$

Value: Noncontingent .21 Contingent .86

Alternative activity (Booklet 2)

Person

$P_1s_1 = .45$	$P_2s_2 = .40$	$P_3s_3 = .35$	$P_4s_4 = .30$	$P_5s_5 = .25$
$Is_1 = 1 - .45 = .55$	$P_1s_2 = .45 \times .40 = .18$	$P_1s_3 = .18 \times .35 = .06$	$P_1s_4 = .06 \times .30 = .02$	$P_1s_5 = .02 \times .25 = .01$
$T_1 = .45 \times .55 = .25$	$Is_2 = 1 - .18 = .82$	$Is_3 = 1 - .06 = .94$	$Is_4 = 1 - .02 = .98$	$Is_5 = 1 - .01 = .99$
$Tr = .25 + .15 + .06 + .02 + .01 = .49$	$Tr_2 = .18 \times .82 = .15$	$Tr_3 = .06 \times .94 = .06$	$Tr_4 = .02 \times .98 = .02$	$Tr_5 = .01 \times .99 = .01$

Value: Noncontingent .25 Contingent .49

Figure 11. Derivation of predictions for persistence in initial immediate activity (Booklet 1) as opposed to changing to an alternative immediate activity (Booklet 2) in contingent paths with initial $P_ns_n = .5$ and subsequent activity of increasingly greater difficulty ($P_ns_n < .5$) as a function of continued immediate success (in Booklet 1). Note that values of resultant achievement motivation Tr are positive when $M_S > M_{AF}$, negative when $M_{AF} > M_S$, and zero when $M_S = M_{AF}$. (See chapter 3 for the details of this study.)

45

that in the contingent condition individuals with $M_S > M_{AF}$ would persist to a greater extent than individuals with $M_{AF} > M_S$, but that in the noncontingent condition the reverse would be found. The calculations of Figure 11 allow us to see why. In the contingent condition, before success, the strength of resultant achievement motivation for the initial activity (Booklet 1) is .56 (based on using five steps in the calculations), while it is only .25 for the alternative activity (Booklet 2). The difference favoring the initial over the alternative activity is $.56 - .25 = .31$. After an initial success, and assuming $P_n s_n$ is increased by .20 units for all activities faced by the subject, resultant achievement motivation is increased for both the initial activity (.86) and the alternative activity (.49). However, the magnitude of increase is greater for the initial activity ($.86 - .56 = .30$) than for the alternative activity ($.49 - .25 = .24$). Consequently, after the initial success, the difference in Tr in the initial booklet in the contingent condition has increased ($.86 - .49 = .37$) in comparison to the difference between the initial and the alternative activity values of Tr prior to success ($.56 - .25 = .31$). Thus, success-oriented subjects are expected to prefer to continue working in the initial activity after continued success. However, since values of Tr are negative for failure-threatened subjects, they are expected to change to the alternative activity rather than continue to work on the initial one. On the other hand, in the noncontingent condition, although the value of Tr is greater for the initial activity than the alternative activity prior to success ($.25 - .19 = .06$), after a success the value of Tr for the alternative activity is greater than that for the initial activity ($.25 - .21 = .04$). Thus, instead of continued persistence, as in the contingent condition, we predict for the success-oriented subjects a change to the alternative activity after successes in the initial activity; the opposite patterns are predicted in the contingent and noncontingent conditions. Analogously, the failure-threatened subjects are expected to behave differently in the contingent and noncontingent conditions, since in the noncontingent condition the negative value of Tr is smaller after success for the initial activity than for the alternative activity.

The investigation of persistence referrred to here is presented in detail in chapter 3. The performance-level results for this persistence study yield the predicted pattern of interaction between motives and contingent and noncontingent future orientation. The persistence data from this study (see chapter 3) show that for the female sample (college students) all the directional hypotheses are consistent with the data. Only the predicted decrement in persistence in the contingent as compared to the noncontingent condition for the low n Achievement-high test anxiety (failure-threatened) subjects did not reach statistical significance. When the male sample is viewed, the results within the contingent condition and the trends across experimental conditions for the high n Achievement-low test anxiety (success-oriented subjects) are consistent with predictions and with the female data. The only difference between the two sexes occurred within the male noncontingent group, where the high n Achievement-low test anxiety group persisted longer than the low n Achievement-high test anxiety group. This is opposite to what was expected for this noncontingent condition. Thus, for men, there is a main effect of motive groups indicating greater persistence of the success-oriented over the failure-threatened group.

Note that predictions for persistence in the face of continued success in a contingent path are opposite to those that would be derived if the initial conceptions of achievement motivation were applied without modification to this situation— they are equivalent to those derived for the noncontingent condition. Since the hypotheses of the elaborated theory were supported by the data, for women the conclusion appears warranted that, at least, contingent future orientation not only increases characteristic achievement motivation (as predicted for performance levels in contingent vs. noncontingent paths, and also obtained in the present persistence research), but also alters the nature of the motivating conditions confronted by in- dividuals.

PERFORMANCE LEVEL IN IMMEDIATE ACTIVITY IN CONTINGENT PATHS THAT VARY IN (CONSTANT) SUBJECTIVE PROBABILITY OF SUCCESS ALONG THE PATH

Raynor and Sorrentino (1972) conducted two studies in which different values of subjective probability of success were induced in contingent paths of equivalent length. The same value of task difficulty was always used at each step of a particular path—hence the reference to "constant subjective probability paths." The hypo- thesis to be tested was that aroused achievement motivation would be strongest (either positive or negative, dependent upon the motives of the person) for imme- diate activity in contingent paths of high constant $P_n s_n$, minimal for immediate activity in contingent paths of low constant $P_n s_n$, and intermediate between these extremes (approximately) for intermediate values of constant $P_n s_n$. Therefore, the predicted higher level of immediate performance of the high n Achievement-low test anxiety group over the low n Achievement-high test anxiety group was expected to be greatest in the high constant $P_n s_n$ path. The results of the first study (see Table 9) in fact revealed that only in the "easy" contingent series (high constant $P_n s_n$) did the high-low group significantly ($p < .05$) outperform the low-high group. This difference was smaller and not significant ($t < 1$, n.s.) for the moderately diffi- cult series (intermediate constant $P_n s_n$) and was reversed for the difficult series (low constant $P_n s_n$). The predicted pattern of interaction was obtained, but with- out the expected main effect of achievement motives. In the second study, different values of constant Ps and different contingent-path instructions were used. (The first study was based on Raynor and Rubin [1971] procedures, with Ps values of .8, .5, and .2 in four-step paths. The second study was based on Entin and Raynor [1973], with Ps values of .9, .5, and .1 in seven-step paths). The results of the second study (see Table 10) were very similar to the positive findings of the first for groups low and high on test anxiety (based on three anxiety groups), but showed no effects of constant $P_n s_n$ differences for groups differing on n Achieve- ment.

Sorrentino, Short, and Raynor (1978) replicated this research, using four-step contingent paths with constant $P_n s_n$ of .8, .5, and .2 at each step, using the Raynor and Rubin (1971) contingent-path instructions. However, in addition, they in- cluded measures of individual differences in uncertainty-related motivation: a (new) projective measure of n uncertainty; the Byrne and Lamberth (1971) acquiescence-

Table 9 Mean Number of Problems Attempted as a Function of Motive Groups and Constant Value of Subjective Probability of Success along Contingent Paths

Motive group	Constant value of Ps along contingent path					
	Low (.2)		Moderate (.5)		High (.8)	
High-low	(5)	12.00	(8)	12.25	(6)	12.83
High-high	(5)	11.80	(7)	10.43	(3)	10.00
Low-low	(8)	12.00	(5)	14.20	(6)	9.83
Low-high	(6)	13.00	(6)	9.83	(10)	8.10

Note. From Raynor and Sorrentino (1972, Study I), with permission.

free measure of authoritarianism, which was taken as an indication of fear of uncertainty; and a resultant uncertainty motivation index obtained by classifying subjects simultaneously on both measures. They report a three-way interaction among achievement motivation, constant value of $P_n s_n$ along a contingent path, and measures of uncertainty-related motivation. The finding suggests that uncertainty-related motivation may also be aroused under contingent-path conditions, and that the determinants of behavior are therefore more complex than presently conceived. Whatever the ultimate explanation, the interaction with uncertainty-related motivation suggests that unless such individual differences are controlled and/or taken into account, it will be difficult to obtain the predicted effects of the more general theory of achievement motivation. Thus we are faced with a situation similar to that found in the Pearlson (1979) findings for task and time hierarchies; another variable not previously considered by the more general theory of achievement motivation determines whether or not the predicted effects are obtained. The results concerning uncertainty-related motivation reported by Sorrentino et al. (1978) suggest that we have more to learn about the determinants of motivation and behavior in contingent-path situations, and that the theory may again have to be modified to account for the obtained results.

Performance Level in Decreasing- and Increasing-Probability Contingent Paths

Two studies (Raynor & Harris, unpublished data) have been conducted in which performance level in the first step of decreasing- and increasing-probability-contingent conditions was viewed. To create the different probability paths, the prob-

Table 10 Mean Number of Problems Attempted as a Function of Test Anxiety and Constant Ps along Contingent Path

Test anxiety	Constant value of Ps along contingent path					
	Low (.1)		Moderate (.5)		High (.9)	
Low	(19)	13.21	(8)	12.38	(13)	15.69
Moderate	(17)	14.00	(10)	14.90	(11)	13.45
High	(13)	13.38	(16)	12.25	(8)	11.25

Note. From Raynor and Sorrentino (1972, study II), with permission.

ability of moving on in the contingent path was manipulated so that, for the decreasing-probability path, subjects were told that those falling in the top 95% of performance scores on Test 1 would be allowed to work Test 2, those falling in the top 65% of performance scores on Test 2 would be allowed to take Test 3, those falling in the top 35% on Test 3 would be allowed to take Test 4, and only those falling in the top 5% on Test 4 would be allowed to take Test 5. The order of these probability values was reversed to create the increasing-probability contingent path. Table 11 presents the derivation of hypotheses for the particular values of $P_n s_n$ used to create the two path conditions. Resultant achievement motivation is derived to be much greater for the first step of the decreasing path of the study (e.g., from Table 11, $Tr = .47$) than for the first step of the increasing path (e.g., from Table 11, $Tr = .09$). Therefore, it was predicted that greater differences in positive and negative achievement motivation Tr would occur in the first step of the decreasing- probability path than in that of the increasing-probability path. Barring overmotivation effects, it was expected that success-oriented subjects would do better and failure-threatened subjects would do worse in immediate activity in the decreasing-probability path. Hence the performance of the success-oriented subjects should be higher than that of the failure-threatened subjects, but this difference should be greater in the decreasing-probability than in the increasing-probability path. Table 12 shows mean problems attempted on the complex (three-step) arithmetic task serving as the first task of the series as a function of motive

Table 11 Calculation of Resultant Achievement Motivation Tr for the First Step of a Decreasing-Probability Contingent Path and an Increasing-Probability Contingent Path, Using the Values of $P_n s_n$ Induced in the Experimental Situation

Step	Increasing-probability path (.05, .35, .65, .95)	Decreasing-probability path (.95, .65, .35, .05)
1	$P_1 s_1 = .05$ $Is_1 = 1 - .05 = .95$ $Tr_1 = .05 \times .95 = .05$	$P_1 s_1 = .95$ $Is_1 = 1 - .95 = .05$ $Tr_1 = .95 \times .05 = .05$
2	$P_2 s_2 = .35$ $P_1 s_2 = .05 \times .35 = .02$ $Is_2 = 1 - .02 = .98$ $Tr_2 = .02 \times .98 = .02$	$P_2 s_2 = .65$ $P_1 s_2 = .95 \times .65 = .62$ $Is_2 = 1 - .62 = .38$ $Tr_2 = .62 \times .38 = .24$
3	$P_3 s_3 = .65$ $P_1 s_3 = .05 \times .35 \times .65 = .01$ $Is_3 = 1 - .01 = .99$ $Tr_3 = .01 \times .99 = .01$	$P_3 s_3 = .35$ $P_1 s_3 = .95 \times .65 \times .35 = .22$ $Is_3 = 1 - .22 = .78$ $Tr_3 = .22 \times .78 = .17$
4	$P_4 s_4 = .95$ $P_1 s_4 = .05 \times .35 \times .65 \times .95 = .01$ $Is_4 = 1 - .01 = .99$ $Tr_4 = .01 \times .99 = .01$	$P_4 s_4 = .05$ $P_1 s_4 = .95 \times .65 \times .35 \times .05 = .01$ $Is_4 = 1 - .01 = .99$ $Tr_4 = .01 \times .99 = .01$
Total	$Tr = .05 + .02 + .01 + .01 = .09$	$Tr = .05 + .24 + .17 + .01 = .47$

Note. Values of Tr are positive for $M_S > M_{AF}$, negative for $M_{AF} > M_S$, and 0 for $M_S = M_{AF}$.

Table 12　Mean Performance Scores Corrected for Standing on Ability as a Function of Motive Groups and Decreasing- versus Increasing-Probability Contingent Paths

	Contingent path			
	Increasing-probability		Decreasing-probability	
$Z\,n$ Achievement $- Z$ test anxiety	N	Mean	N	Mean
Positive	9	10.98^a	7	13.41^b
Negative	8	10.62^c	12	7.49^d

Note. b $-$ d; $t = 2.55^*$, $df = 32$, $p < .01$: (b $-$ d) $-$ (a $-$ c); $t = 1.67$, $df = 32$, $p < .06$

*Based on the mean square error (MS_E) and the adjusted means obtained from the analysis of covariance, with reported mathematical ability group used as the covariate ($r = + .46$, $N = 36$, $p < .01$) between performance scores and ability groups.

groups and experimental conditions. The pattern of results obtained is consistent with expectations: the positive motive group ($Z\,n$ Achievement $-Z$ test anxiety) performed better in the decreasing than in the increasing-probability path. The superiority of the positive over the negative group in performance is clear within the decreasing-probability path. When reported ability groups are used as a covariate in this analysis, the pattern of results is not changed to any great extent. However, the level of statistical significance is now marginal for the overall interaction. But the effects within the decreasing-probability path are still statistically significant ($p < .01$).

This study was replicated with a much larger number of subjects. This made it possible for the first time to be sensitive to the possibility of overmotivation effects within a given contingent path as a function of extreme standing on resultant tendency to achieve *Tr* (rather than on achievement motivation plus extrinsic motivation as in the Sorrentino study described earlier). It would be expected that, with an increase in extreme standing on the motive measures, those individuals with *very* low *n* Achievement-*very* high test anxiety should perform even lower than a less extreme failure-threatened group. This should occur within the decreasing-probability path to a greater extent than in the increasing-probability path. If a moderate level of positive achievement motivation leads to maximum performance efficiency, but still greater positive achievement motivation leads to a performance *decrement* produced by "trying too hard" to do well, then the *very* high *n* Achievement-*very* low test anxiety group should perform at a lower level (rather than a higher level as would be expected if performance level were an increasing *monotonic* function of positive achievement motivation) than a less extreme success-oriented group. This effect should be greater in the decreasing- probability than the increasing-probability path. Table 13 presents the appropriate data. The overall relationship between ability group and performance level was not strong ($r = .20$, $N = 84$). Therefore, the analysis of covariance was dispensed with. The data for the decreasing-probability path (but not the increasing-probability path) show the general pattern that is predicted based on a combination of inhibition-producing decrements for the extreme negative motivation group, and positive motivation for the positive motive group, producing increments, up to a point, and then subsequent decrements in performance level. Specific comparisons reveal significant differences or differences that approach statistical significance within the decreasing-probability path, but little difference in performance between groups within the increasing-probability path.

Thus the Raynor and Harris (study II) data provide evidence inconsistent with predictions (as did the Sorrentino study) if it is assumed that resultant achievement motivation is a monotonic linear determinant of performance level, but consistent with the ad hoc explanation that there is an optimal level of positive motivation beyond which the performance level of success-oriented subjects begins to decline. However, note an important difference between the Raynor and Harris (study II) data and the Sorrentino data. The results for the failure-threatened subjects are not expected to reflect a nonlinear trend if components of resultant achievement motivation produce increased inhibition and this group is not beyond optimal performance in the control or comparison condition (an increasing-probability contingent path in Raynor and Harris; a noncontingent path in Sorrentino). The Raynor and Harris (study II) data suggest such was the case. Unfortunately, in all these attempts to explain the results, we cannot indicate, independently, the particular performance level that reflects the optimal point of motivation, nor can we safely assure that the failure-threatened group was or was not beyond this point in the control or less arousing motivating condition. Until we are able to do so, explana-

Table 13 Mean Number of Problems Attempted in the First Step of Increasing- and Decreasing-Probability Contingent Paths as a Function of Five Levels of Difference in Achievement-Related Motives

Resultant motive group (n Achievement-Test Anxiety)[a]	Contingent path	
	Increasing-probability	Decreasing-probability
Most positive (high-low)	(6) 13.17	(4) 12.25
Positive (high-mod and mod-low)	(13) 14.62	(7) 18.14
Neutral (high-high and mod-mod and low-low)	(16) 13.06	(22) 13.91
Negative (low-mod and mod-high)	(9) 13.22	(6) 15.17
Most negative (low-high)	(6) 15.33	(6) 11.17

[a]To obtain extreme groups, each motive measure was first split to obtain three groups of closest equal size (tritile split). Then numbers were assigned as follows: for n Achievement, high $= +1$, moderate $= 0$, low $= -1$; for test anxiety, high $= -1$, moderate $= 0$, low $= +1$. Then a combined motive group score was obtained by summing the assigned scores for each motive group classification (e.g., high-low on n Achievement-test anxiety $= +1 + (+1) = +2$, high-moderate $= +1 + 0 = +1$). Finally, combined motive groups with the same total score were combined to obtain the five groups listed here.

tions based on the "overmotivation" effect will remain suspect, not providing a firm sense of conviction that, as we claim, the problem in failing to predict according to theory concerns not the theory of motivation but the relationship of motivation to performance efficiency. We are very uncomfortable in appealing to such an explanation. On the other hand, it fits the data, post hoc, and the number of studies that fit such an explanation continues to grow (see Atkinson, 1974a, for a discussion of the kind of research program that is needed to make this overmotivation explanation more plausible). The Raynor and Harris (study II) research is the first to suggest that achievement motivation per se can produce such overmotivation effects.

RISK TAKING IN IMMEDIATE ACTIVITY IN CONTINGENT AND NONCONTINGENT PATHS THAT VARY IN LENGTH

An important impetus for our research on choice was the failure to obtain predicted effects of contingent future orientation on immediate risk taking (Raynor, 1968a). A series of experimental studies was then initiated concerning risk taking in both games of chance and skill. The initial study (Raynor, 1968a) suggested that subjects preferred difficult over easy tasks in contingent (as well as noncontingent) path situations. On the other hand, the elaborated theory predicts that, for relatively long contingent paths, (1) individuals with $M_S > M_{AF}$ will prefer less risk (e.g., higher subjective probability of immediate success) in the first step of a contingent path than either in a noncontingent path or a single activity (a one-step path), (2) individuals with $M_{AF} > M_S$ will prefer more risk (e.g., lower subjective probability of immediate success) in the first step of a contingent path than either in a noncontingent or a one-step path, and (3) individuals with $M_S = M_{AF}$ will prefer the same risk regardless of kind of path in which immediate activity is embedded. The derivation of this set of hypotheses follows from the calculations shown in Table 7 and summarized in Table 8, for constant-probability contingent paths. Similar expectations result when a wide variety of contingent paths are viewed where $P_n s_n$ is allowed to vary from step to step, as, for example, in the calculations given in Figure 9 and summarized in Figure 10. Note, however, that relatively long contingen paths are required before differences in values of resultant achievement motivation Tr become substantial. We did not appreciate this fact in the initial application of the theory to risk preference (e.g., in Raynor, 1968a, contingent paths of only two steps were used).

The fact that in the initial study subjects preferred *more* risk regardless of kind of path, even though the paths were relatively short, coupled with the fact that other evidence suggested that the sample as a whole had $M_S > M_{AF}$, led to a strategy of research in which a game of chance was first used to test hypotheses concerning length of path and immediate risk taking. The elaborated theory was modified for use with a game of chance to eliminate predictions of interaction effects with individual differences in achievement-related motives that are expected for skill but not chance situations. A positive outcome (but no negative outcome) was offered (e.g., points to be won). It was then predicted that immediate risk taking as measured by betting behavior on a version of roulette (where points to be won for a bet were inversely related to the odds of winning that bet) would be *less* risky (as indicated by a choice of higher objective odds of winning fewer points) in immediate activity in a contingent path than either in a (1) noncontingent path of equivalent length, or (2) one-step path. The results (see Table 14, study I) clearly confirmed expectations. A follow-up study replicated the finding (see Table 14, study II). This result was thought equivalent to what would be predicted if only success-oriented individuals (those with $M_S > M_{AF}$) were exposed to an equivalent skill-related path situation.

A second study was then conducted, using the same game of chance, in which the length of path of both contingent and noncontingent betting series was varied. Predictions were that immediate risk taking in a contingent path would become increasingly less risky (e.g., more conservative) as the length of contingent path increased, but this increase would become smaller and smaller as the length of contingent path increased. On the other hand, it was expected that immediate risk taking in a noncontingent path would not be influenced by length of path. Hypotheses were derived from the algebraic statement, assuming all subjects were positively motivated to win points, and the incentive value of points was inversely related to the odds of winning them. Note that the prediction concerning length of path was expected not as a result of inability to choose even more conservative odds, but because the algebraic statement indicates that distant future incentives do not influence the motivation of immediate behavior when the probability of their attainment (in a contingent path) is extremely low (see Tables 7 and 8 for equivalent numerical derivations). The results of the study confirmed predictions (see Table 15). Note that immediate risk taking became more conservative in the contingent but not the noncontingent path, and that the rate of increase in conservative immediate betting leveled off far before the asymptote of increase in (objective) betting odds was reached (a maximum score could be 37). The biggest increase in preference for more conservative odds occurred between steps 2 and 5 of the contingent path ($p < .001$), and length of path did not seem to further increase the preference for more conservative odds beyond a path length of 5.

A third study using the same game of change was conducted for different

Table 14 Mean Betting Scores Indicating Odds of Winning (the Higher the Score the Higher the Odds of Winning) in a Version of Roulette with Points to be Won Set as Inversely Related to the Odds of Winning, as a Function of Length of Path (within-Subjects Factor) and Kind of Path (between-Subjects Factor)

			Length of path		Interaction
			One step	Five steps	
Study I	(N = 43)	Noncontingent	8.56	9.30	$F = 23.24; df = 1/69; p < .001$
	(N = 28)	Contingent	10.68	20.36	
Study II	(N = 33)	Noncontingent	7.97	8.64	$F = 21.01; df = 1/50; p < .001$
	(N = 19)	Contingent	15.00	26.32	

Table 15 Mean Betting Scores as a Function of Length and Kind of Path in the Roulette Game

			Length of Path							
		1		2		5		10		15
Noncontingent	(12)	11.83	(11)	14.18^a	(12)	13.08^b	(12)	11.92	(11)	11.00
Contingent	(13)	12.85	(9)	16.67^c	(10)	23.30^d	(10)	22.00	(9)	22.22

Note. The higher the betting score, the higher the odds of winning. F (linear interaction) $= 1.75, df = 3/76$, n.s.; $d - c$: $t = 3.75, df = 76, p < .001$; $b - a$: $t < 1$, n.s.; $(d - c) - (b - a)$: $t = 2.07, df = 76, p < .025$.

(shorter) contingent path lengths that had not been included in the earlier study. Thus contingent paths of two, three, and four steps were included, along with a one-step control and the five-step path of the earlier study. The results (see Table 16) again show the predicted effect of length of contingent path. Surprisingly, the largest increment in preference for more conservative odds occurred from the step-1 to step-2 condition, with much smaller increments up to step 5. Taken together, the data of Tables 15 and 16 for the contingent paths depict immediate risk taking as becoming more conservative, but at a smaller and smaller rate, as length of contingent path varies from 2 to 15 steps. This general trend conforms to the derivations from theory when individual differences are ignored and a wide variety of anticipated future subjective probabilities are assumed so that values of motivation for immediate choice are obtained. Note that in the free-choice situation of these studies it is not possible to specify the probabilities along the path, for subjects choose only the first bet. More precise research would involve confronting subjects with a choice among paths consisting of sequences of bets, with stated odds of winning each successive bet. Assuming a correspondence between objective and subjective odds (probability) of winning, such studies would allow for the precise derivation of component motivation contributed by each possible future bet, and therefore would yield specific curves to which the obtained data points could be compared.

The positive results of the first study using the game of chance led to development of an analogous game of skill, the "basketball" game, in which points for a win (throwing a tennis ball into a wastepaper basket) were inversely related to the distance of the throw from the basket. Again, in the first studies only points won

Table 16 Mean Betting Scores on the Roulette Game as a Function of Length of Contingent Path, with a One-Step Control

Control		Length of contingent path							
(one-step)		2		3		4			5
(9)	10.67^a	(10)	17.00^b	(10)	20.22	(10)	19.10	(9)	21.44^c

Note. $F = 3.43, df = 4/43, p < .025$; $b - a$: $t = 1.97, df = 43, p < .10$; $c - b$: $t = 1.38$, $df = 43, p < .10$.

for a "basket" were offered. The basketball game was played in the second study on risk taking cited above after subjects had played the game of chance. Thus any result resembling that for the game of chance might be due to an order effect. The fact that risk taking in both games was not correlated in the noncontingent conditions ($r = .07$, $N = 46$) but was in the contingent conditions ($r = .51, N = 38, p < .01$) tends to rule out a sequence-effect explanation. Thus, in the third study cited above, the basketball game was played prior to the roulette game. Comparable conditions in both studies allowed for comparisons of betting scores and throwing (distance) scores, which again led to the conclusion that order did not seem to be influencing the results. The data for the basketball games are shown in Table 17. Here we find much greater variability in data points than for the game of chance. With points to be won inversely related to distance from the basket, it was initially thought that perhaps only positive achievement motivation would be aroused for the task. The variability of the data suggest that there is a slight but not clearly defined tendency for subjects to stand closer to the basket for a first throw in contingent paths of increasing length. This greater variability might be due to unmeasured individual differences in achievement-related motives that might be confounded when a main effect of path length is viewed.

The game of basketball was then modified to include points lost for a miss as well as points won for a basket, so that points won and lost were related to distance to satisfy the conditions known to exist in achievement-related situations. Thus, in this version of the game, a throw from a distance close to the basket (high subjective probability of success is assumed) could win relatively few points but lose a lot of points, while a throw from a great distance (low subjective probability of success is assumed) could win a lot of points but lose only a few points. This is a crude measurement of Ps, but it was felt adequate to test the hypotheses that (1) those individuals with $M_S > M_{AF}$ would become increasingly more conservative (e.g., throw from closer distances) in immediate activity in a contingent path as compared to a one-step control, (2) those individuals with $M_{AF} > M_S$ would become increasingly more risky (as a group) by throwing from increasingly greater distances in immediate activity in a contingent path than in a one-step control, and (3) individuals with $M_S = M_{AF}$ would throw from the same distance regardless of experimental condition. The results (see Table 18) confirm that subjects high in n Achievement and low in test anxiety stood closer in the two-step contingent condition than

Table 17 Mean Throwing Distances from the Basket as a Function of Kind and Length of Path

Study	Length of path						
	1	2	3	4	5	10	15
Study I: Noncontingent	(12) 7.83	(11) 9.18			(12) 8.42	(12) 7.83	(11) 8.64
Study I: Contingent	(13) 9.46	(9) 9.11			(10) 5.70	(10) 5.60	(9) 6.33
Study II: Contingent	(9) 8.44	(10) 5.40	(10) 7.20	(10) 5.70	(9) 6.67		

Note. The larger the score, the greater the distance from the basket.

Table 18   Mean Throwing Distance as a Function of Motives and
Length of Contingent Path with Points Won for a Basket
as a Direct Linear Function of Distance from Basket

			Path			
Motive	One-step		Two-step contingent		Four-step contingent	
High-low	(11)	11.00	(9)	7.22	(8)	7.88
High-high	(10)	9.00	(14)	6.21	(12)	5.00
Low-low	(8)	9.38	(12)	7.83	(17)	5.94
Low-high	(10)	9.10	(8)	8.38	(11)	4.81

Note. ANOVA for length of path: $F = 20.75; df = 2/118; p < .001$.

in the one-step control. Inspection of Table 18 also indicates that the three other motive groups (high-high, low-low, and low-high on n Achievement, test anxiety) moved closer to the basket in the (longer) contingent paths. That is, they behaved as predicted for success-oriented individuals. This clearly *contradicts* the hypothesis formulated for the low n Achievement-high test anxiety group. There are several possible reasons for failure to confirm predictions. First, the real possibility exists that the theory is inadequate. However, the discussion here will suggest that while this certainly is being taken seriously, it may be a premature conclusion. Second, "points to be lost" in this situation did not offer a real threat to subjects, since points lost have no intrinsic (negative) value, and nothing was done to create additional negative value. (But "points to be won" appear to function as though they have intrinsic positive value, independent of any additional attempt to make them valuable, which was not done in this study.) Therefore, the tendency to avoid failure may not have been aroused in this situation. This is a plausible alternative. It suggests that a risk-taking situation be found in which the real threat of failure is apparent. However, it is a weak alternative argument because (1) a miss of the basket was a clear possibility, which, according to theory, should be sufficient to arouse inhibitory motivation, and (2) if this alternative held, there should be a greater tendency for those high than for those low in n Achievement to stand closer to the basket as length of contingent path increased (e.g., high versus low strength of M_S should still interact with length of path). There is no evidence that this occurred. In fact, the opposite is a more accurate summary of results (i.e., low n Achievement stood closer with the longer contingent path).

The above results suggest that all individuals become more conservative in their immediate risk taking, in games of both skill and chance, when the immediate task is contingently related to the opportunity for further activity along the path. They do not support the hypothesis that the individual with $M_{AF} > M_S$ should exhibit the opposite behavior in immediate activity so as to guarantee immediate failure and therefore escape from exposure to further tests of skill. In addition, data obtained in another (unpublished) study seem to confirm this conclusion (see chapter 5 for similar evidence). College students were asked to rate their chances of success in situations where immediate success was necessary or not necessary for their own future career plans to work out. For both chances of "getting a B or better grade in introductory psychology," and for "earning the degree in your chosen major," male students indicated higher subjective probability of success when immediate success was seen as necessary for future success than when it was not. These data are consistent with the results for the basketball game and further suggest that individual differences in achievement-related motives do not interact with contingent future orientation to influence immediate risk taking. Rather, at least for men, all subjects in these studies tended to become more conservative and/or state higher subjective-probability estimates in contingent than in noncontingent paths, and in longer contingent paths.

It is interesting to combine the implications of the two sets of results concerning length of path—risk taking and performance level. If all subjects believe their chances of success are higher in increasingly longer contingent paths and/or their select immediate activity so as to insure that this will be the case, as the risk-taking and assessment data just discussed imply, and the results for "short" time intervals concerning length of path apply, as reported in chapter 6, then the following conclusion seems warranted: Success-oriented individuals select tasks so as to maximize their positive motivation in a contingent path, but, contrary to expectations, failure-threatened subjects select tasks so as to maximize (rather than minimize) their negative motivation in contingent paths. Consequently, failure-threatened subjects pay the subsequent penalty in terms of performance decrements and emotional reaction when confronted with a contingent series that appears relatively easy to them. A similar conclusion concerning the maladaptive behavior of failure-threatened individuals in their conception of their future plans and goals is put forward elsewhere in chapter 5. However, this conclusion must be tempered by the observation that it follows only if "overmotivation effects" do not influence actual accomplishment, and we have seen that there is sufficient evidence to warrant care in expecting a linear relationship between (positive and negative) achievement motivation and actual attainment.

It should be noted that recent changes in theoretical orientation in the area of achievement motivation (Atkinson & Birch, 1974, 1978) suggest that individual differences in achievement motivation may not lead to active inhibition of a maximally positive risk choice. This change in theory would suggest that all subjects would become increasingly more conservative in a contingent path. Of course, the data collected in the present research are consistent with this revised hypothesis.

On the other hand, data collected by Wish and Hasazi (reported in Raynor, 1974a) appear to show not only a clear-cut preference of students with $M_S > M_{AF}$ to choose a concentrate area in a school of management with very high chances for them of earning the degree, but also appear to show that the students with $M_{AF} > M_S$ choose a concentrate area with very low chances for them of earning the degree. This data may merely reflect a difference in "confidence" between the two groups, independent of their actual beliefs in the difficulty of their chosen areas. However, if we assume that a degree in a school of management would be pursued by the majority of students because of its contingent relationship as a prerequisite to entrance into their chosen career, then the data also are consistent with the original hypothesis of the elaborated theory. The Wish and Hasazi results are worth taking seriously because of the plausible argument that *greater real threat* is involved in performance in a school of management than in either the basketball throw of the laboratory studies, or in the choice of concentrate area in college, particularly because virtually no students nowadays are forced out of a liberal arts college curriculum (at the university where the research was done) because of poor grades.

THE FUTURE PLANS OF COLLEGE STUDENTS

The research reported here is an attempt to extend the study of future orientation and achievement motivation in life situations to include relevant variables of the elaborated theory, in addition to the distinction between the high and low "perceived instrumentality" of immediate success and future success. The major data collection involved the assessment of the future plans of college students. Two paper-and-pencil formats were developed for assessment of future plans. In both, the subject was first asked to write down his or her future goal. Then a separate page was provided for describing each step in the path to this future goal. The form provided 15 such step pages (the greatest number used by any subject was 12). For each step page, subjects were asked to write the activity they planned to engage in, the positive outcome of that activity that was desired, and the negative outcome that might result from that activity. A double-lined (open) arrow ($\Rightarrow$) pointed from the activity to the place for writing the positive outcome. Below this arrow was a space for writing the chances (out of 100) that the activity would lead to the desired positive outcome. In one form, subjects were instructed to select only those steps in their path to their future goal that required attainment of the positive outcome for continuation along the path to the future goal. For each step in this form, the arrow from activity to positive outcome was already darkened (filled in like this: $\rightarrow$) when the subject received the form. This is termed the *darkened-arrows* form. In the other form the instructions asked students to write all the steps in the path to their future goal, and to darken each arrow that led from an activity to a positive outcome that was required for continuing along the path to the future goal. Consequently, some steps had darkened arrows while others did not, after the form was completed, but all arrows were open when the form was first received. This is termed the *open-arrows* form.

The attractiveness and repulsiveness of future goal attainment or nonattainment was assessed for all subjects through questions appearing at the back of each form.

Attractiveness and Repulsiveness of Important Future Goals

A more direct check on the validity of the assessment procedures is available by use of the rated attractiveness and repulsiveness of success and failure for students classified high and low in answer to the question (included at the end of the questionnaire), "Right now, how important to you is achievement of this future goal?" The elaborated theory is not directly addressed to the perceived importance of a future goal per se, but rather is concerned primarily with the perceived importance of immediate activity for attainment of a future goal. Thus, no predictions derived from elaborated theory were entertained. However, one would expect that both success and failure would be more attractive and repulsive, respectively, for high important than for low important future goals. The results (see Table 19) show this to be the case to a high degree of statistical reliability. In fact, results for high versus low important future goals are of sufficient interest in their own right so that Table 19 includes the findings for all questions included at the end of the assessment device. It can be seen that students who rate their future goal attainment as relatively more important (1) see success as more attractive, (2) see failure as more repulsive, with regard to attainment or nonattainment of that future goal, (3) are more certain of their future goal, and (4) are willing to work harder to attain it. All these differences are highly reliable ($p < .001$ for each). These data suggest that the assessment procedures did in fact obtain valid indications of motivational arousal with regard to the future plans of these subjects.

Pearlson (1972) analyzed the future-plans data with the general hypothesis that the interaction between achievement-related motives and expected differences used to describe future plans and goals would be greater for high important future goals than for low ones. The data analysis (see chapter 5) generally supports this view.

The data reported in Table 19 appear straightforward and "intuitively obvious"; when future goals are seen as important as compared to less important, individuals are more attracted to success and more repulsed by failure with regard to that future goal, are more certain of their future goal both in terms of what it is and in terms of chances of attaining it, and are more willing to work hard to attain it. How-

Table 19 Mean Ratings for Various Measures as a Function of the Rated Importance of Achieving the Future Goal for Male College Students

	Rated importance of future goal			
Variable description	Low ($N = 78$)	High ($N = 98$)	F ($df = 1/164$)	p
Ps of achieving future goal	62.87	71.38	7.32	$< .01$
Attractiveness of achieving future goal	5.35	6.43	22.98	$< .0001$
Repulsiveness of failure to achieve future goal	4.21	5.50	20.31	$< .0001$
Willingness to work hard to achieve future goal	5.35	6.35	27.49	$< .0001$
Certainty of future goal	3.04	5.68	100.56	$< .0001$
Attractiveness of success in first step, assuming noncontingent path	5.25	5.32	< 1	n.s.
Repulsiveness of failure in first step, assuming noncontingent path	5.06	5.51	2.41	n.s.
Attractiveness of future goal when imagine faced with it	6.19	6.56	4.56	$< .05$
Repulsiveness of failure to achieve future goal when imagine faced with it	4.71	5.58	8.08	$< .01$

ever, several issues raised by these findings are neither obvious nor adequately dealt with by current theory. First, there is no formal status given to the variable "importance of a future goal" in the theory of achievement motivation. The initial theory (e.g., Atkinson & Feather, 1966) would deal with striving to attain a future goal as a single activity or one-step path, and the interaction between subjective probability of success in that activity and individual differences in achievement-related motives in determining resultant achievement motivation would be conceived of as one possible determinant of the perceived "importance" of the future goal. This implies that such future goals would be seen as more important as their subjective probability of attainment approached $Ps = .50$, and less important as Ps deviates from .50. However, the data in Table 19 (for Ps of the future goal) suggest that Ps ratings further from .5 are associated with higher importance so that relatively easy future goals are seen as most important, rather than ones closer to intermediate difficulty. However, the initial theory would more likely suggest that "positive extrinsic motivation" is greater for important future goals, and since an extrinsic incentive and its probability of attainment are not necessarily inversely related to each other, one would expect a positive association between the two when subjects act to maximize the product of expectancy and value by choosing high subjective probabilities of attaining important future goals. This is plausible, and no doubt correct to some or even a great extent, whether or not extrinsic motivation is considered in conjuniction with a one-step future goal or a contingent path to the future goal.

However, appeal to positive extrinsic motivation alone does not appear to be sufficient to explain all the data available at this time. We would expect extrinsic positive motivation to produce a main effect for all subjects so that those who faced important future goals would be more positively motivated to attain them. But the data of chapter 5 show an interaction between importance ratings and achievement-related motives influencing descriptions of future plans and goals, which suggests that the component of motivation that distinguishes important and less important future goals is at least in part achievement related. Otherwise, we would not expect increases in both positive and negative achievement motivation for success-oriented and failure-threatened subjects, as is suggested by their data. In the present context (see chatper 13) the concept of *individual cultural value* is introduced as an additional factor that can produce motivation for striving for a goal and its perceived importance of attainment. Based on the data, it would appear that such differences in importance are both achievement related and independent of the subjective probability of attainment, at the least. Thus we suggest that there are additional determinants of "value" not fixed by the subjective probability of success in attaining that value, but which interact with achievement-related motives to produce aroused achievement motivation. This would account for both the positive association between the importance rating of a future goal and the subjective probability of attaining it, on the one hand, and the interaction between achievement-related motives and importance ratings to influence descriptions of future plans and goals (see chapter 5) on the other. We have no direct evidence at this time to support this contention.

The more general theory of achievement motivation summarized here does not deal directly with the distinction between important and unimportant future goals per se. Rather it is concerned with "future importance" in terms of the individual's perception of the importance (necessity) of doing well in immediate activity for the attainment of some future goal, however important or not the future goal itself may appear to the person. Thus we have been able to induce contingent paths in a laboratory setting, where doing well or "success" earns the opportunity to work on a subsequent task, and doing poorly or "failure" means loss of the opportunity to continue and hence guarantees future failure because future striving is ruled out—without any additional "future", "final," or "ultimate" goal in the contingent-path situation ever having been stated. We might suspect that subjects think that "getting through the contingent path" or "succeeding on the last task" is a goal to be aspired to. However, we do not know this, and our conceptual analysis and research studies thus far have been careful not to address themselves to differences in motivation for the final or ultimate goal of a path per se, so as not to confound motivation aroused by the contingent nature of the path with possible differences in the perceived importance of some final goal at the end of the path. But the assessment procedures for our study of the future plans of college men allowed us to look at life *contingent* paths as well as the importance of future goal attainment.

Attractiveness and Repulsiveness of Future Goals in Contingent Versus Noncontingent Paths

In the future-plans data, the group for whom contingent paths relating immediate activity to their future goal can most readily be inferred consists of those students who darkened all the arrows between activities and positive outcomes along the path of their future goal in filling out the open-arrows form. The group for whom noncontingent paths can best be inferred consists of those students who failed to darken any arrows in their path steps in filling out the open-arrows form. In fact, subjects in the open-arrows assessment group can be broken into approximate thirds if "all or all but one" arrows darkened (or not darkened) is used as a criterion for obtaining contingent and noncontingent groups, respectively, with a middle third consisting of a mixed path group.

The elaborated theory suggests two sets of hypotheses concerning attractiveness-repulsiveness ratings, dependent upon whether these ratings assess *valence* (motive × incentive in the theory) or *tendency* (motive × probability × incentive). If the ratings were measuring valence, the attractiveness of future success should be greater, and the repulsiveness of future failure should be smaller, as the subjective probability of success in achieving the future goal decreases. The subjective probability of achieving the future goal is predicted to decrease in a contingent path owing to the multiplication of probabilities along the path, making the subjective probability of future success lower, in comparison to that in a noncontingent path. This should increase the attractiveness of future success but decrease the repulsiveness of future failure. However, if ratings were measuring tendency, both attractiveness and repulsiveness should be greater as the number of contingent steps increases, since each step in a contingent (but not a noncontingent) path is predicted to add a component of both positive and negative achievement motivation for activity to achieve the future goal. Since the questions asked refer to the view of the future path as seen now (when faced with the first step), measures of tendency should be greater (either positive or negative) for contingent than noncontingent paths, and interactions with achievement-related motives and kind of path as predicted (see below). No a priori argument can be taken as a foolproof check on the validity of which of these two variables (valence or tendency) is assessed by the questions asked. The strategy that was adopted consisted of viewing any positive (e.g., statistically reliable) findings to see whether they tend to confirm predictions based on assumptions that one or the other had taken place.

Analysis of the ratings of attractiveness of achieving the future goal (see Table 20) indicate that all students rated attractiveness of the future goal higher when the path to the future goal consisted of contingent steps as compared to when the path consisted of noncontingent steps (as assessed by the open-arrows form). This difference was statistically reliable as a main effect of noncontingent versus contingent paths for all motive groups ($F = 4.91$, $df = 1/57$, $p < .05$). It is consistent with either the valence or tendency assumption. Motive differences did not interact with kind of path. From Table 21 we see that ratings for the repulsiveness of future failure also are higher in the contingent-path group than in the noncontingent-path groups ($F = 2.83$, $df = 1/57$, $p < .10$). Also, this increase was greater for the low n Achievement-high test anxiety motive group than for the high-low motive group, as shown by the interaction effect between motive groups and noncontingent-contingent paths ($F = 2.36$, $df = 3/57$, $p < .10$), owing primarily to the large increase for the low-high group.

These findings for repulsiveness of future failure are consistent with the tendency assumption but contradict the valence assumption. Thus, from analysis of the attractiveness and repulsiveness ratings of future goal striving taken alone, we can tentatively reject the hypothesis that the ratings were assessing the valence of these outcomes in favor of the hypothesis that they were measuring the amount of resultant achievement motivation (tendency Tr) aroused in striving for the future goal.

Table 20 Mean Ratings of the Attractiveness of Achieving the Future Goal for Men as a Function of Motive Groups and Future Orientation Based on the Number of Darkened Arrows in the Open-Arrows Form

Motive group[a]	Path as determined by open-arrows form		
	Noncontingent	Mixed	Contingent
High-low	(6) 5.50	(11) 6.18	(5) 6.60
High-high	(10) 5.90	(7) 6.43	(13) 6.15
Low-low	(8) 5.88	(9) 6.11	(5) 6.80
Low-high	(10) 5.30	(4) 5.25	(8) 6.50

[a]n Achievement-test anxiety, based on obtained group medians for each motive measure.

Table 21 Mean Ratings of the Repulsiveness of Failure to Achieve
the Future Goal for Men as a Function of Motive Groups
and Future Orientation Based on the Number of Darkened
Arrows in the Open-Arrows Form

Motive group	Path		
	Noncontingent	Mixed	Contingent
High-low	(6) 4.00	(11) 4.45	(5) 4.60
High-high	(10) 3.88	(7) 5.44	(13) 4.40
Low-low	(8) 5.30	(9) 4.57	(5) 4.69
Low-high	(10) 3.70	(4) 5.75	(8) 6.63

If the ratings of future goal striving assess aroused tendency, then a specific pattern of results is predicted when a measure of net attractiveness is utilized. If a mean score for a group is obtained, using + 1 to indicate a positive difference score for attractiveness minus repulsiveness of the future goal, a − 1 to indicate a negative difference score, and 0 to indicate no difference score, then it is expected that the high n Achievement-low test anxiety group should have a larger positive score, and the low-high group a larger negative score (or a smaller positive score), in the contingent- than the noncontingent-path situation, and within the contingent situations the high-low group should have the most positive score, the low-high group the most negative (or least positive) score, with the other motive groups intermediate between these extremes. Inspection of Table 22 indicates that the data show this pattern. The predicted ordering of motive groups is obtained within the contingent-situation group, with the high-low subjects having a mean attractiveness score greater than that of the low-high group ($p < .01$). In addition, the directions of differences between noncontingent and contingent groups are as expected: an increment for high-low and a decrement for low-high, from noncontingent to contingent. Thus the data are more consistent with the assumption that these ratings of the attractiveness and repulsiveness of success and failure in attaining the future goal are a measure of tendency as defined by the elaborated theory and as assessed using the open-arrows form.

Table 22 Means for Net Attractiveness Scores (Attractiveness-Repulsiveness) for Achieving the Future Goal as a Function of Motive Groups and Future Orientation Based on the Number of Darkened Arrows in the Open-Arrows Form

Motive group	Path based on open-arrows form			Darkened-arrows form
	Noncontingent	Mixed	Contingent	
High-low	(6) .67	(11) .64	(5) 1.00[a]	(15) .33[c]
High-high	(10) .30	(7) .86	(8) .62	(23) .22
Low-low	(8) .63	(9) .56	(5) .60	(25) .24
Low-high	(10) .40	(4) .50	(8) .25[b]	(17) .12[d]

Note. +1 = positive difference score; −1 = negative difference score; 0 = no difference.
a − b: $t = 2.68$, $df = 38$, $p < .01$, one-tailed test; c − d; $t < 1$, n.s.

If the darkened-arrows form succeeded in assessing contingent steps in the path to the future goal, then the results concerning the above measure of mean attractiveness and repulsiveness should resemble those obtained for the contingent group of the open-arrows form. The data (see Table 22, right column) show this to be the case. The mean score for the high-low group is highest, that of the low-high group is lowest, and the two other motive groups are intermediate. However, the difference between the extreme motive groups is not statistically reliable for the darkened-arrows form.

Attractiveness and Repulsiveness of the Future Goal as a Function of Ps of Attaining the Future Goal and Number of Steps in the Path

The variables of Ps along a path, and therefore the Ps of attaining the future goal, and the number of steps in a path apply only for *contingent-path* situations. There were insufficient numbers of male subjects to carry out analyses within the contingent group obtained from the open-arrows form. However, separate anlayses for Ps of the future goal and the number of steps in the path are possible for the darkened-arrows form if it is assumed that this procedure in fact assessed contingent future orientation. (The Ns were too small for a complete factorial analysis using both Ps of the future goal and short versus long paths. Thus, a direct test of their joint effects was not carried out.) The net attractiveness scores for the darkened-arrows form are at least consistent with this assumption, since motive group means are ordered as expected (see Table 22).

A check on the distribution of Ps estimates for achieving the future goal indicated that three approximately equal groups were obtainable if Ps from 0 to 55 was considered low, Ps from 60 to 75 was considered intermediate, and Ps from 80 to 100 was considered high. When attractiveness-repulsiveness mean scores are viewed as a function of these differences in Ps for the darkened-arrows form only (see Table 23), we find that within high Ps the groups are ordered as expected (high-low with highest positive scores, low-high with highest negative scores, and the high-high and low-low groups having small positive scores that fall intermediate between the two extremes). In addition, there is a trend for the high-low group to have more positive scores in high than in low Ps groups, while the opposite holds for the low-high group. These trends also yield small differences as expected within moderate Ps, but differences are not statistically reliable for moderate Ps while they are for the high-low versus low-high groups within high Ps ($p < .05$). Note that differences are opposite to those predicted within low Ps. Thus the data are consistent with the prediction of elaborated theory that maximum differences in aroused achievement motivation will occur in contingent paths having relatively high Ps.

A median break was obtained based on the number of steps in a path (1–4 = short path; 5 and over = long path) and used for the darkened-arrows form to determine the effect of length of path on attractiveness–repulsiveness ratings in a contingent situation. The results (see Table 24) are ambiguous, since the mean net

Table 23 Net Attractiveness Scores as a Function of Motive Groups and Rated Subjective Probability *Ps* of Achieving the Future Goal for the Darkened-Arrows Form

Motive group	*Ps* ratings		
	Low (0–55)	Middle (60–75)	High (80–100)
High-low	(6) .33	(6) .17	(2) .50[a]
High-high	(8) .13	(7) .14	(8) .38
Low-low	(8) .63	(9) .00	(8) .13
Low-high	(6) .83	(5) .00	(6) −.50[b]

Note. a − b: $t = 1.72, df = 67, p < .05$, one-tailed test.

attractiveness–repulsiveness ratings fail to yield the expected ordering of motive groups within either the short or the long path. Further inspection of the attractiveness and repulsiveness ratings taken separately (see Table 24) also fails to yield clear-cut evidence for effect of path length. Thus these data provide no support for the expectation that length of path should accentuate characteristic effects of achievement-related motives in contingent paths. Pearlson's (chapter 6) results suggest that number of steps and time to complete them are confounded in this data collection so that failure to obtain the predicted effects of path length may be due to the time hierarchy working in opposition to the task hierarchy. Some indirect evidence is consistent with the possibility of the time effect working. Data from Table 19 show that both anticipated attractiveness of attainment and repulsiveness of nonattainment of the future goal, when faced with it tend to be higher than the corresponding attractiveness–repulsiveness ratings of the future goal when faced with the first step (e.g., right now). This is consistent with the view that closeness to the future goal produces greater motivational arousal, and we are here suggesting that such closeness might refer to closeness in time. The fact that both kinds of analyses (contingent vs. concontingent, and *Ps* along the contingent path) yield results consistent with predictions, but length of path does not, suggests that the task-time confounding, which would influence predictions for path length but not for kind of path or for *Ps* along the contingent path, should be taken seriously.

Table 24 Mean Ratings for Attractiveness and Repulsiveness of Attainment and Nonattainment of the Future Goal as a Function of Motive Groups and Length of Path for the Darkened-Arrows Form (Men Only)

Motive group	Short path			Long path		
	Attractive	Repulsive	Net	Attractive	Repulsive	Net
High-low	(8) 5.88	5.50	.13	(7) 6.14	3.86	.57
High-high	(9) 5.44	4.44	.33	(14) 6.14	5.57	.14
Low-low	(12) 6.58	4.33	.42	(13) 5.77	5.38	.08
Low-high	(9) 5.44	5.88	−.22	(8) 5.63	5.13	.50

COMBINATION OF PROBABILITIES
ALONG A CONTINGENT PATH

A critical assumption of the elaborated theory used to guide the present research is that individuals multiply (or act as though they multiply) the probabilities of success of the individual tasks along a contingent path to yield a final probability that "the immediate activity with eventually lead on to the final success" in that path. This assumption has yielded predictions concerning behavior in contingent paths with different values of $P_n s_n$, yet it is not necessary for general predictions concerning the effects of contingent versus noncontingent paths. In addition, it is not tested by comparing long versus short contingent paths, since other means of combining probabilities might yield predictions concerning the accentuation of motivation effects. Three kinds of studies were conducted that bear on the testing of this multiplicative assumption.

First, the performance-level studies by Raynor and Sorrentino (1972) (see Tables 9 and 10) provide a very indirect test of the model, since the prediction of greatest effects for easy tasks follows from it. The data generally (weakly) support the hypotheses, but alternative explanations that do not involve the multiplicative assumption are plausible. For example, it may be that in contingent paths the incentive value of success and subjective probability of success are independent. If this were so, and if expectancy $\times$ value = motivation (tendency), then it would be predicted that as Ps increased, so would differences between groups differing in achievement motivation. While this explanation does not appear to be tenable, it cannot be ruled out by the Raynor and Sorrentino (1972) data.

Second, predictions for the Raynor an Entin persistence study (chapter 3) and for the Raynor and Harris comparison of performance (described in this chapter) in increasing- and decreasing-probability contingent paths require use of the multiplicative assumption, and it is more difficult to conceive of alternative ways to derive these effects. However, the data are not consistently in support of predictions (only the female data support hypotheses in the Raynor and Entin study, and only study I of the Raynor and Harris research corresponds to initial expectations).

The risk-taking studies involving the game of chance serve as an indirect test of this assumption, since when many different lengths of path are used, it can be derived that when the positive value of points is inversely related to the probability of attaining points, the multiplicative assumption leads to the expectation that individuals should prefer increasingly higher objective probabilities of winning, but at an increasingly smaller rate, as length of path increases. This is an indirect test of the multiplicative assumption, but one that is "nonobvious" and does not seem to follow from other assumptions that could be made concerning how probabilities combine along the path. The data (Tables 15 and 16) are consistent with predictions.

Third, the future-plans study obtained verbal-report data concerning the anticipated individual probabilities of success at each step along the student's own career path, as well as an estimate of the chances of future career success. These data have been analyzed to test directly the multiplicative assumption for those students who also indicated they believed they faced a contingent path versus a noncontingent path, relating the steps along the path to future success. Recall that the data for the darkened-arrows form were obtained by asking students to write down only those steps (and their outcomes) that were contingently related to their future goal. The open-arrows form gave students the task of writing down all steps in their path to their future goal, but they could darken the arrow leading to the positive outcomes if they felt its attainment was contingently related (e.g., necessary) to attain their future goal. All subjects indicated their chances of success for each of the steps in their path. That is, they wrote in the chances (out of 100) that the activity comprising that step would lead to the successful outcome desired for that step. At the end of the questionnaire, each subject indicated the chances of achieving the future goal. Thus a direct test of the multiplicative assumption was possible based on these verbal reports of probabilities of success along a contingent path. For the open-arrows form, subjects were separated into groups who had darkened all or all but one of their arrows (the contingent-path group), darkened none or only one of the arrows (the noncontingent-path group), and where both kinds of arrows appeared (the mixed-contingent group). The data (see Table 25) show the number and percentage of subjects in each group for whom a multiplicative assumption would account for their rating of their probability of future success. That is, the individual probabilities along the path were multiplied to give the Ps estimate based on this model. Then the result was compared to the future-goal Ps estimate. Those products within an arbitrary range ($\pm$ .1) of the future-goal Ps estimate were considered to fit the multiplicative model. In addition, the average of the Ps estimates along the path was also obtained to determine if an "averaging model" might account for the Ps estimates for the future goal. Table 25 also shows the number of subjects for whom the multiplicative and averaging assumptions were equally good in predicting the future-goal Ps estimate, and, finally, the number for whom neither model made a successful prediction. Inspection of Table 25 shows clearly that the multiplicative assumption cannot account for the future Ps estimates, using these questionnaire reports. No more than 8% of the subjects' estimates fit the

Table 25 Number and Proportion of Subjects in Each Future Orientation Group Fitting a Multiplicative versus Averaging Model Relating Individual Subjective Probabilities of Success along the Path to the Overall Estimate of Subjective Probability of Achieving the Future Goal of that Path

	Open-arrows form						Darkened-arrows form	
	Noncontingent		Mixed		Contingent			
Model	N	Proportion	N	Proportion	N	Proportion	N	Proportion
Multiplicative	1	.03	1	.02	3	.08	7	.08
Averaging	14	.36	14	.35	15	.41	30	.33
Neither	22	.58	18	.45	16	.43	51	.55
Both	1	.03	7	.18	3	.08	4	.04
Total N	38		40		37		92	

multiplicative model. On the other hand, the additive model does a much better job of predicting the estimates, with between 33 and 55% fitting this model.

These results raise a critical question concerning the multiplicative assumption of the model that guided some of the present research. It suggests the possibility that the averaging model also determines the functional significance of achievement-related motives, and that future research should include studies to compare a multiplicative versus averaging assumption in terms of behavioral criteria. However, this conclusion is inconsistent with other evidence reported here, and, quite frankly, we do not now believe that the data collection bears on the critical variable of "probability of success as moving on from one step to another" (see chapter 4 for research that separates Ps as "moving on" from "immediate success").

If we take seriously the model termed "averaging," it suggests that the *Ps* for a decreasing-probability contingent path and an increasing-probability contingent path would be equivalent and that behavioral effects in high $P_n s_n$ and low $P_n s_n$ constant-probability contingent paths would be equivalent. Studies reported here suggest that this is not the case (see Tables 9, 10, 12, and 13). Rather, hypotheses derived from the multiplicative assumption appear to be supported to some extent. To us, a more reasonable means of reconciling the discrepancy between the data and theory concerning the multiplicative assumption involves changing the theory to consider the chances of moving on in the contingent path as the variable to which the multiplicative assumption applies, rather than to the chances of success per se in each activity. This distinction has been made and investigated in subsequent research studies (see chapter 4). In addition, preliminary analysis of a more direct attempt to *induce* a contingent path through an imaginative technique to test the multiplicative assumption—where the *Ps* of immediate success and *Ps* of moving on can be more safely assumed to be equivalent—yield evidence that a much greater proportion of subjects' responses fit the multiplicative model (unpublished data). However, future research is clearly needed to resolve this issue.

One such data collection is already available. Entin (in chapter 8) reports a "manipulation check" involving the assessment of chances of success in contingent and noncontingent paths of an experimental study in the laboratory setting. That is, contingent and noncontingent paths were induced for programmed instruction, so that the data are analogous to our experimental data when we induce contingent and noncontingent paths in a contrived laboratory situation. At issue is the implication of the multiplicative model for subjective probabilities in the contingent path; as number of steps increases, the chances of getting through the path decreases. Estimates of success declined for the contingent path but not the noncontingent path; males in the contingent path felt that they had a 72% chance of success on test 2 but only a 62% chance of success on test 4; for females, the corresponding percentages are 49 and 39.

A problem in testing the multiplicative assumption most directly by asking for "joint probabilities" in a contingent path is that we may be assessing subjects' knowledge about the rules of combining probabilities as learned in a course in mathematical probability. Our results might reflect that knowledge as much as or more than subjects' preceptions of the situation they face. We have resisted such direct tests for this reason, and are searching for some convincing evaluation of the multiplicative hypothesis based on a "moving-on criterion" in a contingent path that avoids this problem. For the present we feel that the data are sufficiently consistent with the assumption that "subjects act as though" they multiply probabilities along a contingent path so that no changes in assumptions are contemplated based on what we now know. This could change rather quickly if convincing disconfirming evidence becomes available.

MOTIVATION FOR SUCCESSIVE STEPS OF A CONTINGENT PATH

The equations of the more general theory of achievement motivation can be applied to the prediction of motivation for each successive step of a contingent path as an individual successfully moves through the various steps of the path. Of course, if the person were to fail to meet a moving-on criterion of a contingent path, subsequent striving in that path would be ruled out. Thus we are only concerned with successful movement from step to step. This was done for the derivation of the hypotheses for the study of persistence referred to earlier (see also chapter 3).

There are two ways to treat the situation faced by the individual: (1) We can assume that prior success does not affect subsequent subjective probabilities of success so that the initially perceived values of Ps remain constant, thus simplifying application of the equations of the theory, but probably representing an unrealistic view of functioning in some life situations. (2) We can assume that prior success raises initially perceived values of Ps for subsequent steps along the remaining contingent path (as was done for the persistence research), and make reasonable assumptions about the magnitude of change to be expected, thus using a new set of subjective probabilities after each success in the path. We have pursued both, and will deal with the implications of these in subsequent sections.

In Figure 12 we represent the psychological situation assumed to be faced by an individual who initially believes he or she faces a series of contingent steps each having a high value of subjective probability of success ($P_n s_n = .9$), so that successive successes do not (really cannot) raise Ps for subsequent steps. If we further assume a closed contingent path, so that no additional possibilities for future success are added to the end of the path as a function of more immediate success, we can readily see that the number of steps that will contribute to motivation of activity in each successive step will decrease. However, this does not necessarily mean that motivation for immediate activity (positive or negative, depending upon whether $M_S > M_{AF}$ or $M_{AF} > M_S$) will *always* decrease. It can be derived that such a decrease will always occur when values of Ps remain constant along the path. Thus, in Table 8 we have already displayed immediate motivation based on the values obtained from Table 7, assuming each success reduces the length of the contingent path by one step but does not change Ps for subsequent steps. Note that the situation depicted here is analogous to that first shown in Figure 4. The total amount of motivation (positive or negative) decreases regularly for each successive

Number of successes in the contingent path

No. of successes																
0	Person	+1	+2	+3	+4	+5	+6	+7	+8	+9	+10	+11	+12	+13	+14	+15
1		Person	+1	+2	+3	+4	+5	+6	+7	+8	+9	+10	+11	+12	+13	+14
2			Person	+1	+2	+3	+4	+5	+6	+7	+8	+9	+10	+11	+12	+13
3				Person	+1	+2	+3	+4	+5	+6	+7	+8	+9	+10	+11	+12
4					Person	+1	+2	+3	+4	+5	+6	+7	+8	+9	+10	+11
5						Person	+1	+2	+3	+4	+5	+6	+7	+8	+9	+10
6							Person	+1	+2	+3	+4	+5	+6	+7	+8	+9
7								Person	+1	+2	+3	+4	+5	+6	+7	+8
8									Person	+1	+2	+3	+4	+5	+6	+7
9										Person	+1	+2	+3	+4	+5	+6
10											Person	+1	+2	+3	+4	+5
11												Person	+1	+2	+3	+4
12													Person	+1	+2	+3
13														Person	+1	+2
14															Person	+1

Figure 12 Schematic representation of the number of steps remaining in a contingent path as a function of continued success along the path. Here the initial length of the path is 15 steps, and each success reduces the length of path by one step. We can further assume that the value of $P_n s_n = .9$ at each step of the path, and success does not further increase this value of $P_n s_n$.

new step of the closed contingent path, where the constant value of Ps does not change as a function of immediate success.

Note that different predictions are made for different psychological situations. For example, we have already derived predictions for differences in motivation in the first step of decreasing- and increasing-probability contingent paths (see Table 11). If we assume probabilities do not change as a function of success, and sum over one less step for each success, we find that motivation is predicted to change quite differently in the two paths as a function of successful movement along the path, assuming that both paths remain closed. For a decreasing-probability contingent path (values of $P_n s_n$ of .1, .3, .5, .7, and .9), we first see a rise, followed by a drop in motivation, for each immediate next step of the path, as a function of movement along the path toward the last step, while motivation for the new immediate step regularly decreases for a path with values of $P_n s_n = .9, .7, .5, .9, .7, .5, .3$, and .1 (see Figure 13). Note that differences in motivation for the first step are expected to be reversed by the third step, at which time motivation for both paths continues to drop with further successes (see Figure 14). These predictions have not as yet been experimentally tested.

Atkinson (1978) has viewed the data from the Lehman (1953) study of productivity as a function of age, and the data from the Veroff et al. (1960) national survey study of motivation as a function of age, and has tried to relate these data to predictions derived from the more general theory of achievement motivation. Both the data on creative contributions and the n Achievement score show first an increase, followed by a decrease, as a function of age (see Figure 15).

If we assume age is positively correlated with fewer steps in a closed contingent career path, we can derive these effects as determined by resultant achievement motivation aroused for each successive step of a contingent career path if we make the following assumptions: (1) Creative contributions and the n Achievement score reflect resultant positive achievement motivation. (2) The path faced by the majority of individuals is perceived to be a closed contingent one. (3) The subjective probability of success for each successive step of the career path is anticipated to start at some lower moderate value, and then is either expected to increase as the person gets better in the area of endeavor, or actually increases as a function of continued successful movement along the contingent path, and then either remains constant or decreases. These assumptions are represented when we assume the particular values of Ps for a nine-step path are .4, .5, .6, .7, .8, .9, .9, .9, and .9, and, for this illustration, do not change as a function of immediate success. Another example that gives the same general pattern consists of a closed contingent path with values of Ps (that do not change as a function of success) of .1, .3, .5, .7, .9, .9, .9, .9, and .9; a third has values of Ps of .1, .2, .3, .4, .5, .6, .7, .8, and .9 (an increasing-probability contingent path similar to one shown in Figure 13).

A similar pattern results for the following closed contingent career paths: .2, .2, .3, .4, .5, .5, .5, .5, .5 and .1, .4, .7, .9, .7, .4, .1. In general, the bell-shaped curve represented by the data in Figure 14 for the increasing $P_n s_n$ path seems to result when values of Ps are expected to rise and then level off and/or rise and then drop, whereas a regular decrease in Tr (the data in Figure 14 for the decreasing $P_n s_n$ path)

Number of successes in the contingent path

Increasing-probability contingent path

	$P_1s_1 = .1$	$P_2s_2 = .3$	$P_3s_3 = .5$	$P_4s_4 = .7$	$P_5s_5 = .9$
0 Person	$P_1s_1 = .1$ $Is_1 = 1 - .1 = .9$ $Tr_1 = .1 \times .9 = .09$ $Tr = .09 + .03 + .02 + .01 + .01 = .16$	$P_1s_2 = .1 \times .3 = .03$ $Is_2 = 1 - .03 = .97$ $Tr_2 = .03 \times .97 = .03$	$P_1s_3 = .03 \times .5 = .02$ $Is_3 = 1 - .02 = .98$ $Tr_3 = .02 \times .98 = .02$	$P_1s_4 = .02 \times .7 = .01$ $Is_4 = 1 - .01 = .99$ $Tr_4 = .01 \times .99 = .01$	$P_1s_5 = .01 \times .9 = .01$ $Is_5 = 1 - .01 = .99$ $Tr_5 = .01 \times .99 = .01$
1 Person		$P_1s_1 = .3$ $Is_1 = 1 - .3 = .7$ $Tr_1 = .3 \times .7 = .21$ $Tr = .21 + .13 + .10 + .09 = .53$	$P_1s_2 = .3 \times .5 = .15$ $Is_2 = 1 - .15 = .85$ $Tr_2 = .15 \times .85 = .13$	$P_1s_3 = .15 \times .7 = .11$ $Is_3 = 1 - .11 = .89$ $Tr_3 = .11 \times .89 = .10$	$P_1s_4 = .11 \times .9 = .10$ $Is_4 = 1 - .10 = .90$ $Tr_4 = .10 \times .90 = .09$
2 Person			$P_1s_1 = .5$ $Is_1 = 1 - .5 = .5$ $Tr_1 = .5 \times .5 = .25$ $Tr = .25 + .23 + .22 = .70$	$P_1s_2 = .5 \times .7 = .35$ $Is_2 = 1 - .35 = .65$ $Tr_2 = .35 \times .65 = .23$	$P_1s_3 = .35 \times .9 = .32$ $Is_3 = 1 - .32 = .68$ $Tr_3 = .32 \times .68 = .22$
3 Person				$P_1s_1 = .7$ $Is_1 = 1 - .7 = .3$ $Tr_1 = .7 \times .3 = .21$ $Tr = .21 + .23 = .44$	$P_1s_2 = .7 \times .9 = .63$ $Is_2 = 1 - .63 = .37$ $Tr_2 = .63 \times .37 = .23$
4 Person					$P_1s_1 = .9$ $Is_1 = 1 - .9 = .1$ $Tr = Tr_1 = .9 \times .1 = .09$

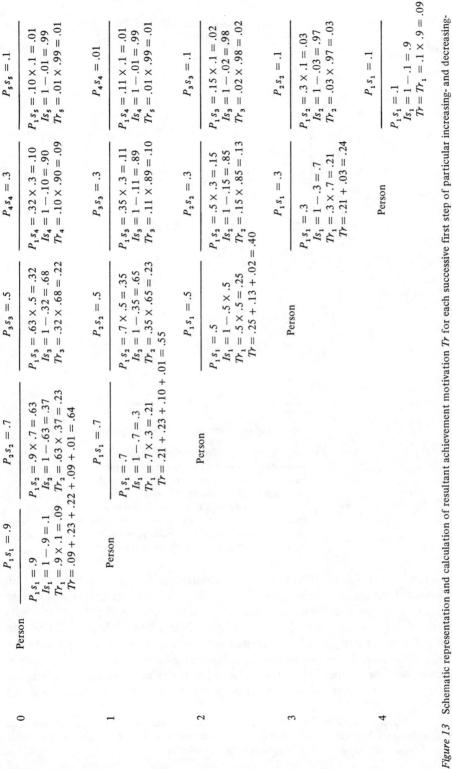

Figure 13 Schematic representation and calculation of resultant achievement motivation Tr for each successive first step of particular increasing- and decreasing-probability contingent paths as a function of the number of prior successes in the path. When $M_S > M_{AF}$, Tr is positive; when $M_{AF} > M_S$, Tr is negative; and when $M_S = M_{AF}$, $Tr = 0$.

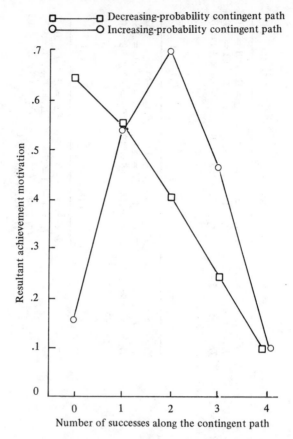

☐━━━━☐ Decreasing-probability contingent path
○━━━━○ Increasing-probability contingent path

Figure 14   Graphic representation of resultant achievement
motivation *Tr* for each successive first step of
particular increasing- and decreasing-probability
contingent paths as shown in Figure 13 (see
figure 13 for calculation of values of *Tr*) as a
function of the number of prior successes in the
path. *Tr* is positive when $M_S > M_{AF}$, negative
when $M_{AF} > M_S$, and 0 when $M_S = M_{AF}$.

is found when values of *Ps* either remain constant for each anticipated step or are
expected to decrease immediately.[4] We believe that the circumstances specified
here that produce the Lehman (1953) and Veroff et al. (1960) patterns of results
(see Figure 15)—consisting of an expected rise followed by a leveling off and/or drop
for $P_n s_n$ along a closed contingent path—are the most reasonable ones that can be
made for individuals who in fact do make creative contributions in the fields of
endeavor: they anticipate and/or initially get better as a function of continued
activity in their area, which is reflected in the increased $P_n s_n$ for anticipated and

[4]We wish to thank Richard Teitelbaum for writing a computer program that allowed us to
investigate the implications of a wide variety of combinations of values of $P_n s_n$ along a contingent path, and for compiling the results of these simulations.

actual later steps; they are success-oriented, more or less, so that *Tr* is positive; they believe that their field will eventually impose limits on their activity, even if this is anticipated as forced retirement, so that they face a closed contingent path. Thus we agree with Atkinson (1978) that the Lehman (1953) and Veroff et al. (1960) data for creative contributions and *n* Achievement score, respectively, are derivable from the more general theory of achievement motivation as the most common pattern, given this set of reasonable assumptions.

Note, however, that a subset of individuals might believe they face (1) an open contingent path, (2) a decreasing $P_n s_n$ contingent path, (3) a constant-probability contingent path, or (4) a noncontingent path. Some might be achievement neutral, and a minority might be failure threatened rather than success oriented. For each of these particular combinations of person and path perception we would derive a pattern of predicted results that differs substantially from the pattern just derived

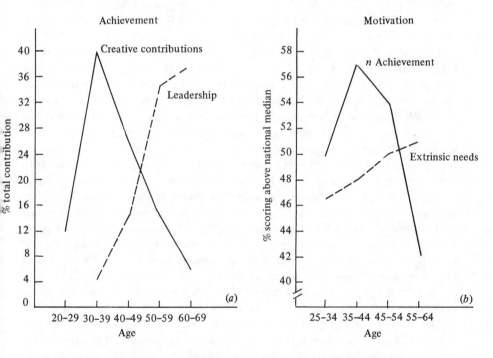

Figure 15   Age, achievement, and motivation to achieve. In (*a*) the curves for creative contributions and leadership are based on medians of fairly recent work in 15 fields of creative endeavor and in 10 fields of governmental, judicial, and military leadership, respectively. (Redrawn after Tables 42 and 43 in Harvey C. Lehman, *Age and Achievement,* published by Princeton University Press (copyright 1953 by the American Philosophical Society), pp. 250–251. Reprinted by permission of Princeton University Press. In (*b*), the curves for TAT *n* Achievement and extrinsic needs (the average of *n* power and *n* affiliation) are based on results from a representative sample of males in the United States in 1957. (From Veroff, J., Atkinson, J. W., Feld, S., and Gurin, G. The use of thematic apperception to assess motivation in a nationwide interview study. *Psychological Monographs,* 1960, *74,* 12, Whole No. 499. Copyright 1960 by the American Psychological Association. Reprinted by permission.

as the expected "majority" pattern. If data were available to allow for analysis of these subgroups, we would no longer expect to see the pattern of an inverted U-shaped curve as a function of age (i.e., continued success), but rather would derive the particular pattern from the particular kind of path and the values of $P_n s_n$ along the path that were believed to hold for that subgroup.

An initial attempt to test experimentally predictions for motivation in each successive step of a contingent path has not been successful because the data yield a very large main effect on performance due to prior practice in each successive step; all subjects did better, regardless of motive type and kind of path induced. We see this at present as a methodological problem—how to create conditions that allow for enough variability so that motive group-path differences can emerge, and/ or how to eliminate practice effects. Possible solutions include use of a different substantive task at each successive step, with comparison of extreme Z scores for each task performance as a function of motive groups and kind of path induced.

We also have explored the implications of theory for positive extrinsic motivation along a closed contingent career path. The major difference in the use of the theory is that the incentive value for the extrinsic reward is not assumed to be inversely related to the (multiplicative) probability that activity in the immediate step of the path will eventually lead on to the extrinsic reward in question. If we assume that the equivalent multiplicative probabilities apply for extrinsic rewards as for achievement incentives, as seems reasonable if we assume that the probability of moving on from step to step determines in part the probability of getting some anticipated future extrinsic reward (since one has to earn the opportunity to strive for the future extrinsic reward in a contingent path in the same way that one has to earn the opportunity to strive for later success in a contingent path), then a family of curves emerges that corresponds to the one shown in Figure 16 for T_{ext}. Here we see that extrinsic motivation T_{ext} generally increases as one approaches the final goal of a closed contingent path, assuming anticipated extrinsic incentives are larger for later steps, but sooner or later also starts to drop off (Figure 16a and b). This dropoff occurs at a later step than the comparable dropoff found for resultant achievement motivation (Tr, also shown for these paths in Figure 16) with equivalent values of $P_n s_n$ for achieving success rather than the extrinsic reward. Thus we derive a general increasing linear trend for extrinsic motivation, although toward the last steps we also expect a start in the drop also predicted for achievement-related motivation for all closed contingent paths. Note, however, that an exception to this trend (see Figure 16c) occurs for a decreasing-probability contingent path. Here both achievement-related and extrinsic motivation decrease as the length of path decreases owing to successful movement along the path, assuming values of $P_n s_n$ do not increase as a function of prior success(es).

Atkinson (1978) has noted the correspondence between the increasing linear trend for leadership contributions in the Lehman (1953) data and the increasing linear trend for the combined n Affiliation and n Power scores, of the Veroff et al. (1960) data, each as a function of increased age, and the prediction made by the more general theory for increased extrinsic motivation (T_{ext}) as a function of successful movement through a contingent path. Again, we agree that Figures 16a and b represent the more probable set of assumptions for these individuals and

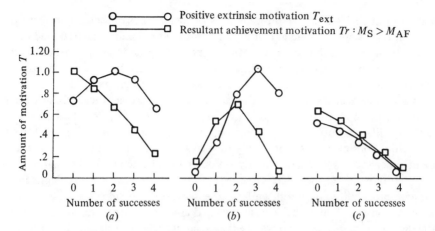

Figure 16 Positive resultant achievement motivation ($M_S > M_{AF}$) and positive extrinsic
motivation (Tr and T_{ext}, respectively) as a function of the number of prior
successes along a contingent path, for three particular contingent paths. (*a*)
.7, .7, .7, .7, .7 path; (*b*) .1, .3, .5, .7, .9 path; (*c*) .9, .7, .5, .3, .1 path.

therefore expect overall trends to correspond to the results obtained (as shown in
Figure 15). Thus the theory, using the entire set of assumptions including that of
multiplication of probabilities along the contingent path, is able to predict trends
for both achievement-related (Tr) and extrinsic (T_{ext}) motivation that correspond
to existing data, given a reasonable set of assumptions. But, again, there are exceptions that are expected if other assumptions hold, particularly for the decreasing-
probability contingent path (Figure 16*c*), which yields a quite different set of predictions for both achievement-related and extrinsic motivation: both are predicted
to decrease as a function of the decrease in length of the contingent path.

The utility of the multiplicative assumption concerning combination of probabilities along the contingent path appears to be enhanced by the correspondence
between predictions based on reasonable assumptions and the data that are thus far
available (e.g., Lehman, 1953, and Veroff et al., 1960). Thus we are reluctant to
abandon it despite the initial disconfirming data from the study of the future plans
of college men reported earlier. The positive data reported in chapter 7 concerning
the implications of the multiplicative assumption for a perceived drop in chances of
success in a contingent path are more encouraging. The multiplicative assumption
remains for us a basic part of the theoretical analysis of contingent future orientation, and data bearing on its validity become of paramount importance.

Implications for Motivation and Career Striving

The analysis of the effects of successful movement through contingent paths
that constitutes career striving in life situations is embedded in a more general
analysis of the functional significance for society of contingent paths and opportunities for advancement and upward social mobility (Raynor, 1974b). It is
assumed that (1) societal gatekeepers are perceived by individuals to function to enforce criteria for moving on in the educational, occupational, and social hierarchies

that exist in society; (2) extrinsic rewards are perceived as becoming increasingly larger in later steps of societal contingent paths; and (3) individuals can and often do use prior success along such a contingent path to upwardly evaluate their degree of possession of the attributes, abilities, and skills that are perceived to be responsible for both prior success and continued success along that path. Thus the implications of our analysis of the relative strengths of achievement-related motivation Tr and extrinsic motivation T_{ext}, as seen in Figure 16a and b, are believed relevant to the qualitative shift in motivation from concern about doing well and advancement along contingent paths of society (due to achievement motivation) to concern about other sources of positive motivation that are reflected in the Lehman (1953) and Veroff et al. (1960) data (Figure 15). When faced with increasing- and/or constant-probability contingent paths, success-oriented individuals are exepcted to be more concerned about achievement-related aspects of career striving than about attainment of the extrinsic rewards that such striving is anticipated to provide. However, as success moves the success-oriented individual toward the original goal of this closed contingent career path, concern with such extrinsic rewards can be expected to dominate over concern about doing well, enhancement of competence-related skills, and/or further promotion and advancement based on merit. While total motivation ($Tr + T_{ext}$) may remain constant or even increase before it starts to drop, we expect this qualitative shift away from concern about doing well as an inevitable consequence of success along the contingent path, so long as the path remains a closed one—that is, so long as the original goal of the path remains fixed so that fewer and fewer achievement steps are perceived to remain between the individual and attainment of the original goal. On the other hand, if the path were to remain an open one, where prior success suggests new achievement goals that are added on to the contingent path so that the old final goal becomes just another goal on the way to still a newer final goal, then decrements in achievement motivation are no longer predicted.

The correspondence between theoretical predictions given reasonable assumptions and the available data (the Lehman, 1953, and Veroff et al., 1960, studies) suggests that our post hoc explanations concerning qualitative shifts from achievement-related to extrinsic motivation in closed contingent paths should be taken seriously as a set of hypotheses to be tested a priori in research where values of $P_{n}s_{n}$, $P_{n}ext_{n}$, $Iext_{n}$, and the open-closed nature of contingent paths faced by the individual are used to predict subsequent achievement-related performance and concern about doing well and advancement. At present we merely note the correspondence between theory and existing data and encourage research in life situations that would bear on these hypotheses. But just as important, we have used the implications of the eventual drop in motivation (both Tr and T_{ext}) as an individual approaches the final goal of a contingent path in a more general theory of personality functioning and change (see chapter 13) as it relates both to stages of career striving and to self-identity tied to such stages of striving. The equations of the more general theory of achievement motivation will eventually require explicit application to the situations involving both the *retrospected past* and the *anticipated future*. We are encouraged by the correspondence between expectations and data thus far obtained that such an extension is firmly enough embedded in empirical support so as to make such an effort worthwhile.

CONCEPTUAL CHANGES TO RESULT
FROM THE PRESENT RESEARCH

The elaboration of the theory of achievement motivation that has guided the present research represented a logical extension of the previous expectancy × value theory of achievement motivation and rested on the best evidence available at the time concerning the role of future orientation in the motivation of immediate action. It resulted in a research paradigm (e.g., the concept of "contingent path") that had not previously been the subject of systematic experimental investigation. The present research was primarily concerned with the study of contingent future orientation. It would be surprising, indeed, if this initial extension of the theory were to find extensive empirical support in its present form. Good scientific theory is so explicitly stated as to be subject to disproof and changes as a function of new (better) knowledge. It is therefore appropriate to speculate on possible conceptual changes in the guiding theory that might result from the present research.

The Functional Significance of Explicit Noncontingent Paths

The concept of noncontingent path was initially developed merely to provide an experimental control situation so that length of path per se rather than contingent future orientation would not be implicated in studies of the effects of future orientation on motivation of immediate activity. It was simply assumed that non-contingent paths would arouse motivation equivalent to one-step situations. Put another way, the initial theory of achievement motivation (e.g., Atkinson & Feather, 1966) was assumed to predict behavior in noncontingent-path situations. *It now appears that this assumption was in error.* Rather, it is likely that the explicit denial that immediate success or failure has any bearing on the opportunity to strive for future success functions to create a nonachievement-oriented situation in which achievement-oriented motives are not aroused and hence not related to behavior. Most of the studies thus far conducted (e.g., see chapters 3, 7, 11, and 12) show either (1) no relationship between motive measures and behavior under non-contingent conditions, or (2) a reversal of the performance and persistence relationships that are predicted for contingent conditions. Why the latter occurs is still not clear. All the possible explanations that are being considered to account for these reversals involve the consideration of factors other than arousal of achievement motivation by noncontingent cues. These include (1) higher ability brought to the situation by failure-threatened individuals, (2) stronger extrinsic motivation aroused in the situation for failure-threatened individuals, and (3) greater inertial tendency (positive achievement motivation) carried over to the present situation by the failure-threatened individual. Each of these possibilities is worth following up in subsequent research.

Only the results reported by Sorrentino (1971) for a noncontingent condition, where group incentives were thought present and in which only individuals high in *n* affiliation were considered, give evidence of significantly higher performance of success-oriented over failure-threatened individuals. This is the only instance where it might be definitely concluded that arousal of achievement motivation did not seem to be prevented by noncontingent instructions.

The Role of Too Much Positive Motivation in Producing Performance Decrements

It is now clear that the initial theory erred in the assumption of a monotonic relationship between motivation and performance efficiency. The results of Sorrentino (1971) and Raynor and Harris (study II) suggest that a very large increase in aroused achievement motivation produced by contingent future orientation has the effects of producing performance decrements for *all* subjects; the decrement for the failure-threatened subjects is predicted and consistent with theory, presumably the result of greater resistance (producing the experience of greater anxiety) to achievement-oriented activity. On the other hand, an increment, but not a subsequent decrement for success-oriented individuals due to (too much) positive motivation, was expected in the initial research, but an overmotivation effect clearly should have been suspected if more attention had been paid to recent studies in the area (cf. Atkinson, 1974a).

The Raynor-Harris study II should also have a bearing on a controversy that has developed concerning the reason why this performance decrement occurs. Horner (1968) has speculated that the decrement is produced when success-oriented individuals also high in *n* affiliation try to engage in incompatible behaviors—pleasing another person or trying to maintain a friendly attitude toward that person while trying to win at a competitive activity. Since all previous research has implicated high *n* affiliation as the source of positive motivation producing performance decrements, this is a reasonable hypothesis. However, the Raynor-Harris (study II) data show the performance decrement in a decreasing-probability contingent path, with no reference to *n* affiliation or an additional interpersonal competitive incentive, but rather merely associated with extreme standing on high *n* Achievement-low test anxiety. This finding is not compatible with Horner's explanation of the performance decrement.

The Multiplication of Probabilities along a Contingent Path

A more serious set of contradictory findings concerns evidence that subjective probabilities of success along a contingent path are not reported as multiplying to determine the total subjective probability of future success in that path. Consideration of this negative finding, along with more recent research findings that were conducted within the framework of the present theory (see chapter 4), clearly suggests that the theory should be changed to indicate that the concept of "success" in the elaborated theory refers to "success as moving on" in the contingent path, rather than success in the immediate activity per se. The distinction between the two meanings of success was made in original statements of the theory (cf. Raynor, 1968a) but then lost when it was assumed that the subjective probability of immediate success defined for the subject the subjective probability of moving on in the path. However, a more recent analysis of the function of contingent paths in society (cf. Raynor, 1974b) indicated that the "gatekeeper" of a contingent path might define the criteria that must be met if one is to be allowed to move on to the next step in the contingent sequence. The individual faced with the contingent hurdle and the gatekeeper whose job it is to enforce the gate may have different standards of good performance that they will take as defining success in that situation. For example, in the Raynor and Rubin (1971) study, the operational definition of success as moving on was 20 of 25 problems solved in $2\frac{1}{2}$ minutes. However, a subject might define "success to me" (rather than to the gatekeeper) as only 10 of 25 problems in $2\frac{1}{2}$ min, or 25 of 25 in $2\frac{1}{2}$ min. The fact is that the elaborated theory should be limited to consideration of "success as moving on" in the contingent path. Research has begun to determine if interactions and/or separate effects result when the two variables are not equivalent in a given situation (see chapter 4), and the preliminary work suggests that the situation is rather complicated.

We now assume that the theoretical statements about psychological distance and incentive values along a contingent path are determined by the multiplication of the subjective probabilities of moving from one step to another rather than the subjective probabilities of success at each of the steps of the path. The research in the present program has implicitly assumed this, and in fact all the operational definitions of subjective probability in experimentally induced contingent paths have used "moving on" to define immediate success. The problem is that the field studies have not. And field studies have been used thus far to test the multiplicative relationship. Hence the comparability of studies has to be reassessed, with both kinds of study making this distinction between success as moving on and some other personal criterion. In field studies only the subjective probability of personal success has been assessed. In experimental studies only the subjective probability of moving on has been induced. We now need to test the multiplicative assumption in field studies of moving on from one step to another.

The Prediction of Risk Preference.

The data suggest that theory might be changed to take account of risk reference, indicating all individuals (rather than just success-oriented individuals) become more conservative in immediate activity in contingent paths. If this turns out to be the experimental finding, as the present studies have shown, then the following conceptual changes might be made. First, the derivation by Atkinson and Birch (1974) is that the *ratio* of tendencies (in the language of the present theory) rather than the *difference* between tendencies determines risk preference. This leads to the conclusion that with little or no extrinsic motivation aroused, all individuals should equally prefer higher subjective probabilities of immediate success (e.g., become more conservative) in contingent than in one-step situations, and do so to a greater extent as the length of the contingent path increases. This would account for the present findings. Alternatively, the motive to avoid failure might not be aroused in contemplating a choice of alternatives, but function only after the individual has been self-committed to that course of action (see chapter 11 for a discussion of this possibility). A third possibility for explaining the results is that the elaborated theory is correct, but that an additional factor overrides its effects. This factor might concern how all individuals view their own competence as a part of their self-image, which might function as an additional source of positive motivation to ensure that individuals who believe that they are trying to fulfill a long-term "sense of self" in a contingent path act so as to guarantee that they stay in the contingent path long enough to fulfill this future sense of self (see chapter 13).

The Self-Image as a Future Goal
in a Contingent Path

The finding of a positive relationship between the importance of doing well in an activity for future success and the importance of doing well in an activity for positive self-evaluation (Raynor, Atkinson, & Brown, 1974; Raynor (1974; see also chapters 10 and 11), plus consideration of the role of societal contingent career paths in providing "roles" that individuals often use as sources of personal identity (cf. Raynor, 1974b), suggests the important conceptual addition that "becoming a sense of self" (e.g., becoming a psychologist) along a contingent path provides for large sources of achievement-related motivation that accentuate characteristic differences between success-oriented and failure-threatened individuals. This possibility is of major importance in the study of motivation, for it may provide the means of integrating the general study of personality and its functioning with the study of achievement motivation via use of the self-concept as an integrating variable (see chapter 13).

3

Achievement Motivation as a Determinant of Persistence in Contingent and Noncontingent Paths

Joel O. Raynor and Elliot E. Entin

Previous investigations of the relationship between achievement-related motivation and persistence (cf. Atkinson & Litwin, 1960; French & Thomas, 1958; Winterbottom, 1958; Feather, 1961; Smith, 1964; Weiner, 1965; Brown, 1967) have shown that the relationship between the two depends upon such factors as initial subjective probability of success Ps, success or failure feedback, the nature and Ps of the alternative task, and the subject's level of intelligence. Also, in previous experimental studies of persistence, the subjects could move on to the next task whether or not they succeeded or failed in the first. This would seem to correspond to a noncontingent path, although it is not usually explicitly pointed out as such to the subject. The present research is concerned with persistence in immediate activity of both a noncontingent and a contingent path in the face of continued success. Three tasks with various numbers of subitems were presented in each condition. The first task was purportedly of intermediate difficulty ($Ps = .5$), with the second and third tasks described as being of increasingly greater difficulty ($Ps <$ .5). Subjects were then given success feedback (cf. Weiner, 1965; Brown, 1967) on each subitem of each of the tasks. The number of subitems worked in the first task before the subject chose to move on to the second task was taken as the measure of persistence in the first. Mean level of performance in the first task was also obtained.

Explicit hypotheses follow from the application of the elaborated theory of achievement motivation (see chapter 2) to the specific situations described above. The noncontingent path used here corresponds to structural arrangements used in previous research in which the initial theory of achievement motivation successfully predicted persistence, with the possibly important difference that in the present research (but not in earlier work) the nature of the noncontingent arrangement is explicitly pointed out to the subject. If previous theory were to apply to explicit noncontingent situations (it may not—see chapter 4), then individuals in whom the motive to achieve is relatively stronger than the motive to avoid failure ($M_S > M_{AF}$) should be more positively motivated for immediate activity when $Ps = .5$, and motivation should decrease with departures of Ps from this intermediate value (cf. Atkinson & Feather, 1966, chap. 20). Continued success should reduce positive motivation for the initial activity as Ps becomes greater than .5.

Success should also increase Ps for the (similar) alternative (second) activity, first presented as having $Ps < .5$. Therefore, positive motivation for the alternative (second) activity should increase while decreasing for the initial one, resulting in an early change of activity from the first to the second. On the other hand, for individuals in whom $M_{AF} > M_S$, negative (inhibitory) motivation should be initially greater for the first task than for the second, but success feedback should reverse their relative strengths. Thus, changes in Ps produced by success feedback should result in individuals with $M_{AF} > M_S$ persisting longer than individuals with $M_S > M_{AF}$ in the immediate activity of the noncontingent series. This reasoning is identical to that used by Feather (1961, 1963) to derive hypotheses in what appear to have been noncontingent-path situation.

Predictions for the contingent path are the opposite of those for the noncontingent path. Resultant achievement motivation should be more positive or negative, depending upon whether M_S is stronger or weaker than M_{AF}, when Ps is substantially higher than .5 than when it equals .5. For the particular situation investigated here, success feedback should first increase (but much later decrease) aroused achievement motivation for the first task. While the same should occur for the second task, the initial difference and rate of increase should produce more aroused motivation for the first than for the second task (see chapter 2, Figure 11, for the derivation discussed here). Success-oriented individuals should persist in the first task for a relatively long period of time. Failure-threatened individuals should stop work relatively early to move on to the second task, for continued success in the first task of the contingent path should increase their negative (inhibitory) motivation for it. Thus success-oriented subjects should persist longer than failure-threatened subjects in immediate activity in the contingent path investigated here.

It follows from the above that individuals in whom $M_S > M_{AF}$ should persist longer in immediate activity in the contingent than in the noncontingent condition, whereas individuals in whom $M_{AF} > M_S$ should persist less in the contingent than in the noncontingent condition. These within-motive group expectations can be viewed as reflecting the theoretical expectation that resultant achievement motivation will be more positive and more negative, respectively, for these motive groups, in immediate activity in the contingent than in the noncontingent paths with the initial values of Ps investigated here and with continued success feedback.

In the present research the behavior of both male and female subjects was investigated. The problem of sex differences in achievement motivation has recently received substantial attention. However, the controversy seems to be more concerned with the effects of different arousal instructions and cue characteristics of pictures on projective thought samples coded for n Achievement and/or fear of success, than with the relationship of these scores to behavior (cf. Horner, 1968, 1974). In a previous study (cf. Raynor, 1968a) it was found that the pattern of interaction between achievement-related motives and future orientation on level of academic performance was very similar for male and female college students (see chapter 2, Table 1). Consequently, it was predicted that results for men and women would be identical in the present research. That is, when differences in future orientation are taken into account, the functional significance of motive scores of men and women are expected to be equivalent.

STUDY I

Method

Subjects

All subjects were male volunteers from an introductory psychology course at Ohio University. For participating, the subjects were awarded experimental credit that could increase their course grade. Complete data were obtained from 82 subjects.

Assessment of Motives

The motive to achieve success (M_S) was assessed by the technique developed by McClelland, Atkinson, Clark, and Lowell (1953), using sentences rather than pictures to elicit stories (cf. Raynor and Rubin, 1971). Stories were scored by an expert (E.E.E.) according to the *n* Achievement scoring manual (cf. McClelland, Atkinson, Clark, and Lowell, 1958). The first third of the Test Anxiety Questionnaire (Mandler & Sarason, 1952) was used to assess the motive to avoid failure (M_{AF}). This section of 12 items has been found to correlate between .84 and .90 with the total score (cf. Smith, 1964). A graphic rating scale appeared below each item. The scale was divided into fifths and scored so that 5 indicated highest and 1 indicated lowest anxiety. Total scores were obtained by summing over the 12 items.

Motive groups were obtained by first breaking the distribution of *n* Achievement and test anxiety scores at their respective medians and then categorizing each subject simultaneously high and low on both. This yielded four motive groups: high (*n* Achievement)–low (test anxiety), low–high, high–high, and low–low. It was assumed that subjects in the high-low group would have $M_S > M_{AF}$, and those in the low-high group would have $M_{AF} > M_S$.

The product moment correlation between *n* Achievement and test anxiety scores was −.03 ($N = 82$).

The Performance Task

The performance task was composed of three booklets of three-step arithmetic problems (cf. Wendt, 1955; Raynor & Rubin, 1971). The first, second, and third booklets were labeled Item 1, Item 2, and Item 3, and consisted of 35, 30, and 25 pages, respectively. Each page had 12 problems.

Procedure

After the assessment of motives was completed by the male experimenter (E.E.E.), the experimental induction began. In preparation for working the tasks, all subjects were told:

We are collecting final data for some similar kinds of items. These are arithmetic problems taken from a larger abilities test thought to be a culture-free measure of ability. The items are ordered so that the first should be easiest, the second more difficult, and the last most difficult. However, since these items come from the last part of the test, even the first kind of item you will work on is not easy. Our research has shown that it should be of moderate difficulty for a college group of this age and ability.

Each item booklet is composed of many subsets, one set per page, of a particular kind of item. As in many tests of this nature, this one is constructed so that failure at a particular subset of an item marks one's level of ability. Failure is defined here as doing below the established average for that particular subset and trial.

Those subjects in the noncontingent condition were then told the following, including the information not printed in italics but not including that in parentheses, while those in the contingent condition were told the same, except that all non-italicized phrases were omitted and all in parentheses were included:

The probability is small that you will be able to solve more difficult items in the allotted time after failure, but today you can continue beyond that point *(thus there is no object in continuing beyond that point).*

You can have as many tries, i.e., do as many subsets as you want of a particular item, even if you happen to fail on a particular subset *(as long as you are successful). When you feel you have mastered a kind of item, you can go on to the next more difficult kind. However, you cannot return to an easier kind of item once you begin to work at a more difficult kind, so make sure you are good enough before you move on. When you leave the blue—first booklet—book to work on the green—second booklet—book, you are not free to go back. Remember the blue booklet is moderately difficult, the green a bit more difficult, and the white more difficult still.*

As we progress through the experiment, the time that you have to work may change. I will tell you in advance of such a change. For the beginning, you will have about one minute to work on each subset.

The instructions to the problem are. . .

Instructions for the three-step arithmetic problems were given at this point. The experimental induction then continued:

When time is called at the end of a subset, you will have a few seconds to count the number of problems you have done for that page. Compare that number to the one I print on the board. If your number done is larger or equal to that number there is a very high probability you have done an average number correct. You are successful. You can continue. (If your number done is less, you have failed. You are to stop work.) When we score the booklets later, only the number correct will matter, so be sure you work for correctness.

You have three booklets marked Item 1—a blue book—Item 2—a green book—and Item 3—a white book. You are asked to start with Item 1—the blue book. However, you can move on to the next booklet any time you want. Just close the booklet you are working on and select the new one. Even if you fail, continue to work. *(If you fail, stop work and sit quietly.) Are there any questions?*

Thirty-five 75-sec trials were conducted. At the end of every five trials the following was said: "Remember you are free to go on to the next item in the sequence when you feel you have mastered the item you are working on." The numbers written on the board at the end of each trial ranged from 1 to 4 with a median of 3. This was well below the average number of problems that subjects could do in 75 sec. Thus all subjects experienced constant success, i.e., success on each try in the first booklet (and the second, if necessary). After the 35th trial the experiment was ended and subjects were completely debriefed. This procedure allowed persistence scores in the first booklet to range from 1 to 35.

STUDY II

Method

Subjects

Seventy-eight female students from an introductory psychology class volunteered to participate in the experiment, for which they received credit that could increase their class grade.

Assessment of Motives

Need achievement and test anxiety scores were obtained and scored as in study I. Motive groups were obtained by using the median breaks on n Achievement and test anxiety found in this sample of females to classify subjects simultaneously high and low to obtain the four motive groups referred to in study I.

The correlation between n Achievement and test anxiety was .00 ($N = 78$).

The Performance Task

The performance task was identical to that employed in study I; three booklets consisting of 35, 30, and 25 pages of three-step arithmetic problems.

Procedure

The assessment of motives and induction of the experimental manipulations were carried out by a female experimenter.[1] All introductory remarks and materials were identical to those used in study I, as were the instructions used to create the experimental conditions. The only procedural differences between this study and study I were that now 60-sec trials were conducted and no reminder was given at the end of blocks of five trials informing subjects that they could move on when they wished. Again the numbers written on the board at the end of each trial ranged from 1 to 4, with a median of 3, which was still well below the average number of problems that subjects could do in 60 sec.

RESULTS

Performance Level

There was no basis for expecting that the difference in procedures concerning the way persistence data were obtained would have an effect on the pattern of in-

[1] The authors wish to thank Judy Wheat for collecting the data for this study.

teraction predicted for level of performance. However, to check on this possibility, performance scores were treated in terms of a factorial design including sex as one of the variables. Thus, the mean number of problems attempted in the first task was analyzed as a function of extreme motive group (high-low vs. low-high), experimental condition, and sex. The data are shown in Table 1. There was a main effect due to sex ($F = 4.93$, $df = 1/80$, $p < .05$), indicating that men attempted more problems than women. But sex did not interact with either motives or conditions, alone or taken together. Inspection of the means of Table 1 indicates that the pattern of interaction is very similar for the two sexes. For both male and female subjects, the data support the same three of four directional hypotheses that can be specified: the high-low group tried more problems in the contingent than in the noncontingent condition, while the reverse was the case for the low-high group, with the high-low group outperforming the low-high group within the contingent condition. The overall analysis of variance shows that the extreme motive groups X conditions interaction is significant ($F = 4.54$, $df = 1/80$, $p < .05$) but that the interaction between extreme motives, conditions, and sex does not approach significance ($F < 1$, n.s.). Thus it appears safe to conclude from these results that (1) the relative levels of performance of comparable motive groups across different experimental conditions were as predicted, and (2) the difference in prompting about moving on after five trials, which was included for males but not for females, did not affect these relative levels of performance. Note, however, a reversal of expected results for both men and women was obtained within the noncontingent conditions, where the low-high groups tried more problems than the high-low groups. We would expect the predicted superiority of the high-low over the low-high group would be *smaller* in the noncontingent than in the contingent condition, rather than reversed.

Further inspection of Table 1 suggests that the effects just described for the two

Table 1 Number of Problems Attempted in the First Task (Performance Level) as a Function of Motive Groups, Experimental Conditions, and Sex

| | Males | | | | Females | | | |
| | Noncontingent | | Contingent | | Noncontingent | | Contingent | |
	N	Mean	N	Mean	N	Mean	N	Mean
n Achievement								
High	23	6.24	20	6.55	21	5.63	14	5.95
Low	15	6.64	25	6.43	18	5.51	25	5.27
Test anxiety								
Low	18	6.12	22	6.89	20	5.42	19	5.93
High	12	6.65	23	6.11	19	5.75	20	5.12
n Achievement -test anxiety								
High-low	10	6.13	11	6.78	11	5.43	10	6.44
High-high	13	6.33	9	6.27	10	5.87	4	4.73
Low-low	8	6.12	11	6.99	9	5.41	9	5.37
Low-high	7	7.23	14	6.00	9	5.62	16	5.21

Table 2 Number of Pages Attempted in the First Task (Persistence) as a Function of Motive
Groups, Experimental Conditions, and Sex

	Males				Females			
	Noncontingent		Contingent		Noncontingent		Contingent	
	N	Mean	N	Mean	N	Mean	N	Mean
n Achievement								
High	23	7.26	20	9.60	21	11.52	14	18.29
Low	15	7.60	25	7.84	18	12.50	25	13.20
Test anxiety								
Low	18	9.33	22	10.32	20	9.50	19	18.11
High	20	5.65	23	7.00	19	14.58	20	12.10
n Achievement-test anxiety								
High-low	10	9.00	11	11.90	11	8.64	10	21.70
High-high	13	5.92	9	6.68	10	14.70	4	9.75
Low-low	8	9.75	11	8.73	9	10.56	9	14.11
Low-high	7	5.14	14	7.14	9	14.44	16	12.69

extreme motive groups are primarily due to differences in test anxiety rather than
n Achievement. To check on this possibility, an additional ANOVA was carried out
using *n* Achievement (high vs. low) and test anxiety (high vs. low) as separate
factors in the analysis, along with conditions and sex. The analysis and its appropriate means tables (see Table 1) confirm the fact that test anxiety alone is largely
responsible for the pattern of results that was obtained. There was a significant
TAQ $\times$ condition interaction ($F = 4.44, df = 1/145, p < .05$) while the interaction
between *n* Achievement and conditions did not approach significance ($F < 1$, n.s.)
For both sexes the pattern is identical, disregarding a main effect of sex ($F = 9.90$,
$df = 1/145$, $p < .005$), indicating that males outperformed females. There is an
increment for the low test-anxiety groups coupled with a decrement of about equal
magnitude for the high test-anxiety groups from the noncontingent to the contingent conditions. The low test-anxiety groups performed higher than the high test-
anxiety groups within the contingent conditions, but the reverse is found within the
noncontingent conditions.

Persistence

The data for persistence were analyzed in a way similar to that for performance
level. Persistence scores were first subject to analysis of variance as a function of
extreme motive group, experiment condition, and sex. The mean data are presented
in Table 2. There was a main effect due to sex indicating that women persisted
longer than men ($F = 8.52$, $df = 1/80$, $p < .005$). This is most probably interpre-
table as due to the difference in procedure whereby the men but not the women
were reminded after every five trials that at any time they could move on to the
next booklet in the series. Of greater relevance for the hypotheses of the present re-

search is an evaluation of the interaction effects for the extreme motive groups. The overall analysis of variance reveals an extreme motives X conditions interaction ($F = 3.58$, $df = 1/80$, $p = .05$), but also shows an interaction between extreme motive groups, conditions, and sex ($F = 2.80$, $df = 1/80$, $p < .10$). Inspection of the means of Table 2 indicates that the predicted pattern of interaction is present for the females but not for the males. Consequently the data for the two sexes were analyzed separately to evaluate specific hypotheses. For the female sample alone, the interaction effect between extreme motive groups and conditions was significant ($F = 4.71$, $df = 1/42$, $p < .05$). Specific directional hypotheses were then evaluated for the sample of females using a priori comparisons (t tests). The prediction that in the contingent condition the high-low group would persist longer than the low-high group is confirmed ($t = 2.64$, $df = 42$, $p < .01$, one-tailed test). It was also predicted and found that the high-low group would persist longer in the contingent than in the noncontingent condition ($t = 1.97$, $df = 42$, $p < .05$, one-tailed test). Inspection of the data in Table 2 indicates that the trend of results is consistent with the other two hypotheses: that in the noncontingent condition the low-high group would persist longer than the high-low group, and within the low-high group persistence would be greater in the noncontingent than in the contingent condition. However, neither trend approaches statistical significance ($ts = 1.14$ and 1, respectively, n.s.).

Analysis of variance of the persistence data for the male sample separately yields a main effect due to extreme motives ($F = 3.85$, $df = 1/38$, $p = .05$). None of the other effects approached significance. Inspection of Table 2 shows that, for the males, the high-low group persisted longer than the low-high group regardless of experimental condition. While there is some tendency for both groups to persist more in the contingent than the noncontingent condition, the effect of the conditions does not approach statistical significance ($F = 1.25$, $df = 1/38$, $p < .30$, n.s.).

Further inspection of Table 2 suggests again that effects for the two extreme motive groups are primarily due to differences in test anxiety rather than n Achievement. Therefore the ANOVA using n Achievement (high vs. low) and test anxiety (high vs. low) as separate factors along with conditions and sex was again employed. The results confirm the fact that test anxiety alone pretty much accounts for the pattern of results. There was a significant TAQ X condition X sex interaction affecting persistence scores ($F = 3.82$, $df = 1/145$, $p = .05$) whereas none of the effects involving n Achievement approached statistical significance. Note (see Table 2) that for the females we observe the increment in persistence as predicted for the low test-anxiety group coupled with the very small decrement for the high test-anxiety group, from the noncontingent to the contingent condition. The low test-anxiety females persisted longer than the high test-anxiety females in the contingent condition, but the reverse is found within the noncontingent condition. On the other hand, for the males we find the low test-anxiety groups persisting longer than the high test-anxiety groups in both the contingent and noncontingent conditions.

DISCUSSION

Independent assessment of level of performance provides a pattern of interaction between motive measures and conditions that was generally predicted by theory and found in previous research (cf. Raynor & Rubin, 1971; Entin & Raynor, 1973; chapters 7 and 13). Persistence results provide evidence consistent with expectations for the females but not the males. The *n* Achievement scores alone do not significantly relate to either performance levels or persistence. Results for extreme motive groups obtained using *n* Achievement-test anxiety are also consistent with hypotheses for performance level and persistence for females. Since the performance-level data for men and women are similar and are consistent with expectations, we should take seriously the difference in the pattern of persistence results for men and women. The performance-level data provide independent validity evidence for the assessment of motives and the experimental procedures of the present research. The main effect of test anxiety on persistence for men but the interaction between test anxiety and conditions on persistence for women suggests that an additional factor was operating to influence persistence but not performance for men to produce the greater persistence of low test-anxiety and high-low (success-oriented) over high test-anxiety and low-high (failure-threatened) subjects.

One factor not considered in the present research might be that subjects who placed a higher value on possession of the substantive skill (mathematical ability) purportedly assessed here were more concerned with obtaining information about their level of possession of this valued ability than they were concerned about doing well per se. Such information seeking about one's ability (cf. Trope & Brickman, 1975; Trope, 1976; chapter 11) might override the predicted effects for men but not women because men may place a much greater value on possession of mathematical ability than do women. Continued persistence in either the noncontingent or contingent condition should yield more information about one's level of ability through success/failure feedback on each item than moving on without feedback on earlier items. And presumably the success-oriented men were more concerned about finding out about possession of this ability than the failure-threatened men. While we have no direct evidence for this post hoc interpretation of the results for men, it is a plausible one that merits further investigation. In chapter 11 we present theory that is constructed to deal with assessment of ability in achievement-oriented situations.

One bit of indirect evidence that is consistent with a greater overall arousal of motivation for men than women is the finding of a substantial main effect of sex on performance such that men had higher performance scores than women. While the main effect of sex on persistence is probably due to the difference in prompting to move on in the procedures for men and women samples, we do not have a plausible explanation as to why this should also have produced a main effect on performance levels. This difference might reflect the overall greater value of mathematical ability perceived by the men in comparison to the women of the present sample.

Note that any such interpretation of the results must also account for the fact that the performance-level data for men also reflect an interaction between test anxiety, or extreme combined motive groups, and conditions—while the persistence data do not. We suspect that the decision to persist or move on for the men was influenced by cognitive factors concerning information seeking that also produced the main effect on performance, whereas for the women this cognitive factor was minimal for persistence (as well as performance) because assessment or possession of mathematical ability was less important overall due to less positive value of this ability in general for college-age women subjects of the present research. If we were able to isolate those men who did not value possession of mathematical ability to any great extent, and women who did, then we would expect that within levels of value of possession the results for persistence for the two sexes would then be equivalent, and the main effect on performance would disappear.

4

Success versus Moving
on in Contingent Paths

Elliot E. Entin and Joel O. Raynor

An important feature of Raynor's (1969, 1978a) elaboration of the theory of achievement motivation (see chapter 2) is the concept of contingent path. A *path* is defined as a sequence of anticipated activities or tasks where each activity represents a step in that path. A path is said to be *contingent* if success at the immediate step of a path is necessary to guarantee the opportunity to strive for success at the next step, while immediate failure precludes such an opportunity. When immediate success or failure at a step has no bearing on the opportunity to engage in subsequent activities, the path is said to be *noncontingent*.

In the elaborated theory, Raynor (1978a) proposes (see also chapter 2) that individuals who are assumed to be motivated to achieve success, that is, individuals in whom the motive to achieve is stronger than the motive to avoid failure ($M_S >$ M_{AF}), should perform better in a contingent than in a noncontingent path. For these individuals a contingent path arouses future as well as immediate tendencies to achieve, while a noncontingent path arouses only immediate tendencies to succeed. By contrast, individuals who are assumed inhibited by the threat of failure in achievement activities, that is, individuals in whom the motive to avoid failure is stronger than the motive to achieve success ($M_{AF} > M_S$), should perform better in a noncontingent than a contingent path. For these individuals, a contingent path arouses inhibition associated with possible future as well as immediate threats of failure, while a noncontingent path arouses inhibition associated only with immediate threats of failure.

Empirical findings have supported these hypotheses (Raynor & Rubin, 1971; Entin & Raynor, 1973; see chapter 2). In these studies, subjects were led to believe that attaining some criterion, and thus success, earned for them the opportunity to move on to the next step in the contingent path. Specifically, subjects were told that they had to achieve an objective criterion, such as completing 20 of 25 items in $2\frac{1}{2}$ min, or a relative criterion, such as placing above the mean performance of the group. "Success" and "continuing on" in a contingent path were thus made synonymous. Stated another way, reaching the stated criterion defined success, and success was the necessary condition to be allowed to continue on in the path.

This, however, need not be the case. Success and earning the opportunity to continue on in a contingent path need not be confounded. The preceding definition of a contingent path can be interpreted more loosely. Being successful, that is, measuring up to some internal or external criterion and taking pride in the accomplishment, does not have to guarantee continuance in a contingent path. One can, for example, do well in college (i.e., Dean's list) and rightly take pride in the accomplishment, yet this accomplishment may still not be at a level high enough to obtain admission to medical school. On the other hand, one may not achieve the internal or external success criteria, feel little or no pride of accomplishment, yet find the criteria for certain fields, say salesperson, to be below the achieved level. Thus, continuance in such a contingent path is possible.

Such a situation, where the criterion for success can be disassociated from that required for continuing in a contingent path, will be referred to as the "gatekeeper" effect (see Raynor, 1974b, p. 372). The gatekeeper (some person or agency) has the power to establish what will be required to continue in a path and thus can decide whether it will be above, below, or at what is usually accepted by the individual engaged in the activity as successful performance. Furthermore, the gatekeeper can base the criteria on task-relevant or task-irrelevant attributes. In the medical-school example, the gatekeeper has selected a task-relevant criterion, academic achievement. The gatekeeper is able, however, to base continuance in the path on such task-irrelevant attributes as skin color, religion, and nationality.

Two studies were designed to examine the gatekeeper effect. In study I a task-relevant criterion for continuation in the contingent path took on two levels, as did the success criterion—high and low. In study II both the success and moving-on criteria could take on three values: an easily reachable criterion, one moderate in difficulty, and one quite difficult to attain. Due to the highly empirical nature of these studies, no specific hypotheses were made concerning the success versus moving-on criterion other than those usually subsumed under the theory of achievement motivation.

STUDY I[1]

Method

Subjects

Male college students enrolled in introductory psychology classes at Ohio University served as subjects. Students received extra credit points that could augment their course grade for participation. Complete data were available for 138 students.

Assessment of Motives

The Resultant Achievement Motivation Scale (RAMS) (Mehrabian, 1968), a purported self-report measure of achievement motivation, and the first third of the Test Anxiety Questionnaire (TAQ) (Mandler and Sarason, 1952) were administered to all students under neutral conditions. Both instruments were administered and coded according to the literature pertinent to each. Smith (1964) has pointed out that the first third of the TAQ correlates .84 with the full scale and can be used in

---

[1] Study I is based in part on an unpublished master's thesis (Rosenthal, 1973) completed at Ohio University.

lieu of the whole scale with little loss of reliability. The resulting distributions were each rank ordered and trichotomized. Those students in the upper third on RAMS were assumed $M_S > M_{AF}$ while students in the lower third on RAMS were assumed $M_{AF} > M_S$. In a similar manner, students in the lower third of the TAQ distribution were considered $M_S > M_{AF}$, while those in the upper third were considered $M_{AF} > M_S$. Atkinson (1964, p. 250) has already presented an explanation of how resultant achievement motivation can be inferrred from TAQ alone.

Dependent Measures

The performance measure consisted of four-letter anagrams (adapted from Lowell, 1952). Sixty anagrams were placed on a page, and four such pages were organized into a test booklet. In addition to the anagrams, questions assumed to assess the attitudes students held about the test and testing situation were also arranged in booklet form. Only three of those questions concern us here. They were: (1) "On a scale from 0 to 100 what do you feel your probability is of attaining the success criterion"; (2) "On a scale from 0 to 100 what do you feel your probability is of attaining the opportunity-to-move-on criterion"; (3) "Which goal is more important to you: Being successful or moving on?"

Procedure

After the assessment of motives, the anagram and questionnaire booklets were distributed. Students in the first experimental condition both read and heard the following:

> This booklet consists of four subtests of verbal ability. These tests have been adjusted to be of moderate difficulty for people of your age and abilities. On the first test and each test thereafter, to be considered successful you are required to complete 54 problems out of 60. To earn the opportunity to move on to the next test you are required to complete 6 problems out of 60. Those of you who do not complete the number of problems required to move on will remain seated until all four tests are finished. You will have five minutes for each test.
>
> Remember that to be considered successful you are required to complete 54 out of 60 problems. To move on to the next test you are required to complete 6 out of 60 problems.

The students in the other three experimental conditions read and heard the same instructions except for changes in the number of problems required to meet each criterion. That is, individuals in the second experimental condition were told they had to correctly solve 54 problems out of 60 to be successful and 54 out of 60 to earn the opportunity to move on to the next test; students in the third experimental condition heard they had to correctly solve 6 out of 60 problems to be considered successful; 6 out of 60 problems were necessary to earn the opportunity to move on; and in the fourth experimental condition students were informed that 6 out of 60 problems worked correctly was necessary to be considered successful but 54 out of 60 was required to earn the opportunity to move on.

Instructions on how to solve the anagrams and 10 sample problems followed the induction instructions. Just prior to the performance task, students completed the

11-item questionnaire. This was followed by a short reiteration of the induction instruction and the first anagrams test. The 5-min time interval allotted to do Test 1 precluded all but a very few individuals from attempting 54 problems. Immediately after Test 1, students completed another form of the 11-item questionnaire. The same 11 items were used except now they were worded to refer to Test 2. The experiment was then terminated, all materials collected, and the students debriefed.

Results

The two measures of resultant achievement motivation, RAMS and TAQ, were employed in separate analyses. In this way the RAMS could be compared to the more traditional TAQ, and any differences between them evaluated.

The number of anagrams attempted and worked correctly were analyzed using analysis of variance with RAMS (2) X success criteria (2) X moving-on criteria (2) as factors. A similar analysis was computed with TAQ substituted for RAMS. Individuals in the intermediate groups of the RAMS and TAQ distributions were deleted. Thus only the relatively purer motivation groups remained, allowing for easier interpretation of interactions.

Table 1 presents the means for the number of anagrams attempted and solved correctly as a function of RAMS, success criterion, and moving-on criterion. The ANOVA, summarized in Table 2, shows no main effects for either dependent variable. A success criterion X opportunity-to-move-on criterion interaction did prove significant for number of anagrams attempted and correct ($F = 3.52$, $df = 1/82$, $p < .07$ and $F = 6.02$, $df = 1/82$, $p < .05$, respectively). Performance appeared to be better when the two criteria were different (that is, when the success criterion was 54 out of 60 and the moving-on criterion was 6 out of 60, or the success criterion was 6 out of 60 and the moving-on criterion was 54 out of 60) than when the two criteria were the same. None of the other interactions was significant.

The means for number of anagrams attempted and solved correctly, analyzed by TAQ, success criteria, and opportunity to move on are shown in Table 3, and the summary of the ANOVA is shown in Table 4. Again, no main effects were found

Table 1 Number of Anagrams Attempted and Worked Correctly as a Function of RAMS, Success Criterion, and the Opportunity-to-Move-on Criterion

RAMS	Success	Moving on	n	Number attempted	Number correct
High	6 of 60	6 of 60	11	23.18	20.36
	6 of 60	54 of 60	13	29.31	26.62
	54 of 60	6 of 60	10	26.00	24.10
	54 of 60	54 of 60	10	20.10	16.70
Low	6 of 60	6 of 60	10	24.10	18.80
	6 of 60	54 of 60	9	25.56	21.33
	54 of 60	6 of 60	14	24.21	21.93
	54 of 60	54 of 60	13	23.77	19.85

Table 2 Number of Anagrams Attempted and Worked Correctly Analyzed as a Function of
RAMS, Success Criterion, and Opportunity-to-Move-on Criterion

		Mean square		F	
Source	df	Number attempted	Number correct	Number attempted	Number correct
RAMS (A)	1	1.20	47.38	< 1	< 1
Success (B)	1	89.33	28.31	1.18	< 1
Opportunity to move on (C)	1	2.11	.65	< 1	< 1
A × B	1	30.64	84.10	< 1	1.10
A × C	1	.86	3.54	< 1	< 1
B × C	1	266.66	458.85	3.52*	6.02**
A × B × C	1	140.98	112.24	1.86	1.47
Within	82	75.69	76.28		

*Significant at the .07 level.
**Significant at the .05 level.

for any variable. A TAQ × success criterion interaction was found for number correct ($F = 3.93$, $df = 1/83$, $p < .05$). Low-TAQ individuals performed better when the success criterion was 54 out of 60 than when it was 6 out of 60, while high-TAQ individuals showed the opposite trend and performed better when the success criterion was 6 out of 60 than when it was 54 out of 60. Number of anagrams attempted showed a TAQ × moving-on criterion interaction ($F = 3.56$, $df = 1/84$, $p < .06$). Low-TAQ students tried more problems when the moving-on criterion was 6 out of 60 than when it was 54 out of 60, and high-TAQ students attempted more when the moving-on criterion was 54 out of 60 than when it was 6 out of 60.

Finally, a three-dimensional chi-square analysis using TAQ × opportunity to move on × goal preference on Test 1 was computed to determine if anxiety level and moving-on criterion affected preference for the success or moving-on criterion on Test 1. Thus, the ratings taken after Test 1 were used. Using a method proposed

Table 3 Number of Anagrams Attempted and Worked Correctly as a Function of TAQ,
Success Criterion, and Opportunity-to-Move-on Criterion

TAQ	Success	Moving on	n	Number attempted	Number correct
High	6 of 60	6 of 60	13	24.23	21.23
	6 of 60	54 of 60	13	28.23	24.08
	54 of 60	6 of 60	9	20.44	18.22
	54 of 60	54 of 60	8	22.88	18.00
Low	6 of 60	6 of 60	11	26.82	21.36
	6 of 60	54 of 60	11	25.27	22.27
	54 of 60	6 of 60	17	30.24	28.71
	54 of 60	54 of 60	10	23.40	21.20

Table 4 Number of Anagrams Attempted and Worked Correctly Analyzed as a Function of TAQ, Success Criterion, and Opportunity-to-Move-on Criterion

| | | Mean square | | F | |
Source	df	Number attempted	Number correct	Number attempted	Number correct
TAQ (A)	1	149.87	195.55	1.77	2.25
Success (B)	1	18.11	5.83	< 1	< 1
Opportunity to move on (C)	1	17.45	51.23	< 1	< 1
A × B	1	165.56	341.82	1.96	3.93**
A × C	1	322.98	135.28	3.82*	1.55
B × C	1	148.84	296.99	1.76	3.41
A × B × C	1	18.95	39.12	< 1	< 1
Within	84	84.47	87.06		

*Significant at the .06 level.
**Significant at the .05 level.

by Goodman (1964), a chi-square of 9.98 ($p < .005$) was obtained for the frequency distribution shown in Table 5. These results show that when the opportunity-to-move-on criterion was 54 out of 60, high-TAQ individuals felt the success criterion was more important than the moving-on criterion, while low-TAQ individuals felt the opportunity-to-move-on criterion more important than the success criterion. On the other hand, when the opportunity-to-move-on criterion was 6 out of 60, high-TAQ individuals showed no clear preference, and low-TAQ individuals felt success more important than the opportunity-to-move-on criterion. A similar analysis was performed for TAQ × success criterion × goal preference but did not prove significant.

Discussion

The pattern of results obtained showed that each criterion interacted with personality and each interaction had its unique effect on performance. Individuals in whom $M_S > M_{AF}$, as assessed by test anxiety, solved more anagrams correctly when the success criterion was set high than when it was set low. Those in whom

Table 5 Distribution of Subjects as a Function of TAQ, Moving on, and Goal Choice

| | Moving on | | | |
| | 6 out of 60 Goal choice | | 54 out of 60 Goal choice | |
TAQ	Success	Moving on	Success	Moving on
High	10	11	13	5
Low	20	8	6	15

$M_{AF} > M_S$ showed the opposite pattern of results, performing better when the success criterion was low rather than high. It would appear that when proceeding on in a contingent path is not at issue, $M_S > M_{AF}$ individuals work more efficiently when confronted with the more difficult success criterion than with the easier one, and $M_{AF} > M_S$ individuals are less inhibited by the easier than by the more difficult success criterion.

Analysis of the questionnnaire item that asked students to estimate their probability of reaching the success criterion showed that students low in test anxiety viewed the 54 out of 60 condition as easy ($p = .72$) prior to performance and moderately difficult ($p = .48$) after performance. The 6 out of 60 condition was viewed by the same motive group as moderately easy (about .64) both prior to and after performance. According to the initial theory of achievement motivation, as probability of success falls into the intermediate range, $M_S > M_{AF}$ individuals should experience an increase in the positive achievement tendency and performance should increase. This apparently occurred in the 54 out of 60 condition. In contrast, the initial probability estimates remained unchanged in the 6 out of 60 condition, and were viewed as moderately easy. They thus would be expected to generate a relatively constant, weak-approach tendency. These conditions presumably produced the observed higher performance of the low test-anxiety group in the 54 out of 60 than in the 6 out of 60 condition.

On the other hand, students high in test anxiety rated the 54 out of 60 condition moderately difficult (i.e., .59) prior to performance and difficult (i.e., .32) after performance. The 6 out of 60 condition was seen as moderately easy (about .62) both prior to and after performance. In other words, students high in test anxiety perceived the probability of success as dropping through the intermediate-difficulty range, predicted to produce for these individuals considerable inhibition and thus lower performance when compared to the 6 out of 60 condition. In this latter condition, the probability of success was viewed as moderately easy throughout, thus tending to minimize inhibition. This presumably produced the observed higher performance of individuals high in test anxiety in the 6 out of 60 than in the 54 out of 60 condition.

As for the opportunity to move on by TAQ interaction, it seemed that students low in test anxiety ($M_S > M_{AF}$) tried harder (i.e., attempted more anagrams) when the opportunity to move on was objectively easier (6 out of 60) than more difficult (54 out of 60), while students high in test anxiety ($M_{AF} > M_S$) appeared less inhibited when the opportunity to move on was objectively more difficult to attain (54 out of 60) rather than easier to attain (6 out of 60). These results conform to predictions derivable from Raynor's (1969, 1974a) elaborated theory of achievement motivation if the criterion necessary to earn the opportunity to move on is considered the contingent element in the path. It is, after all, the criterion to earn the opportunity to move on that must be achieved on each step to go on to the next step. The elaborated theory predicts that for $M_S > M_{AF}$ individuals a path composed of easier as opposed to more difficult tasks (steps) will produce a relatively greater future-oriented resultant achievement tendency and therefore higher performance (see chapter 2). For $M_{AF} > M_S$ individuals, the elaborated theory predicts that a path composed of more difficult tasks will produce less future-oriented inhibition when compared to a path composed of easier tasks. Less inhibition leads to relatively better performance for $M_{AF} > M_S$ individuals. Results of the item that requested students to give their probability of reaching the moving-on criterion lend support to this interpretation by showing that students low in test anxiety viewed the 6 out of 60 condition as relatively easy (about .74) both prior to and after performance, and the 54 out of 60 condition was viewed as moderately difficult (i.e., .59) and difficult (i.e., .30) before and after performance, respectively. Those high in test anxiety rated the 6 out of 60 condition as moderately easy (about .62) both prior to and after performance, while the 54 out of 60 condition was rated as moderately easy (i.e., .62) before performance but dropped to difficult after performance (i.e., .36).

Results of the three-way chi-square analysis also are consistent with this interpretation. Students in whom $M_S > M_{AF}$ favored the success criterion when opportunity to move on in the path appeared unlikely, and favored the opportunity-to-move-on criterion only when it was likely to be attained. That is, when remaining in the path appeared doubtful, $M_S > M_{AF}$ individuals saw success in the task as more important but favored the opportunity to move on when its attainment was highly probable. In contrast, students in whom $M_{AF} > M_S$ showed a pattern of avoidance. They chose the goal of success on the task as important when attainment of the opportunity to move on was likely, but preferred the goal of moving on only when it was relatively unattainable. Such choices minimize inhibition for them.

The results depicting the interaction between the success criterion and opportunity-to-move-on criterion indicate that, overall, subjects faced with an easy achievement of the success criterion (solving only 6 out of 60 anagrams) tried hardest and worked most efficiently when success at a difficult task (like solving 54 out of 60 anagrams) was required to remain in the path. When success appeared difficult to attain, subjects generally performed better when moving on in the contingent path appeared easy. Presumably this happened because subjects were motivated to attain another chance to strive for the success criterion.

In reviewing the results, it is interesting to note that no statistically reliable main effects or interactions involved the RAMS measure. This tends to cast some doubt on the scale as a measure of resultant achievement-oriented tendency.

The interpretation of the results employing TAQ as the measure of resultant achievement motivation strongly supports the notion of the gatekeeper effect. In life, earning success and feeling pride in that accomplishment does not always earn one the opportunity to continue on in a contingent path. If further studies prove these results reliable, it might be more advantageous to define a contingent path as a series of steps in which attainment of the moving-on criterion is the necessary condition to remain in the path, and nonattainment precludes striving in the path.

Study I provided some very useful information and insights into the gatekeeper effect, but it was not without its weaknesses. After examination of the subjective probability estimates of reaching the success and moving-on criteria, some anomalies presented themselves. For example, the low-anxiety subjects rated their probability of reaching the success criterion in the 54 out of 60 condition as easy (.72) prior to performance, but the low-anxiety group in the 6 out of 60 condition viewed their probability of reaching success only moderately easy (about .64) before doing the test. In addition, the mean probability of reaching the moving-on criterion was .62 for the high-anxiety groups in both the 54 out of 60 and 6 out of 60 conditions. These reversals make one wonder about the manipulation of Ps.

After a review of the induction instructions, a possible point of confusion emerged. The instructions first informed the students that the tests were of moderate difficulty for them and then went on to state the particular success and moving-on criteria. What does it mean to say that the tests are of moderate difficulty and then say one must solve 54 out of 60 problems to be considered successful? It is unfortunate that this confusion of probabilities was not recognized before the study was conducted. It seems likely that this ambiguity caused the reversals obtained for the mean probability estimates—higher probability estimates for the objectively more difficult criterion.

In the first study we attempted to use a self-report measure of resultant achievement motivation (Mehrabian, 1968), the RAMS. But this instrument yielded no statistically reliable results, and only the TAQ was available to discriminate $M_S > M_{AF}$ from $M_{AF} > M_S$ subjects. While it has been argued (and we agree) that use of a valid measure for each motive derived independently is superior to either used alone (Atkinson & Litwin, 1960), the results of study I do not provide any positive evidence for the validity of the RAMS instrument. (See Part II of this volume for further evidence on this point.)

Summing up, then, difficulty with the induction, a weak assessment of resultant achievement motivation, the post hoc nature of the interpretations, and the non-overwhelming levels of significance all argued for a second study. To this end, study II was designed and run.

Considerable time went into the design of the second experiment and, specifically, the induction instruction. For this reason, study I and study II were separated by a year.

The induction instructions were considerably longer and different in form. First, subjects were given a rationale as to why two different criteria might exist to specify success at a single task. It was also explained that some individuals might see one criterion as more important or they might prefer to strive to attain one over another. Careful attention was given to the statement of the criteria so as to eliminate any confusion. To assess resultant achievement motivation, the traditional projective measure of n Achievement was used along with the TAQ. It was also decided to assess the probabilities of reaching the success and moving-on criteria only once, before the performance measure. It was hoped that these changes would strengthen the manipulations and tighten the overall design.

Although study I supplied important information, it was still felt that the empirical nature of the research precluded specific hypotheses. However, based on the results of study I, we felt three global hypotheses could be stated. Other things equal, $M_S > M_{AF}$ individuals should strive hardest when the criterion to move on in a contingent path was low (i.e., they faced an easy moving-on criterion). When moving on was very difficult, $M_S > M_{AF}$ individuals should strive hardest when the success criterion was high (i.e., they faced a difficult success criterion). In general, $M_{AF} > M_S$ individuals should show the reverse trends.

STUDY II

Method

Subjects

The subjects were 220 male introductory psychology students who volunteered to earn extra credit points that could augment their class grades.

Assessment of Motives

The projective measure of the achievement motive (McClelland, Atkinson, Clark, & Lowell, 1953) and the TAQ (Mandler & Sarason, 1952) were administered to all students under neutral conditions to assess motive to approach success M_S and motive to avoid failure M_{AF}, respectively. In accordance with current practice, sentence leads and not pictures were used to elicit stories. Repeated use of sentence leads has shown them to be a valid alternative to pictures (see Raynor & Rubin, 1971, or Entin & Raynor, 1973), and Entin (1973) has provided evidence that n Achievement scores elicited by sentence leads are functionally equivalent to those elicited by pictures.

The protocols were scored by an established expert (E.E.E.) who correlates .90 with another expert. Scoring was done according to the abbreviated scoring procedure described by Entin and Freedman (1978), where AI, TI, and UI are the only categories coded for each story. Entin and Freedman (1978) present evidence that using the abbreviated score is virtually identical to using the whole score.

The TAQ was administered and scored in the same manner as described for study I. A correlation between the scores of the projective measure and the TAQ confirmed the assumption that the two motives were independent ($r = .01$, $N = 220$). Each motive distribution was standardized, and the standard score for the TAQ was subtracted from the standard score for n Achievement. In this way a resultant achievement motivation score was derived for each subject. Individuals scoring in the top third of the resultant achievement motivation distribution were considered high, or $M_S > M_{AF}$; those placing in the bottom third was considered low, or $M_{AF} > M_S$; and individuals falling in the middle third were considered intermediate, or $M_S = M_{AF}$. For some analyses it became necessary to dichotomize the distribution, in which case those above the median were considered high and those below the median were considered low in resultant achievement motivation.

Dependent Measures

Study II employed the same anagrams task as described for study I. A questionnaire composed of eight self-report questions was also prepared. Only one of those questions is germane to this report: "Which goal do not prefer to strive for?" Available responses were: "Being able to consider yourself successful" and "To be able to move on to the next test."

A third booklet containing the written induction materials, an 18-item mood adjective checklist, and two items designed to measure perceived difficulty in reaching the success and moving-on criteria, respectively, were prepared.

Procedure

The procedure used in this study was, in general, similar to that described for study I. One important difference between the two studies was in the number of experimental conditions used. In study I the success and moving-on criteria took on only the extreme values of 54 out of 60 and 6 out of 60 anagrams worked correctly. The design of study II called for the addition of an intermediate value of 30 out of 60 anagrams worked correctly. Thus, nine experimental conditions were created: the three levels of the success criterion, each within the three levels of the moving-on criterion. Prior to the beginning of the experiment, the order of presentation of the nine conditions was randomized.

The experimenter conducting the sessions was conservatively dressed, naive to the hypotheses, and informed of which condition he was to conduct only several minutes before the session began. After assessment of motives, the booklet containing the written induction was passed out. For each session the form of the induction material corresponded to the experimental condition. The experimental conditions, in order of presentation, were (success criterion followed by moving-on criterion): (1) 30 out of 60, 54 out of 60; (2) 6 out of 60, 6 out of 60; (3) 54 out of 60, 6 out of 60; (4) 30 out of 60, 30 out of 60; (5) 6 out of 60, 30 out of 60; (6) 54 out of 60, 54 out of 60; (7) 54 out of 60, 30 out of 60; (8) 30 out of 60, 6 out of 60; and (9) 6 out of 60, 54 out of 60.

The induction began by describing how success, in terms of personal satisfaction, might be independent of and different from the criterion imposed by some outside person or agency for continuing on to later tests or activities. A brief discussion of the four tests of verbal ability followed. Specifically, those in the first experimental condition heard:

> In the present research various tests of verbal ability are used to create a situation where these different meanings of success are realistically presented to you. The test booklets you have received contain four tests, and each test is comprised of 60 separate anagrams or scrambled word problems. On the first and each test thereafter, to consider yourself successful on any of these four tests, you should complete 30 problems out of 60. These tests have been adjusted for people of your age and ability so completing 30 out of 60 anagrams should be moderately difficult. About 50% of you should be able to do this, so to consider yourself successful should be moderately difficult.
>
> To move on to the next test you are required to complete 54 out of 60 problems. Only about 10% of people of your age and ability should be able to do this, so moving on to the next test should be difficult for people of your age and ability.
>
> Those of you who do not complete the number of problems required to move on obviously cannot do the next test in the series and must remain seated until all four tests are finished. You will have 5 minutes for each test.
>
> Remember, to consider yourself successful you should complete 30 out of 60 problems, which should be moderately difficult for you, and to move on to the next test you are required to complete 54 out of 60 problems, which should be difficult for you.

Students in the other experiment conditions read and heard the same instructions except for changes in the numbers of anagrams to be solved for each criteria according to the particular condition they were in.

Following this, the test booklets and the questionnaire containing the eight self-report questions were handed out. Subjects were then given instruction in how to do the anagrams test, allowed to complete the mood-adjective checklist, and rated their perceived difficulty in reaching the two criteria. A short reiteration of the induction was read, and subjects were then given 5 min to work the anagrams on the first of the four tests. Immediately following the first test, all students completed the eight self-report questions. The experiment was then ended, and all subjects debriefed.

Results

Just prior to the performance task, subjects were asked to rate their perceived difficulty in reaching the stated success criterion and the stated moving-on criterion. The accompanying response scales went from zero (easy) to 10 (difficult). As a manipulation check, these data were subjected to a success criterion (3) X moving-on criterion (3) ANOVA. The results showed a main effect for both the success and moving-on criteria. As the levels of the success criterion increased in difficulty from 6 out of 60 to 30 of 60 to 54 of 60, so did the students' ratings of how difficult they felt it would be to complete that many problems correctly. Means for the three levels of the success criterion were 4.28, 5.93, and 6.96, respectively ($F = 26.61$, $df = 2/193$, $p < .0001$). Results for the main effect of moving on were similar. Means for the three levels of the moving-on criterion were 4.41, 5.66, and 7.01, respectively ($F = 21.54$, $df = 2/193$, $p < .0001$). No interactions were found. Manipulations dealing with the establishment of the success and moving-on criteria clearly appear to have been effective.

Initial Analyses

The number of anagrams attempted and solved correctly were each analyzed in a resultant achievement motivation (3) X success criterion (3) X moving-on criterion (3) least-squares ANOVA (Statistical Analysis System, 1976). The means are depicted in Table 6, while summaries of the ANOVAs are shown in Table 7. Inspection of Tables 6 and 7 shows that as resultant achievement motivation increased, the number of anagrams solved correctly also increased ($F = 5.80$, $df = 1/127$, $p < .02$.) A second main effect shows that as the levels of the success criterion increased in difficulty from 6 out of 60 to 30 of 60 to 54 of 60, the number of anagrams attempted increased ($F = 2.66$, $df = 2/193$, $p < .07$). A success X moving-on effect was found for both dependent variables; $F = 2.80$, $df = 2/193$, $p < .03$ for number correct, and $F = 2.93$, $df = 2/193$, $p < .03$ for number attempted. The patterns of results for both dependent variables are virtually identical. Thus only the interaction for number correct is presented graphically in Figure 1. A V-shaped pattern of results can be seen for the individuals in the 54 out of 60 success condition when performance scores are plotted across the three levels of the moving-on

Table 6 Mean Number of Anagrams Attempted and Worked Correctly as a Function of
Resultant Achievement Motivation and the Number of Problems to Solve out of 60
for the Success and Moving-on Criteria

| | | | | | | Moving-on criterion | | | | |
| | | | 6 | | | 30 | | | 54 | |
Motivation	Success criterion	N	Attempted	Correct	N	Attempted	Correct	N	Attempted	Correct
High	6	8	22.00	28.88	9	37.67	35.11	12	29.42	25.25
	30	11	26.37	24.36	6	35.83	32.50	6	37.50	33.67
	54	8	31.25	26.63	8	29.63	27.88	4	38.75	34.25
Moderate	6	11	24.82	21.54	6	26.33	24.83	10	35.70	32.40
	30	6	28.67	23.33	9	33.11	26.89	10	29.60	24.80
	54	8	37.38	33.50	5	19.40	13.80	10	35.70	31.10
Low	6	10	30.50	27.50	11	23.91	20.18	4	21.75	19.25
	30	9	23.67	18.22	7	31.14	26.14	6	33.67	24.33
	54	5	38.00	29.20	10	30.80	23.40	11	23.27	27.64

criterion. Performance is about equal and highest in the 54 out of 60 and 6 out of
60 moving-on conditions, and lowest when the level of moving on is 30 out of 60.
Figure 1 also shows a decline in performance for the 6 out of 60 success condition
across the levels of the moving-on criterion, and the performance of individuals in
the 30 out of 60 success condition is higher in the 30 out of 60 than in the 54 out
of 60 moving-on condition and then shows a sharp drop in the 6 out of 60 moving-
on condition.

Further inspection of Tables 6 and 7 reveals a resultant achievement motivation

Table 7 ANOVA Summary Tables for Number of Anagrams Attempted and Worked
Correctly

| | | Mean square | | F | |
Source	df	Number attempted	Number correct	Number attempted	Number correct
Resultant achievement					
Motivation (A)	2	113.65	409.97	.83	3.20**
Success criterion (B)	2	366.43	87.73	2.66*	.69
Moving-on criterion (C)	2	231.92	170.21	1.69	1.33
A × B	4	67.67	56.64	.49	.44
A × C	4	303.12	292.99	2.20*	2.29*
B × C	4	402.74	358.08	2.93**	2.80**
A × B × C	8	204.60	190.97	1.49	1.49
Within	193	137.51	128.01		

*$p < .07$.
**$p < .03$.

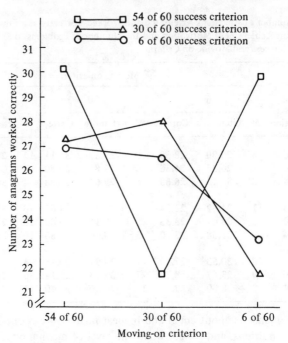

Figure 1 Number of anagrams worked correctly as a function
of the success and moving-on criteria.

by moving-on interaction for both number of anagrams correct ($F = 2.30$, $df = 4/193$, $p < .06$) and number of anagrams attempted ($F = 2.20$, $df = 4/193$, $p < .07$). When the moderate achievement motivation group is removed and the ANOVA recomputed, the F ratios are increased for both number correct and attempted ($F = 2.95$, and $F = 3.09$, $df = 2/127$, $p < .05$, respectively). Figure 2 depicts data only for number correct, as the two patterns of results were highly similar. Figure 2 shows that the number of anagrams worked correctly by individuals low or moderate in resultant achievement motivation traces a V-shaped pattern across the levels of the moving-on criterion, while individuals high in resultant achievement motivation showed an inverted V across the same three levels. None of the other effects proved significant.

From the results to this point, it appears that performance tends to be highest where the level of the success or moving-on criterion is most difficult (54 out of 60), and that students high in resultant achievement motivation perform best when the level of the moving-on criterion is intermediate (30 out of 60), while those low in achievement motivation perform worst at this point. There appears to be little difference in performance among the motive groups when the moving-on level is 6 out of 60, and a moderate difference exists between individuals high and low in achievement motivation when the moving-on level is 54 out of 60.

Overall, these results do not parallel those of study I. However, the induction instructions of study II did more than clarify the probability issue raised concerning the first study. The inductions employed here stressed and strengthened the notion of goal preference. That is, some people might come to prefer personal success, and others might come to prefer moving on to the next test as their measure of success. The cognitive representation of such a preference might have an important bearing on how hard or vigorously one might work. The next set of analyses were designed to explore these issues and assess the effect of goal preference.

Secondary Analyses

A goal preference (2) X resultant achievement motivation (2) X success criterion (3) X moving-on criterion (3) least-squares ANOVA was computed for number of anagrams attempted and correct. In addition, separate ANOVAs were computed for each dependent variable at each level of goal preference, employing the remaining independent variables.

The 2 X 2 X 3 X 3 ANOVAs showed that preference had a pronounced effect on performance. Subjects who expressed a preference for moving on to the next test worked more anagrams correctly and attempted more ($F = 7.08$, $df = 1/179$, $p <$ .009 and $F = 5.21$, $df = 1/179$, $p < .03$, respectively) than those who preferred to

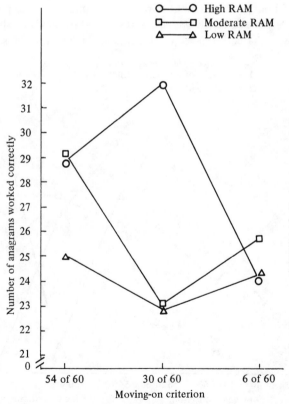

Figure 2 Number of anagrams worked correctly as a function of resultant achievement motivation (RAM) and moving-on criterion.

strive to consider themselves successful. As before, performance increased as the levels of the success criterion increased in difficulty from 6 out of 60 to 54 out of 60 ($F = 3.74$, $df = 2/113$, $p < .03$ and $F = 5.58$, $df = 2/113$, $p < .005$ for number correct and attempted, respectively).

The significant interaction reported in the first analyses between success and moving on also appeared to be dependent on criterion preference. The interaction was observed only for those who preferred to move on to the next test ($F = 5.08$, $df = 4/65$, $p < .002$ for number correct and $F = 4.28$, $df = 4/65$, $p < .004$ for number attempted). The pattern of means obtained for this preference group was reminiscent of that reported in study I. That is, when the success criterion was 54 out of 60, performance was higher when the moving-on criterion was 6 out of 60 than when it was 54 out of 60; however, when the success criterion was 6 out of 60, performance was higher when the moving-on criterion was 54 out of 60 than when it was 6 out of 60. Figure 3 depicts the pattern of results when all three levels of each criterion are considered, for both preference groups. Once again only the results for number of anagrams worked correctly are graphed, as the patterns of results for both dependent variables are nearly identical. The performance means of students in the 54 out of 60 and 6 out of 60 success conditions who preferred striving for success describes a rough V shape across the three levels of the moving-on criterion. However, the performance of students in the 54 out of 60 success condi-

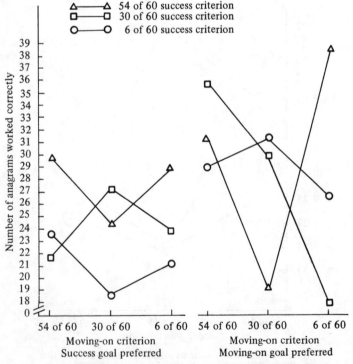

Figure 3   Number of anagrams worked correctly as a function of goal preference, success criterion, and moving-on criterion.

tion was superior at each level of the moving-on criterion to that of students in the 6 out of 60 success condition. Meanwhile, the 30 out of 60 success condition traces a rough inverted V across the levels of the moving-on criterion.

Figure 3 also shows the performance of students who preferred to strive to move on. The pattern of results from the 54 out of 60 success condition also describes a V shape. In this case performance first declines from the 54 out of 60 to the 30 out of 60 moving-on condition and then shows a dramatic increase when the moving-on condition is 6 out of 60. Students in the 30 out of 60 success condition showed an almost linear decline in performance from the 54 out of 60 to the 6 out of 60 moving-on condition. Results for the 6 out of 60 success condition traced an inverted V over the three levels of the moving-on criterion.

When the results are viewed simultaneously in terms of both the distinctions between performance criterion (success vs. moving on) and goal preferred (success vs. moving on) as a function of differences in resultant achievement motivation, they can be related to the conceptual framework of the elaborated theory of achievement motivation (see Figure 4). Note that the basic pattern of results of Figure 4 reveals generally higher performance for both motive groups as the criterion becomes more difficult, regardless of whether it is the performance criterion or the goal preference. For the groups low in resultant achievement motivation, Figures 4*a, b,* and *d* all suggest a fairly linear trend; as performance criterion becomes more difficult to attain (e.g., a greater number of problems must be solved to meet it), performance scores increase. A similar linear trend appears for those high in resultant achievement motivation, as shown in Figures 4*a, c,* and *d*. However, there is an important exception that is critical from the point of view of theory—Figure 4*b* shows a regular *increase* in performance of the high-RAM group as the success criterion becomes *less* difficult to attain. Given what might be expected based on the results of study I, this trend would be predicted for the moving-on criterion rather than the success criterion—within those high-RAM subjects who preferred the moving-on goal. Thus the difference in results for the high-RAM group between Figure 4*b* and *d* represents what might be considered unexpected results, despite the fact that no specific directional hypotheses directly derivable from theory were entertained. The pattern shown in Figure 4*b* is the pattern we would expect for the moving-on criterion when it is the preferred goal (Figure 4*d*). That is, we would expect an interaction between preference for the moving-on criterion and the moving-on performance criterion, rather than an interaction between preference for moving on and the success performance criterion. High-RAM subjects would be expected to perform at a higher level, and low-RAM subjects at a lower level, as the moving-on (rather than the success) performance criterion became less stringent— for those who preferred as a goal the moving-on criterion.

Statistically, the difference between the patterns of results in Figure 4*a* and *b* yields a significant interaction between resultant motive group and goal preference for the success criterion for performance ($F = 3.79$, $df = 2/179$, $p < .03$ for number correct, and $F = 3.87$, $df = 2/179$, $p < .03$ for number attempted). This interaction no longer approaches statistical significance when the moving-on criterion is viewed (Figure 4*c* and *d*); all groups tend to perform at the higher level as the moving-on performance criterion becomes increasingly more stringent. The only apparently serious departure from these linear trends appears for the low-RAM group in Figure 4c, where performance is lower for the moderately difficult moving-on performance criterion than for the extremes.

General Discussion

The analyses of study II, examining the probability estimates, demonstrated that an important part of the manipulation, specifically the setting of the success and moving-on conditions, was effective. Students' estimates of difficulty increased as the number of anagrams to be solved increased, and this was true independently for the levels of both the success criteria and moving-on criteria. Analysis of the number of anagrams worked correctly showed that achievement motivation had been successfully aroused. Individuals higher in RAM performed better than those lower in RAM. Also, this effect was stronger when only those students in the high and low thirds of the RAM distribution were compared. Thus, the data provided support for the manipulation procedures and the arousal of achievement motivation in study II.

The bulk of the findings derived from the first analyses of study II proved difficult to interpret. In general, it appeared (with a few exceptions) that as the criteria to be attained increased in difficulty, performance increased. The students high in RAM performed better when the moving-on criterion was high (54 out of 60) and particularly when it was intermediate (30 out of 60) than when it was low (6 out of 60). Such results run counter to those reported in study I, where low-TAQ students (assumed high-RAM) performed better when the moving-on condition was low than when it was high. The findings for the low-RAM individuals were approximately reversed between the two studies.

Inspection of the success X moving-on interaction of study II revealed that when success and moving on were both difficult to attain, performance was quite high. This finding is at variance with the results reported in study I, in which the performance of this group was low. In the condition of study II where success was difficult and moving on was easy, performance was also high, a finding similar to the outcome in study I. In comparing the two conditions, one where both the success and moving-on criteria are difficult to achieve and one where success is difficult and moving on easy to attain, we had anticipated that the dynamics in these two conditions should differ and that, consequently, performance should differ as well. Such was the finding in study I, but not in study II. This difference, in combination with other anomalies in the data of study II, suggested to us that an explanation positing a single cause to account for the findings was unlikely. This led to a careful review of the methodology and logic of study II.

Several issues came to light. The induction instructions, as previously indicated, stressed that some individuals might perceive the attainment of the success criterion as "success," while others might feel that attainment of the moving-on criterion represented success. This clear dichotomizing of the two criteria in the instructions was used as a way of legitimizing (to the subjects) the partitioning of the success

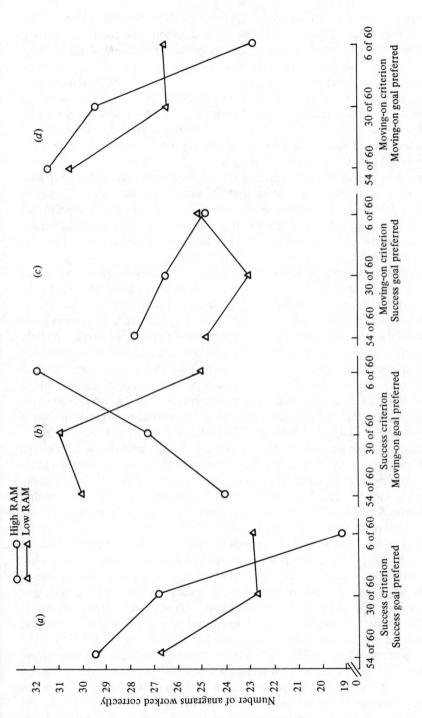

Figure 4 Number of anagrams worked correctly as a function of goal preference, RAM, and performance criterion.

111

and moving-on criteria. But we now believe that the induction instructions created a cognitive set in the subjects concerning which criterion would come to represent success for them. Furthermore, to dispel any doubt concerning the ease of difficulty of reaching the criteria, they were stated quite explicitly. If the criterion was the solving of 6 out of 60 anagrams, the students were told it should be easy for them to attain the criterion. If the criterion was 30 out of 60, they were told this was moderate in difficulty; and if the criterion was 54 out of 60, they were informed that this would be quite difficult to achieve. This clear-cut explanation of the success criteria may have created a cognitive set concerning how hard the student would have to work to attain the goal.

What, then, happened when these two factors were taken together? If preference was for the moving-on criterion, then students would strive to achieve this goal in preference to the other and the contingency of the path would be sharpened. We call these students *path* success strivers. If preference was for the success criterion, this would be the goal to achieve, and the contingency of the path would be mitigated. These subjects are called *personal* success strivers.

Two findings lend partial support to this distinction between path and personal success. First, the analyses incorporating goal preference as a factor showed it to be an important influence on performance. Path success strivers (those who favored striving to move on as their goal) performed more problems and worked more problems correctly than personal success strivers (those who preferred striving to attain the success criterion). Second, the goal preference X success criterion interaction showed that personal success strivers performed better as the success criterion became more difficult. The overall interaction of goal preference and moving on was not significant. Among path success strivers, however, a weak interaction existed, showing that performance increased as the moving-on criterion increased in difficulty ($F = 3.01$, $df = 2/65$, $p < .06$ and $F = 2.51$, $df = 2.65$, $p < .09$, respectively, for anagrams attempted and correct). A comparison between the high and low moving-on conditions of this group revealed that the 54-out-of-60-condition group worked more problems and solved more correctly than the 6-out-of-60-condition (t's $= 2.15$ and 2.05, $df = 65$, $p < .05$, respectively). It would seem that a preference for one or the other success criterion produced effort commensurate with the level of difficulty confronted.

Among path success strivers, those high in RAM attempted and correctly solved more problems as the number of anagrams to be worked, as specified by the success criterion, decreased, but the opposite trend is found as the moving-on criterion decreased. Increasingly more difficult success and moving-on criteria produced better performance for those low in RAM. There exists a loose similarity between these latter findings of study II and those of study I, which showed that when moving on in a contingent path was not an issue, high-RAM (low-TAQ) students performed better when confronted with the more difficult success criterion than with the easier one. Low-RAM individuals, however, appeared less inhibited by the easier than by the more difficult success criterion and demonstrated better performance than the high-RAM students. But the pattern of results revealed by the goal preference X success X moving-on interaction in study II cannot be easily or fully explained with the more general theory of achievement motivation as currently stated.

In conclusion, it seems that goal preference is an important factor in the gate-keeper effect. Path and success strivers by definition perceive the importance of attaining the success and moving-on criteria differently. The overall effects for the path success strivers in study II were in part consistent with results found in study I. However, the picture is far from clear, particularly when differences in achievement-related motives are taken into account. We do not believe that all the important factors of the gatekeeper effect have been accounted for or controlled. More research is required to clarify the functional significance of what appears to be an important distinction—that between personal success and success as moving on in a contingent path.

Two potentially important points for future research should be noted at this time. In the research reported here we have tried to induce a personal standard of success for subjects so as to create an unconfounded experimental design that systematically views levels of personal success within different levels of moving-on criterion. Also, the manipulation involved the use of problems attempted as the criterion for moving on, rather than allowing a pause to score for problems correct. Perhaps a more meaningful situation is created for the subject when the moving-on criterion is varied by the experimenter, but subjects are left to choose the level of the personal success criterion they wish to strive for—similar to a study of level of aspiration—and then problems correctly solved are used to determine moving on. Such a situation might correspond more closely to the life situations in which external gatekeepers usually impose criteria for moving on in a contingent path, and then enforce them using quality rather than quantity of performance, while the individual entertains a personal standard of success that may or may not be different from the moving-on criterion. This is the situation referred to in our introductory remarks concerning the gatekeeper effect. We did not investigate it in this way in these studies because we wanted to create groups with relatively equal numbers of subjects in all the success X moving-on combinations (3 X 3) of study II, and the use of a scoring procedure for problems correct precludes group testing. It may be that the assessment rather than the induction of the personal success criterion and/or actual clear-cut indications that quality rather than quantity of performance will be evaluated are required to clarify the functional significance of the distinction between personal success and moving on.

5

Motivational Analysis of the Future Plans of College Men: Imagery Used to Describe Future Plans and Goals

Howard B. Pearlson and Joel O. Raynor

Two methods were used to carry out a motivational analysis of the future plans of college men. This chapter is concerned with the first method; the types of imagery used to describe future plans and goals are viewed as a function of individual differences in achievement-related motive measures (*n* Achievement and test anxiety) and the rated importance of the future goal.

The elaborated theory of achievement motivation (see chapter 2) does not directly pertain to the types of imagery persons will employ in describing their future plans. However, it suggests that success-oriented persons are likely to perceive their future in more achievement-related terms. In the present study some general hypotheses were entertained:

1. Success-oriented persons should express their future career goals in more achievement-related terms than do their failure-threatened counterparts.
2. Success-oriented persons should structure their future plans with a greater number of achievement-related steps.
3. The above-mentioned differences should be accentuated when the path to the goal is perceived as contingent.

Although not directly derived from the elaborated theory of achievement motivation, hypotheses are entertained concerning the importance of attaining the future goal. We suggest that when an individual perceives the attainment of a career goal as important, achievement-related motives are likely to be aroused. Thus, for success-oriented persons, the predominant orientation to succeed should be aroused. Steps even remotely associated with the attainment of a career goal should be colored with achievement. In contrast, failure-threatened persons should become more inhibited. They will be even less likely to perceive component steps in terms of achievement. Such perceptions could only serve to increase apprehension concerning the prospect of failure to attain a career goal.

This research was supported by NSF Grant GS-2863; Joel O. Raynor, principal investigatc

The following additional hypotheses are offered:

4. As the attainment of a career goal assumes greater importance to success-oriented individuals, the number of achievement-related steps anticipated in the future plans and the degree to which the future goal is perceived in achievement-related terms should increase.

5. As the attainment of a career goal assumes greater importance for failure-threatened individuals, the number of achievement-related steps anticipated in their future plans and the degree to which the future goal is perceived in achievement-related terms should decrease.

METHOD

Subjects and Assessment of Motives

The subjects were 182 males, all enrolled in two introductory psychology classes at the State University of New York at Buffalo. Subjects were given the projective measure of n Achievement (McClelland, Atkinson, Clark, & Lowell, 1953) and the first third of the Test Anxiety Questionnaire (TAQ) (Mandler & Sarason, 1952). Both instruments were administered during large testing sessions. At that time subjects were presented with a battery of tests representing the assessment needs of particular research groups associated with the Psychology Department, State University of New York at Buffalo. Separate testing sessions were conducted for each of two introductory psychology classes.

The n Achievement and TAQ instruments were administered under neutral conditions and scored according to the pertinent literature concerning each (McClelland, Atkinson, Clark, & Lowell, 1958; Atkinson, 1958, app. III; Mandler & Sarason, 1952). The n Achievement instrument was administered first. Sentences rather than pictures (cf. Entin, 1973) were used to elicit stories for the following cues: two men in a factory are working at a machine; a man is working with a typewriter and books; an older man is talking to a younger man; a boy is standing, vague operation scene in the background. Stories were coded for n Achievement by an expert scorer (J.O.R.), who has correlated above .90 with the n Achievement practice materials of Smith and Field (1958).

The TAQ was administered subsequent to the n Achievement instrument. It was randomly distributed among other tests in the battery. Only the first third of the TAQ, consisting of 12 items and 3 fillers, was administered. This section correlates between .84 and .90 with the total score (cf. Smith, 1964). The response scale for each item was divided into five parts such that a score of five indicated most anxiety, and one least. Total scores were computed by summing over the 12 items. Scores for the TAQ correlated .09 (n.s.) with those for n Achievement.

Subjects were classified into motive groups by first obtaining the closest median breaks on n Achievement and test anxiety separately, based on the scores from one mass testing session (hereafter referred to as session I). Subjects in the entire sample were then simultaneously classified as either above or below the group medians established for each motive.

Assessment of Future Plans

Two forms of a Future Plans Questionnaire were randomly distributed among the test batteries. In both, the subjects were first asked to write in their future goals. Then a separate page was provided for describing each "step" in the "path" to this future goal. The form provided 15 such step pages (the greatest number used by any subject was 12). For each step page, subjects were asked to write in the activity they planned to engage in, the positive outcome of that activity that was desired, and the negative outcome that might result from that activity. A double-lined arrow (➡) pointed from the activity to the place for writing in the positive outcome. Below this arrow was a space for writing in the chances (out of 100) that the activity would lead on to the desired positive outcome. In the contingent form, subjects were instructed to select only those steps in their path to the future goal that required attainment of the positive outcome to continue along the path to the future goal. For each step in this form, the arrow from activity to positive outcome was already darkened (filled in like this: ➡) when the subject received the form. In the open-arrows (or open-ended) form the instructions asked students to write in all the steps in the path to their future goal, and to darken each arrow that led from an activity to a positive outcome that was required to continue along the path to the future goal. Consequently some steps had darkened arrows and others did not, after completion of the form, but all arrows were open when the form was first received. Prior to indicating their future goal and accompanying steps, subjects were provided with descriptive material and instructions for two instances, one involving becoming a nuclear physicist, another having a successful printing business.

After filling out their career paths, all subjects answered a series of questions.

Assessment of Importance

Question 8 pertained to the importance of attaining the future goal: "Right now, how important to you is achieving this future goal?" Subjects were required to indicate the importance of achieving their future goal by checking the appropriate segment of a Likert-like continuum that ranged from not at all important to very important. Responses were scored on a seven-point scale. The distribution of scores was split at the median such that subjects scoring six or seven comprised the high importance group while those scoring five or lower comprised the low importance group.

Scoring of Steps and Future Goal

Protocols from session 1 of the mass testing were used to develop a scoring system that was then applied to protocols obtained from session II. Future goals from all protocols were listed on a separate page. Similarly, all activities and positive and negative outcomes were compiled. A number of scoring categories was developed to differentiate responses within each list. Negative outcome responses proved too homogeneous for this task—they tended to be positive outcomes with *not* as the prefix. A scoring system for future goals, activities, and positive outcomes was developed. Excerpts from that scoring system are now presented.

The future goal was scored for the following categories: achievement imagery (AI), task imagery (TI), and unrelated imagery (UI). To be scored for achievement imagery (AI),[1] a future goal had to reflect concern with a standard of excellence. In addition, the premise that the individual is responsible for his or her own success or failure must not have been contradicted. Two criteria were used for scoring AI: (1) The individual used good, better, or best to describe a future goal. Examples are "good lawyer" and "best accountant in Chicago." (2) The person indicated quality in his or her description of a future goal. Examples are "sound law practice," "successful law degree," and "earn a law degree." A future goal that could be related to achievement concerns but did not clearly indicate so was scored for task imagery. The following criteria were used in determining task imagery: (1) Any goal that has no verb or modifier (adjective or adverb), but has the possibility of being achievement related. Examples are "doctor" and "lawyer." (2) A goal that has mundane modifiers, not directly implying achievement but nonetheless having the possibility of being achievement related. Examples are "get law practice," "receive law practice," and "learn law." A goal in which nonachievement-related motives clearly predominated was scored for unrelated imagery. The fact that a goal was nonachievement related was often implied by accompanying verbs or modifiers. Examples of goals scored for unrelated imagery are "happy person," "be happy," and "happiness." A goal that had quality modifiers was scored for unrelated imagery under two circumstances: (1) The goal does not seem related to achievement concerns. An example would be "successful millionaire." (2) The goal is very general and is more related to concern about life than to the achievement motive. An example of this would be "a good world."

Activities were scored for the following categories: quality (Q), intensity (I), task imagery (TI), unrelated imagery (UR), and transitional imagery (TR). The Q category was similar to AI. A quality activity indicated concern for achievement or doing well. Quality activities were indicated by modifiers that directly implied quality. They were also indicated by modifiers that indirectly implied quality. An example of the former would be "try to be a *good* student." An example of the latter would be "try to *earn* a degree." Activities that denoted intensity of action but not necessarily quality were scored I. The most common example of this would be "work hard." Activities that did not directly indicate quality but offered the possibility that concern with quality exists were scored TI. An example would be "try to pass a course." Activities clearly pertaining to nonachievement-related motives were scored UI. Examples are "try to find myself" and "try to attain happiness." TR was scored when the sole purpose of an activity was to place the individual in position to enter the next step. Such activities offer little intrinsic reward. The most common examples of transitional activities are applications to schools, i.e., "apply to medical school."

[1] Note that the authors' definition of achievement imagery is more limited than that provided in the scoring manual for *n* Achievement (McClelland et al. 1953). The relatively unelaborated responses in the protocols precluded the development of more extensive criteria.

Positive outcomes were scored for the following categories: achievement imagery (AI), task imagery (TI), unrelated imagery (UI), and transitional imagery (TR). The first three categories were scored according to the criteria established for corresponding future goal categories. However, the imagery refers to outcomes rather than future goals. Transitional outcomes were typically the result of transitional activities. An example would be "getting into medical school."[2]

To put the scoring system in perspective, consider the individual who has the goal of becoming a doctor and anticipates the following series of steps: study hard in undergraduate school, do well in courses; apply to medical school, get accepted; work hard in anatomy, pass the course; find a girlfriend, get married; try to set up a good practice, do well. The future goal would be scored TI. The activity and outcome of the first step would be scored I and AI, respectively. The second step would be scored TR, TR; the third I, TI; the fourth UI, UI; and the fifth Q, AI.

Protocols from session I were scored by one author (H.B.P.) and a second scorer.[3] Scoring reliability was established by comparing scores for the first step of all protocols. The percentage agreement was 97% for first-step activities and 95% for first-step outcomes. The second scorer proceeded to score all protocols from session II. Only protocols from session II were used in later data analysis.

In scoring protocols for future goal, 1 was indicated for AI, 0 for TI, and −1 for UI. For each protocol, the number and percentage of steps containing each activity and outcome scoring category were calculated.

Treatment of data

ANOVAs were applied to each form separately, with motive and importance as independent factors for each scoring category. These results are supplemented by information concerning significant three-factor interactions when form was used as an additional variable. All data were analyzed by NYBMUL (Finn, 1969), which performs exact multivariate least-squares solutions for equal and unequal and proportionate and disproportionate cell frequencies.[4] A priori comparisons (t tests) used mean square error and degrees of freedom from the appropriate analysis of variance (Winer, 1962, p. 244) and one-tailed tests of significance to evaluate directional hypotheses.

RESULTS

Future Goal

Analyses employing resultant motive groups (high-low vs. low-high on n Achievement-test anxiety) indicate a different pattern of results for each form (see Table 1).

---

[2] Future goals, activities, and positive outcomes can be scored for more than one category. Thus, the activity "try to do well in school and be happy" would be scored for both Q (do well) and UI (be happy).

[3] The authors wish to thank Linda Brown for her help in scoring the protocols.

[4] The two ANOVAs for future goal proved computationally simple. Hence, they were computed by hand using the unweighted-means solution provided by Winer (1962, p. 242).

Table 1   Proportion of Future Goals Scored as Achievement Imagery (AI) as a Function of
Achievement-Related Motives and Rated Importance of the Future Goal, for the
Contingent and Open-Ended Forms

| | Contingent form | | | | Open-ended form | | | |
| | Low importance | | High importance | | Low importance | | High importance | |
Motive group	N	Mean	N	Mean	N	Mean	N	Mean
n Achievement								
High	8	.125	19	.105	14	−.143	15	.067
Low	15	−.067	13	−.231	15	.000	16	−.250
Test anxiety								
Low	13	.000	14	−.214	20	−.118	15	−.067
High	10	.000	18	.111	15	.000	18	−.125
n Achievement-test anxiety								
High-low	6	.167	5	.000	7	−.286	7	.000
Low-high	8	.000	4	.000	5	.000	8	−.375

Note. See text for definition of scoring category AI.

Within the open-arrows form, a significant motive X importance interaction
($F = 4.96$, $df = 1/23$, $p < .05$) was found. As predicted, the high-low persons perceive their future goal in more achievement-related terms when attainment of that
goal is important. In contrast, the low-high persons perceive their future goal in less
achievement-related terms when attainment of that goal is important. The predicted
main effect for motive was not found. However, within the high importance condition, high-low *n* Achievement-test anxiety persons perceive their future goal in
significantly more achievement-related terms than do their low-high counterparts
($t = 1.91$, $df = 23$, $p < .05$).

Analysis of the contingent form indicates no significant effects for resultant (*n*
Achievment-test anxiety) motive groups. The differences between forms (signifi-
cant interaction vs. no effects) are reflected in the corresponding three-factor
ANOVA. The motive X importance X form interaction approaches significance
($p < .07$).

Supplementary analyses indicate that *n* Achievement conforms more closely to
expectations than does test anxiety (see Table 1). Within the open-ended form, the
n Achievement X importance interaction is significant in the predicted direction
($p < .025$). Specific comparisons indicate a predicted motive difference within the
high importance condition ($t = 3.39$, $df = 56$, $p < .01$); those high in *n* Achievement perceive their future goal in more achievement-related terms.

Within the contingent form, a predicted main effect for motives was found ($p <$
.025). Once again, those high in *n* Achievement perceive their future goal in more
achievement-related terms. Specific comparisons indicate that motive differences
are significant only within the high importance condition ($t = 2.37$, $df = 51$, $p <$
.025).

Results for test anxiety did not support expectations (see Table 1). No significant effects were found within the open-ended form. Within the contingent form, the data indicate a motive difference for the high importance groups that is opposite to that predicted. Subjects scoring high in test anxiety have a more achievement-related future goal. The above-mentioned form differences led to a motive X importance X form interaction in the corresponding three-factor ANOVA that approaches significance ($p < .10$).

Number of Achievement-Related Steps

A composite measure was developed to reflect the number of achievement-related steps in the individual's path. A step was considered achievement-related either if the outcome was scored achievement-related (AI) or if the activity was scored quality (Q). Analyses using resultant motive groups (see Table 2) indicate a significant motive X importance interaction within the open-ended form ($p < .04$). As predicted, high n Achievement-low test anxiety persons have a greater number of achievement-related steps when attainment of their future goal is perceived as important. In contrast, the low n Achievement-high test anxiety persons have fewer achievement-related steps when attainment of the future goal is perceived as important. The main effect for motives is nonsignificant. However, specific comparisons indicate a trend toward the predicted motive difference within the high importance condition ($t = 1.63, df = 27, p < .10$). Thus, within the high importance condition of the open-ended form, high n Achievement-low test anxiety subjects tended to have a greater number of achievement-related steps.

The motive X importance interaction was not significant within the contingent form. A predicted motive difference was also not significant within the high importance condition.

Supplementary analyses were computed for n Achievement alone (see Table 2).

Table 2 Mean Number of Achievement-Related Steps to the Future Goal as a Function of Achievement-Related Motives and Rated Importance of the Future Goal, for the Contingent and Open-Ended Forms

	Contingent form				Open-ended form			
	Low importance		High importance		Low importance		High importance	
Motive group	N	Mean	N	Mean	N	Mean	N	Mean
n Achievement								
High	10	1.90	20	1.95	17	1.65	17	2.29
Low	15	1.53	13	1.39	18	1.50	16	1.25
Test anxiety								
Low	14	1.36	14	1.71	20	1.15	15	1.67
High	11	2.09	19	1.74	15	2.13	18	1.89
n Achievement-test anxiety								
High-low	7	1.74	5	2.00	9	1.00	7	2.43
Low-high	8	2.00	4	1.00	7	1.86	8	1.50

Within the open-ended form, a predicted main effect for motive approaches significance ($p < .10$). Specific comparisons indicate a predicted motive effect only within the high importance condition ($t = 2.39, df = 64, p < .025$). Similarly, a predicted motive effect was found within the high importance condition of the contingent form ($t = 1.99, df = 54, p < .06$). Thus, when attainment of the future goal is important, those high in n Achievement have a greater number of achievement-related steps than those low in n Achievement.

Results for test anxiety did not support expectations (see Table 2). Within the open-ended form, the motive × importance interaction is nonsignificant but in the predicted direction. A main effect for motive in the direction opposite to predictions ($p < .07$) suggests that students high in test anxiety have a greater number of achievement-related steps, particularly in the low importance condition.

Number of Intensity Activities

Results for number of intensity activities (see Table 3) resemble those for achievement-related scoring categories. Analyses using resultant motive groups indicate a significant motive × importance interaction within the open-ended form ($p < .05$). Subjects high in n Achievement and low in test anxiety have a greater number of intensity activities when attainment of the future goal is important. In contrast, subjects low in n Achievement and high in test anxiety have fewer intensity activities when attainment of the future goal is important. No significant effects were found within the contingent form.

Similar results were obtained for n Achievement alone, but no significant effects were found for test anxiety in either form (see Table 3).

Table 3   Mean Number of Intensity Activities in the Path to the Future Goal as a Function of Achievement-Related Motives and Rated Importance of the Future Goal, for the Contingent and Open-Ended Forms

	Contingent form				Open-ended form			
	Low importance		High importance		Low importance		High importance	
Motive group	N	Mean	N	Mean	N	Mean	N	Mean
n Achievement								
High	9	.56	17	1.06	17	.83	15	1.20
Low	13	.62	13	.92	18	1.44	16	.69
Test anxiety								
Low	13	.62	14	1.00	20	.80	14	.86
High	9	.56	16	1.00	15	1.60	17	1.00
n Achievement-test anxiety								
High-low	7	.57	5	1.20	9	.44	6	1.33
Low-high	7	.57	4	1.00	7	2.00	8	.88

Number of Task Imagery (TI) Activities and Outcome

No significant effects were found for the number of TI activities.

With respect to number of TI outcomes, significant effects were found only in the contingent form. Analyses using resultant motive groups indicate a significant motive × importance interaction ($p < .005$). The pattern of this interaction is opposite to those found for achievement-related scoring categories. Subjects high in n Achievement and low in test anxiety have *fewer* task imagery outcomes when attainment of the future goal is important. In contrast, subjects low in n Achievement and high in test anxiety have more task imagery outcomes when attainment of the future goal is important. In addition, a main effect for motive of borderline significance was found ($p < .10$) such that subjects high in n Achievement and low in test anxiety have a greater number of task imagery outcomes. Within the high importance condition, subjects low in n Achievement and high in test anxiety tend to have a greater number of task imagery outcomes. The fact that there are no significant effects in the open-ended form versus several significant effects in the contingent form explains the significant motive × importance × form interaction found within the corresponding three-factor ANOVA ($p < .02$).

Number of Transitional (TR) Outcomes

No significant main effects or interactions were found for the number of TR outcomes, except that a main effect for importance was found in all analyses pertaining to the contingent form. Subjects in the high importance condition tend to have a greater number of transitional outcomes ($p < .02$ in the analysis for resultant motive groups).

DISCUSSION

The cumulative evidence suggests that success-oriented and failure-threatened persons perceive their futures in quite different terms, particularly when attainment of the future goal is important. The predominantly positive tendencies of success-oriented persons are aroused when attainment of the future goal is important. As such, they are more likely to focus on achievement, that is, doing well in component steps (evidence for this is found in both forms), working hard (evidence from analyses of intensity activities in the open-ended form), and applying for various positions presumably related to eventual attainment of the future goal (evidence from analyses pertaining to use of transitional imagery in both forms). They are less likely to perceive their future in such mundane terms as getting through and passing the course (evidence from analyses pertaining to the use of task imagery in the contingent form).

The reverse occurs for failure-threatened persons. When attainment of the future goal is unimportant, their plans are colored with constructive steps pertaining to achievement, hard work, and applying for various positions. When attainment of the future goal is important, there is less emphasis on positive constructive steps and more on mundanely getting through, that is a C rather than an A in a course, and passing rather than doing well.

If the descriptions of future plans elicited in the questionnaires are valid indices of behavior, it would appear that failure-threatened persons are unrealistic with respect to future planning. They plan to exert maximum effort when attainment of the future goal is unimportant, and minimal effort when attainment of the future goal is important.

Why do important goals seem to arouse achievement-related tendencies? Backman and Secord (1968) suggest that aspired-to occupations are important to the extent that they appear congruent with the individual's perceived self-concept. If so, attainment of important future goals may serve to validate perceived or aspired-to competencies. Thus, individuals who believe they can reason abstractly and value that ability may aspire to become physicists because they consider physicists to be abstract thinkers. If they succeed in attaining this occupational goal, a valued domain of competence is at least partially validated. If they fail, a valued domain of competence is potentially invalidated. Success-oriented persons should be motivated to undertake positive steps to attain such goals. In contrast, failure-threatened persons should be motivated to avoid failure and potential invalidation of a perceived or aspired-to domain of competence. As such, they may reduce anxiety by coloring future steps with nonachievement-related perceptions. (See parts III and IV of this volume for a more extended discussion of competences and the self-concept.)

II

EMPIRICAL
EXTENSIONS

The research studies presented in this part have two aspects in common: (1) they employ the direct (questionnaire) measure of resultant achievement motivation developed by Mehrabian (1968, 1969) in an attempt to provide evidence for its construct validity under well-controlled experimental conditions, and (2) they investigate problems that are related to but not explicitly addressed by the more general theory of achievement motivation (see chapter 2).

The theory of achievement motivation does not include the effects of time to attain a goal on motivation of immediate activity. Rather, it explicitly treats psychological distance as a series of tasks in sequence (cf. Raynor, 1974a). Thus, it makes no predictions about the possible effects of differences in anticipated time to attain a goal on the arousal of motivation to strive for that goal. In chapter 6, the joint influence of psychological distance as time and psychological distance as a series of tasks in a contingent path on the arousal of motivation of immediate activity is investigated, using performance on a digit-symbol substitution task and a measure of resultant achievement-related effect to infer aroused motivation. In life situations it is almost always the case that as the number of tasks in a contingent path increases, so does the (anticipated) time to move successfully through the path. Thus, time and task variables are systematically confounded. They can be expected to have opposite effects on the arousal of motivation of immediate activity. Miller's (1944) goal gradient hypothesis suggests, and previous research on acheivement motivation confirms (Gjemse, 1974), that as the anticipated distance in time from a goal increases, aroused achievement motivation decreases—success-oriented individuals become less positively motivated, and failure-threatened individuals become less negatively motivated. The more general theory of achievement motivation (Raynor, 1974a; see chapter 2) derives that as the number of steps in a contingent path increases, aroused achievement motivation for the immediate next step of the contingent path should increase—success-oriented individuals should become more positively motivated, but failure-threatened individuals more inhibited. But since an increase in the number of steps increases the anticipated elapsed time for "getting through the path" and/or for "success at the last step," these effects of time and task, if correctly identified, should work against each other (i.e., in opposite directions) so that it would be difficult to validate predictions for length of contingent path when motivational effects due to anticipated time should reduce or wash out effects due to anticipated steps. However, in chapter 6 an experimental situation is discussed in which the normal confounding of time and task variables was broken; for two different amounts of time (20 and 40 min), two- and four-step contingent paths were created where the amount of elapsed time for the two paths was held constant. In this design the effects of time and the effects of tasks could be viewed separately, as could their joint impact on immediate behavior. In employing the Mehrabian measure and a resultant measure using Mehrabian and test anxiety, Pearlson (chapter 6) found evidence consistent with three sets of expectations. (1) There was a motive × time interaction: as time decreased, success-oriented subjects became more positively motivated while failure-threatened subjects became more negatively motivated. (2) There was a motive × task interaction: as steps increased, success-oriented subjects became more positively motivated, but failure-threatened subjects became more negatively motivated. (3) A motive × time × task interaction was found: the motive × time interaction held only for the longer (four-step) contingent path, while the motive × task interaction held only for the short (20-min) paths, and therefore predictions of the more general theory of achievement motivation were supported only for the short time condition.

These results have extremely important implications. First, for the first time there is clear-cut support for predictions concerning the effect of length of contingent path on motivation of immediate activity—an increase in the number of contingent steps has different but predictable effects depending upon individual differences in achievement-related motives. Second, the long-accepted conception of the goal gradient (Miller, 1944) in which the gradient of avoidance is assumed steeper than the gradient of approach is again shown to be inadequate in the area of achievement-oriented action; consistent with Gjesme's (1974) results, such an assumption applies only for those individuals dominated by the motive to avoid failure. More strongly supported in terms of statistical evidence is the implication that for success-oriented individuals the gradient of approach is stronger than the gradient of avoidance (really, the "do it" tendency increases at a faster rate than the "don't do it" tendency as time to an achievement-related outcome decreases). Third, both the Miller (1944) and Raynor (1974a) conceptions need to be revised to account for the three-factor interaction among time, task, and motives and/or the findings for the motive × time interaction. In terms of an expectancy × value approach, does time function through a change in the expectancy of success, through a change in the value of success, or through both? If time changes expectancy, does value remain independent of such changes or does the inverse relationship between expectancy and value produce a corresponding change in value? These are critical questions that Pearlson's positive results raise, which must be addressed in subsequent research.

In chapter 7 the joint influence of two dimensions of motive engagement are systematically investigated—high versus low achievement arousal, and contingent versus noncontingent future orientation, holding subjective probability of success constant. The more general theory of achievement motivation (chapter 2) originally evolved in part as an attempt to account for the fact that so-called aroused (achievement-oriented) conditions seemed to produce the predicted effects of achievement-related motives to a greater extent than did so-called relaxed conditions (see Atkinson, 1964; Raynor, 1974a), and previous theory could only account for such findings by assuming that under achievement-oriented conditions the subjective probability of success was closer to a moderate value (.5)—an implausible but possible explanation in the absence of data bearing on the issue. Subsequent research (see chapter 2) showed that effects previously found under achievement-oriented conditions are found under contingent-path conditions, and effects previously found under relaxed conditions are obtained under noncontingent-path conditions. The research in chapter 7 addresses the question as to whether or not contingent future orientation completely accounts for the relaxed-aroused distinction. The results for a combined measure of Mehrabian score and test anxiety score, and the test anxiety score alone, suggest that both dimensions of motive engagement need to be taken into account in predicting the correct number of problems solved on the task employed, although the effects for the motive X contingent versus noncontingent interaction appear more clear-cut. This research raises questions as to how to account for a motive X arousal interaction, holding both subjective probability of success and future orientation constant. The concept of individual cultural value introduced later (see chapters 11 and 13) may be needed to account for these data as well as those presented in chapter 5, where differences in ratings of the importance of a future goal interact with n Achievement scores in a manner analogous to the motives X arousal effect just referred to. We suggest that success-oriented individuals come to see achievement in terms of the positive value of success that it offers, while failure-threatened individuals come to see achievement in terms of the negative value of failure that it offers, and that these differences in perceptions of resultant cultural value function when "important" achievement is at stake, as when high achievement arousal is created or when an important future goal is pursued. Future research that directly investigates individual differences in what can be called "achievement values" (cf. Rosen, 1955) needs to be undertaken to see if this is a viable explanation for such effects.

In chapter 8 the relationship between theory of achievement motivation as it applies to contingent and noncontingent path behavior and learning (acquisition) is viewed. Do predictions concerning utilization of already acquired information (e.g., performance) hold for acquisition of information as well? The issue is complicated by the fact that learning must be inferred from some performance meant to assess it. The findings are mixed. They clearly indicate that the distinction between contingent and noncontingent arrangements of tasks in sequence is a useful one to make in studying learning. In fact, they provide some evidence that individual differences in achievement-related motives (as inferred from test anxiety in study I and the Mehrabian measure in study II) interact as predicted with the nature of the path of which the immediate learning-performance task is a part. However, when a more explicit distinction is made between acquisition and utilization of knowledge (study III), the data suggest that while the predicted interaction is found for utilization of knowledge already acquired in a previous learning period, contingent-path acquisition may be disruptive to learning for all subjects. This is a new finding that is reminiscent of the overmotivation effects found in some contingent paths (see chapter 2 for the Sorrentino study and its implications), and whatever its explanation, it raises the important point that application of the theory of achievement motivation to the study of learning (as opposed to the motivation of performance using already acquired information and/or skills) may involve additional complications. On the other hand, the data reported in chapter 8 provide additional evidence for predictions derived for performance in contingent versus noncontingent paths, and they increase our confidence that at least for some learning tasks the elaborated theory of achievement motivation is applicable.

In Chapter 9 we return to an investigation of the so-called Zeigarnik effect—the recall of interrupted and completed tasks—so as to integrate previous study of achievement motivation with the study of future orientation. Thus, recall is viewed under relaxed, achievement, and contingent path conditions for individuals differing in achievement-related motives. Study of the Zeigarnik effect by Atkinson (1950, 1953) apparently had resolved a controversy concerning the Lewinian prediction of persistent tendency (tension) that influenced thought (recall) and action (resumption) after success versus failure: Atkinson showed that individuals high in n Achievement recalled a greater proportion of incompleted (failure) than completed (success) tasks under achievement-oriented, then neutral, then relaxed conditions, but that the reverse was found for those low in n Achievement. He also reported a greater recall of completed items for all subjects in the achievement, then neutral, then relaxed conditions. And it is here that our newer study and his work diverge in terms of findings. The study presented in chapter 9 was originally carried out with the limited objective of showing that these trends would be continued and accentuated in a contingent-path situation, thereby establishing the link between earlier work and the study of achievement motivation and future orientation. The results do just this for recall of incompleted tasks. However, they also yield a pattern for recall of completed tasks similar to that for incompleted tasks, so that the trend reported for the failure-threatened group of the Atkinson research to recall more completed tasks with increased achievement arousal (weakly found for both studies from the relaxed to achievement conditions in each) is reversed in our contingent condition and recall of completed tasks is substantially lower in the contingent condition than the achievement condition of our research. Thus, viewing separately the Mehrabian measure and the test anxiety score, as well as a resultant measure utilizing both, we find that a measure of total recall best reflects the effects of our experimental conditions on recall; total recall for success-oriented subjects increases, although total recall for failure-threatened subjects decreases, from relaxed to achievement to contingent conditions. Thus we replicate Atkinson's findings; but when the supposedly higher achievement-arousing properties of a contingent path are also included for the first time, we find a suprising effect for total recall (due to recall of completed items) not found in earlier research. And the fact that similar patterns are found for the Mehrabian measure and the test anxiety measure, each used separately, suggests that we take the results seriously. If we do, we are confronted with what may turn out to be the need to reconceptualize the role of recall as influenced by motivational variables. Clearly, our data are not consistent with a simple explanation in terms of persistent positive achievement motivation that follows from the extension of Lewinian ideas to the derivations in the theory of the dynamics of action (Atkinson & Birch, 1978a, 1978b). Rather, they suggest that either Weiner's (1965) idea that resultant achievement motivation rather than just positive achievement motivation persists after failure is in part correct, or that some other explanation is required to reflect resultant motivation effects not only on recall of incompleted items (which Weiner's idea could handle) but on completed items as well (which Weiner's idea cannot account for). What is needed now is a study of resumption of activity (rather than recall) in the face of success and failure in contingent and other conditions, because the use of retrospected recall is now expected to be complicated by the status of immediate activity as occurring early, later, or terminally in a sequential arrangement of contingent-path steps (see chapters 13 and 15 for a discussion of stages of striving along a contingent path).

Our tentative explanation for the findings concerning total recall involves the assumption that the information value (see chapter 13) of both a success and a failure that occurred in the past is greater the more likely it is that such information is perceived by the individual to be instrumental to later achievement of success. Thus the instrumental value of past activity is implicated in an increase in total recall that is most pronounced in the contingent condition of our research for success-oriented subjects, and least pronounced for failure-threatened subjects—the latter because past achievement activity has negative instrumental value for individuals more inhibited by the prospect of failure than excited by the prospect of success. Our data are consistent with this explanation in that differences in total recall for individuals differing on the combined Mehrabian–test-anxiety measure are negligible in the achievement condition, and reversed in the relaxed condition. This suggests that the effect of recall proposed here is found only when instrumental value is relevant—that is, only when subjects know that recall of what they did on a first series of tasks can make a difference for later performance (in the second task of the contingent series). Our newer theoretical perspective (chapter 13) suggests further that if subjects were allowed to successfully move through a contingent series and then be faced with a task as the final step, recall would consist predominately of completed (success) items, since no further instrumental value is involved when no further steps of a contingent series are perceived. Thus the concept of instrumental value in recall at the end of a contingent path reverses the original Lewinian predictions for the Zeigarnik effect. This leads us to expect an interaction between achievement-related motives and stage of striving along a contingent path: At the end of a contingent path, with no further activity possible, success-oriented individuals should recall more success items than failure items and resume tasks that involved previous success; failure-threatened individuals should "repress" (not recall through a cognitive strategy) more failure items than success items, but resume tasks involving previous success. At the beginning of striving along a contingent path, recall of both success and failure items should be greater for the success-oriented individual, and resumption higher for a previously worked task regardless of success or failure than for a task not previously worked; recall of both success and failure items should be less for the failure-threatened individual, and resumption of tasks should indicate preference for a task not previously worked rather than for a previously tried task, regardless of success or failure on it.

6

Effects of Temporal Distance from a Goal and Number of Tasks Required for Goal Attainment on Achievement-related Behavior

Howard B. Pearlson

Two conceptions of time perspective can be identified in the achievement motivation literature: task time perspective and temporal time perspective. The former emphasizes the implications for immediate achievement-related behavior of the quality and number of anticipated future goals, while the latter emphasizes the individual's temporal distance from the attainment or lack of attainment of achievement-related goals. Psychologists have only recently begun to investigate the joint effects of these two variables (Pearlson, 1975).

TASK TIME PERSPECTIVE

Historical Background

The literature on task time perspective is the product of 30 years of programmatic research on the functional significance of individual differences in achievement motivation (paraphrased from Atkinson & Raynor, 1978). Raynor's elaboration (1968a, 1969, 1974a) represents an attempt to extend the expectancy X value theory of achievement motivation so as to be able to account for behavior in contingent path situations (see chapter 2) such as that faced by one who is climbing the corporate ladder, where an individual is confronted with a series of achievement-related tasks and must succeed on each prior task to earn the opportunity to move on in the sequence. The elaborated theory predicts that contingent path situations accentuate the individual's characteristic pattern of motivational arousal. Thus, high RAMs (those high on resultant achievement motivation) are assumed to become more positively motivated, and low RAMs are assumed to become more in-

This chapter is based upon an unpublished doctoral dissertation of the same title.

hibited, when placed in contingent-path situations. (A more extensive discussion of this critical issue is presented in chapter 2.)

The accentuation of motivation that occurs in contingent paths is partly a function of the individual's relative strength of achievement-related motives and the number of tasks in the contingent path. For high RAMs ($M_S > M_{AF}$), the components of resultant achievement motivation aroused by each achievement-related task of the contingent path are predominantly positive. As such, increasing the number of tasks in the path will increase the positive resultant achievement motivation of high RAMs. For low RAMs ($M_{AF} > M_S$), the components of resultant achievement motivation aroused by each achievement-related task of the path are predominantly negative. As such, increasing the number of tasks in the contingent path will increase the predominantly inhibitory motivation of low RAMs. For moderate RAMs ($M_S = M_{AF}$), the components of positive and inhibitory motivation aroused by each achievement-related task in the contingent path are relatively equal in strength. As such, increasing the number of tasks in the contingent path will not make the total resultant achievement motivation more positive or more inhibitory (see chapter 2, Equation 10).

TEMPORAL TIME PERSPECTIVE

The literature on temporal time perspective derives its theoretical impetus from the goal-gradient hypothesis proposed by Miller (1944). Miller made three basic assumptions derived from his extension of Hullian theory.

1. The approach tendency grows stronger as organisms approach positively valent goals (e.g., food) in time and space.
2. The avoidance tendency grows stronger as organisms approach negatively valent goals (e.g., shock) in time and space.
3. The slope of the avoidance gradient is steeper than that of the approach gradient.

Subsequent research has confirmed the first two assumptions, but the third has received only marginal empirical support. The research on temporal time perspective can be broken into two categories: studies that are not directly relevant to the arousal of achievement-related motives and studies that are. Only the latter are reviewed here (see Pearlson, 1979.)

Research Directly Relevant to the Arousal of Achievement-Related Motives

Gjesme (1974) investigated the relationship between temporal distance from a goal and achievement-related performance. Subjects were given problems described as practice for the schoolwide achievement tests to be administered the next day, in 1 week, in 1 month, or in 1 year. High-RAM subjects (high approach scores and low avoidance scores on the Achievement Motives Scale [Gjesme & Nygard, 1970]) were found to have a significant approach gradient, with the number of problems solved increasing linearly with the temporal closeness of the experimental procedure to the date of the actual exam. Low-RAM subjects (low approach scores and high avoidance scores on the Achievement Motives Scale) were found to have a significant avoidance gradient, with the number of problems sovled decreasing linearly with the temporal closeness of the experimental procedure to the date of the actual exam. The avoidance gradient found for low-RAM subjects was not steeper than the approach gradient found for high-RAM subjects.

Two pilot studies conducted by the author (Pearlson, 1975) suggest that both time and task variables interact to determine the arousal of achievement-related affect. To the author's knowledge, these were the first studies to assess the effects of both time and task variables in the same data collection. In study I, subjects assessed on the motive to avoid failure (high and low on test anxiety) were asked to imagine themselves moving closer in time to hypothetical course examinations for which performance had progressively greater future implications. As compared to subjects low on the motive to avoid failure, subjects high on the motive to avoid failure experienced a greater increase in anxiety as they imagined themselves moving temporally closer to the examinations and as performance on the examinations was perceived as having progressively greater future implications.

In study II both enthusiasm and anxiety were periodically assessed as subjects moved temporally closer to the date of their final exam in introductory psychology. In conjunction with this assessment, subjects were asked to indicate the extent to which good grades in introductory psychology were perceived as important for the attainment of their future goals. Predicted motives X time and motives X task interactions were found for enthusiasm ratings. High-RAM subjects (high on *n* Achievement, low on test anxiety) had a greater increase in enthusiasm than low-RAM subjects (low on *n* Achievement, high on test anxiety) as they approached temporally closer to the date of their examination and as good grades were perceived as more important for the attainment of future goals. The expected motives X time and motives X contingency interactions were nonsignificant for anxiety ratings. Although low-RAM subjects were higher than high-RAM subjects on all ratings of anxiety, they did not experience a greater increment in anxiety than high-RAM subjects as they approached temporally closer to the date of their final examination. Nor did they experience a greater increment in rated anxiety than high-RAM subjects as good grades were perceived as more important for the attainment of future goals.

TIME AND TASK VARIABLES: A REQUIRED INTEGRATION

The literature reviewed clearly indicates that time and task variables interact with achievement-related motives to effect achievement-related behavior. The literature does not, however, address itself to the basic confounding that exists between time and task variables as they occur in nature. Increasing the number of tasks intervening between an individual and some future goal also increases the time required to attain that future goal. As such, the strength of motivation (both positive and negative) aroused in the immediate first step of a contingent path is expected to increase owing to a greater number of tasks but should decrease owing to the greater amount of time required to complete the path and thus attain the future goal. Likewise, decreasing the number of tasks in a contingent path should decrease the extent of motivation aroused by task (fewer tasks) but increase the extent of motivation aroused by time (the individual is temporally closer to completing the path and attaining the future goal). Under these circumstances, it thus becomes impossible to precisely determine the relative effects and higher-order interactions of time and task variables.

Confounding of time and task could account for the nonsignificant or marginally significant results of studies investigating the relationships between the number of tasks in the path and the arousal of achievement-related motives (Brecher, 1972, 1975; Raynor, Entin, & Raynor, 1972). In increasing the number of tasks, these researchers increased the time required to complete the path and, unwittingly, may have decreased the total arousal of motivation due to time effects. The decrements in aroused motivation due to time effects may have canceled out or decreased the increments in aroused motivation due to task effects.

The present investigation was designed to disentangle the effects of time and task on achievement-related behavior by systematically exposing subjects to contingent paths of varying numbers of tasks requiring either short or long periods of time to complete. Predictions were made with regard to performance on the first task of a contingent path and the arousal of achievement-related affect prior to engaging in the achievement-related task. They were based upon the assumptions that increasing the number of tasks in the contingent path and decreasing the time required to complete the contingent path would: (1) add predominantly positive components of motivation for high-RAM subjects, (2) add predominantly negative or inhibitory components of motivation for low-RAM subjects, and (3) add equal components of positive and negative motivation for moderate-RAM subjects. These changes in positive and negative (inhibitory) motivation as mediated by changes in time and task were expected to affect performance and achievement-related affect as follows:

1. Motives × number of tasks in the path: As the number of tasks in the contingent path increases, (a) the performance and positive affect of high RAMs should increase, (b) the performance of low RAMs should decrease and negative affect should increase, and (c) the performance and affect of moderate RAMs should remain constant.

2. Motives × time required to complete the path: As the time required to complete the contingent path decreases, (a) the performance and positive affect of high RAMs should increase, (b) the performance of low RAMs should decrease and negative affect should increase, and (c) the performance and affect of moderate RAMs should remain the same.

3. Motives × time × task: (a) The expected motives × task interaction should be stronger when the time required to complete the contingent path decreases, and (b)

the expected motives X time interaction should be stronger when the number of tasks in the path increases.

The reader should note that the predicted triple-order interactions for perform-ance and achievement-related affect are based upon the assumption that each task in a contingent path functions to provide additional incentives and threats for immediate performance. As such, the motives X task interaction should be stronger when the time required to complete the contingent path is reduced. Under these conditions (1) the time required to complete each component task is reduced, (2) anticipated success or failure on each task of the path is moved temporally closer to the present, and, most important (3) the components of motivation (both positive and negative depending upon the individual's resultant achievement moti-vation) aroused by each task in the sequence are increased. Since the path with the greater number of tasks has more components of motivation to be summed, it should be associated with a greater increment in aroused motivation as the time required to complete the contingent path decreases. Thus, the increments in moti-vation (positive for high RAMs, negative for low RAMs) expected to occur as the number of tasks in the path are increased should be accentuated when the time re-quired to complete the contingent path is relatively brief.

Similarly, the motives X time interaction should be stronger for paths of greater task length (greater number of tasks). Under conditions of relatively long task length a greater number of components of motivation are summed when the time required to complete the contingent path is reduced. As such, the expected incre-ments in aroused motivation (positive for high RAMs, negative for low RAMs) asso-ciated with temporally shorter paths should be accentuated for paths of greater task length.

It should also be noted that the present study has been designed so that the experimenter can determine the effects of time and task variables on achievement-related behavior both for conditions similar to the confounding between time and task that occurs in nature (paths with greater task length take longer to complete than paths with lesser task length) and conditions in which time and task are not confounded (paths with different task lengths require the same amount of time to complete). Since the effects of task are masked by the effects of time in confounded conditions (increasing the number of tasks increases the motivation aroused by task but decreases the motivation aroused by time; decreasing the number of tasks in the path decreases the motivation aroused by task but increases the motivation aroused by time), it is expected that the motives X task interaction will be stronger for con-ditions in which time and task are not confounded than for conditions in which time and task are confounded. This issue will be discussed at greater length in the design section that follows.

METHOD

Design

The six experimental conditions used in the study are illustrated in Table 1. The italic numbers used to describe the experimental conditions in Table 1 represent the

Table 1   Six Experimental Conditions Used to Vary the Number of Tasks in the Contingent
Path and the Time Required to Complete Each Task

Experimental condition	Number of tasks and time required to complete each task			
	Time (min) for task 1	Time (min) for task 2	Time (min) for task 3	Time (min) for task 4
One (h,m,l)[a]	5[b]	5		
Two (h,m,l)	5	5	5	5
Three (h,m,l)	5	15		
Four (h,m,l)	10	10		
Five (h,m,l)	10	10	10	10
Six (h,m,l)	10	30		

[a]The letters h,m,l stand, respectively, for high, moderate, and low resultant achievement
motivation groups nested within each experimental condition.
[b]The italic numbers represent the number of minutes required to complete a component
task in a given experimental condition.

time required to complete each component task of a designated contingent-path
sequence. Experimental conditions one, two, and three operationalize temporally
short paths; conditions one *(5,5)* and two *(5,5,5,5)* respectively are two-and four-
task paths with 5 min required to complete each task of each sequence, and condition three *(5,15)* is a two-task path with 5 min required to complete the first task
and 15 min required to complete the second task. Experimental conditions four,
five, and six operationalize temporally long paths; conditions four *(10,10)* and five
(10,10,10,10) respectively are two- and four-task paths with 10 min required to
complete each task of each sequence, and condition six *(10,30)* is a two-task path
with 10 min required to complete the first task and 30 min required to complete
the second task.

Experimental conditions one, two, four, and five *(5,5; 5,5,5,5; 10,10;* and *10,10,*
10,10) were used to constitute a 3 X 2 X 2 "confounded" design (analogous to confounding in nature) in which two-task paths require less time to complete than corresponding four-task paths. The design includes three levels of resultant achievement motivation (high, moderate, and low) nested within experimental conditions,
two levels of time required to complete the path (temporally short and temporally
long paths), and two levels of task (two- and four-task paths).

Experimental conditions two, three, five, and six *(5,5,5,5; 5,15; 10,10,10,10;*
and *10,30)* were used to constitute a 3 X 2 X 2 "unconfounded" design in which
two- and four-task paths require the same amount of time to complete. The unconfounded design is similar to the confounded design in that it employs three levels
of resultant achievement motivation (high, moderate, and low) nested within each
experimental condition, two levels of time required to complete the path
(temporally short and temporally long paths), and two levels of task (two- and four-
task paths).

Subjects and Assessment of Motives

The subjects were 117 males recruited from a pool of 301 introductory psychology stud·nts at SUNY/AB who had completed the 26-item Mehrabian Scale of Achievement Motivation (Mehrabian, 1968, 1969) and the first third of the Test Anxiety Questionnaire (Mandler & Sarason, 1952) during mass testing sessions conducted at the beginning of the spring 1977 semester.

Subjects scoring in the top and bottom thirds of the distribution of Mehrabian scores (high scores are assumed indicative of a stronger motive to approach success than motive to avoid failure, and low scores are assumed indicative of a stronger motive to avoid failure than motive to approach success) were contacted by telephone and asked by the experimenter (H.B.P.) for their cooperation in participating in an experiment entitled "Time Perception and Cognitive Processes." No description of the experimental procedure was provided. However, subjects were informed that the experiment would take less than an hour of their time and that they would receive one experimental credit for their participation. (Introductory psychology students at SUNY/AB are required to either earn three units of experimental participation credits or write a psychology paper as partial requirement for passing the introductory course.)

Assignment of Subjects to Experimental Conditions

The experimenter attempted to include equal numbers of subjects from the top and bottom thirds of the Mehrabian distribution in each experimental session. However, scheduling difficulties resulted in experimental sessions ranging from four to nine subjects, with the ratio of high to low Mehrabian subjects in a given session ranging from 3:2 to 2:3.

Three sessions were conducted for each experimental condition. The sessions were conducted in sequences such that all experimental conditions would have been run before a given experimental condition could be repeated. The order in which experimental conditions were run was randomized within each sequence. Data collection was completed within 5 weeks.

Experimental Procedure

The experimental procedure consisted of (1) introductory remarks, (2) specification of the number of tasks in the sequence and the time required (temporal length) to complete the contingent path, (3) instructions intended to minimize pacing effects, (4) specification of contingent properties of task sequence, (5) specification of performance tasks, (6) summatory reiteration of experimental instructions, and after-performance completion of a (7) posttest questionnaire and debriefing. (A complete text of the instructions for each experimental condition is available in Pearlson, 1979.)

Prior to the beginning of each experimental session, subjects were greeted by the experimenter, who was professionally dressed in a suit and tie. Subjects were handed two sharpened pencils and an experimental packet containing a code sheet with an identifying code number, two or four "Digit Symbol" test booklets depending upon the experimental condition, and a posttest questionnaire. (Sample protocols are available in Pearlson, 1979.) Subjects were asked to place their names on the code sheet and were assured that the data would be referred to by code number rather than name to protect the confidentiality of respondents.

Specification of Number of Tasks in the Sequence and the Temporal Length of the Contingent Path

The number of tasks and time per task were specified as follows:

> Now that you have filled in this preliminary information I will go into further detail about today's experiment: We are interested in how people perform under various competitive conditions. As such we have developed a (two, four) test sequence consisting of items adapted from the Wechsler-Bellvue Intelligence Test Battery. You will have (5,5; 5,5,5,5: five minutes to work on each test; 5,15: five minutes to work on the first test and fifteen minutes to work on the second test; 10,10; 10,10,10,10: ten minutes to work on each test; 10,30: ten minutes to work on the first test and thirty minutes to work on the second test). You should find these tests to be fairly easy. Each test has been designed so that most college students like yourself can complete correctly at least three-quarters of the items within the allotted time period. This assumes of course that they work hard and put forth maximum effort. The second (latter) test(s) has (have) been adjusted for practice and learning effects so as to maintain the same level of difficulty as the first test.

Subjects were instructed to work as quickly as possible and not pace themselves. They were informed that they would be given a few seconds to rest and catch their breath after each 5 min of work. Pacing instructions were intended to control for differential pacing effects in which subjects confronted with paths taking a relatively long period of time to complete might slow down and conserve their energy more than subjects confronted with paths taking a relatively short period of time to complete.

Specification of Contingent Properties of Task Sequence

The contingent properties of the various two-task sequences (5,5; 5,15; 10,10; 10,30) were specified as follows:

> The opportunity to move on to the second test of the sequence depends upon your prior performance. Those of you who fail to complete correctly at least three-fourths of the items on the first test within the allotted time period will not be allowed to go on to the second test. If and when you are eliminated from the competition, you will spend the remainder of the experimental period working on a noncompetitive task involving the rating of magazine articles for aesthetic value.

The contingent properties of the four-test sequences (5,5,5,5; 10,10,10,10) were specified as follows:

> The opportunity to move on to the second, third, and fourth tests of the sequence depends upon your prior performance. If you fail to complete correctly at least three-

fourths of the items on any given test within the allotted time limit, you will not be allowed to go on to the next test or any of the tests, which follow. Those of you who fail to complete correctly at least three-fourths of the items on the first test will not be allowed to go on to the second, third, and fourth tests. Those of you who succeed on the first test but fail on a later test will be eliminated from the competition at the point at which you fail (i.e., if you succeed on the first test but fail on the second test, you will not be allowed to take tests 3 and 4; if you succeed on the first two tests but fail on the third test, you will not be allowed to take test 4). If and when you are eliminated from the competition, you will spend the remainder of the experimental period working on a noncompetitive task involving the rating of magazine articles for aesthetic value.

As the experimenter explained the noncompetitive alternative task for those failing to go on in the contingent path, he pointed to a stack of *Apartment Life* magazines and a stack of booklets, each having the words "Magazine Rating Task" printed on the cover sheet.

Specification of Performance Tasks

After reading aloud the experimental procedures, the experimenter instructed subjects to take the booklet marked "Digit Symbol Substitution Test 1" out of the packet. The booklet contained, in order of appearance: instructions, practice problems, a measure of achievement-related affect validated in pilot studies and previous research (Raynor, Atkinson, & Brown, 1974), and a performance task consisting of digit-symbol substitution problems similar to those used by Brown (1969), Meichenbaum (1972), and Wechsler (1958). The number of items on each performance task was varied in direct proportion to the length of time subjects were alloted to complete the first task in the various experimental conditions. The performance task was designed (based upon pilot research) such that no subjects could complete three-fourths of the items within the allotted time period. Depending upon the experimental condition, each experimental packet contained additional booklets labeled "Digit Symbol Substitution Test 2" (and 3 and 4 where required). Each subsequent test booklet contained progressively more complex symbols and a greater proportion of test items per unit of time allotted for completion.

The experimenter read performance test instructions aloud as the subjects followed along in their test booklets. The subjects then proceeded to work on sample test problems. After completing the sample test items, the subjects were read a brief reiteration of the experimental instructions. The experimenter wound a stopwatch while reading the reiterations. Following the reiteration of experimental instructions, subjects completed a scale of achievement-related affect, immediately after which they were instructed to begin working on Test 1.

Completion of Posttest Questionnaire and Debriefing

Subjects were allowed 5 min to work on Test 1. After 5 min the experiment was terminated. Subjects were asked to complete a post test questionnaire and were then debriefed as to the predictions and rationale of the experiment. (A sample of the post test questionnaire is available in Pearlson, 1979.)

Treatment of Data

Classification of Achievement-Related Motives

Following the initial mass-testing data collection, all males in the subject pool were assigned Z scores to reflect their respective positions on the distributions of Mehrabian and test anxiety scores. Each person's Z scores on the Test Anxiety Questionnaire was then subtracted from his Z score on the Mehrabian Scale. The total distribution of Z Mehrabian $-Z$ TAQ ($Z-Z$) was then computed and split into tripartite sections. Persons scoring in the top third of the $Z-Z$ distribution were considered to be high in resultant achievement motivation; persons scoring in the middle third of the $Z-Z$ distribution were considered to be moderate in resultant achievement motivation; and persons scoring in the bottom third were considered to be low in resultant achievement motivation.

Performance

Two dependent measures were used: number of problems attempted and number of problems correct.

Resultant Achievement-Related Affect

Resultant achievement-related affect was determined by summing the scores subjects obtained on three adjectives cued for positive achievement-related affect (eager, enthusiastic, and interested) and three adjectives cued for negative achievement-related affect (clutched-up, fearful, and jittery). Positively and negatively cued adjectives were selected on the basis of pilot data (see Table 2 for the correlation matrix from the pilot data) that indicated substantial positive correlations among positively cued items, substantial positive correlations among negatively cued items, and essentially no correlation between positively and negatively cued items.

The distribution of scores for each adjective was determined and split at the median. Subjects received a score of 1 or 0 for each positively cued adjective, depending upon whether their score was above or below the respective median. Likewise, subjects received a score of -1 or 0 for each negatively cued adjective, depending upon whether their score was above or below the respective median. This resulted in a distribution of scores ranging from 3 (very positive resultant achieve-

Table 2   Pilot-Data Correlation Matrix for Items Chosen to Measure Positive and Negative Resultant Achievement-Related Affect ($n = 49$)

	Eager	Enthusiastic	Interested	Nervous	Fearful	Jittery
Eager	1.00	.47	.46	.14	−.02	.15
Enthusiastic		1.00	.49	.01	−.08	−.23
Interested			1.00	−.10	−.10	−.07
Nervous				1.00	.63	.52
Fearful					1.00	.65
Jittery						1.00

Table 3   A. Confounded Experimental Design for which Two-Task Paths Require Less Time to Complete than Four-Task Paths

Temporally short paths		Temporally long paths	
Two-task path	Four-task path	Two-task path	Four-task path
1.[a] $(5,5)$[b] h,m,l[c]	2. $(5,5,5,5)$ h,m,l	4. $(10,10)$ h,m,l	5. $(10,10,10,10)$ h,m,l

Table 3   B. Unconfounded Experimental Design for which Two-Task Paths Require the Same Amount of Time to Complete as Four-Task Paths

Temporally short paths		Temporally long paths	
Two-task path	Four-task path	Two-task path	Four-task path
3.[a] $(5,15)$[b] h,m,l[c]	2. $(5,5,5,5)$ h,m,l	6. $(10,30)$ h,m,l	5. $(10,10,10,10)$ h,m,l

[a]Numbers followed by periods indicate experimental conditions.
[b]Italic numbers indicate the time (in minutes) required to complete each component task in a given experimental condition.
[c]The letters h,m, and l respectively stand for high, moderate, and low resultant achievement motivation groups nested within each experimental condition.

ment-related affect) to -3 (very negative resultant achievement-related affect). The rationale for using this method to obtain resultant achievement-related affect scores is based upon the positive results obtained by Raynor et al. (1974) in using this derived score.

A Priori Tests of Hypotheses

The data were analyzed both with time and task in their natural confoundings (experimental conditions one, two, four, and five; see Table 3A) and with time and task unconfounded (experimental conditions two, three, five, and six; see Table 3B).

In the unconfounded sets of experimental conditions the time required to complete the path was held constant across experimental conditions, and the two- and four-task paths required the same amount of time to complete. As such, the temporally short two-task $(5,15)$ and four-task $(5,5,5,5)$ paths required the same amount of time to complete. Similarly, the temporally long two-task $(10,30)$ and four-task $(10,10,10,10)$ paths required the same amount of time to complete.

Hypotheses were tested by the use of a priori comparisons (*t* tests) using the total within-cell error term for all six experimental conditions, weighted by the number of subjects in each comparison (Winer, 1962, p. 244). One-tailed comparisons were used to test predicted directional effects for subjects high and low in

142 EMPIRICAL EXTENSIONS

resultant achievement motivation. Since no directional hypotheses were made for subjects moderate in resultant achievement motivation, effects for the moderate motives group were tested with two-tailed comparisons. Interaction effects were tested by comparing the differential effects of time and task variables for subjects high and low in resultant achievement motivation (RAM).

RESULTS

Manipulation Checks

The posttest questionnaire (PTQ) data were analyzed as a check on the effectiveness of experimental manipulations of number of tasks in the path, time required to complete the path, and experimental attempts to eliminate differential pacing (performing at less than one's capacity during the initial part of the performance period so as to conserve energy for the latter part of the performance period) across experimental conditions. Analyses of subjects' PTQ estimates of the number of tasks in the path indicate that this manipulation was effective. Subjects in the four-task path conditions perceived their path as having a significantly greater number of tasks than did subjects in the two-task path conditions ($F = 23.56$, $df = 1/97$, $p < .005$). Analyses of subject PTQ estimates of the time required to complete the path indicates that subjects in the 20-min conditions perceived the path as taking significantly less time to complete than did subjects in the 40-min path conditions ($t = 1.44$, $df = 94$, $p < .10$, one-tailed). Although subjects in the 10-min path condition perceived their path as taking less time to complete than did subjects in the 20-min path condition, the difference was not statistically significant. Thus, while the ordering of experimental conditions with respect to subject perceptions of the time required to complete the path was consistent with intended induced effects, the manipulation of time was not supported as being very strong. Subject self-reports on the extent of pacing during the performance task indicate that there was no differential pacing effect across experimental conditions.

Inspection of the task protocols indicates that 14 subjects did not answer problems in consecutive order as requested in the experimental instructions. Using Sandler's A statistic for matched or correlated samples, the performance of these 14 subjects was found to be significantly lower ($\overline{X} = 148.36$) than that of a comparison group matched for $Z-Z$ score and experimental condition ($\overline{X} = 183.29$) ($A = 0.13$, $df = 11$, $p < .01$, two-tailed). In light of this substantial performance difference, the 14 subjects not answering problems in consecutive order were excluded from subsequent data analyses.

Performance: Number of Problems Correct

A Pearson correlation coefficient computed to determine the relationship between the two performance measures (number of problems attempted and number of problems correct) indicates that they were almost perfectly correlated ($r = .99$). Therefore, only results for number of problems correct are presented here. The

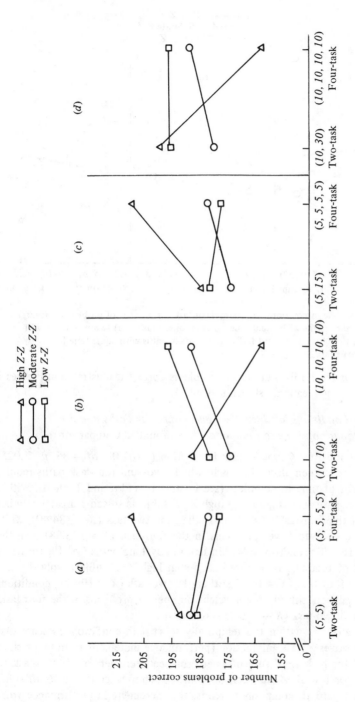

Figure 1 Motive × time × task interaction and component motive × task interactions within levels of time for number of problems correct. (*a*) and (*c*), short time; (*b*) and (*d*), long time, (*a*) vs. (*b*), experimental conditions for which two-task paths require less time to complete than four-task paths (confounded comparisons). (*c*) vs. (*d*): experimental conditions for which two- and four-task paths require the same amount of time to complete (unconfounded comparisons).

143

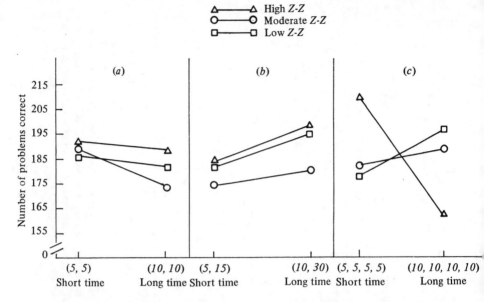

Figure 2 Motive X time interactions within levels of task for number of problems correct. (a) Two-task paths with equal time for component tasks; (b) two-task paths with unequal time for component tasks; (c) four-task paths with equal time for component tasks.

overall pattern of results for number of problems correct is illustrated in Figures 1 and 2. Corresponding means are shown in Table 4.

Analyses for Conditions in which Two- and Four-Task Paths Require the Same Amount of Time to Complete (Unconfounded Comparisons)

A significant motives X time X task interaction ($t = 2.08, df = 85, p < .025$) was found for experimental conditions in which two- and four-task paths require the same amount of time to complete (see Figures 1c and d and Table 4). Within temporally short paths (see Figure 1c) high $Z-Z$ subjects solved a greater number of problems in the four-task ($\bar{X} = 210.67$) than the two-task ($\bar{X} = 184.40$), while low $Z-Z$ subjects solved fewer problems in the four-task ($\bar{X} = 178.88$) than the two-task ($\bar{X} = 183.78$) conditions. Within temporally long paths (see Figure 1d), a partial reversal of predictions occurred such that high $Z-Z$ subjects solved fewer problems in the four-task ($\bar{X} = 162.25$) than the two-task ($\bar{X} = 199.71$) conditions and low $Z-Z$ subjects solved an equivalent number of problems in the four-task, ($\bar{X} = 196.71$) and two-task ($\bar{X} = 196.25$) conditions.

Subsequent analyses within the temporally short path conditions indicate that the expected motives X task interaction (performance increment from two-task to four-task path for high $Z-Z$ subjects; performance decrement from two-task to four-task path for low $Z-Z$ subjects) approached significance ($t = 1.36, df = 85, p < .10$). With regard to component trends, the increment in performance from two-task to four-task paths approached significance for high $Z-Z$ subjects ($t =$

Table 4 Mean Performance Scores for Number of Problems Correct as a Function of Resultant Achievement Motivation, Time to Complete Contingent Path, and Number of Tasks in the Contingent Path

| | Ten minutes | | Twenty minutes | | | | | | Forty minutes | | | |
| | 1.[a] $(5,5)$[b] = two-task | | 3. $(5,15)$ = two-task | | 2. $(5,5,5,5)$ = four-task | | 4. $(10,10)$ = two-task | | 6. $(10,30)$ = two-task | | 5. $(10,10,10,10)$ = four-task | |
	N	Mean	N	Mean	N	Mean	N	Mean	N	Mean	N	Mean
Z Meh − Z TAQ												
High Z−Z	6	191.33	5	184.40	6	210.67	2	188.00	7	199.71	4	162.25
Moderate Z−Z	5	188.20	6	174.84	6	183.83	3	173.00	4	180.50	6	189.50
Low Z−Z	3	186.00	9	183.78	8	178.88	8	182.38	8	196.25	7	196.71
Mehrabian												
High	8	184.88	9	177.56	9	199.56	3	193.33	11	201.18	8	181.00
Low	6	193.50	11	184.22	11	182.00	10	177.40	8	184.63	9	190.56
Test anxiety												
High	5	191.80	13	178.62	10	185.30	8	190.62	11	197.26	11	196.80
Low	9	187.55	7	187.57	10	194.80	5	165.80	8	192.09	7	172.00

[a]Numbers followed by periods indicate experimental conditions.
[b]Numbers in parenthesis indicate the time required to complete each task in a given experimental condition.

145

1.48, $df = 85$, $p < .10$) while the decrement in performance from two-task to four-task paths found for low $Z-Z$ subjects was nonsignificant. No significant task effect was found for moderate $Z-Z$ subjects.

Subsequent analyses within the long time to complete the path conditions indicate that the predicted $Z-Z \times$ task interaction was nonsignificant, as were component trends for high and low $Z-Z$ subjects. Once again, no significant task effect was found for moderate $Z-Z$ subjects.

Motives × Time Interactions within Levels of Task

Comparisons were made to determine the significance of expected motives × time interactions within various levels of task. Comparisons within the two-task conditions for which the component tasks of the path took equal amounts of time to complete (see Figure 2a) indicate that the expected motives × time interaction (performance increment from temporally long to temporally short paths for high $Z-Z$ subjects; performance decrement from temporally long to temporally short paths for low $Z-Z$ subjects) was nonsignificant. Component trends for high, moderate, and low $Z-Z$ subjects across levels were also nonsignificant.

Comparisons within two-task conditions for which the component tasks of the path took unequal amounts of time to complete (see Figure 2b) indicate that the motives × time interaction was nonsignificant. Taken separately, performance trends for high, moderate, and low $Z-Z$ subjects across levels of time required to complete the path were all nonsignificant.

Comparisons within four-task conditions (see Figure 2c) indicate that the expected motives × time interaction was highly significant ($t = 2.71$, $df = 85$, $p < .005$). High $Z-Z$ subjects solved a greater number of problems in the temporally short four-task path ($\bar{X} = 210.67$) than in the temporally long four-task path ($\bar{X} = 162.25$). Low $Z-Z$ subjects solved fewer problems in the temporally short four-task path ($\bar{X} = 178.88$) than in the temporally long four-task path ($\bar{X} = 196.71$). With regard to component trends, the performance increment for high $Z-Z$ subjects from temporally long to temporally short four-task paths was highly signficant ($t = 2.52$, $df = 85$, $p < .01$). The performance decrement for low $Z-Z$ subjects from temporally long to temporally short four-task paths was nonsignificant, though in the expected direction. Subjects moderate in $Z-Z$ did not differ in performance across temporally short and temporally long four-task paths.

Results for the confounded comparisons are in general similar to those for the unconfounded conparisons but tend not to be as statistically significant. Thus, for both confounded and unconfounded comparisons, (1) the predicted motives × task interaction (increase in performance from two-task to four-task path for high $Z-Z$ subjects, decrease in performance from two-task to four-task path for low $Z-Z$ subjects) was stronger within temporally short than within temporally long paths; (2) the predicted motives × task interaction was stronger for unconfounded than for confounded comparisons; (3) the predicted motives × time interaction (increase in performance from temporally long to temporally short paths for high $Z-Z$ subjects, decrease in performance from temporally long to temporally short paths for low $Z-Z$ subjects) was stronger within four-task than two-task paths; and

(4) component trends for both motives X task and motives X time interactions were stronger for high $Z-Z$ than for moderate or low $Z-Z$ subjects.

Resultant Achievement-Related Affect

Results for resultant achievement-related affect roughly parallel those for number of problems correct. Means are shown in Table 5. The data indicate that (1) the predicted motives X task interaction (increase in positive resultant achievement-related affect from two-task to four-task paths for high $Z-Z$ subjects, increase in negative resultant achievement-related affect from two-task to four-task paths for low $Z-Z$ subjects) was stronger for the unconfounded than for the confounded comparisons; (2) the predicted motives X task interaction was stronger within temporally short than within temporally long paths (for unconfounded conditions); (3) the predicted motives X time interaction was nonsignificant (more positive resultant achievement-related affect from temporally long to temporally short paths for high $Z-Z$ subjects, more negative resultant achievement-related affect from temporally long to temporally short paths for low $Z-Z$ subjects) within both two- and four-task paths, but the pattern of means was more consistent with predictions within four-task paths; and (4) component trends for both motives X task and motives X time interactions were generally stronger for high $Z-Z$ than for moderate or low $Z-Z$ subjects (see Pearlson, 1979, for specific a priori comparisons).

DISCUSSION

The significant motives X time X task interactions found for both performance and resultant achievement-related affect suggest that task time perspective and temporal time perspective must be considered *jointly* if one is to gain an accurate understanding of the effects of future goals on achievement-related behavior. The differential motivational effects predicted for number of tasks in the path were found only for conditions in which the time required to complete the contingent path was relatively brief. Similarly, the differential motivational effects for time required to complete the contingent path were found only for paths with a relatively high number (4) of component tasks.

The experimental design enabled the researcher to determine the effects of time and task on achievement-related behavior both for confounded comparisons in which two-task paths require less time to complete than four-task paths and unconfounded comparisons in which two- and four-task paths require the same amount of time to complete. Since task effects are masked or canceled by time effects in the confounded comparisons and not masked or canceled by time effects in the unconfounded comparisons, the predicted motives X task interactions were expected to be stronger for the unconfounded than for the confounded comparisons. Inspection of the data indicates that such was the case. The expected motives X task interaction for performance (within temporally short paths) was significant for unconfounded comparisons in which two- and four-task paths required the same amount of time to complete, but nonsignficant for confounded comparisons in

Table 5 Mean Resultant Achievement-related Affect as a Function of Resultant Achievement Motivation, Time to Complete Contingent Path, and Number of Tasks in the Contingent Path

| | Ten minutes | | Twenty minutes | | | | | | Forty minutes | | | |
| | 1.[a] (5,5)[b] = two-task | | 3. (5,15) = two-task | | 2. (5,5,5,5) = four-task | | 4. (10,10) = two-task | | 6. (10,30) = two-task | | 5. (10,10,10,10) = four-task | |
	N	Mean	N	Mean	N	Mean	N	Mean	N	Mean	N	Mean
Z Meh – Z TAQ												
High Z–Z	6	.167	5	.000	6	1.667	2	.500	7	1.429	4	.750
Moderate Z–Z	5	.200	6	–.833	6	–.333	3	.667	4	–.250	6	–.333
Low Z–Z	3	–1.607	9	–.333	8	–.625	8	–.375	8	–.375	7	–.286
Mehrabian												
High	8	.250	9	–.333	9	1.000	3	.333	11	.455	8	.250
Low	6	–.833	11	–.455	11	–.545	10	–.100	8	.125	9	–.333
Test anxiety												
High	5	–.600	13	–.385	10	.200	8	–.375	11	–.375	10	.100
Low	9	.000	7	–.429	10	.100	5	.600	8	.818	7	–.286

[a] Numbers followed by periods indicate experimental conditions.
[b] Numbers in parenthesis indicate the time required to complete each task in a given experimental condition.

which two-task paths required less time to complete than four-task paths. Likewise, the expected motives X task interaction for resultant achievement-related affect was significant for unconfounded comparisons in which two- and four-task paths required the same amount of time to complete, and nonsignificant for confounded comparisons in which two-task paths required less time to complete than four-task paths.

A comparison of the relative strengths of the motives X task interactions for conditions in which time and task were and were not confounded suggests the extent to which the effects of task length may be masked in the "real world." That is, while the number of tasks in a contingent path does interact with achievement-related motives to affect achievement-related behavior (the implication of significant motives X task interaction found in unconfounded comparisons), the effects are minimized in confounded real-world situations where paths of greater task length generally take longer to complete (the implication of lack of significance of motives X task interaction in confounded comparisons). The results also suggest that previous researchers (Brecher, 1972, 1975; Raynor, Entin, & Raynor, 1972) failed to find significant effects of number of tasks in the contingent path because they failed to control for the effects of the time required to complete the path.

As expected, subjects high in $Z-Z$ had significantly better performance and significantly more positive resultant achievement-related affect as the number of tasks in the path increased (within temporally short paths) and the time required to complete the path decreased (within four-task paths). Likewise, the expectation that moderate RAMs would not differ in performance and achievement-related affect over levels of time and task was confirmed. However, there was a consistent lack of significance of trends for subjects low in $Z-Z$. Subjects low in $Z-Z$ solved fewer problems and had more negative resultant achievement-related affect in the four-task than in the two-task paths (within temporally short paths), but the trends were nonsignificant. Similarly, subjects low in $Z-Z$ solved fewer problems and had more negative resultant achievement-related affect in the temporally short than in the temporally long paths (within four-task paths), but again the trends were nonsignificant. This failure is similar to earlier ones in research on achievement motivation (see Atkinson & Raynor, 1974).

The data were analyzed using three indices of resultant achievement motivation: high, moderate, and low $Z-Z$ (Z Mehrabian $-Z$ test anxiety); high (top third) and low (bottom third) Mehrabian scores; and high (above median) and low (below median) test anxiety scores. Hypotheses were most strongly supported when the composite $Z-Z$ measure of resultant achievement motivation was used. Results were similar but less significant when hypotheses were tested using the Mehrabian measure, and least significant using the test anxiety measure (see Pearlson, 1979).

Miller's (1944) goal-gradient hypothesis postulated that the slope of the avoidance gradient is steeper than that of the approach gradient. An obvious implication is that persons should have progressively more negative resultant achievement-related affect and progressively poorer performance as they approach goals in time and space.

The data indicate that Miller's hypothesis is valid for subjects low in resultant achievement motivation but not valid for subjects high in resultant achievement motivation. Within four-task paths, only subjects low in $Z-Z$ decreased in performance (see Table 4) and experienced more negative resultant achievement-related affect (see Table 5) as the time required to complete the contingent path decreased. In contrast to Miller's goal-gradient hypothesis, subjects high in $Z-Z$ had performance increments (see Table 4) and experienced more positive resultant achievement-related affect (see Table 5) as the time required to complete the contingent path decreased. This suggests that for subjects high in $Z-Z$ (high in resultant achievement motivation), the approach gradient for time is in fact steeper than the avoidance gradient for time.

The data present further construct validation of the achievement-related affect scale used in the study. Results for resultant achievement-related affect generally parallel results for performance. Note that the expected motives X task interactions were stronger for resultant achievement-related affect than for either the positive or negative component measures of resultant achievement-related affect taken separately (see Pearlson, 1979, for an elaboration of predictions and results for positive and negative resultant achievement-related affect taken separately). This is consistent with the expected strength of interactions for the composite and component measures of resultant achievement-related affect.

At the present time, the author has no viable explanation to account for the reversal of predictions found within the temporally long path conditions. It should be noted, however, that other studies in the achievement motivation literature have found reversals of predictions where weak effects were predicted in accordance with either the expectancy-value theory of achievement motivation (Atkinson & Feather, 1966) or Raynor's elaboration of the expectancy-value theory of achievement motivation (Raynor, 1969, 1974a; see chapter 2). Thus, Raynor (1974a) cited two studies indicating that when introductory grades in psychology were perceived as having relatively little instrumentality for future career success, low RAMs (subjects scoring low on a distribution of n Ach scores and high on a distribution of TAQ scores) received higher marks in Introductory Psychology than did high RAMs (subjects scoring high on a distribution of n Ach scores and low on a distribution of TAQ scores) (see Tables 1 and 4, chapter 2). Similarly, Sorrentino (1971) found that when the opportunity to go on in a sequence of performance tasks was *not* contingent upon prior performance (noncontingent path), low RAMs performed better than high RAMs (with resultant achievement motivation again being determined by relative standing on the distributions of n Ach and TAQ scores) (see Figure 6, chapter 2). Further research is necessary to account for these reversals, obtained in experimental conditions and field situations thought to operationalize a relatively weak arousal of achievement-related motives. (See also chapters 3, 7, and 12 for data showing this reversal, and chapter 2 for a discussion of its theoretical significance.)

7

Effects of High versus Low Achievement Arousal on Level of Performance in Contingent and Noncontingent Paths

Joel O. Raynor and Elliot E. Entin

Early research on achievement motivation was concerned with the effects of "relaxed" versus "aroused" conditions on imaginative thought samples (McClelland et al., 1949, Atkinson, 1950; McClelland, Atkinson, Clark, & Lowell, 1953), which led to the development of the *n* Achievement measure of the achievement motive. Later research was concerned with how individual differences in *n* Achievement scores obtained under neutral conditions might relate differently to other achievement-oriented behavior under relaxed versus aroused conditions (Atkinson, 1953; Atkinson & Raphelson, 1956; Atkinson & Reitman, 1956; Smith, 1963; Raynor & Smith, 1966). Although there are some exceptions, these studies showed in general that relationships were stronger in the expected directions under aroused conditions and were weaker or reversed under relaxed conditions. Further research, which also incorporated the test anxiety measure of the motive to avoid failure as well as the *n* Achievement measure of the motive to achieve (Atkinson, Bastian, Earl, & Litwin, 1960), showed, as predicted, that under aroused achievement-oriented conditions, individuals high in *n* Achievement, low in test anxiety, and/or high-low in a combined measure of *n* Achievement and test anxiety (motive to achieve M_S assumed stronger than motive to avoid failure M_{AF}), performed at a higher level than did individuals low in *n* Achievement, high in test anxiety, and/or low-high on the combined measure ($M_{AF} > M_S$).

Early statements of the expectancy $\times$ value theory of achievement motivation (e.g., Atkinson, 1964) accounted for the stronger relationships under aroused conditions by assuming that under relaxed conditions there is no incentive to achieve, so that the motive to achieve (and the motive to avoid failure) are not engaged. This argument assumed that expectancy of success was the only situational variable that could influence the strength of relationship between achievement-related motives and achievement-oriented behavior, holding extrinsic sources of motivation constant. This relationship should be nonexistent when expectancy of success is irrelevant, as in a relaxed condition, and strongest when $Ps = .5$ in an aroused achievement-oriented condition.

Raynor (1969, 1974a) has elaborated the expectancy $\times$ value theory of achievement motivation (see also chapter 2) to include the concepts of noncontingent and contingent future orientation. Both experimental and field studies have generally shown that in a contingent path, individuals with $M_S > M_{AF}$ are more concerned about doing well than anxious about failure (Raynor, Atkinson, & Brown, 1974) and/or perform at a higher level (Raynor, 1970, study I; Raynor & Rubin, 1971; Entin & Raynor, 1973; Raynor, 1974a; see also chapter 2).

It has been assumed that behavior under noncontingent conditions would be the same as in previously investigated achievement-oriented situations where, conceptually, an isolated activity-outcome (step) is usually provided (cf. Raynor, 1974a). That is, predictions derived from initial statements of the expectancy $\times$ value theory of achievement motivation (cf. Atkinson & Feather, 1966, chap. 20; Atkinson, 1978b) were expected to hold in noncontingent-path situations. However, both experimental and field studies have generally failed to show the predicted higher performance of individuals with $M_S > M_{AF}$ over those with $M_{AF} > M_S$ in these noncontingent situations, whereas this comparison has yielded statistically reliable differences in the predicted direction in immediate activity of contingent paths.

The question remains as to why behavior under noncontingent conditions is not predicted by achievement-related motives as expected. When a test is presented under such a condition with a stated performance criterion and the chances of attaining it are not zero but are given as .5, there is every reason to believe that the incentive values of success and failure are not zero so that achievement motivation should be aroused in such a noncontingent path. However, perhaps the noncontingent instructions themselves prevent achievement arousal because of the fact that they explicitly state that immediate success or failure has no bearing on the opportunity to move on along the path. If moving on to the next step were seen as an important achievement goal of the situation, the noncontingent instruction might effectively prevent motive arousal. On the other hand, perhaps in previous research on future orientation not enough emphasis has been placed on cues that produce a full-blown "achievement-oriented" condition when noncontingent paths are induced, since in these studies concern has been more with the contingent versus noncontingent distinction than with a high-arousal versus low-arousal continuum that is implied by the achievement-oriented versus relaxed distinction.

In the present research, contingent and noncontingent paths were created under two conditions of motivation arousal. In one, termed a low-arousal (achievement-oriented) condition, the task was described as a test with a known and specified probability (.5) of attaining a certain criterion of immediate performance. However, all other achievement-related cues were either omitted or explicitly de-emphasized. In the other, a high-arousal (achievement-oriented) condition, most of the cues that have been previously used to create strong achievement arousal were either included or emphasized (cf. McClelland et al., 1949, 1953; Atkinson & Reitman, 1956; Raynor & Smith, 1966). The upper part of Table 1 summarizes the instructions used to create these two levels of achievement arousal.

Note that to create comparable path conditions it is necessary to state the same explicit performance criterion in both noncontingent and contingent paths (cf. Entin & Raynor, 1973). In the present research the criterion of "immediate success" of the noncontingent condition was used both as a criterion of immediate success

Table 1 Comparison of Procedures and Instructions Used to Create Each Dimension of Motivation Arousal

Low Achievement Arousal	High Achievement Arousal
Male experimenters are informally dressed (slacks and sport coat).	Male experimenters are formally dressed (suit, coat, and tie).
Subject is told that undergraduates are conducting the session.	No mention that experimenters are undergraduates.
"We are . . . doing standardization of the data on the four tests you are about to take.	"You are about to take a series of very challenging tests designed to measure your ability to work mathematical problems in your head."
"Please do not write your name on the test; use only the code number you were given . . . you will remain anonymous."	"Please print your full name on each page of the test as you take it."
"Do not worry about how well you do on these tests." R-N	"The object of this test is to do as well as you can."
"We are not concerned with your individual ability on the test." R-C	"Your performance will be taken as the full measure of your ability."
	A-N "Do your best and do as many problems as you can."
	A-C "Work hard and do your best to complete 20 out of 25 items on each test."

Noncontingent condition	Contingent condition
"Completing 20 out of 25 items correctly on any test is considered successful performance, but you will have an opportunity to take each test regardless of your performance on any one of them."	"Completion of 20 out of 25 problems correctly is required to go on to the next test in the series. In other words, to go on to tests 3 and 4, you are to complete 20 out of 25 items on tests 2 and 3, respectively, within the time limit."
	A-N "If you don't complete 20 out of 25 items on any test, don't become concerned; just sit quietly until the test period is over."
	A-C "If you fail to complete 20 out of 25 problems on any test in the allotted time, you will not be permitted to continue on to the next test. Instead you must remain in your seat until the end of the test period.

Note. R = low arousal; A = high arousal; N = noncontingent; C = contingent.

and as a criterion for "moving on" to the next step of the contingent path so that only a single performance norm needed to be specified in each condition (see chapter 4). The lower part of Table 1 summarizes the instructions used to create the two kinds of paths, contingent and noncontingent.

No explicit hypotheses were made concerning the possible interaction of low and high achievement arousal and noncontingent and contingent path conditions.

However, we were prepared to draw conclusions from two particular patterns of results. (1) If noncontingent performance was as originally predicted by the elaborated theory of achievement motivation (individuals with $M_S > M_{AF}$ scoring higher than those with $M_{AF} > M_S$, with performance of $M_S = M_{AF}$ individuals intermediate) under both low and high achievement arousal, we would reject the notion that noncontingent cues rule out the engagement of achievement-related motives, particularly if predicted results were obtained under high-arousal-noncontingent conditions. (2) If predicted differences in performance levels were not obtained under either high or low achievement arousal in the noncontingent condition but were as predicted in the contingent condition, we would accept the notion that noncontingent cues rule out engagement of achievement-related motives, particularly if predicted results were not obtained under high-arousal-noncontingent conditions but were obtained under low-arousal-contingent conditions.

Regardless of the degree of achievement arousal, a specific pattern of interaction was expected in comparing the performance of $M_S > M_{AF}$ and $M_{AF} > M_S$ groups under different contingency conditions: The $M_S > M_{AF}$ group should perform at a higher level while the $M_{AF} > M_S$ group should perform at a lower level in immediate activity in the contingent path than in the noncontingent path so that the expected superiority of the $M_S > M_{AF}$ over the $M_{AF} > M_S$ group should be greater within the contingent condition (with $M_S = M_{AF}$ intermediate), regardless of the results obtained under noncontingent conditions (cf. Raynor, 1974a).

Regardless of contingency condition, a pattern of interaction similar to that described above for the motives $\times$ contingency condition interaction was expected in comparing performance in low and high achievement arousal conditions: An increment for the $M_S > M_{AF}$ group coupled with a decrement for the $M_{AF} > M_S$ group from low to high achievement arousal conditions so that, within high arousal, performance is higher for $M_S > M_{AF}$ than for $M_{AF} > M_S$ groups (with $M_S \approx M_{AF}$ intermediate), regardless of performance under low arousal conditions (cf. Atkinson et al., 1960).

The usual assessment of achievement-related motives (cf. Atkinson & Raynor, 1974) involves use of the n Achievement measure of the motive to achieve (cf. Atkinson, 1958, chap. 12 and app. III) and a test anxiety measure of the motive to avoid failure (e.g., the Mandler-Sarason [1952] Test Anxiety Questionnaire). However, there is substantial evidence that a group of individuals classified low on a test anxiety measure behave as though they have $M_S > M_{AF}$, and the theoretical explanation for this result is consistent with this interpretation (cf. Atkinson, 1964, chap. 9; Atkinson & Feather, 1966, chap. 20; Atkinson, 1978a). In addition, Mehrabian (1968, 1969) has devised and presented some (questionable) validity evidence for a measure of resultant achievement motivation. Since the administration and scoring of the Mehrabian measure is simpler and more convenient than that of the n Achievement measure, its potential construct validity is of some concern to researchers in this area. Since in the present research we have two explicit patterns of interaction against which to validate a measure of achievement-related motives, we included the Mehrabian measure instead of the n Achievement measure, along with the Test Anxiety Questionnaire (TAQ). We expected the TAQ measure to provide evidence concerning the issues discussed above, and equivalent results for the Mehrabian measure alone and in conjunction with TAQ to provide evidence concerning the construct validity of the former.

METHOD

Subjects

The subjects were 160 male students drawn from two ninth-grade and two tenth-grade physical education classes of a high school located in a small Midwestern city.[1] The tenth-grade students ($N = 80$) were tested 3 weeks after data were obtained from the ninth-grade students ($N = 80$). Complete data were available from 147 subjects.

Assessment of Motives

The Mehrabian (1968, 1969) measure of resultant achievement motivation (RAM) and the Test Anxiety Questionnaire (Mandler & Sarason, 1952) were administered to all subjects under neutral testing conditions. The RAM is a self-report measure asking subjects to indicate their strength of agreement with each of 34 items. This is done by circling for each item an integer ranging from -3 to $+3$. In coding, the scale is transformed to a 7-to-1 scale with 7 indicating the most and 1 the least achievement-oriented response. A subject's achievement motivation score was the sum over the 34 items.

The first 15 items of the TAQ (of which the first 3 are fillers) were employed to assess test anxiety. These items comprise the first third of the TAQ. They have been found to correlate between .84 and .90 with the total TAQ score (cf. Smith, 1964). The graphic response scale for each item was divided into five equal parts and coded so that 5 indicated the most and 1 the least anxious response. A subject's test anxiety score was the total score over the 12 items. The resulting distributions for RAM and TAQ were rank ordered and split at their respective medians. Those above the median on each were considered high, and those below the median on each were considered low. Subjects high on RAM, subjects low in TAQ, and those high on RAM and low on TAQ were considered to have motive to achieve relatively stronger than motive to avoid failure ($M_S > M_{AF}$). Subjects low on RAM, high on TAQ, and those low on RAM and high on TAQ were considered to have motive to avoid failure relatively stronger than motive to achieve ($M_{AF} > M_S$).

Assessment of Performance Level

A complex (three-step) arithmetic task (Wendt, 1955) that has been previously used in both the Raynor and Rubin (1971) and Entin and Raynor (1973) studies

[1] The authors thank Robert Grill for assistance in data collection.

provided the measure of performance level. The task requires the solution of a series of three-step addition and subtraction problems. These were arranged 25 to a page. Four different pages of problems were constructed. The same page order was used throughout all test booklets. As in previous research, the number of problems attempted and the number of problems solved correctly on the first page were used as measures of performance level.

Procedure and Experimental Instructions

After the RAM and TAQ measures were administered, all subjects were read instructions adapted from Raynor and Rubin (1971) to induce equivalent perceptions of task difficulty:

> On the basis of lots of experiments using lots of students at other public schools, four tests have been developed. Each test is made up of 25 separate problems. The items on each test have been chosen to give you a 50-50 chance of doing at least 20 of the 25 items in two and one-half minutes. The later tests have been adjusted for practice and learning effects to maintain this 50% level of difficulty. This estimate of your chances of success is based on a computer analysis of the performance of a large number of students. Later experiments have confirmed the truth of these estimates. That is, within each test approximately 50% of the students were able to complete 20 out of 25 items.

Following these instructions subjects were shown how to solve the three-step arithmetic problems. Then one of the four experimental conditions was induced. Table 1 summarized the differences among instructions used for the various conditions. As an example, the verbatim instructions for the high-arousal contingent condition were:

> You will now take a series of very challenging tests. These tests are designed to measure your ability to work mathematical problems in your head. The object is to do as well as you can. Your performance on each of the four tests will be taken as the full measure of your ability. You will have two and one-half minutes to work on each test. Do not begin any test in the booklet until you are told to do so. Do not write anything in the test booklet except the final answer. The opportunity for you to work on the next test in the series depends on how many of the problems you complete on the previous test. You must complete 20 out of 25 problems in test one in order to take test two and so on. If you fail to complete 20 out of 25 problems on any test in the allotted time, you will not be permitted to continue on to the next test. Instead, you must remain in your seat until the end of the test period. Work hard and do your best to complete 20 out of 25 items on each test. Be sure your name is on each page.

All subjects were allowed $2\frac{1}{2}$ min to work on the first test. Previous results with this task showed that it was unlikely that anyone could do all the problems in this time. At the conclusion of the first test the experiment was ended and all subjects were debriefed.

The experimental groups were composed of about 20 subjects each, and each of the four experimental conditions were conducted within both the ninth and tenth grades. The ordering of experimental conditions was determined by chance prior to testing.

We adopted the following validity criteria to determine the extent to which a given motive classification functions as predicted by theory: First, with regard to the pattern of mean performance within a given experimental condition, are the motive groups ordered as expected (for the Mehrabian measure, high Mehrabian higher than low Mehrabian; for test anxiety, low test anxiety higher than high test anxiety; for a joint measure of Mehrabian and test anxiety, high-low highest, low-high lowest, with high-high and low-low intermediate between the extremes)? Second, for the joint motive classification, within a given experimental condition, to what extent is one, the other, or both measures contributing to the results? That is, if the two middle motive groups (high-high and low-low) are equidistant between the extreme motive groups (high-low and low-high), then both motive measures contribute equally to the predicted result. If the middle groups fall closer to one or the other of the extreme motive groups, then the particular pattern reveals which of the motive measures accounts for the results; e.g., if the high-high motive group falls closest to the high-low motive group, and the low-low motive group falls closest to the low-high group, then differences in Mehrabian rather than test anxiety account for the results, whereas if the high-high group falls closest to the low-high group, and the low-low group falls closest to the high-low group, then differences in test anxiety rather than Mehrabian account for the results. Third, with regard to patterns of interaction, to what extent does one, the other, or both motive measures yield the predicted motive X contingency and/or motive X arousal interactions already mentioned? Fourth, with regard to statistical significance, to what extent does use of each motive measure separately as a factor in the overall analysis of variance (ANOVA) yield statistically reliable effects ($p < .05$) or effects that approach statistical significance ($p < .10$)? Finally, with regard to statistical significance, to what extent do a priori comparisons for predicted directional results yield evidence supporting a particular pattern of results for a motive measure, either alone or in joint classification?

RESULTS

The Mehrabian measure of resultant achievement motivation and the test anxiety measure were included as separate factors in an overall analysis of variance that also included the two experimentally manipulated dimensions of motive engagement (contingency and arousal). This resulted in a 2 X 2 X 2 X 2 ANOVA involving Mehrabian (high vs. low), TAQ (high vs. low), contingency condition (noncontingent vs. contingent), and arousal condition (low vs. high). Individual group means for number of problems attempted and solved are shown in Table 2 for all motive groups. Table 3 presents a summary of the ANOVA.

Inspection of the means of Table 2 within experimental conditions indicates that the expected ordering of combined motive groups (high-low highest, low-high lowest, and high-high and low-low intermediate) occurred in high arousal contingent conditions but not in either of the noncontingent conditions. Further inspection of data within the contingent conditions suggests that differences are due

Table 2   Mean Number of Problems Attempted and Solved as a Function of Motive Groups, Arousal Condition, and Contingency Condition

	Low achievement arousal						High achievement arousal					
	Noncontingent			Contingent			Noncontingent			Contingent		
Motive measure	N	Attempted	Solved	N	Attempted	Solved	N	Attempted	Solved	N	Attempted	Solved
Mehrabian												
High	22	9.91	5.14	16	8.69	5.31	10	9.20	6.60	24	10.08	6.71
Low	16	11.50	5.56	22	8.45	5.00	23	8.35	4.00	14	9.07	6.00
Test anxiety												
Low	21	11.52	5.05	19	10.53	6.63	12	7.75	5.25	25	9.92	7.48
High	17	9.41	5.65	19	6.58	3.63	21	9.10	4.52	13	9.31	4.46
Mehrabian-test anxiety												
High-low	12	10.59	4.58	8	12.13	7.38	4	7.50	4.25	14	10.14	8.21
High-high	10	9.10	5.80	8	5.25	3.25	6	10.33	8.17	10	10.00	4.60
Low-low	9	12.78	5.67	11	9.36	6.09	8	7.88	5.75	11	9.64	6.55
Low-high	7	9.86	5.43	11	7.55	3.91	15	8.60	3.07	3	7.00	4.00

Table 3   Summary of Analysis of Variance for Number of Problems
Attempted and Solved as a Function of Mehrabian, Test Anxiety,
Contingency Condition, and Arousal Condition

| | | Value of F | |
Source	df	Attempted	Solved
Mehrabian (A)	1	< 1	1.39
Test Anxiety (B)	1	2.71*	4.93**
Contingency (C)	1	< 1	1.07
Arousal (D)	1	< 1	< 1
A × B	1	< 1	< 1
A × C	1	< 1	< 1
A × D	1	< 1	1.93
B × C	1	1.09	4.62**
B × D	1	3.39***	< 1
C × D	1	3.11***	1.83
A × B × C	1	< 1	3.13***
A × B × D	1	1.14	1.01
A × C × D	1	< 1	< 1
B × C × D	1	< 1	< 1
A × B × C × D	1	< 1	< 1

Note. Mean square error: attempted, 28.816, $df = 131$; solved, 17.015,
$df = 131$.
   *$p = .10$.
  **$p < .05$.
 ***$p < .10$.

primarily to TAQ rather than Mehrabian. Inspection of means for the two motive measures taken separately indicates the expected ordering showing higher scores for high than for low Mehrabian groups in all but the low-arousal-noncontingent condition. Inspection of the data for test anxiety groups indicates the expected higher performance of the low-TAQ group over the high-TAQ group within the two contingent conditions, whereas in the two noncontingent conditions the results depend upon which performance measure, attempted or solved, is viewed. Thus, according to our first validity criterion, both motive measures taken alone gain some validity, whereas according to the second validity criterion, the evidence favors the effect of test anxiety alone.

Inspection of Table 3 indicates that only one of the possible effects of Mehrabian by itself on performance approaches statistical significance; Mehrabian did not have a main effect on performance, nor did Mehrabian scores alone interact with either contingency conditions or arousal conditions, or the two experimental dimensions taken together. Thus, according to the fourth criterion, Mehrabian by itself has no construct validity in the present study. However, the interaction between Mehrabian, TAQ, and contingency condition approaches statistical significance ($F = 3.13$, $df = 1/131$, $p < .10$) for number of problems solved. This pattern of results is discussed shortly.

There was a significant main effect of TAQ on number of problems solved ($F =$

Table 4   Mean Number of Problems Attempted and Solved as a Function of Motive Groups
and Contingency Condition, Collapsed over Arousal Condition

		Contingency condition				
		Noncontingent			Contingent	
Motive measure	N	Attempted	Solved	N	Attempted	Solved
Mehrabian						
High	32	9.69	5.59	40	9.53	6.15
Low	39	9.64	4.64	36	8.69	5.39
Test anxiety (TAQ)						
Low	33	10.15	5.12	44	10.18	7.11
High	38	9.24	5.03	32	7.69	3.97
Mehrabian-TAQ						
High-low	16	9.81	4.50	22	10.86	7.91
High-high	16	9.56	6.69	18	7.89	4.00
Low-low	17	10.47	5.71	22	9.50	6.32
Low-high	22	9.00	3.82	14	7.43	3.93

4.93, $df = 1/131$, $p < .05$). As expected, those low in TAQ solved more problems
(6.26) than those high in TAQ (4.54). Results for problems attempted are in the
same direction (10.17 vs. 8.53) and approach statistical reliability ($F = 2.71$, $df = 1/131$, $p = .10$). There was also a significant interaction between TAQ and contingency condition for problems solved ($F = 4.62$, $df = 1/131$, $p < .05$), and, as
already noted, an interaction between Mehrabian, TAQ, and contingency condition
on problems solved. Table 4 presents the group means for the motive × contingency condition interactions. Inspection for test anxiety alone indicates that within
the contingent condition the low-TAQ group solved more problems than the high-TAQ group ($t = 3.10$, $p < .001$),[2] while this difference within the noncontingent
condition does not approach significance ($t < 1$, n.s.). Within anxiety groups, there
was an increase as predicted in problems solved for the low-TAQ groups from the
noncontingent to the contingent condition ($t = 1.95$, $p < .05$), while the predicted
decrease for the high-TAQ group from noncontingent to contingent is not significant ($t = 1.07$, n.s.). With regard to the third criterion, TAQ alone gains in construct validity since the overall pattern of results is consistent with expectations and
tests of significance confirm some of the predicted directional effects.

In terms of the substantive issues of the present study, the pattern of results for
the significant TAQ × contingency interaction (Table 4) suggests that the contingency condition rather than the arousal condition accounts for the engagement of
achievement-related motives (as inferred here from test anxiety) and that the
effects are due primarily to TAQ rather than to Mehrabian. In particular, from
Table 2 we see that the low-TAQ group solved more problems than the high-TAQ
group in the contingent-low-arousal condition ($t = 2.24$, $p < .025$) as well as in the

---

[2] Directional hypotheses are evaluated using one-tailed t tests of significance and degrees of
freedom of the corresponding analysis of variance ($df = 131$ for MSE).

contingent-high-arousal condition ($t = 2.14$, $p < .025$), but that this difference is not significant in the noncontingent-low-arousal condition (the means are reversed) and, particularly, is not significant in the noncontingent-high-arousal condition ($t < 1$, n.s.). This pattern is consistent with the evidence needed to accept the notion that noncontingent cues prevent the engagement of achievement-related motives, as inferred from TAQ.

The ANOVA failed to yield effects approaching statistical significance concerning the interaction between motive measures and arousal conditions. The means for the motive X arousal interaction are shown in Table 5. Inspection of these data suggests that the ANOVA results may be somewhat misleading, since for number of problems solved, both the Mehrabian measure alone and the test anxiety measure alone yield a pattern of interaction suggesting the predicted accentuation within high arousal as compared to low arousal, although neither F value for these effects approaches statistical significance. The combined motive measure yields a pattern of interaction for problems solved for the Mehrabian X TAQ X arousal interaction that is similar to that found for the Mehrabian X TAQ X contingency interaction, with the added similarity that the effect of test anxiety is greater than that of Mehrabian. Despite the fact that neither the Mehrabian X TAQ X contingency interaction nor that for Mehrabian X TAQ X arousal yields significant ($p < .05$) F values, a priori comparisons reveal that (1) within high arousal the number of problems solved tends to be greater for the high-low motive group than for the low-high motive group ($t = 1.54$, $p < .10$), within low arousal this difference does not approach significance ($t < 1$, n.s.); (2) within the contingent condition the number of problems solved was significantly greater for the high-low than for the low-high motive group ($t = 2.36$, $p < .025$), within the noncontingent condition this difference does not approach significance ($t < 1$, n.s.), and the difference between the differences the interaction effect is significant ($t = 1.65$, $p < .05$).

Table 5 Mean Number of Problems Attempted and Solved as a Function of Motive Groups and Arousal Condition, Collapsed over Contingency Condition

Motive measure		Arousal condition				
		Low achievement			High achievement	
	N	Attempted	Solved	N	Attempted	Solved
Mehrabian						
High	38	9.39	5.21	34	9.82	6.68
Low	38	9.74	5.24	37	8.62	4.76
Test anxiety (TAQ)						
Low	40	11.05	5.80	37	9.22	6.76
High	36	7.92	4.53	34	9.18	4.50
Mehrabian-TAQ						
High-low	20	11.20	5.70	18	9.56	7.33
High-high	18	7.39	4.67	16	10.13	5.94
Low-low	20	10.90	5.90	19	8.89	6.21
Low-high	18	8.44	4.50	18	8.33	3.22

These results suggest that both dimensions of motive engagement influenced performance as measured by problems solved, and that the combined Mehrabian-TAQ motive measure as well as the TAQ alone yielded patterns of interaction for both the contingency dimension and the arousal dimension consistent with theoretical expectations and previous experimental findings. Unfortunately, the data for the Mehrabian measure alone suggest that by itself it cannot be used as a valid assessment of individual differences in strength of achievement-related motives.

DISCUSSION

Differences in performance levels are predicted by the theory of achievement motivation and have been found in previous research—individuals with $M_S > M_{AF}$ should perform better than individuals with $M_{AF} > M_S$, with the $M_S \approx M_{AF}$ group intermediate. If problems solved in the present research is used as the performance measure, then the present research is clear in suggesting that noncontingent-path cues function to prevent this motive engagement, as inferred from differences in test anxiety and from differences in a combined measure of Mehrabian score of resultant achievement motivation and test anxiety. No predicted differences in performance level in either the low-arousal or the high-arousal *noncontingent* conditions approached statistical significance.

The results are consistent with Atkinson's (1964) general argument that other environmental cues besides a "relaxed condition" can rule out what he termed motive arousal, and what we have termed motive engagement. The results suggest that the explicit reference to the fact that immediate success or failure has no bearing on the opportunity to move on, so that moving on is in fact guaranteed regardless of the quality and quantity of immediate performance, as in an explicitly noncontingent condition, functions to rule out pride of accomplishment or shame in failure. Note, however, that this is different from saying that there is "no incentive" to achieve or to avoid failure. It is now clear that Atkinson (1964) referred to the idea that it must be possible for activity on a (first) task to result in a level of performance that the person is prepared to define as success in that situation for motive engagement to occur, rather than the idea per se that $Ps = 0$ so that $Is = 0$ and therefore resultant achievement motivation is also zero. It is now also clear that Raynor (1969a) did not anticipate the distinction between success as "doing well" and success as "moving on" in a contingent path (see chapter 4).

We suggest that the data of the present study can be interpreted to mean that (1) subjects in the contingent condition interpreted moving on as the goal that would define immediate success, so that the primary goal in the contingent condition was to earn the opportunity to work on the second task rather than merely to do well in the immediate activity per se; (2) setting performance norms with $Ps = .5$ in the contingent condition defined the subjective probability of moving on as .5, which in this situation was equivalent to saying that the subjective probability of immediate success was .5 because immediate success determined moving on; (3) in the noncontingent condition the explicit reference to the fact that immediate success or failure had no bearing on the opportunity to move on in the path, so that moving on was actually guaranteed, served as a cue to indicate that immediate success or failure was not possible, since immediate success and moving on are seen as equivalent.

If this interpretation is correct, future orientation in the form of a contingent path may often involve more than the accentuation of characteristic differences in achievment-related motives, as originally supposed in the elaborated theory. Rather, it can play a critical role in defining what will be seen as an achievement-related situation by indicating a moving-on criterion to be used to define immediate success in a performance situation. In a contingent path, moving on may represent the primary achievement goal rather than doing well per se, so that low-arousal-contingent performance engages achievement-related motives. In an explicit noncontingent condition the fact that moving on is not at issue prevents motive engagement, even in a high-arousal-noncontingent condition, where doing well per se is still possible. Several changes in theory are suggested if this interpretation is valid: (1) noncontingent conditions should not be taken as equivalent to one-step or isolated activities; (2) the distinction between success in terms of the performance task per se and success in terms of moving on to a next step of a path needs to be made; and (3) the subjective probability of moving on rather than the subjective probability of immediate success in terms of the performance task is the variable that should be manipulated to test predictions of the elaborated theory of achievement motivation involving different levels of subjective probability of success.

8

Achievement Motivation, Future Orientation, and Acquisition

Elliot E. Entin

From their inceptions the initial and elaborated theories of achievement motivation (see chapter 2) have been primarily concerned with the prediction of task performance. Little systematic research has brought achievement motivation theory to bear on the learning or acquisition phase. Historically, however, motivation and learning theories have been intimately related. One has only to look back at the mechanistic theories of Hull, Spence, or Tolman to find variables of motivation and learning presented in the same model. More recent research endeavors have appeared to separate the two for intense but isolated study, with the results that models of learning or motivation rarely make references to each other. But there is little doubt that the motivational forces that affect performance also have their effect on learning or acquisition.

The language of the everyday world acknowledges this relationship. We speak of persisting or working hard at studying, implying a motivational state oriented toward learning. We might also hear an individual indicate that he or she is working hard or expending a great deal of effort trying to grasp a concept, again implying a motivational state to learn. It seems reasonable to assume that we work hard and are motivated when we learn just as we work hard and are motivated when we perform.

Some time ago Zajonc (1965) referred to the effect of social facilitation or acquisition as separated from performance. His work shows the differential effect that social facilitation can have on the efficiency or time it takes to acquire a particular skill. Zajonc also demonstrated how conditions existing at the time of acquisition could affect subsequent performance. Just as Zajonc studied and postulated the effect of social facilitation on learning as opposed to performance, we too would like to examine the effects on acquisition of individual differences in achievement motivation and differences in the future orientation of a situation.

Study I is based on an undergraduate project Gary Frank completed with E. E. Entin and then subsequently presented at the Southeastern Psychology Association conference in Hollywood, Fla., in May, 1974. Similarly, study II is derived from undergraduate work Lisa L. Barnhouse and Marianne Luch did with E. E. Entin and presented at the American Educational Research Association conference in Chicago, in April, 1974. Study III is based on a portion of an unpublished masters thesis (Humphrey, 1973) at Ohio University.

The author would like to express his thanks and gratitude to Joel Raynor for his ideas and helpful comments through all phases of this work.

There are only a few studies examining the relationship of the theory of achievement motivation to learning. One study examining the relationship between speed of learning and strength of achievement motivation dates to one of the earliest attempts at validating the *n* Achievement measure of the achievement motive. Lowell (1952) found that the number of unscrambled words increased significantly over trials for high *n* Achievement but not for low *n* Achievement subjects. Lowell interpreted these results to mean that high *n* Achievement subjects were learning a strategy for unscrambling the words, while those low in *n* Achievement were not.

Anxiety and speed of verbal learning has long been a topic of research. The work in this area by Spence and his colleagues (e.g., Spence, Farber, & McFann, 1956) is well known. In a more recent study, Weiner (1966) showed the relationship to be more complex than originally thought. In this study low anxious students learned an easy paired-associate list faster in a treatment condition that led them to believe they were failing than did high anxious students. These results are more in line with the cognitive approach to achievement motivation than traditional drive theory in that the nature of the feedback, and not the habit hierarchy, seemed to be the important aspect of the situation that interacted with anxiety.

No direct attempt has been made as yet to relate the predictions of the elaborated theory of achievement motivation to acquisition. A study by Raynor (1970), however, bears on the problem. College students were asked to indicate how important getting a good grade in introductory psychology was for their future plans to work out. The pattern that emerged (see chapter 2) indicated that success-oriented students (individuals in whom the motive to approach success is relatively stronger than the motive to avoid failure) received higher grades in the course than failure-threatened students (individuals in whom the motive to avoid failure is relatively stronger than the motive to approach success) when they perceived their performance as important to future success. On the other hand, failure-threatened students performed better than success-oriented students when the grade was perceived as having little future importance. A course grade is a multiply determined measure, but it is reasonable to assume that among its many components, acquisition or speed of learning figures prominently.

STUDY I

The first of several studies to be presented here was devised to examine the acquisition of a verbal task composed of paired associates within the context of a contingent and a noncontingent path. It was hypothesized that success-oriented subjects would show better acquisition—that is, recall more words—in the contingent than in the noncontingent path, while failure-threatened subjects would show better acquisition in the noncontingent than in the contingent path. It was also expected that success-oriented individuals would exhibit better recall than failure-threatened individuals in the contingent but not the noncontingent path. In other words, the predictions made for acquisition in an achievement-oriented situation paralleled the predictions made for task performance.

Method

Subjects

The subjects were 69 male and 27 female suburban high-school students. All students were enrolled in the program "Education Through Inquiry," which is designed for students who have difficulty in normal classroom programming.

Procedure

Because of class-time limitations (the design had to fit a 45-min class period) we decided to administer only the Test Anxiety Questionnaire (TAQ) for high-school students (Sarason, Davidson, Lighthall, Waite, & Ruebush, 1960) as a measure of achievement motivation. The resulting distribution of anxiety scores was ranked ordered and split into tritiles. Then, in accordance with the argument presented by Atkinson (1964, p. 250), students placing in the highest third were assumed to be failure-threatened (motive to avoid failure relatively stronger than motive to approach success), while those falling in the lowest third were assumed to be success-oriented (motive to approach success relatively stronger than motive to avoid failure). Individuals placing in the middle third of the distribution were assumed to be moderates (motive to approach success approximately equal to motive to avoid failure.)

We tried to stay close to traditional verbal learning design. We selected a learning task consisting of three-letter paired associates chosen according to high meaning-fulness and low similarity (e.g., far-mit, cab-sun) (Tulving, 1964). A list of 16 such paired associates was prepared and arranged in three random orders. Each randomized list was photographed on a 2 X 2-in slide. The lists were presented by projecting them on a wall screen in a large study hall using a Kodak Carousel slide projector.

Each subject was provided a 10-page test booklet. Pages 1, 4, and 7 contained 72 "two-digit added to two-digit" problems. These were employed to prevent rehearsal of the verbal task and as a manipulation control. Pages 2, 5, and 8 presented three randomized lists of the 16 stimulus words followed by a blank where the student was asked to write in the correct response term. Blank pages marked the end of each trial.

Groups of subjects were randomly assigned by coin toss to one of the two experimental conditions. After the anxiety measure (TAQ) was administered, the students were read the induction instructions. Individuals in both experimental conditions were told that there would be four tests in the battery and that each test was composed of three trials. They were led to believe that the tests were of moderate difficulty for students of their age and ability—that is, that there existed a 50-50 chance of their learning all 16 word pairs correctly by the third trial of each test.

Subjects in the contingent condition were told that to work on Test 2 they had to have been successful at Test 1. Likewise, to earn the opportunity to work at Tests 3 and 4 they had to have been successful at the previous test. Success was described as placing above the average for that group. In other words, those who scored below the average established for that test and group would be considered failures and could not go on to the next test. Instead, they would have to remain in their seats until all testing was completed. Those who scored above the established average for that test and group would be considered successful and could go on to the next test.

Subjects in the noncontingent condition were informed that if they scored above the average established for that test and group they could consider themselves successful, but if they fell below the established average they would have failed. However, they were further told that whether they succeeded or failed would have no bearing on their opportunity to go on to the next test. In other words, they would be allowed to take all four tests.

Subjects were allowed to view the 16 word pairs projected on the screen for 30 sec. Immediately thereafter, they worked the addition problems for 1 min. Such a time interval precluded anyone from finishing all 72 problems. After working the arithmetic problems, subjects were asked to turn to the next page and to provide as many of the 16 missing response words to the 16 stimulus words as they could. Two minutes were allowed for recall. The next two trials of Test 1 proceeded in an identical fashion. The same 16 word pairs were presented in different orders. Each page of arithmetic problems, however, was unique. After Test 1, the experiment was terminated and subjects were debriefed.

Results

As a manipulation check, the arithmetic problems (used to prevent rehearsal) were scored by totaling the number of problems performed correctly over all three trials. Table 1 shows the mean number of arithmetic problems correctly solved as a function of test anxiety and experimental condition. Examination of the top and bottom thirds of the motive distribution (no specific hypotheses are made for the middle group) shows, as expected, that success-oriented subjects performed better in the contingent than the noncontingent condition while failure-threatened subjects performed better in the noncontingent than the contingent condition ($F =$

Table 1   Mean Number of Arithmetic Problems Correctly Solved as a Function of Test Anxiety and Experimental Condition

	Path			
Test anxiety	Noncontingent		Contingent	
	N	Mean	N	Mean
Low	10	49.10	16	58.06
Moderate	12	51.17	12	43.33
High	10	52.30	18	42.28

Table 2   Mean Number of Words Correctly Recalled for Each Trial as a Function of Test
Anxiety and Experimental Condition

Test Anxiety	Path											
	Noncontingent						Contingent					
	Trial 1		Trial 2		Trial 3		Trial 1		Trial 2		Trial 3	
	N	Mean	N	Mean	N	Mean	N	Mean	N	Mean	N	Mean
Low	10	0.60	10	1.80	10	3.10	16	2.25	16	2.44	16	3.68
Moderate	12	0.58	12	1.75	12	2.66	12	1.00	12	1.08	12	1.75
High	10	1.20	10	1.00	10	2.20	18	1.50	18	1.17	18	2.61

4.06, $df = 1/50$, $p < .05$). It was also found that the characteristic difference between success-oriented and failure-threatened individuals was significant in the contingent condition ($t = 2.75$, $df = 50$, $p < .005$) while it was reversed in the noncontingent path condition. Such results parallel those reported by Entin and Raynor (1973) and Raynor and Rubin (1971) for performance on an achievement-oriented task and confirm the effectiveness of experimental induction in creating contingent and noncontingent arousal effects.

For the acquisition results, the number of words correctly recalled was computed for each of the three trials. The data for each trial were subjected to a two-way ANOVA (three levels of TAQ by two levels of experimental condition). The means for the analysis are depicted in Table 2. One-tailed a priori t tests were also computed to test specific hypotheses. Inspection of the top and bottom thirds of the motive distribution for Trial 1 show, as predicted, that within the contingent condition success-oriented individuals recalled more words than failure-threatened individuals, while within the noncontingent condition failure-threatened individuals showed superior recall to success-oriented individuals ($t = 1.64$, $df = 50$, $p < .05$). Such an interaction pattern is not apparent in Trials 2 and 3. However, as expected, success-oriented individuals recalled significantly more words than failure-threatened individuals in the contingent condition for both Trials 2 and 3 ($t = 2.42$, $df = 50$, $p < .01$ and $t = 1.34$, $df = 50$, $p < .10$, respectively) while the same contrasts within the noncontingent condition yielded nonsignificant results ($ts < 1.0$, n.s.).

To examine the results over trials, an experimental condition (two levels, between) $\times$ TAQ (two levels, between) $\times$ trials (three levels, within) ANOVA was computed. The analysis showed a significant improvement in the number of words recalled over the three trials ($F = 28.0$, $df = 2/100$, $p < .001$). Interestingly, a trial $\times$ anxiety interaction (depicted graphically in Figure 1) was also revealed ($F = 3.15$, $df = 2/100$, $p < .05$). Although an analysis of trends showed significant linear components for both the success-oriented and failure-threatened individuals across trials, the rate of increase (learning) for the success-oriented individuals was $2\frac{1}{2}$ times that of the failure-threatened individuals.

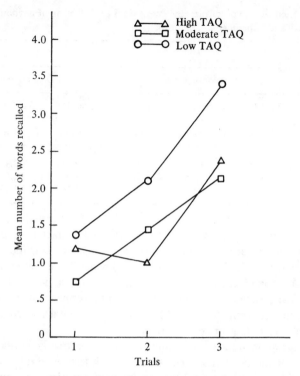

Figure 1 Number of words recalled by trials and test anxiety.

Discussion

These results support the argument that individual differences in achievement motivation and future orientation influence acquisition behavior. When present success was necessary to earn the opportunity to strive for future success, success-oriented individuals exhibited better recall of words than failure-threatened individuals. However, in the noncontingent condition, when present success was not linked to future success, inhibition for the failure-threatened individual was diminished, and recall improved. While the exact mechanism by which acquisition was affected by motivation cannot be discerned from this design, a likely explanation is that achievement motivation sharpens or heightens the attention an individual pays to the task. The positive motivating forces of the success-oriented individuals, further heightened in the contingent condition, leads to increased attentiveness. The individual is eager and prepared, and thus the word pairs are efficiently encoded into long-term memory. An increase in inhibitions as suffered by failure-threatened individuals is further intensified in the contingent condition. This leads to interference and lowers attendance to the task. Thus, the word pairs are not as efficiently encoded and not as well remembered.

STUDY II

In the second experiment, subjects studied a programmed-learning task under achievement-oriented noncontingent (not future oriented) or contingent (future oriented) experimental conditions. They were then called upon to apply what they had learned on a subsequent test on the material studied.

It has been suggested (Shrable & Sassemath, 1970; Weiner, 1967) that programmed-learning situations represent a kind of task for which the theory of achievement motivation (Atkinson & Feather, 1966, chap. 20) is well suited. The initial achievement model (see chapter 2) specifies that for success-oriented persons, resultant achievement motivation is positive, and the tendency to undertake the task is strongest when the task is considered to be one of intermediate difficulty. For the failure-threatened person, resultant achievement motivation is negative, and inhibition to undertake the task is strongest when the task is one of intermediate difficulty. The initial achievement model, therefore, suggests that in a programmed-learning situation, in which item difficulty is typically very low, success-oriented individuals will not be highly motivated to perform. For failure-threatened individuals expectation of failure will be slight, thus minimizing their inhibition to undertake the task.

When future orientation is introduced, the resulting interaction with achievement motivation produces a different cognitive representation of the situation, and thus a change in expected outcome. Specifically, elaborated achievement theory (see chapter 2) predicts that "for any length of contingent path (two- or more-step paths), an individual's achievement motivation should become stronger with an increase in magnitude of constant subjective probability of success along the path in conjunction with an increase in the length of the path" (Raynor, 1974a, p. 139). In other words, success-oriented individuals should perform best in contingent paths comprised of easy tasks, when path length is at least moderate, and such paths should serve to further inhibit failure-threatened individuals. We further predicted that when programmed-learning tasks are viewed by students as being contingent paths, then success-oriented individuals should be highly motivated to perform, particularly if item difficulty is low (as it usually is in programmed learning), and individuals who are failure threatened should be strongly inhibited to undertake such a task. However, if students perceive the programmed-learning task as being a noncontingent path and item difficulty is at its usual very low level, then inhibition should be at its lowest, and failure-threatened individuals should be far more willing to undertake the task. In such a path, each item is viewed relatively independently of the other, and the task remains easy—a situation that is not very arousing to individuals who are success oriented. Hence, in a noncontingent path composed of easy tasks, the characteristic difference between success-oriented and failure-threatened persons should be "washed out" at least, or the failure-threatened person's performance might even be superior to that of the success-oriented individual.

Method

Subjects

Thirty one male and 30 female senior-high-school students served as subjects in this study.

Procedure

Each student completed Mehrabian's (1968, 1969) Resultant Achievement Motivation Scale (RAMS). Those placing in the top third of the RAMS distribution were considered success oriented, and those falling in the bottom third were considered failure threatened. Students occupying the middle third were viewed as neither success oriented nor failure threatened.

A programmed-learning task was adapted from the introductory psychology text, *The Analysis of Behavior* (Holland & Skinner, 1961, frames 1 to 54). A test, consisting of 17 questions chosen mostly from terminal frames present in the first 54 frames, was administered to measure the performance of students on the programmed task.

About three days after the administration of the Mehrabian scale the programmed-learning task was administered under an ego-involved contingent or noncontingent set of instruction. Students in the contingent condition were led to believe that there were four units (steps) comprising the programmed lesson, each accompanied by a test. They were told that for students of their ability, their chance of success on each of the four tests was 90% and that their probability of correctly answering a frame was also about 90%. They were further informed that only those who correctly answered all the questions on Test 1 could go on to Unit 2, only those who answered all the questions on Test 2 could go on to Unit 3, and so on. Those who failed anywhere along the way would be given an alternative task concerned with the correction of faulty study habits. Students in the noncontingent-path condition were read similar instructions, except they were told that regardless of success or failure on any test they would be allowed to continue and study each unit and take each test.

After the induction instructions, students were given 30 min to complete the first unit. At the end of the allotted time, the programmed-learning booklets were collected and the achievement test was administered. When all test papers had been collected, supposedly to be graded, students estimated their probabilities of success for Tests 2, 3, and 4, respectively, on scales provided. The experiment was then terminated, and all students were debriefed.

Results

As a manipulation check, the probability of success estimated for Tests 2 through 4 were analyzed to see if the subjects viewed the two kinds of paths appropriately. Mehrabian RAM (3) X path condition (2) X test (3) (between, between, within) ANOVAs were computed for the success estimates made by the men and women comprising the sample. As expected, estimates of success declined from

Test 2 through Test 4 in the contingent condition but not in the noncontingent condition, where success was not necessary to move on to the next unit. Males in the contingent path felt they had a 72% chance of success on Test 2 but only a 62% chance of success on Test 4 ($t = 2.44$, $df = 48$, $p < .05$). Similarly, females stated a 49% chance of success on Test 2 but dropped to 39% for Test 4 ($t = 2.04$, $df = 48$, $p < .05$). Judging from these results, it seems that the students generally viewed the contingent and noncontingent conditions in accordance with our expectations.

Analysis of the Dependent Variable

The number of test questions answered correctly on Test 1 was analyzed in a sex (2) X Mehrabian RAM (3) X experimental condition (2) ANOVA. However, since no specific hypotheses were made for individuals intermediate in achievement motivation, a priori comparisons were computed to test the specific contrasts concerning the extreme motive groups.

The means, presented in Table 3, show that males did not differ from females in the number of questions answered correctly. Nor were there any overall differences between the experimental conditions. A comparison between the means for individuals high and low in Mehrabian RAM also revealed no difference. This often occurs when a significant interaction exists between resultant achievement motivation and type of path, as it does in this study. As predicted, success-oriented students (high on Mehrabian score) performed better in the contingent than the noncontingent path, but failure-threatened students (low on Mehrabian score) performed better in the noncontingent than the contingent path ($t = 1.58$, $df = 49$, $p < .06$).

Further inspection of the means shows that this pattern of results was true for the men in the sample but not for the women. The simple effects contrast for resultant achievement motivation X experimental condition for men showed the anticipated interaction to be significant ($t = 1.73$, $df = 49$, $p < .05$), but a similar contrast for the women fell short of significance ($t < 1.0$, n.s.). Females high in Mehrabian resultant achievement motivation did tend to perform better in the contingent than in the noncontingent condition, but not significantly better, and the performance of females low in Mehrabian RAM was almost identical for the two path conditions.

Table 3   Number of Test Questions Answered Correctly, by Sex, Resultant Achievement Motivation (Mehrabian Score), and Experimental Condition

| | Males | | | | Females | | | |
| | Noncontingent | | Contingent | | Noncontingent | | Contingent | |
Mehrabian Score	N	Mean	N	Mean	N	Mean	N	Mean
High	5	10.60	5	15.00	5	10.33	5	12.40
Moderate	6	11.00	3	15.25	5	11.75	5	13.00
Low	3	14.33	8	11.13	5	12.29	5	12.33

Discussion

It would appear from these results that success-oriented individuals acquired more from the programmed lesson and hence exhibited higher test scores when moving on to the next learning unit was contingent upon success than when success was not contingently related to moving on. Failure-threatened individuals, on the other hand, appeared to benefit from the lower inhibition when success was not contingently related to proceeding on to the next learning unit, performing better in that situation than when success was necessary for moving on. To be cautious, we should add that this may not be true for women. However, we have reason to believe that the Mehrabian method used to assess resultant achievement motivation for the women in the sample may be at fault. Our research has shown the Mehrabian (1969) scales to be weak at assessing resultant achievement motivation, and this seems to be particularly true for the women's scale.

STUDY III

This third study is derived from Humphrey's (1973) Master's thesis. Humphrey devised a design that allowed her to examine the acquisition of material in either a contingent or noncontingent path, as well as the subsequent application of that information. Thus, three effects could be studied: the effect of achievement motivation and future orientation on acquisition; the effect of achievement motivation and future orientation on performance; and the interaction of acquisition contingency with performance contingency. Humphrey noted that Raynor's (1970) grade study might indirectly bear on such issues. Students acquired information in one phase of a class and were then asked to apply it in another phase. However, there was no way of telling if students perceived themselves more in a contingent or non-contingent situation when they acquired the information and whether those perceptions changed or remained the same when the students were called upon to perform. Humphrey speculated that the usual interaction between achievement motivation and future orientation observed for performance would prevail for acquisition. The outcomes from the interaction of the acquisition and performance contingencies, on the other hand, were considered too speculative, and no hypotheses were drawn.

Method

Subjects

One hundred sixty-six male and female students drawn from the introductory psychology pool were asked to complete the first third of the Mandler and Sarason (1952) Test Anxiety Questionnaire (TAQ). As noted previously in this paper, this measure can be used to estimate resultant achievement motivation. Students placing in the lowest tritile of the anxiety measure were considered success oriented; those in the middle tritile were considered neither motivated to approach success nor to avoid failure (very strongly); and those in the highest tritile were considered failure threatened.

Procedure

To begin the induction, all students were told that they would be taking a series of four tests designed to assess learning and memory. They were further informed that the tests consisted of two parts, a memorization test and a test of reasoning ability. It was stated that to be considered successful on the test, a certain goal had to be met. Failure to do so would be interpreted as failing the test. The students were also told that their chances of succeeding were intermediate (i.e., a 50-50 chance).

Within groups, a random half of the students were led to believe that whether they succeeded or failed at the first part of Test 1, they would still be allowed to continue, thus establishing the noncontingent acquisition condition. The remaining students were told that only those meeting the specified goal for the first part of Test 1 would be allowed to continue, while the rest would remain seated until the experiment was completed. This created the contingent acquisition condition.

All students were then read the instructions for a paired-associate learning task, along with a criterion of success specific to each condition. The task consisted of a nine-item paired-associate list of high-imagery nouns adapted from Hays (1966). Students were given 12 trials in which to learn the list, and the total number of correct responses served as the acquisition score.

A random half of the students in the noncontingent acquisition condition were led to believe that it would now be necessary for them to meet a specified goal to be considered successful in the second part of Test 1, and to earn the opportunity to take Test 2. The remaining noncontingent students heard a reiteration of the noncontingent induction. In a similar manner, half the students in the contingent acquisition condition were told that, regardless of whether or not they met a specific goal for the second part of Test 1, they would be allowed to take Test 2. Students in the remainder of the contingent condition were read a reiteration of the contingent induction stating that they must reach the goal for the second part of Test 1 to earn the opportunity to take Test 2.

All students were next informed that the associations they had just learned were in fact a list of spys' names and the communication connections within a spy ring. Their task was to get a message from spy A through spy B to spy C, using as few of the connections as possible. The students were shown slides of three sample problems and their solutions as warmups. Following this, each student was given 10 min to solve 20 such problems. The number of problems worked correctly served as the performance score.

Results

Table 4 presents the acquisition scores as a function of path contingency and TAQ. A two-factor ANOVA revealed that students lower in anxiety earned higher acquisition scores than those higher in anxiety ($F = 3.01, df = 2/160, p < .05$), but no interaction between TAQ and path contingency existed. A contrast between low and high anxious students within each path condition did show that in the contin-

Table 4   Mean Acquisition Scores for Path Contingency and Test
            Anxiety

| | Acquisition path | | | |
| | Noncontingent | | Contingent | |
Test anxiety	*N*	Mean	*N*	Mean
Low	23	76.22	29	72.45
Moderate	34	68.85	23	62.91
High	24	67.75	33	62.06

gent path individuals low in anxiety received higher acquisition scores than individuals high in anxiety ($t = 2.09$, $df = 160$, $p < .02$), although a similar comparison in the noncontingent path yielded nonsignificant results ($t = 1.49$, $df = 160$, n.s.). However, care must be taken in interpreting these results. Individuals low in test anxiety tend to be performing better in the noncontingent and *not* the contingent path as expected. Acquisition in contingent paths might be somewhat disruptive. Note that all subjects had lower acquisition scores in the contingent than in the noncontingent path.

The results of the application phase can be seen by examining the performance means shown in Table 5. The simple interaction effects contrast of test anxiety X path condition (the individuals moderate in TAQ were deleted, as no specific prediction was made for them) revealed a significant interaction ($t = 2.26$, $df = 160$, $p < .02$). As expected, students low in test anxiety solved more problems correctly in the contingent than in the noncontingent path, but students high in test anxiety solved more problems correctly in the noncontingent than in the contingent path. The performance outcome of this experiment parallels the performance results of Raynor and Rubin (1971) and Entin and Raynor (1973).

The mean performance scores for the acquisition contingency X performance contingency X test anxiety analysis are given in Table 6. Only a main effect of test anxiety and an interaction between performance contingency and test anxiety were found. Individuals low in test anxiety performed better than those high in test

Table 5   Mean Number of Problems Solved Correctly for Path
            Contingency and Test Anxiety: Application Phase

| | Performance path | | | |
| | Noncontingent | | Contingent | |
Test anxiety	*N*	Mean	*N*	Mean
Low	28	3.84	25	7.55
Moderate	29	5.54	28	3.14
High	33	3.42	23	2.80

Table 6   Mean Number of Correct Problems as a Function of Acquisition, Performance Paths, and Test Anxiety

	Acquisition contingency							
	Noncontingent				Contingent			
	Performance contingency				Performance contingency			
	Noncontingent		Contingent		Noncontingent		Contingent	
Test anxiety	N	Mean	N	Mean	N	Mean	N	Mean
Low	11	4.27	12	9.17	17	3.41	13	5.92
Moderate	20	3.75	14	3.00	9	7.33	14	3.28
High	12	3.75	12	3.42	21	3.09	11	2.18

anxiety ($F = 3.30$, $df = 1/154$, $p < .05$), and there was an interaction between test anxiety groups and path contingency ($F = 4.84$, $df = 2/154$, $p < .01$). The results showed highest performance scores for low test anxious students who acquired their knowledge in a noncontingent path but applied that knowledge in a contingent path. Their mean performance was higher than low test anxious subjects who had acquired and performed in a contingent path ($t = 1.66$, $df = 154$, $p < .05$). Besides this, there appeared to be no other evidence that the path in which acquisition took place interacted with the path in which performance occurred. Furthermore, it appeared to us that the joint effect of achievement motivation and path had a much stronger impact on performance than on acquisition.

OVERALL CONCLUSIONS

An issue that should be discussed is the dichotomy between learning and performance. Learning is an unseen process, an intervening variable whose effect is measured by its impact on performance. In the usual learning experiment, the rate or effect of learning is measured by recall, trials to criterion, recognition, etc., in other words, some performance measure that is tied very closely in temporal contiguity to the acquisition process or to the encoding process. In the usual experiment concerned with performance, it is assumed that the skill has been learned at some time in the past and thus temporal contiguity and encoding are not at issue.

Our experiments were an attempt to examine the effect of motivation and future orientation on learning. The results show that there is some effect, but not an overwhelming one. Undoubtedly, motivation affects learning, perhaps in the form of attention, interest, set, or anxiety. We took a very global approach—that the interaction of motivation and future orientation would affect learning. But we did not systematically observe temporal contiguity apart from encoding. Nor did we separate encoding from decoding. In short, our experimental designs were not refined or specific enough to make such discriminations in measurement. All we could hope to detect was a global effect and, in fact, we did.

9

Recall of Incompleted and Completed Tasks under Relaxed, Achievement, and Contingent Conditions

Richard C. Teitelbaum, Joel O. Raynor, and Elliot E. Entin

The Zeigarnik (1927) effect refers to the greater recall of incompleted than completed tasks. Lewin (1938) hypothesized that an intention to reach a goal corresponds to a tension within an individual that persists until reduced by attainment of that goal. This tension is predicted to have consequences at the behavioral level for *resumption* of incompleted tasks and at the psychological level for *recall* of incompleted tasks. The Zeigarnik (1927) procedure involved motivating individuals to complete a series of tasks, followed by interruption for some tasks and completion for others. It follows that subjects should recall more incompleted than completed tasks, resulting in a large Zeigarnik quotient, and Zeigarnik (1927) reported a ratio of 2:1 for recall of interrupted to completed tasks in a formal test atmosphere. Marrow (1938) replicated this Zeigarnik effect and extended the conceptual analysis to "success" and "failure" rather than mere interruption versus completion per se. Marrow (1938) instructed subjects to interpret interruption during task performance prior to completion to mean that they were solving the problems correctly, while completion in the allotted time meant they were on the wrong track. Marrow (1938) then found greater recall of completed tasks than incompleted tasks. This suggested that recall is greater for past failure than for past success.

Rosenzweig (1943), Glixman (1949), and Lewis and Franklin (1944) attempted to replicate these results but generally obtained the reverse of the Zeigarnik effect under stressful conditions while replicating it under relaxed conditions. To account for these results it was hypothesized that repression of incompleted (failure) items is stronger in the stressful condition, while persisting tension is stronger in the relaxed condition (Rosenzweig, 1943).

Atkinson (1950) classified subjects as high and low on *n* Achievement (McClelland et al. 1953) and showed that under stressful test conditions (i.e., achievement oriented) recall of incompleted tasks was greater than recall of completed tasks (the

Portions of this paper were presented at the meetings of the Eastern Psychological Association, Philadelphia, April, 1979.

Zeigarnik effect) for those high on n Achievement and that the reverse applied for those low on n Achievement. Atkinson (1950) reviewed the previous research and suggested that the nature of the subject samples in previous work could be presumed to differ in the proportions of individuals high and low in n Achievement, with the Zeigarnik effect resulting when volunteers (presumably high in n Achievement) predominate in the sample (i.e., Marrow, 1938) and the reverse Zeigarnik effect resulting when draftees (presumably low in n Achievement) predominate in the sample (i.e., Rosensweig, 1943; Glixman, 1949; Lewin & Franklin, 1944). According to Atkinson (1950), individual differences in achievement-related motives determine whether recall of failure or success will result under achievement-oriented conditions; success-oriented individuals (high in n Achievement, low in test anxiety, or high in n Achievement and low in test anxiety) are expected to recall more failure than success items, while failure-threatened individuals (low in n Achievement, high in test anxiety, or low in n Achievement and high in test anxiety) are expected to recall more success than failure items.

The objective of the present work was to replicate and extend Atkinson's (1950) results to the more general theory of achievement motivation (Raynor, 1969, 1974a, 1978a; see chapter 2). The more general theory suggests that a contingent-path condition should prove to be at least as motivationally arousing—and result in a Zeigarnik effect for success-oriented subjects and reverse Zeigarnik effect for failure-threatened subjects—as Atkinson's (1950) achievment-oriented condition (a one-step path). That is, if the continuum notion of increasing motivational arousal as a function of increasing number of steps is valid, then an enhancement of prevailing motive characteristics should be observed in a contingent as opposed to an achievement-oriented (one-step) situation. This enhancement would be expected to take the form of a larger Zeigarnik effect for success-oriented subjects and a larger reversal of the Zeigarnik effect for failure-threatened subjects.

There is an additional empirical point that bears mention in regard to our attempt to replicate Atkinson's (1950) results and extend the task recall paradigm to the elaborated theory of achievement motivation in contingent-path situations. Although Atkinson (1950) obtained the Zeigarnik effect for high n Achievement subjects in an achievement-oriented condition, this can be seen to result from the recall of incompleted tasks increasing faster than the recall of completed tasks. Note that for Atkinson's (1950) subjects, the recall of completed tasks did *not* diminish but rather increased as well, from relaxed to achievement-oriented conditions, but at a slower rate. On the other hand, for his low n Achievement subjects, the reverse Zeigarnik effect resulted not only from an increased recall of completed tasks from the relaxed to the achievement-oriented condition (the magnitude was only 4%), but also from an additional (6%) decrease in recall for incompleted tasks. This suggests that an additional method for investigating motivational differences in this paradigm consists of a simple index of *total* recall, without regard to type of item.

METHOD

Subjects

Subjects were 72 male college students[1] recruited from an Introductory Psychology course at Ohio University,[2] for which participation in an experiment earned extra credit points to augment their course grade.

Procedure

The experimental task items and two of the three test conditions (relaxed and achievement oriented) were adapted from Atkinson (1950). The sequence of events was identical for all test conditions. The difference among them lies in the instructions and atmosphere in which the experiment was administered. Subjects for a particular condition arrived and were seated at desks containing a manila envelope within which were the test materials. They were then asked to complete the Mehrabian (1969) measure of resultant achievement motivation. Following scale completion, 16 experimental tasks were administered. Following the tasks, subjects completed the Test Anxiety Questionnaire and performed an interpolated task for 10 min. After the interpolated task, subjects were asked to recall as many of the 16 tasks as they could. After a 10-min free recall period, subjects were given a post experimental questionnaire. Subjects were then debriefed and dismissed. The entire session lasted slightly less than 2 hours.

The manipulations used in creating the test conditions can be summarized as follows: For the relaxed condition, the experimenter was relaxed and informal with the subjects, joking with them, etc. The experimental tasks were introduced as new, with the main interest on developing the task items themselves, and not on the subjects' performance. The timing between items was handled as unobtrusively as possible. For the achievement-oriented condition, the experimenter was formal and businesslike, not speaking with the subjects unless asked. The experimental task items were called "test items" taken from a "general intellectual abilities test." Subjects were asked to write their current GPA or college admissions test scores, names, and majors on their folders. It was emphasized that performance on these test items would be interpreted as representing their ability. The timing of items was business-

[1] Additional subjects were run in two additional conditions in which time for incomplete and completed items were not equivalent. Data for these conditions are not reported here, except that all subjects' responses were used in the manipulation checks comparing relaxed, achievement, and contingent conditions.

[2] The authors wish to thank Larry McAllister and Tom Caffee for their assistance in collecting the data and Lynn Mitchel, Linda Stein, Julie Tevis, and Judy Ustick for scoring, coding, and key punching the data.

like and obvious. For the contingent condition, the experimenter was formal and businesslike as in the achievement-oriented condition. The experimental items were again referred to as test items taken from a "general intellectual abilities test." Subjects were also asked to write down their GPA or college admissions test scores, name, and major on their folders. Subjects were also instructed that these test items formed a test that was the first in a series of increasingly harder tests that they would be allowed to move on to if they scored above 60% on these initial items. It was mentioned that previous work indicated that only a handful of the group would make it to the next, shorter but harder, test. The timing of items was businesslike and obvious, as in the achievement condition.

Materials

The test items themselves are identical to the stimulus materials used by Atkinson (1950). These items were fashioned after Marrow (1938). All items were slightly modified in length to accommodate the specific items utilized in the present study. There were a short and a long version of each particular item. The short version could be completed in about $2\frac{1}{2}$ min while the long version was rarely completed in this time. The tests were constructed by randomly distributing 8 long versions of some items and 8 short versions of the rest of the items for 16 different orders of the 16-item tests. Another 16 forms were constructed from these initial randomly distributed forms by replacing a long-version item with its associated short version, and vice versa. Thus, there were 32 different orders in two forms of these tests: a set of 16 forms containing one version (long or short) of the items in randomized orders, and a set of 16 forms containing the converse version of each item from the original set. These were randomly distributed to subjects within each test condition, each subject receiving a different order or form from all the others.

RESULTS

After standardizing the distributions of Mehrabian and Test Anxiety Questionnaire (TAQ) scores, difference scores were obtained (Z Mehrabian $- Z$ TAQ) to derive groups on resultant motivation. This distribution of scores was then trichotomized to create high, moderate, and low resultant motive groups. The high resultant motive group was assumed to be primarily motivated to achieve success ($M_S > M_{AF}$), while the low resultant motive group was assumed to be primarily motivated to avoid failure ($M_{AF} > M_S$). The moderate resultant group was assumed to contain individuals intermediate between these extremes and was subsequently dropped from further statistical analyses involving the critical dependent measures, although data for the moderate groups on each motive measure are reported.

All recall data were calculated as the percent recall of the type of item, except for total recall. These data were then transformed using the arcsin $\sqrt{\%}$ (or $\sqrt{\text{percentage}}$) transformation for subsequent data analysis.

Manipulation Checks

The postexperimental questionnaire allowed a check on the instructional atmosphere for the varying test conditions. Responses were obtained (on a scale from 1 to 7) to questions asking the extent of the experimenter's friendliness, courtesy, and formality. The experimenter was found to be more friendly $[F(2/194) = 105.26, p < .001]$, more courteous $[F(2/194) = 45.54, p < .001]$, less formal $[F(2/194) = 31.31, p < .001]$, and less businesslike $[F(2/194) = 29.03, p < .001]$ in the relaxed condition than in either the achievement or contingent condition, which did not differ significantly from each other. Subjects in the relaxed condition were also more relaxed than their counterparts in either the achievement or contingent condition $[F(2/194) = 2.41, p < .09]$.

Mean data for the four dependent measures of the present study are shown in Table 1.

Recall of Incompleted Items

Percent recall of incompleted items as a function of motive groups and experimental conditions is shown graphically in Figure 1. Percent recall of incompleted items increased as expected for the high Z Mehrabian $-Z$ TAQ (success-oriented) subjects and decreased as expected for the low Z Mehrabian $-Z$ TAQ (failure-threatened) subjects from the relaxed to the achievement-oriented to the contingent condition. Analysis of variance for recall as a function of extreme motive groups and experimental conditions yields a main effect due to motive groups that is statistically reliable $(F = 3.73, df = 1/43, p = .06)$ and an interaction effect that approaches significance $(F = 2.44, df = 2/43, p < .10)$. A priori comparisons yield significant (one-tailed test) differences in the predicted direction indicating greater recall of incompleted items for the high than the low Z Mehrabian $-Z$ TAQ group in the achievement condition $(t = 1.90, p < .05)^3$ and in the contingent condition $(t = 2.62, p < .01)$. Further a priori comparisons indicate that differences between adjacent groups of high Z Mehrabian $-Z$ TAQ subjects are not reliable (relaxed vs. achievement, $t = 1.20$, n.s.; achievement vs. contingent, $t < 1$, n.s.), while the difference between extreme groups (relaxed vs. contingent) of high Z Mehrabian $-Z$ TAQ approach significance $(t = 1.37, p < .10)$. Differences between adjacent groups of failure-threatened subjects are again not reliable (relaxed vs. achievement and achievement vs. contingent, $ts < 1$, n.s.), while the difference between extreme groups of failure-threatened subjects was significant $(t = 1.69, p < .05)$.

Results for test anxiety alone most closely correspond to the expected pattern and that found for the resultant measure (see Figure 1). Results for those high in test anxiety show the regular decrease in recall of incompleted items across experimental conditions, as do results for those low in Mehrabian. Results for those low

---

^{3} Degrees of freedom used for all a priori comparisons are those in the corresponding MSE of the ANOVA (in this case, $df = 43$).

Table 1 Recall of Percent Incompleted Items, Percent Completed Items, and the Difference between Percent Incompleted and Percent Completed, and Total Number of Items Recalled, as a Function of Achievement-Related Motives and Experimental Conditions

Motive group	Test condition														
	Relaxed					Achievement					Contingent				
	N	%I[a]	%C[b]	%I-%C[c]	T[d]	N	%I	%C	%I-%C	T	N	%I	%C	%I-%C	T
Mehrabian (Meh)															
High	8	67.2	54.7	12.5	9.8	8	67.2	57.8	9.4	10.0	9	63.9	62.5	1.4	10.1
Moderate	12	54.2	54.2	0	8.7	10	61.3	57.5	3.8	9.5	6	62.5	62.5	0	10.0
Low	9	63.9	66.7	-2.8	10.4	4	56.3	62.5	-6.3	9.5	6	45.8	47.9	-2.1	7.5
Test anxiety (TAQ)															
Low	7	62.5	53.6	8.9	9.3	10	66.3	61.3	5.0	10.2	6	66.7	66.7	0.0	10.7
Moderate	9	56.9	63.9	-6.9	9.7	6	62.5	54.2	8.3	9.3	6	56.3	58.3	-2.1	9.2
High	13	62.5	56.7	5.8	9.5	6	56.3	58.3	-2.1	9.2	9	54.2	52.8	1.4	8.6
Z Meh - Z TAQ															
High	7	58.9	46.4	12.5	8.4	10	67.5	57.5	10.0	10.0	8	70.3	65.6	4.7	10.9
Moderate	11	60.2	62.5	-2.3	9.8	5	62.5	52.5	10.0	9.2	7	51.8	57.1	-5.4	8.7
Low	11	62.5	61.4	1.1	9.9	7	55.4	64.3	-8.9	9.6	6	50.0	50.0	0	8.0

[a] Percent incomplete.
[b] Percent completed.
[c] Difference between percent incomplete and completed.
[d] Total.

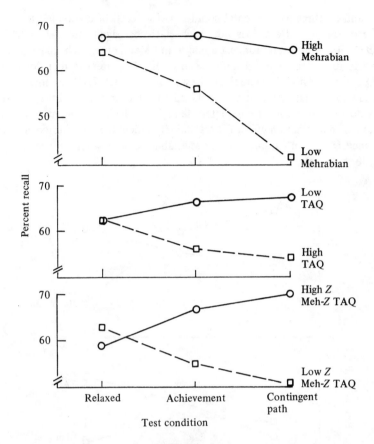

Figure 1   Percent recall of incompleted items as a function of motive
measures and experimental conditions.

in test anxiety and high in Mehrabian show a weaker trend for increase in recall of
incompleted tasks across experimental conditions. However, the interaction effect
for test anxiety alone is not significant ($F = 1.06$, $df = 2/45$, n.s.); nor is that for
Mehrabian ($F < 1$, n.s.).

Recall of Completed Items

Percent recall of completed items is shown graphically in Figure 2. Results for
the relaxed and achievement conditions replicate findings reported by Atkinson
(1950) in that a tendency is again found for increase in percent recall of completed
items from relaxed to achievement conditions for the majority of motive groups.
However, results for the contingent condition show a continued increase in recall of
completed items for the high Z Mehrabian $- Z$ TAQ subjects, but a decrease for the
low Z Mehrabian $- Z$ TAQ subjects. Results were not evaluated using planned comparisons because no explicit predictions were made concerning trends for recall of
completed tasks alone. The ANOVA for extreme motive groups on Z Mehrabian $-$

Z TAQ and all three experimental conditions for recall of completed items shows that the interaction effect does not reach statistical significance ($F = 2.14$, $df = 2/43$, $p < .20$). The results for test anxiety and Mehrabian, each taken separately, show fairly linear trends for an increase in recall of completed items for those low in TAQ and those high in Mehrabian. Results for the high-TAQ and low-Mehrabian groups are somewhat different from relaxed to achievement condition, while both show a decrease in recall of completed items from the achievement to contingent condition. The interaction effect for test anxiety alone does not approach statistical significance ($F < 1$, n.s.), but that for Mehrabian is somewhat stronger ($F = 2.09$, $df = 2/38$, $p < .20$).

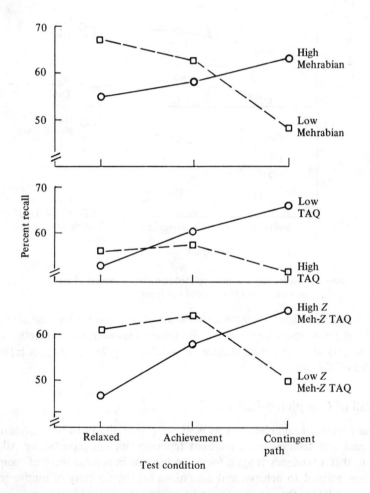

Figure 2   Percent recall of completed items as a function of motive
measures and experimental conditions.

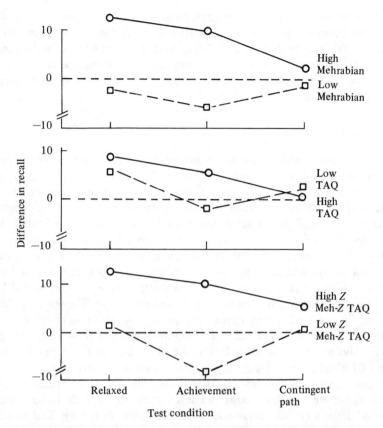

Figure 3 Difference in percent recall of incompleted and completed items as a function of motive measures and experimental conditions.

Recall of Incompleted Tasks versus Completed Tasks: The Zeigarnik Effect

The difference in recall between incompleted and completed tasks is shown graphically in Figure 3. Here a positive number indicates greater recall of incompleted tasks, while a negative number indicates greater recall of completed tasks. Results do not replicate findings reported by Atkinson (1953) for the Zeigarnik effect for success-oriented subjects. In the present data, for all three motive measures of success orientation (high Mehrabian, low TAQ, high Z Mehrabian $- Z$ TAQ), the increase in recall of completed tasks from relaxed to achievement-oriented conditions is greater (rather than less, as found by Atkinson) than that for the corresponding increase in recall of incompleted tasks. Thus the success-oriented subjects show an increase in negative difference score (incomplete-complete) from relaxed to achievement to contingent condition. The corresponding effect for the failure-threatened subjects is nonlinear, first showing a decrease in the difference score (between incomplete and complete) from relaxed to achievement condition, and then an increase. Thus, the overall pattern of results does not conform either to the pattern obtained by Atkinson (1950) or to that expected based on the assumption that this difference score reflects a continuum of motivational arousal that interacts with achievement-related motive measures. None of the linear interaction effects approaches significance (all $Fs < 1$, n.s.).

Total Recall

The fact that similar patterns of interaction were found between motive measures and experimental conditions for recall of both incompleted and completed items suggested that total recall best reflects the empirical results. With the exception of the failure-threatened subjects' increase in percent recall of completed items from the relaxed to the achievement condition, the patterns of recall within each motive group for recall of incompleted and completed items are in the same direction. Thus a measure of total recall should summarize and best reflect recall in the present study. Statistical support for this interpretation is obtained from a three-way ANOVA (motive group X test condition X type of item) in which the type of item recalled was treated as a within-subjects factor. The results yielded a significant interaction between motive groups and experimental conditions when extreme groups on Z Mehrabian $- Z$ TAQ are employed ($F = 3.82$, $df = 2/43$, $p < .03$). Also of interest is the lack of a reliable three-factor (item type X extreme motive [Z Mehrabian $- Z$ TAQ] group X test condition) interaction ($F < 1$, n.s.). This is consistent with the idea that type of item did not differentially affect the interaction between motive groups and test conditions for total recall. Figure 4 depicts Atkinson's (1950) redrawn data demonstrating increasing total recall for high n Achievement subjects and decreasing total recall for low n Achievement subjects. The present study replicates Atkinson's (1950) results for total recall for the two comparable conditions (relaxed and achievement; see Figure 5). In addition, the contingent condition shows a further increase in total recall for success-oriented subjects and a further decrease in total recall for failure-threatened subjects. A two-way (motive group X test condition) ANOVA using total recall as the dependent measure (depicted in Figure 5) yields a significant motive X test condition interaction ($F = 3.82$, $df = 2/43$, $p < .03$). No other effects on total recall were significant ($F < 1$, n.s.). As with the recall of completed items, these results were not evaluated using planned comparisons, since explicit predictions were not made concerning trends for total recall.

Data for total recall are similar for the test anxiety and Mehrabian measures taken separately. Each by itself shows the two opposite trends in total recall across experimental conditions, with the results for test anxiety showing equal increments for those low and decrements for those high, while the data for the Mehrabian measure show a larger decrement for those low than an increment for those high (see Figure 5). The interaction effect for test anxiety alone is not significant ($F = 1.09$, $df = 2/45$, n.s.) while that for Mehrabian approaches significance ($F = 2.44$, $df = 2/38$, $p = .10$).

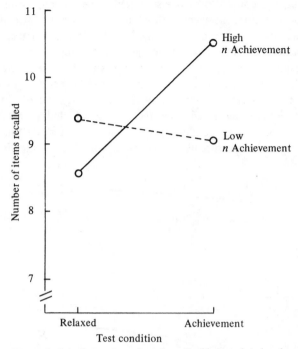

Figure 4 Reconstruction of total recall of incompleted and completed items in a relaxed and an achievement test condition. (From Atkinson, 1950.)

DISCUSSION

Responses from the postexperimental questionnaire indicate that the instructional manipulations, which varied the atmosphere under which the experiment was performed, were successful. Subjects were more relaxed and at ease in the relaxed condition than in either the achievement or contingent-path conditions, where the experimenter was successful in creating a formal, businesslike test-taking situation, one that could be inferred to engage achievement-related motives.

The results for recall of incompleted items are statistically reliable and are similar to those obtained by Atkinson (1950), where the *n* Achievement score was used as the measure of individual differences in the achievement motive. Thus, the evidence concerning recall of incompleted tasks is fairly consistent—success-oriented subjects recall more incompleted tasks (perceived as failures), while failure-threatened subjects recall fewer incompleted tasks, as the experimental condition is more likely to engage achievement-related motives (relaxed vs. achievement). Also, the results for the contingent condition for recall of incompleted items are in the direction predicted by the more general theory of achievement motivation. Overall, for the three conditions, opposite linear trends that extend from relaxed to achievement to contingent condition suggest that the contingent condition appears to arouse characteristic achievement motivation at least as well as, and perhaps to a greater extent than, the conventional one-step achievement-related situation. We predict that use of a longer contingent path would accentuate the effects of contingent future orientation even more, but this hypothesis was not tested in the present research (see chapter 5 for research on the effects of path length).

For recall of completed tasks, the pattern of results in the present investigation somewhat resembles those data obtained by Atkinson (1950) for the comparable test conditions, but results are not statistically reliable. As in the earlier study, the majority of motive groups increased their recall of completed items from the relaxed to the achievement test condition, but in the present study this depends somewhat on the particular measure used. Since results are not statistically reliable,

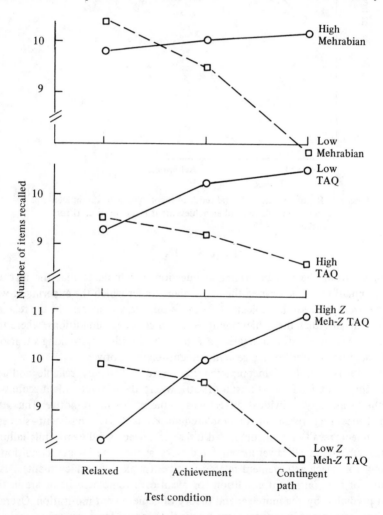

Figure 5 Total recall of incompleted and completed items as a function of motive measures and experimental conditions.

we do not have a clear-cut answer concerning the effects of arousal condition on recall of completed items.

The results in the present study for the Zeigarnik effect clearly are at variance with those reported by Atkinson (1950). He obtained an increasing Zeigarnik quotient for high n Achievement subjects and a decreasing quotient for low n Achievement subjects, from relaxed to achievement condition. In our data the trends for low test anxiety, high Mehrabian, and high resultant (Z Mehrabian $-Z$ TAQ) motive groups are opposite to those found by Atkinson (1950) for high n Achievement, while the lower Zeigarnik effect from relaxed to achievement condition replicates the Atkinson findings for those considered to be failure threatened.

In light of this discrepancy as regards the results for the Zeigarnik effect, the suggestion that failures and successes may not play a differential role in the recall strategies of subjects of differing motivational tendencies takes on added interest. Thus, recall of both types of items may be a more appropriate index of motivational differences. However, the trend for the failure-threatened subjects for recall of completed items does not continue from achievement to contingent condition as it begins from relaxed to achievement condition, so that it is not clear what the finding represents in terms of effects of degrees of motivational arousal.

The data of the present study replicate the findings for total recall obtained by Atkinson (1950) and show linear extensions from the relaxed to achievement to contingent condition. In our study the patterns for both incompleted and completed items are similar across experimental conditions, so that both contribute to the overall effect, which is statistically reliable. Thus the Atkinson (1950) study and the present study suggest that a reliable effect of increased achievement arousal is to increase total recall of task items for success-oriented subjects, but to reduce total recall for failure-threatened subjects.

III

ABILITIES,
ATTRIBUTES,
AND
SELF-ATTRIBUTION

The theory and research reported in this section are primarily concerned with the role of an individual's assessment of the degree of possession of attributes, abilities, and competences· that are believed both prerequisites for success in, and simultaneously assessed by, skill-demanding activity, and the relationship of "self-possession" to both future orientation and self-evaluation. A series of empirical findings over the past decade (reviewed in chapter 11) has suggested that self-evaluation is at stake when success in immediate activity is believed necessary to achieve future success, and that the degree of possession of prerequisite competences that are needed for immediate success is positively associated with a belief that immediate activity is related to future success (that requires such competence) and to positive self-esteem. After one such study is presented (chapter 10), an attempt is made to review and then incorporate these findings within the existing theory of achievement motivation (chapter 11). The distinction is made between an individual's motivation to assess some competence on some (formal or informal) test, and the utilization of that competence to do well in some skill-demanding activity—which itself may serve as an assessment of competence—to achieve some future goal or a more immediate successful outcome. To do so, it is necessary to extend the existing theory of achievement motivation by conceptualizing the determinants of willingness or resistence to undertake an evaluation of some attribute, ability, or competence that has value to the individual beyond that value determined by the subjective probability of success in the task (or series of tasks) faced by the individual. Here we foreshadow changes in theory that are integrated into the more general theory of personality functioning and change presented in chapter 13. Thus the value of a competence to the individual, and the value of a test of competence to the individual, are viewed in the more general cultural context that gives meaning to the degree of possession of various attributes of personality (later called individual cultural value). This, in conjunction with the perceived validity of the test and the individual's expectation of demonstrating increments or decrements in the degree of possession of the attribute—where perceived validity influences the expectancy of obtaining information from the test—are combined to provide what is called a theory of *competence motivation*. This theory can be seen as a subset of the more general theory presented in chapter 13, dealing as it does with the evaluated present. Attempts to resolve issues concerning the relationships among future importance, self-importance, and self-possession that are indirectly addressed here are more fully worked out when the more general theory is proposed. Therefore, the ideas presented here should be viewed as dealing with only one aspect of motivation and action, and taken in the context of the more general conception.

Chapter 12 presents the first experimental investigation of the study of causal attributions of success and failure in contingent and noncontingent experimental conditions. We try to determine if differences in future orientation influence the attribution process. The fact that a four-factor interaction is found among individual differences in achievement-related motives, outcome (success vs. failure), kind of attribution (ability, effort, task difficulty, and luck) and nature of path (contingent vs. noncontingent) points to the general need to view the study of causal attribution within the context of the more general problem of motivation. Findings that fail to replicate previous studies that only viewed some of these dimensions suggest that causal attribution cannot be divorced from the study of personality and motivation, and that "main effects" attributable to various causal dimensions may be misleading. We reserve for the chapter itself the particular (and complex) pattern of results that were obtained.

We hope that Chapter 12 will foreshadow a greater concern with the distinction that we now make between *retrospective* causal ascriptions and *anticipatory* causal ascriptions. Previous work on causal attribution has been primarily concerned with retrospective causal attribution—how an individual, after having been confronted with the success or failure of some other individual's action, or that individual's own, then accounts for that success or failure in terms of the dimensions of ability, effort, task difficulty, and/or luck (cf. Weiner, 1972, 1974). More recent concerns with ego-defensive or ego-enhancement theories put forward to account for these patterns of retrospective ascription (see chapter 12 for a review and discussion of these issues) must be viewed within the context of a more general theory of personality functioning and change (chapter 13). The theory specifies the conditions under which attempts to maximize positive value and/or minimize negative value will differentially affect the behavior of individuals differing in positive (success-oriented) or negative (failure-threatened) motive dispositions, given the arousal of the self-system to influence action versus cognitive evaluations in important versus unimportant situations—both when further action along a contingent path is anticipated, and when such action is no longer believed to be possible. We need to know, for example, what the effects on motivation of immediate activity are of anticipation that success in such activity will be due to high ability, great effort, facing an easy task, and/or luck—if they exist. And if they do, do individual motive dispositions differentially influence that effect—the effect of that causal ascription on action—as would be expected based on the theory of achievement motivation? Put another way, what is the functional significance of differences in causal ascriptions for subsequent action? We need more research concerned with such anticipatory causal ascriptions to determine how to modify existing theory to account for such effects, given that they are obtained. For example, can these be conceptualized as influencing the subjective probability of success for subsequent action? Do a willingness to ascribe success to high ability and the belief that the individual possesses a great deal of that ability result in more confidence when the individual is faced with the task than if attribution is anticipated to be to hard work and/or luck? If so, does that change in expectancy influence action as predicted by existing theory?

The problem is best seen in light of our distinction between time-linked sources of value and their influence on the motivation of immediate activity (chapter 13). The expectancy × value theory of achievement motivation has been almost exclusively concerned with the anticipated future, and in chapter 11 it is extended so as to be able to deal with the immediate evaluated present, while it has neglected the possible role of the retrospected past on motivation of immediate activity. We believe that the study of causal ascription has suffered from the opposite kind of problem—it has focused on the retrospected past, with little attention (if any) to how such retrospections might influence motivation of subsequent (immediate) activity, particularly when that activity is perceived by the individual to have important long-term future implications.

10

Relationships among Self-Importance, Future Importance, and Self-Possession

Joel O. Raynor and Louis D. English

The data reported in this chapter were collected as part of a larger study concerned with the effects of achievement-related motives, self-attributes, and the willingness (or not) to work hard on performance on a laboratory task (see English, 1974). The first part of this data collection (the data presented here) served an important function independent of the concerns of the experimental investigation of performance level. We were interested in replicating in a much more general way the finding reported by Raynor, Atkinson, and Brown (1974) that if a student rated a final course examination as important to future goals, the student also rated that final exam as important for positive self-evaluation. That is, Raynor et al. (1974) found a substantial positive correlation between the self-importance and the future importance of a final course examination.

Raynor (1969, 1974a; see also chapter 2) has interpreted this future-importance question to indicate the extent to which immediate success is believed necessary to earn the opportunity to strive for one's own future goals. Evidence indicates that differences in academic performance between groups that differ in strength of achievement-related motives are sometimes accentuated when good grades are seen as important and/or necessary to achieve future success (cf. Raynor, 1970; also chapter 2). The fact that future importance and self-importance were found to be positively correlated by Raynor et al. (1974) raises questions concerning the interpretation of previous grade studies. In addition, it raises a more general question concerning the conditions under which one might expect to find future importance and self-importance to be positively correlated.

The present data collection was designed to see to what extent, if any, there is a positive correlation between self-importance and future importance for ratings that deal with personality attributes or self-attribution of personality descriptors, specifically the following: a popular personality, a hard worker, competent in skill-demanding tasks, lucky, competitive in skill-demanding tasks, influential. Selection of these attributes was based on two considerations. First, we wanted to pursue the study of achievement motivation and attribution that Weiner (1972, 1974) had begun. However, instead of studying the determinants of attributions of others' success and failure as a function of effort, ability, task difficulty, and luck, we wanted to see to what extent self-attribution of person-related characteristics (luck, effort, and ability) would be related to self-importance and future importance, and

(2) we wanted to include obviously "nonachievement-related" attributes (popular, influential) to provide some indication of "discriminant validity" concerning the intercorrelation of these attributes. We did not anticipate similar patterns of relationships among self-possession, self-importance, and future importance for what we considered to be achievement-related attributes (a hard worker, competent, competitive) and non-achievement-related attributes (luck, popular, influential).

In the later part of this study a more direct replication of the Raynor et al. (1974) study was made by asking students to rate the self-importance and future importance of performance on the laboratory task they were about to do. Thus, two kinds of data were obtained concerning the relationship between self-importance and future importance, one concerning the personality attributes and the other concerning doing well on a specific task.

METHOD

One hundred six male and female undergraduates enrolled in an Introductory Psychology course at the State University of New York at Buffalo participated in the study. Participation was in partial fulfillment of course requirements. Three subjects failed to complete all data and were not included in the data analysis, resulting in a sample size of 103. The study was conducted over a 1-week period of the spring of 1973. It was called "Career Attitudes and Behavior Study." Group sizes ranged from 5 to 20 (mean of 13.3). The projective measure of n Achievement was administered first, followed by the Test Anxiety Questionnaire. They were administered and scored in the usual manner (cf. Raynor & Rubin, 1971). The subjects were then handed a questionnaire asking about their self-concepts, career goals, and what they thought was important to make these goals become reality. While this material was gathered in preparation for the major experimental part of the study, the present paper is concerned with results obtained from these questionnaire responses.

Assessment of Self-Importance, Future Importance, and Self-Possession

The self-rating questionnaire consisted of four pages of questions. At the top of the first page appeared the statement "Please rate yourself on the extent to which you see yourself as being:" This was followed by six descriptors in the following order: a popular personality, a hard worker, competent in skill-demanding tasks, lucky, competitive in skill-demanding tasks, and influential. Below each descriptor appeared a graphic rating scale anchored at the left end by "very much" and at the right end by "not at all." A slash appeared in the middle of the scale, below which appeared the word "midpoint." All scales were keyed in the same direction. This was done so that subjects would not become confused as to which end was which. Responses to these questions are taken to be the assessment of extent of self-possession of the six attributes, hereafter referred to as popular, hard worker, competent, lucky, competitive, and influential, respectively.

At the top of the second page appeared the statement "Please indicate to what extent each of the following is important for your own positive self-evaluation:" followed by the descriptors being lucky, being a hard worker, a popular personality, being competent, being competitive, being influential. Graphic rating scales were anchored by "very important" at the left and "not at all important" at the right, with a slash and "midpoint" in the middle. Again, all were keyed in the same direction. Responses to these questions are taken as the assessment of self-importance of these attributes.

Page 3 of the questionnaire contained eight questions that referred to various aspects of the student's future career plans. On the top of page 4 appeared the statement "Please indicate to what extent each of the following is important for attaining your own future goals:" and the descriptors being lucky, being a hard worker, being competent, being competitive, being a popular personality, being influential. "Very important" and "not important at all" anchored each graphic rating scale, all of which were keyed in the same direction. These responses were taken as the assessment of the future-importance of each attribute.

We explicitly chose to key all scales in the same direction on each page for self-importance, future importance, and self-possession so that we could be sure that subjects did not mismark their questionnaires in a rush to finish. This creates the possibility, however, that positive correlations within items for each kind of question (i.e., for a given page) might be due to this method of data collection and therefore be spurious. It is less likely, but still possible, that a "response set" might produce spurious correlations within a given attribute across the three kinds of ratings, despite the fact that they appeared on different pages. To check on these possibilities we present data not only for what we consider to be relevant correlations (e.g., extent of correlation of self-importance, future importance, and self-possession for a given attribute), but for what we considered irrelevant correlations (i.e., correlations of responses for one attribute with responses for the other attributes). We reasoned that if correlations for relevant items are large, positive, and larger than correlations for irrelevant items, then we could conclude that responses to the three kinds of items are positively related for this sample, despite any common methods variance. On the other hand, if correlations for the relevant items were no larger than the correlations for the irrelevant items, we would conclude that methods factors could account for the results and that we would not be safe in claiming a positive association for the three kinds of items. This procedure is conservative in that it might treat meaningful irrelevant correlations as mere methods variance.

RESULTS

Personality Attributes

Self-Importance and Future Importance

Table 1 presents the intercorrelation matrix between the ratings of self-importance and future importance for each of the six personality attributes used in

Table 1   Correlations between Items Assessing Future Importance and Self-Importance of Six
Personality Descriptors

	Future importance					
Self-importance	Lucky	Hard worker	Popular	Competent	Competitive	Influential
Lucky	.62	.03	.34	.02	.18	.29
Hard worker	−.16	.52	.09	.26	.21	.05
Popular	.26	.11	.62	.15	.19	.56
Competent	.07	.36	.20	.49	.34	.13
Competitive	.19	.19	.24	.29	.75	.21
Influential	.39	.08	.53	.19	.27	.67

Note. Boxed values indicate correlations of future importance and self-importance for the *same* attribute.

this study. The correlations on the diagonal, which appear in a box, indicate the correlation between corresponding attributes. For example, the boxed correlation in the upper left (.62) indicates the extent to which there was a correlation between the rated importance of being lucky for "attaining your own future goals" and for "your own positive self-evaluation." The correlation just to the right in the first row (.03) indicates the extent of correlation between the importance of being lucky for attaining future goals and the importance of seeing oneself as a hard worker for positive self-evaluation. The correlation just below, in the first column (−.16), indicates the extent to which seeing oneself as a hard worker for positive self-evaluation was correlated with ratings of being lucky as important for having future plans work out. Thus the boxed correlations indicate the extent of self-future relationship for each of the six personality descriptors, while the off-diagonal correlations may be taken either to indicate real relationships between noncorresponding attributes, or, as we have done, as indicating the extent to which common methods variance has contributed to the magnitude of the boxed (relevant) correlations.

Inspection of the boxed correlations of Table 1 indicates substantial positive values that far surpass in magnitude those commonly found in research on achievement motivation. They indicate a uniformly strong positive correlation between self-importance and future importance for each of the six attitude descriptors used in this study. Their magnitude made us very much aware of the possibility that these correlations might merely reflect methods variance rather than the substance of the questions that were asked.

To be conservative, we assume that any off-diagonal correlation represents a methodological influence rather than a genuine relationship. This is conservative, since some of these correlations make good "sense" in terms of the substance of the questions they refer to. Note that in every case the boxed correlation is larger than any other correlation found in the row or column of which it is a part. For example, for "lucky," the highest row correlation is .34 and the highest column correlation is .39, while the box value is .62 for self–future for lucky. Further inspection indicates that without exception the boxed correlation is the highest for each of the other row-column combinations for that attribute. The median value for the off-diagonal correlations is +.19, while the median value for the diagonal (boxed) correlations is +.62. Thus we conclude that the positive correlations between self-importance and future importance for these six personality attributes reflect the substance of the questions from which the data were obtained, rather than some common methods factor.

Self-Possession and Future Importance

Table 2 shows the intercorrelation matrix for self-possession of attributes and their future importance. Again, as in Table 1, the relevant correlations are shown as the diagonal and are boxed. Inspection again indicates that, without exception, the boxed correlation is higher than any other correlation of its row or column. The magnitudes of the boxed correlations are not as great as in Table 1 (median = +.41). But note that the median off-diagonal correlation was found to be +.10 rather than +.19. It therefore appears safe to conclude that there is a positive relationship between the extent to which these subjects indicated that they possess each of these attributes and the extent to which they believe that possession of it is important for attainment of their future goals. This is a new finding. It would appear that the relationship between self-evaluation and future importance is somewhat stronger than the relationship between self-possession and future importance.

Self-Possession and Self-Importance

Table 3 shows the complete correlation matrix for the importance of self-possession of attributes and their importance for self-evaluation. Again, the corresponding correlations for each attribute appear as the diagonal and are boxed. The median off-diagonal correlation for this matrix is +.10, while the median diagonal $r = +.34$—the smallest median value for the diagonal correlations reported thus far. Note that one of the six boxed correlations of Table 3 is not statistically reliable: seeing oneself as lucky is not significantly related to the extent to which luck is seen as impor-

Table 2 Correlations between Items Assessing Future Importance and Self-Possession of Six Personality Descriptors

Self-possession	Future importance					
	Lucky	Hard worker	Popular	Competent	Competitive	Influential
Lucky	.30	−.02	.28	.08	.03	.17
Hard worker	−.05	.41	.05	.25	.15	.05
Popular	.11	−.02	.40	−.01	.01	.33
Competent	−.05	.14	.09	.31	.24	.12
Competitive	.16	.03	.19	.24	.39	.20
Influential	.04	.02	.38	.09	.14	.42

Note. Boxed values indicate correlations for the *same* attribute.

Table 3   Correlations between Items Assessing Self-Importance and Self-Possession of Six Personality Descriptors

	Self-importance					
Self-possession	Lucky	Hard worker	Popular	Competent	Competitive	Influential
Lucky	.14	−.05	.06	.09	−.07	.16
Hard worker	.13	.50	.02	.22	.09	.00
Popular	.00	.11	.35	.08	−.06	.21
Competent	−.05	.15	−.02	.33	.16	.11
Competitive	.16	.03	.15	.35	.46	.15
Influential	.00	.12	.23	.17	.09	.23

Note. Boxed values indicate correlations for the *same* attribute.

tant for self-evaluation ($r = .14$, n.s.). For the other five attributes (hard worker, popular, competent, competitive, influential) the diagonal correlations are statistically reliable ($r = .23$, $p < .025$, two-tailed test) and are larger than any of the other row-column values for that attribute.

Self-Importance and Future Importance for a Laboratory Task Performance

Questions concerning the future importance and self-importance of the performance task were asked twice: once in referring to "these tests" as important for self-evaluation and for future goals, and later, just before actual performance, in referring to "doing well on this test" for self-evaluation and for future goals. Table 4 shows the correlations between these responses for these four questions. Examination indicates that for questions referring to "the tests," there is a correlation of .43 ($p < .01$, two-tailed test), and for those referring to "doing well on the tests" this relationship is .58 ($p < .01$, two-tailed test). Thus, there apparently is a substantial positive correlation between self-importance and future importance concerning these tests and/or doing well on them.

Another way to assess this relationship is to first consider the correlation between responses for the "tests" and "doing well on the tests" as reliability coeffi-

Table 4   Correlations of Self-Importance and Future Importance for Questions Concerning "the Tests" and "Doing Well on the Tests"

	Future importance (.42)	
Self-importance (.50)	Of tests	Of doing well on tests
Of tests	.43	.36
Of doing well on tests	.38	.58

cients for the self-importance question (.50) and for the future-importance question (.42). Then the correlation between the self "tests" question and the future "doing well on the tests" question can be taken as one index of the relationship between self-importance and future importance (.36), with the future "tests" question and the self "doing well on the tests" question serving as a second index of this self-future relationship (.38). When these values (median of .37) are compared to the earlier ones (.43 and .58) that show the relationship, we find them smaller but still substantial, and when compared to the "reliability coefficients" of .50 and .42 we find they account for about $.37^2/.45^2$ or 68% of the possible variance, given this reliability ceiling. Whichever index of the relationship is used, the data suggest a substantial positive relationship between self-importance and future importance for the specific laboratory task and replicate the findings of Raynor et al. (1974).

Self-importance, Future Importance, and Affective Reactions to Anticipated Performance on a Laboratory Task

In the second part of the study subjects were asked to work on a performance task under two different conditions as part of another aspect of our research. In one condition, subjects were told that "quantity rather than quality was important—so attempt as many problems as possible." In the other condition, subjects were told that "quality rather than quantity was important, so try to get as many problems correct as possible." Results from this part have been reported elsewhere (English, 1974). Our purpose here was to see if there was some overall relationship between aroused affect and self-importance and future importance when data were collapsed over experimental conditions.

Two questions assessed affective reactions in the testing situation. The first asked "To what extent do you feel enthusiastic about working on these tests?" A graphic rating scale appeared below, anchored by "feel very enthusiastic" and "do not feel at all enthusiastic," with "midpoint" in the middle. The second asked, "To what extent are you worried about how you will do on these tests?" The graphic rating scale was anchored by "not at all" and "a lot," with "midpoint" in the middle. These questions correspond to the self-importance and future-importance questions for the "tests".

Table 5 shows the correlations between these ratings of enthusiasm and worry, and both the corresponding self-importance and future-importance questions concerning the "tests" and those concerning self-importance and future importance for "doing well on the tests." Inspection indicates that all correlations are positive and statistically reliable.

DISCUSSION

The results presented here replicate the positive correlation between self-importance and future importance reported by Raynor et al. (1974), who found that the rated importance of the final examination in a college Introductory Psychology course was positively correlated with the rated importance of the exam for one's self-evaluation. Here we extended the relationship between self-importance

Table 5   Correlations between Self-Importance and Affective
Reactions, and between Future Importance and Affective
Reactions

	Affective reaction	
	Enthusiasm	Worry
Self-importance		
Of tests	.32	.40
Of doing well on tests	.29	.33
Future importance		
Of tests	.30	.39
Of doing well on tests	.26	.31

and future importance to self-descriptors or attributes of personality, rather than the results of performance on an examination. In addition, the extent of possession of the attribute is also positively related to future importance for all six descriptors used, and is positively related to self-importance at least for seeing oneself as a hard worker, as competent and competitive in skill-demanding activity, and as popular. We did not necessarily anticipate the role of self-possession, although we were not surprised at the result. We were much more surprised by two other aspects of the findings. First, "lucky," "popular," and "influential" were included in the questionnaire because we wanted to obtain discriminate validity between achievement-related and non-achievement-related items. That is, we expected positive relationships between self-importance and future importance for those self-descriptors having to do with achievement-related activity, such as hard worker, competent, and competitive. However, it did not occur to us that other self-descriptors might show a similar pattern of results. "Popular" surprised us in that its correlation coefficients are as substantial as for the achievement-related attributes. In retrospect, the findings for "popular" began us on the path toward a more general theory of personality functioning (see part IV) because our conception of the determinants of achievement-related behavior had no way in which to incorporate such a finding.

Results for "lucky," while not significant for the self-possession–self-importance relationship, are substantial for the self-importance–future-importance relationship and significant for self-possession–future importance. We did not anticipate that an attribute that appears to deny the individual's own responsibility, effort, and/or skill—as we interpret the notion of "luck" to imply—would show us this pattern of results.

The implications of the results for "popular" and "luck" with regard to future orientation seemed clear: If an attribute is believed by a person to be related to future career success, then it tends to be seen as important to that person for his or her own self-evaluation, independent of its classification by us as "achievement related" or not. It seems that the presence of perceived instrumentality of the attribute for attainment of future goals is the relevant factor rather than *the way* in which it was instrumental, as we had previously considered it. For example, if we set up a chance-related task, such as in a gambling situation, then we expect that relationships usually obtained under achievement-oriented conditions—where one believes oneself responsible for the outcome of action through one's own ability, effort, and/or skill—will not hold. Previous research had clearly suggested such a distinction (cf. Raynor & Smith, 1965). The present results do not. In this regard they are similar to results for studies of gambling in different kinds of paths (contingent vs. noncontingent) and for various lengths of contingent paths. (See chapter 2, where we also obtained results for a so-called "chance-related" outcome similar to those for the "achievement-related" outcome. Recall that all subjects became more conservative in their immediate risk-taking behavior in a contingent than in a noncontingent path, and as the length of contingent path increased, regardless of whether the game was "roulette" or "basket throw.")

We now see that both the gambling results and the results reported here for "lucky" suggest something about the *instrumentality*, (independent of the kind of activity,) of the outcome of the activity and/or self-attributes *that ensure moving on* to a later opportunity for "success"; both may function equivalently, in that when they are seen as related to future goals, they take on importance for self-evaluation because attainment of the future goal is necessary to continue on. But note that for "lucky," unlike the achievement-related attributes, there is little relationship between self-possession and self-importance. One does not necessarily feel good about oneself because one sees oneself as a lucky person, while for the other attributes, when self-importance and future importance are positively related, self-possession is also positively related to each of the others. Why? Could it be that the nature of some self-descriptions makes them less valuable so that good feelings do not necessarily follow from merely *having* them? For such attributes, only when they are instrumental to (important) future goals are good feelings about the self implicated.

We concluded that attributes must differ in their ability to make one feel good about oneself when one believes one possesses them, independently of the good feeling that one gets when one believes that possession of an attribute will be instrumental to career success. This eventually led to the addition of "cultural value" as a theoretical variable in our subsequent conceptual efforts (see chapter 11) to account for differences in the perceived value of possessing different attributes.

11

Self-Possession of Attributes, Self-Evaluation, and Future Orientation: A Theory of Adult Competence Motivation

Joel O. Raynor

OVERVIEW

In this chapter we summarize and begin the conceptual analysis of some research findings concerning relationships among the self-possession, future importance, and self-importance of personality attributes, on the one hand (see chapter 10), and the relationship between the future-importance and self-importance of outcomes of action (success and failure), on the other. In addition, the functional significance for motivation of immediate activity of future importance, self-importance, and self-possession is discussed. An initial theory is presented concerning information-seeking behavior in undertaking tests of competence to obtain knowledge about the degree of possession and/or the increment in degree of possession of competences that are positively valued by the individual. We anticipate a later, more systematic treatment presented in part IV concerning what is then called the *present self-image*, defined in terms of the perceived degree of possession of prerequisite attributes that provide for positive value and/or self-esteem.

ATTRIBUTES AND SELF-ATTRIBUTION

There were two major sources of impetus for the present work. One stemmed from an attempt to utilize Weiner's (1972, 1974) early approach to attribution and achievement motivation within a motivational rather than social psychological perspective. At that time, this meant to us that one's perceptions of the extent to which one possessed an attribute such as "ability" or "competence"—or seeing oneself as competitive or a hard worker—might be important as a determinant of one's subsequent achievement-oriented behavior. That is, from the start, we were interested in how *self-attribution,* defined as the degree or extent to which a person believes he or she possesses a particular attribute, might influence motivation. A second impetus stemmed from the work reported by Raynor, Atkinson, and Brown (1974), who predicted and found that students assumed to be success-oriented (high in *n* Achievement and low in test anxiety) showed an increase in concern about doing well relative to reported anxiety, while students assumed to be failure-threatened (low in n Achievement and high in test anxiety) showed an increase in reported anxiety relative to concern about doing well, when a final course examination was seen as important to their own future goals as compared to when it was not. In addition, they reported a positive relationship between the perceived relatedness of the exam for students' future goals and the extent to which students believe that the exam grade was related to their own positive self-evaluation. The result was obtained for all motive groups and is best reflected statistically by a main effect of low, moderate, and high relatedness to future goals on mean scores on importance for self-evaluation ($p < .001$).

A follow-up study (Raynor & English; see chapter 10) extended the approach concerning the attribution theory of achievement motivation (cf. Weiner, 1972, 1974) to investigate the relationship between self-attribution of various descriptors and the importance of possession of that attribute for both self-evaluation and attaining one's own future goals. Six self-descriptors were used in the study: seeing oneself as a hard worker, as competent, as lucky (these were based on Weiner's attributional analysis), and as competitive, popular, and influential. Three questions were asked about each of these self-descriptions: (1) "To what extent do you see yourself as . . . ; (2) "How important is seeing yourself as . . . for your own positive self-evaluation?; and (3) "How important to you is being . . . for achievement of your own future goals?" The basic findings were as follows: There was a positive correlation between each of these questions for most of the six self-descriptors (except lucky) which was larger than would be accounted for in terms of possible common methods variance due to response sets and/or response keying of the items (see chapter 10). Thus the Raynor and English data replicated and extended the findings first reported by Raynor et al. (1974) concerning the relationship between self-importance and future importance, with self-possession of attributes as part of this positive correlational matrix.

The Raynor and English study provided a second means of replication of the relationship between self-importance and future importance for a particular task. After completing the above-described rating tasks, subjects were presented with a two-step contingent path involving complex arithmetic tests. Subjects were given questions very similar to those used by Raynor et al. (1974): "To what extent are these tests important for your own self-evaluation?"; "To what extent are these tests important for your own future goals?"; "To what extent is doing well on these tests important for your own self-evaluation?"; To what extent is doing well on these tests important for your own future goals?" Again, positive correlations were obtained for these items (but not other items, suggesting that methods variance cannot account for the results), despite the fact that the subjects of the experiment (male college students) knew that results of these tests would in no way be used to evaluate their standing in the university or in any other meaningful life activity.

The Raynor and English study also included questions concerning rated enthusiasm and worry that allow an evaluation of the extent to which "importance" is associated with greater reported affective arousal. It was found that as importance for self-evaluation increases, so does feeling enthusiastic about working on the tests increase. Similarly, as the importance for self-evaluation increases, so does worry about how one will do on the tests. When importance for future goals is viewed, the same picture is obtained; enthusiasm increases with increased importance for future goals, and worry increases with increased importance for future goals. Thus, the study not only replicates the positive relationship between self-importance and future importance but provides evidence that both have equivalent relationships to reports of affective arousal.

Two additional studies provide evidence bearing on this issue. Gazzo (1974) investigated the relationship between self-possession of an attribute (competence vs. nurturance as applied to a specific tutorial program that was described to the subject) and the future relatedness of that attribute. The specific questions asked (among others) were the following: (1) "To what extent do you believe yourself to possess the qualities necessary to perform in the tutorial capacity described above (regardless of whether you had the opportunity to do so or not)?"; (2) "To what extent do you believe that possessing the qualities referred to above is necessary for you to achieve your own future goals?" Thus Gazzo's questions are able to evaluate the relationship between extent of self-possession of an attribute of self and extent of perceived necessity of possession of that attribute for future success. She found a positive association between extent of self-possession of the attribute (disregarding whether the attribute was competence or nurturance) and extent of perceived necessity of possession of that attribute for future success ($ps < .05$, for men and women, separately). Subsequent analysis of her data viewed the relationship of self-possession and future importance to rated interest in, and willingness to volunteer for, the tutorial program. Both interest and willingness to volunteer were positively related to both self-possession and future importance.

Raynor and Mitchell (reported in Raynor, 1974c) asked college students the following two questions at the beginning of the academic semester: (1) "To what extent is it necessary for you to get at least a B in Introductory Psychology for having your future career plans work out?"; (2) "To what extent is it necessary for getting a B or better in Introductory Psychology for your self-esteem (feeling good about yourself)?" This study provides a direct replication of the Raynor (1970) data with two improvements: (1) a B grade is specifically referred to, whereas in the earlier study the implication was that some "good grade" on the exam is what is related to the student's future goals; (2) the *necessity* of the grades is assessed, to provide a direct link to theory concerning *contingent* future orientation. Median breaks on both questions were obtained to view their effects in conjunction with achievement-related motives on the actual grade obtained in the course at the end of the semester. Again, the positive relationship between necessity for self and necessity for future is apparent ($p < .005$), but for men only. In this study, there is little relationship between the two measures for the women.

The results of the Raynor and Mitchell study show that future necessity and self-necessity both functioned in an equivalent manner, for both sexes; for men, each produced the predicted effects of achievement-related motives, while for women, each produced the predicted effect for success-oriented individuals but failed to produce the expected effect for failure-threatened individuals. Table 1 shows the results for future necessity alone, and for self-necessity alone, using proportion of B or better grades as the dependent measure. Table 2 shows the joint influence of future and self-necessity, this time using proportion of B or better grades and mean grades, since the latter are more stable given the relatively small number of subjects in some of the subgroups. Results for the two different measures of academic performance (proportion of B grades and mean grades) are in general similar throughout the data analyses. They all show that as future necessity increases, or self-necessity, or both, both success-oriented men and women tend to receive higher grades, while as both future and/or self-necessity increases for the failure-threatened group, grades drop for men but remain pretty much the same for women. Here we find the only apparent discrepancy between analyses for the proportion of B grades and the mean grade measures of performance—for the latter, there is some evidence that the joint influence of future and self-necessity is to lower the grades of the low- n Achievement-high test-anxiety (failure-threatened) women (3.17 in low-low vs. 2.71 in high-high future and self-necessity), while for the former, there is little difference between these groups (.67 vs. .57). Neither of these differences approaches statistical significance. In addition, for both measures, the ordering of motive groups within high-high future and self-necessity for the women suggests that the low- n Achievement-high test-anxiety group is higher than would be expected based on (1) the ordering within the men, and (2) the ordering within the women for the first three motive groups—high-low highest, with high-high and low-low lower as for men. Thus the data are consistent in suggesting a very important difference between the data for men and those for women as far as theoretical interpretation is concerned—the failure-threatened women do not show the comparable decrement in performance while most of the other data for the women show trends similar to those for the men.

Table 1   Proportion of B or Better Grades in Introductory Psychology as a Function of Motive Group and Sex for the Rated Necessity of a B or Better Grade for Future Career Plans to Work Out and for Self-Esteem

Motive group: n Achievement-test anxiety	Men				Women			
	Low		High		Low		High	
	N	Prop.	N	Prop.	N	Prop.	N	Prop.
Future necessity								
High-low	11	.10	11	.64	13	.31	8	.50
High-high	14	.43	8	.38	9	.89	18	.39
Low-low	28	.25	14	.43	13	.38	11	.27
Low-high	20	.45	11	.09	11	.55	16	.56
Self-necessity								
High-low	15	.33	7	.57	11	.27	10	.50
High-high	12	.42	10	.40	13	.57	13	.54
Low-low	29	.24	13	.46	17	.24	7	.57
Low-high	19	.47	12	.08	15	.60	12	.58

Table 2 Academic Performance in Introductory Psychology as a Joint Function of Future and Self-Necessity for Men and Women Differing in Achievement-Related Motives for Proportion of B or Better Grades and Mean Grades

	Self-future necessity															
	Men								Women							
	Low-low		Low-high		High-low		High-high		Low-low		Low-high		High-low		High-high	
n Achievement-test anxiety	N	Prop.	N	Prop.	N	Prop.	N	Prop.	N	Prop.	N	Prop.	N	Prop.	N	Prop.
	Proportion of B or better grades															
High-low	10	.20	5	.60	1	1.00	6	.67	7	.29	4	.25	6	.33	4	.75
High-high	9	.33	3	.67	5	.60	5	.20	6	1.00	8	.25	3	.67	10	.50
Low-low	21	.19	8	.38	7	.43	6	.50	10	.20	7	.29	3	1.00	4	.25
Low-high	5	.53	4	.25	5	.20	7	.00	6	.67	9	.56	5	.60	7	.57
	Mean grades[a]															
High-low	10	2.30	5	2.00	1	2.00	6	3.17	7	2.29	4	1.25	6	2.50	4	3.00
High-high	9	2.44	3	3.00	5	2.80	5	2.00	6	3.67	8	2.25	3	3.00	10	2.50
Low-low	21	2.10	8	2.38	7	2.57	6	2.50	10	1.50	7	2.14	3	3.00	4	2.00
Low-high	15	2.53	4	2.25	5	2.00	7	1.86	6	3.17	9	2.44	5	3.20	7	2.71

[a] A = 4, B = 3, C = 2, D = 1, and F = 0

It should be noted that for the overall ANOVA on mean grades with n Achievement, test anxiety, self-necessity, future necessity, and sex as factors ($2 \times 2 \times 2 \times 2 \times 2$), the four-factor interaction among these variables disregarding sex is statistically reliable ($F = 5.69, df = 1/184, p < .02$), but the five-factor interaction is not ($F = 0.67$, n.s.). Thus the ANOVA may be insensitive in failing to detect what to us is a critical theoretical difference in trends across future-self necessity for the low n-Achievement high test-anxiety (failure-threatened) group as described above. In fact, this significant four-factor interaction, but not the five-factor one, reflects the nearly identical pattern of results for men and women in the other cells shown in Table 2.

The data for mean grades in Table 2 are clear in suggesting that only when both future and self-necessity are high do we get the predicted superiority in the academic performance of success-oriented (high on n Achievement low on test anxiety) over failure-threatened (low on n Achievement-high on test anxiety) students, for both men and women. For men, this difference is indeed large—over a B average (3.17) for the success-oriented students as compared to below a C average (1.86) for the failure-threatened students ($t = 5.04, p < .001$), while for women this difference (3.00 vs. 2.71) does not approach statistical significance ($t < 1$, n.s.). However, the data for proportion of B or better grades, while yielding comparable levels of significance for the comparisons just referred to, is not as clear in suggesting that only when future-self necessity is high is performance of the success-oriented students superior to that of the failure-threatened students.

We present data from this study in such detail, and using both possible measures of academic performance, because we believe these findings to be crucial for subsequent theoretical analysis of the determinants of immediate achievement-oriented activity, particularly the findings suggesting that immediate performance must be seen by the individual as related to that individual's own positive self-evaluation before individual differences in the predicted direction among persons differing in achievement-related motives become apparent. If such findings are replicated, they suggest a new set of conditions that must be conceptualized as being necessary for the arousal of achievement-related motives—self-evaluation as the condition defining "ego involvement" and hence engagement of resultant achievement motivation to influence action, in addition to and in conjunction with future contingent orientation. The implication of this finding is pursued in chapter 13.

EVALUATION OF COMPETENCE
AND SELF–FUTURE IMPORTANCE

The series of findings concerning self-importance, future importance, and self-possession tentatively suggest the following theoretical points: (1) Achievement arousal is tied to both the future implications of immediate activity and the implications of that activity for a person's self-esteem; concern about doing well, worry, interest, and willingness to undertake activity seem increased by future importance and/or self-importance or self-possession. (2) Both importance for future goals and self-esteem may function to produce the characteristic effects of achievement-related motives that are predicted by expectancy X value theory of achievement motivation. (3) The extent of self-possession of particular skills, abilities, and attributes is related to the belief in both self-importance and future importance. Why the latter? Perhaps it is because skill activity is believed to implicate the assessment of relevant skills, abilities, and competences that are believed to be instrumental to the attainment of long-term future goals and/or which serve as means of esteem-income owing to their desirability of being possessed.

The suggestive inferences outlined above are consistent with several other kinds of empirical data and theoretical arguments that emphasize the evaluation of competence as the factor that is critically responsible for the arousal of achievement motivation. Taken together, these arguments and evidence have provided the impetus for a revision of the theory of achievement motivation to emphasize evaluation of valued attributes through some skill-demanding activity (either formally when called a "test of ability" or more informally when implicated in life striving that is evaluated in terms of possession of that competence) as the basis for arousal of achievement-related motives—presented in this chapter—and involving self-evaluation—presented in chapter 13.

Several questions immediately must be faced. Is it necessary for a task to be perceived as being influenced by an attribute or competence that has value to the individual before achievement motivation will be aroused by the task? If so, should not information as to the validity of the evaluation, and the actual amount of information expected, also play a role in arousal of achievement motivation? A recent study by Weinberg (1975) suggests "yes" as the answer to the first question. A recent study by Trope and Brickman (1975) suggests "yes" as the answer to the second.

Evaluation of Competence in Skill-Demanding Activity

Recall that in the Raynor and English study (chapter 10) subjects who rated the test performance as related to future goals also rated it as related to self-evaluation, despite the fact that there was no obvious contingent path relating test performance to these students' own future goals. This might have been produced by the two-step contingent path that was used to present the actual tasks, but a recent unpublished doctoral dissertation (Weinberg, 1975) suggests that this was not the case. In the Weinberg (1975) study, athletes and nonathletes worked on a pursuit rotor task under achievement-oriented and relaxed conditions. Standing on achievement-related motives was assessed from the Mehrabian (1968) measure of resultant achievement motivation (RAM). The importance of doing well on the task for future goals and for self-evaluation were both assessed, for one sample prior to performance on the task, and in the actual experiment after performance on the task in either the achievement-oriented or relaxed condition. The results showed (1) a substantial correlation between self-importance and future importance, (2) mean ratings on both were substantially higher under achievement-oriented than relaxed conditions, (3) athletes were significantly higher on both self-importance and future importance for the pursuit rotor than nonathletes, and (4) the success-oriented athletes did best, while the failure-threatened athletes tended to do worst, with both success-oriented and failure-threatened nonathletes intermediate, in performance on the pursuit rotor task under achievement-oriented conditions.

The implications of these results seem fairly clear: pursuit rotor is perceived to assess an attribute relevant to athletic pursuits; this attribute (physical coordination?) is related to the future goals of athletes more than nonathletes and is related more to the self-image of athletes than that of nonathletes because it is a prerequisite competence for both success in an athletic career (future goal) and seeing oneself as an athlete (self-esteem); consequently, performance on pursuit rotor is more "ego involving" for athletes than nonathletes; and finally, achievement-related motives are better able to predict performance under so-called "achievement-oriented conditions" because these conditions often provide diagnostic tests of valued competences in which feedback as to "how good I am" (how much of this competence I possess) is expected.

Without the assumption that "achievement arousal" provides for evaluation of valued competences, we are left with no answer as to why students in an experimental situation believe (in both the Raynor-English and Weinberg studies) that it is important for them to do well on the task at hand to attain their own future goals. It seems hard to imagine that subjects are so suspicious of experimental psychologists that they would seriously think that these psychologists would use their task performance to influence life decisions about their subsequent careers, to determine whether or not they will be allowed to move on to the next step in the path to their future goals. And if we assume for the moment that students do not believe that this performance represents the first (next) step in a contingent life path, then for what other reason could they believe that good performance on the task is necessary for having their future plans work out? The answer may rest in students' belief that the test they are confronted with is a valid diagnostic test of a valued attribute or competence whose possession they believe is a necessary prerequisite for their own future career success. "Physical coordination" for athletes and "mathematical ability" for the average college student might be the competences that are perceived, in the two studies cited above, that students believe to be assessed by the tests they are confronted with in the laboratory situation. The critical point is that they anticipate obtaining information about their own competences, quite independently of the information to be obtained by the experimenter, and while they most probably believe that the experimenter would not and will not use this information in a career gatekeeper function, the students anticipate that they might use this information, depending upon its validity, to assess their own chances of future career success that requires possession of this competence. Thus a student who wants to become a professional athlete or continue a career as a college athlete and who therefore believes that "physical coordination" is a necessary prerequisite for attaining future goals (because physical coordination is believed a necessary prerequisite for success as an athlete) would rate as highly important the possession of physical coordination as necessary for future career plans to work out. And if the student identified himself or herself as a "potential professional athlete," then feeling good about his or her own self-image would be dependent upon the extent of possession of "physical coordination," because it is possible to continue to see oneself as an "athlete" and a "potential pro" only to the extent that one possesses the prerequisites of this "role" (read "self-image"). We could then also understand why good performance on the test would be rated as highly important for feeling good about oneself.

For students whose future goals do not require physical coordination for their attainment, the possession of this attribute is not a prerequisite, so that it would be rated as relatively unimportant for attaining the future goal. Since the individual's sense of self would not involve this attribute to as great an extent as the athlete referred to earlier, we would expect a lower rating on extent of importance for doing well on this task (really, on extent of possession of this attribute) for feeling good about oneself.

The implication of this argument is that the equations of the elaborated theory of achievement motivation (see chapter 2) confound (1) the utilization of competences that are required and (2) their assessment in the (testing) situation that the individual is confronted with. Utilization of particular valued skills seems to describe the "activity" (r_1) that the individual is engaged in, where the goal seems to be to demonstrate one's effectiveness in the situation by successfully accomplishing the goal of the situation (as seen by the person) through utilization of the required skills. Thus, at the same time, the individual is utilizing particular competences and having them assessed (re-evaluated). The appropriate phrase for the latter behavior is "competence testing," and the appropriate description of factors sustaining it is "competence motivation."

THE AROUSAL OF ACHIEVEMENT MOTIVATION IN COMPETENCE TESTING

We have already noted that, according to the elaborated theory of achievement motivation, either an increase in one's evaluation of one's own ability (competence) or a decrease in the perceived task difficulty, or both, could result in an increase in subjective probability of success $(P_n s_n)$ along a contingent path and therefore in the accentuation of achievement-related motivation sustaining immediate activity along that path (see chapter 2). In addition, we have already noted (see Raynor, 1974a) that this increase in perceived ability and/or task ease is expected to increase an individual's future orientation by moving the phenomenal goal and/or phenomenal threat of immediate activity to a more distant step along the contingent path. Thus we have theoretical machinery to incorporate the findings reviewed above concerning the correlation obtained between extent of perceived possession of attributes that are related to skill-demanding activity and extent of the rated necessity and/or importance of (doing well in) activity that assesses the attributes for attainment of the individual's future goals. Also, what is needed, initially, is the further assumption that evaluation of that competence at a higher level will raise the subjective probability of success in subsequent activity requiring that competence as a prerequisite for immediate success.

The data clearly suggest that an increase in the extent of perceived possession of a competence is related to an increase in the extent to which that ability is used as a means of positive self-evaluation or self-esteem. But not for all attributes. This relationship did not apply for "luck" in the research reviewed earlier. This suggests the more general point that only attributes that in a given culture are seen as desirable attributes (as well as ones that are perceived as instrumental to the attainment of future goals) come to arouse positive competence motivation. We suggest, therefore, that skill-demanding activities that are believed to provide valid assessments of attributes arouse achievement motivation in direct proportion to the value of the attribute to the individual. "Intelligence" is one of the attributes that, in Western culture, is valued to a great extent by many (but not all) members of the culture. Some individuals value possession of intelligence to a much greater extent than others. For them, possession of intelligence provides a source of positive self-evaluation, and lack of intelligence provides a source of negative self-evaluation. For such an individual, anticipation of performance on a skill-demanding activity that is known to provide a valid assessment of intelligence is therefore expected to arouse the individual's characteristic strength of achievement-related motives, if the individual is constrained to perform on such a test. The individual will then be enthusiastic about doing well, worried about doing poorly, and rate doing well on the task as necessary for positive self-esteem and as necessary for attainment of future goals. The former results because the individual tends to see himself or herself as an "intelligent person," and the latter results because the individual tends to strive to utilize his or her attribute of intelligence in movement along a career path of society in which the possession of intelligence is believed the necessary ingredient to achieve future success. This argument is developed more fully in chapter 13.

We do not mean to imply that all individuals conceptualize some global, non-differentiated entity referred to as "intelligence" as their most valued competence-related attribute. On the contrary, we expect individuals to differentiate to a great extent the particular skills and competences that they use to provide a basis for esteem income in the arena of skill-demanding activity. Anecdotal information concerning the many and varied roles of criminals, the increasing technological specialization of society, and the tendency of individuals to develop and pursue specialized avocations and hobbies all suggest that individuals will vary widely in the extent that any particular competence will be highly valued. Nevertheless, we expect that "intelligence" will be the single attribute that is more highly valued by the greatest number of individuals in Western culture. As a consequence, we expect, based on this analysis, the maximal arousal of achievement-related motivation on activities perceived to be valid tests of intelligence.

We believe that this alteration in the theory of achievement motivation to emphasize assessment of valued competences is consistent with most of what is known about the conditions under which arousal of achievement-related motives is to be expected. The extent to which other (than intelligence-related) skill-demanding activities are believed to provide assessment of valued attributes is the extent to which they will also arouse achievement motivation. Activities are then considered to be "trivial" by individuals to the extent that these activities fail to assess valued competences. They can arouse achievement motivation, but do so to a minimal extent because only the perceived difficulty of the task (and not the importance of the task for self-evaluation and for attainment of future goals) provides for the arousal of components of resultant achievement motivation.

There are many precedents for the general emphasis on evaluation of competence as an important factor in the arousal of achievement motivation. Festinger (1954) argued that individuals are motivated to evaluate themselves upwardly in comparison to others with regard to competence. Feather (1967) has argued that the value of skill-demanding activity is not completely determined by task difficulty, but by one's belief that one's own initiative and effort can produce that outcome. DeCharms (1968) argued that one's effectiveness in producing outcomes (being an "origin") is the critical factor in arousal of achievement motivation. Moulton (1967, 1974) argued that assessment of specific competences is what is critical about the 50-50 risk option and choice of contingent paths, in selection of tasks and concern about doing well in them. Pearlson and English (unpublished papers) have, in the present program of research, suggested that the value of the competence or attribute being evaluated by a test of skill should be incorporated into the theory of achievement motivation, and they suggest several ways in which this might be done. Finally, Trope and Brickman (1975) and Trope (1975) have shown that, when the information value and the difficulty of a task of ability are separated, individuals exhibit a strong preference for working on the version of the test with the greatest information about one's standing on ability, rather than on the version offering the 50-50 risk option.

If replicated, the Trope and Brickman (1975) results are important because they suggest (1) that expectancy X value theory may be inadequate to conceptualize the effects of competence testing, and (2) that all individuals are more or less motivated to select the informative test of ability. Their results are consistent with the failure to show that failure-threatened individuals avoid tasks of moderate risk in one-step paths (cf. Atkinson, 1974b) and the failure to find avoidance of high Ps immediate tasks in contingent-path situations (cf. Raynor, 1974a and chapter 2). That is, all individuals may be attracted to tests of competence, regardless of their achievement-related motivation.

The assumption that individuals are motivated to test their socially valued abilities at higher and higher levels of consensual difficulty (cf. Festinger, 1954; Moulton, 1974) helps account for the general trend of research findings concerning preference among potential tasks involving effort and/or skill. However, this assumption by itself has been, and remains, inadequate to account for other substantive findings in research on achievement motivation, particularly those concerning performance level, persistence in an already selected task, and affective reactions to and changes in level of aspiration caused by success and failure (cf. Atkinson & Feather, 1966; Atkinson & Raynor, 1974). Although it is now assumed here that all individuals are motivated to test their competence (although not necessarily in the same kind of ability), we assume that the commitment to upward evaluation of ability produces differential effects on the aroused level of achievement motivation sustaining the activity—once the individual is constrained to engage in it or is so self-constrained psychologically. That is, once an individual is committed to such a test of a valued competence, the characteristic effects of achievement-related motives are predicted to become apparent as (1) an accentuation of positive motivation for those individuals considered to be success-oriented $(M_S > M_{AF})$, (2) an accentuation of negative (inhibitory) motivation for those individuals considered to be failure-threatened $(M_{AF} > M_S)$, and (3) a continuation of indifference to and no change in aroused achievement motivation for individuals with equal strengths of the two achievement-related motives $(M_S \approx M_{AF})$. The choice of a test of competence, and motivation to do well in it after such a commitment, are here assumed to function differently because only after commitment to evaluation of one's abilities are the inhibitory effects of resistance to engaging in such a test (so as not to demonstrate one's incompetence) expected to be relatively strong. Such effects of inhibition are expected only when one (1) places a substantial positive value on possession of the competences being assessed by the skill-demanding test, and a substantial negative value on their lack of possession, and (2) defines oneself in terms of possession of that competence. We expect that under these conditions the individual will also (3) see the test of competence as a means of positive or negative self-evaluation and (4) see the test as important to the attainment of future goals because either doing well on the test is believed to be necessary to earn the opportunity for competence testing at a higher level of consensual difficulty to fulfill a future sense of self, or performance on the test is believed diagnostic for how the individual would do on a later test of competence at a higher level of consensual difficulty (see chapter 13).

The conditions noted above are all fulfilled when an individual strives along a contingent career path of a society. We believe that the above factors, when taken together, account for the substantive findings in the area of research on achievement motivation. There is a long history of previous theory and research in which the present reconceptualization is embedded (cf. Lewin et al., 1944; McClelland et al., 1953; Atkinson, 1958; McClelland, 1961; Atkinson & Feather, 1966; Atkinson & Raynor, 1974). The research and theory have at various times and in various ways dealt with the above issues, for example, in comparisons of "ego-involved" versus "non-ego-involved" conditions, "stress" versus "nonstress," "aroused" versus "relaxed," "interpersonal" versus "noninterpersonal," and "contingent" versus "noncontingent." In all this research it is now apparent that there has been a systematic confounding of the arousal of achievement motivation for particular tasks, on the one hand, and the value of the task performance as a test of valued competences that the person sees as prerequisites for future success and for seeing himself or herself in a positive way, on the other.

FUTURE ORIENTATION AND SELF-EVALUATION AS DETERMINANTS OF COMPETENCE MOTIVATION

The Determinants of Value of a Competence to the Individual

Since we assume that "competence testing" is the critical factor engaging achievement-related motives, it is worthwhile to begin with the conceptual analysis of the determinants of the "value of a competence to the individual," for this should determine the attractiveness of an opportunity for a valid test of that competence. We suggest that there are three components of the determinants of the value of a competence to the individual: (1) the extent of belief that the competence is a necessary prerequisite for attainment of valued (future) extrinsic incentives of the society, (2) the extent of belief that the competence is a necessary prerequisite for the successful mastery of a particular task faced by the individual, which may or may not be a step in a path to some long-term extrinsic incentive or achievement goal, and (3) the extent of belief that the competence is a component part of a self-image that the individual is striving to attain, which is, in turn, determined by the individual's cultural valuation of this "role image" associated with the particular career pursuit. Put another way, item 3 above refers to the extent of belief that possession of a competence is seen by one as "good" in the society of which one sees oneself as part. Since all the above factors should contribute to the rating of the importance of the possession of a competence, we expect that this question will provide an independent means of assessment of the value of a competence to the individual. That is, the value of a competence is derived from its instrumental value in (1) attaining valued extrinsic rewards in the society, (2) mastery of a particular skill-demanding activity, and (3) fulfillment of a future self-image. This value of a competence is reflected in the extent of belief that possession of the competence is seen as "important"—important for the attainment of extrinsic incentives, important for the attainment of success in skill-demanding activity, and important for the fulfillment of one's sense of self.

Since for many in Western culture a central part of a valued self-image is the ability to attain one's future goals (regardless of whether they are extrinsic, achievement related, or self-related), all these sources of value of a competence often contribute to the importance of possession of the competence for self-evaluation. Seeing oneself as an effective agent ("origin") may be the critical factor here (cf. DeCharms, 1968).

The Determinants of the Value of a Test of Competence to the Individual

The value of a competence is one determinant of the value to the individual of a particular *test of competence;* the higher the value of the competence to the individual, the greater the valence or attractiveness of an opportunity to test one's standing on extent of possession of that competence.

We include two other factors that determine the value of a test of competence: the extent of perceived validity of the test and the extent of information expected from the test. The greater the belief in the validity of the test, the greater its (positive or negative) value. The greater the information gain expected from the test of competence, the greater its (positive or negative) value.

DETERMINANTS OF MOTIVATION TO UNDERTAKE
OR TO RESIST UNDERTAKING A TEST OF COMPETENCE

We suggest that the extent to which the person believes that a valid test of competence can (will) show an increase in the degree of possession of an attribute, along with the (positive) value of that competence to the individual, determines the strength of motivation to undertake the test of competence. A maximally arousing test of competence is one where the individual believes he or she can demonstrate a substantial increment in possession of a substantially valued competence. On the other hand, the test of competence will provide no motivation to undertake it (above and beyond what it would if presented merely as any other skill-demanding activity) when it is believed that that test of competence can merely confirm the extent of possession of the competence at a level that has already been validly established. Furthermore, the test of competence will arouse negative motivation (negation tendency) to the extent that it is believed that the outcome of such a test of competence can provide valid information indicating a substantial drop in the degree of possession of a positively valued attribute in comparison to a previously validated level of competence; the most negatively valent test of competence should be a test of a positively valued competence that is expected to demonstrate a substantial decrement in degree of possession of that attribute.

The subjective probability that the test will provide this information is the other relevant factor. It, in turn, is influenced by the perceived validity of the test of competence and the expectation that knowledge of the results is anticipated.

We are now able to specify the predicted conditions that will determine the extent to which an individual will be motivated to undertake a test of competence: maximum positive motivation to evaluate one's competence will be aroused when one believes one can find a completely valid test of that competence that will provide greatest information in terms of an increase in the extent of possession of that attribute (as compared to a previous test of that competence), where the attribute is a highly valued one because its possession means a high subjective probability of (1) attaining valued extrinsic rewards, (2) mastery of skill-demanding activity requiring that competence, and (3) fulfillment of a future self-image.

We are now also able to specify the conditions that will determine the extent to which an individual will be inhibited (resistant) to undertaking a test of competence: inhibition will be aroused when a completely valid and informative test of a highly valued competence is expected to indicate a substantial drop in the extent of possession of that competence. (These predictions apply for a positively valued attribute. A negatively valued attribute [e.g., stupidity] will arouse a tendency not to take the test so as not to find out one possesses more of the attribute than previously thought, and the test is perceived as a valid one; if a decrement in possession of a negatively valued attribute is expected, then less inhibition is expected to be aroused than when an increment in the perceived possession of a negatively valued attribute is expected to result.)

In short, the individual will be motivated to test a competence, other things equal, when that test is expected to result in a higher standing on that competence, but will be resistant to that test when it is expected to result in a lower standing on that competence. If we define these outcomes as "success" and "failure," respectively, with regard to competence testing, then the hypotheses reduce to the simple prediction that when a successful test of competence is anticipated the individual will be motivated to test the competence, but when failure in competence testing is anticipated the indivdual will be resistant to a test of the competence. If we define these outcomes as "demonstration of competence" and "demonstration of incompetence" (for anticipation of showing a higher level of competence than previously validated, and for anticipation of showing a lower level of competence than previously validated, respectively), then we can phrase the hypotheses in terms of motivation to demonstrate one's competence and motivation not to demonstrate one's incompetence.

It should be clear that we are not limiting the conceptual analysis to "formal" tests of a competence such as provided by a psychological testing service. Any perceived test of competence involving validity, information, and a valued competence should arouse motivation to undertake or not to undertake it, providing there is a previously obtained valid assessment of that competence that provides a basis for anticipated feedback concerning possible increments or decrements in possession of that competence.

We have considered the situation where the individual already has participated in a valid test of a competence so that this criterion of degree of possession of that competence serves as the level of past performance on a test of that competence to provide the point of comparison for anticipation of success or failure in the possible demonstration of an increase or decrease in possession of that competence. When no such standard of extent of possession is available, we expect that all individuals will be positively motivated to "discover" where they stand on extent of possession of a competence, to the extent that the competence is percieved to have positive value to the individual. When the individual has previously tested a valued competence but believes that the test was invalid, or less than completely valid, the individual will be motivated to undertake a (more) valid test of the competence. When the individual believes that the previous test was valid, but lacked diagnostic information concerning just how much of the competence is possessed, then the individual will be motivated to undertake a more informative test of the competence, other things equal. That is, we assume the individual is motivated to seek out information about the extent of possession of a competence that is valued (i.e., to know about oneself) until that individual obtains a valid test that is informative of the extent of possession of the competence. Then the individual will be motivated ot undertake tests of competence to the extent that a valid and informative test is expected to yield an increment in the possession of that competence, but will be resistant to undertake tests of competence to the extent that a valid and informative test is expected to yield a decrement in the possession of the competence.

IMPLICATIONS OF THE PRESENT CONCEPTION
OF COMPETENCE MOTIVATION

When previous information about one's level of competence is lacking, all individuals will be motivated to undertake a test of that competence to discover where they stand. "How good am I?" really means "How much of this ability do I possess?"

If previous information about one's level of competence is suspected of being invalid, or lacking in validity, all individuals will be motivated to undertake a more valid test of competence; the greater the expected increment in validity, the greater the motivation to undertake the test of competence.

If valid information about one's level of competence is believed to define one's level of possession of a particular competence, positive motivation to undertake a further assessment of that competence will vary directly with the expected increment in possession of competence that is believed will result from such new (valid) competence testing. Conversely, resistance to undertaking a further test of competence will vary directly with the expected decrement that is believed will result from such new (valid) competence testing. That is, an interaction is expected between the validity of a test of competence and the expected change in assessment of competence: the increment in perceived validity of a test should accentuate the motivation to undertake or to resist undertaking that test of competence. For tests whose validity is suspect, motivation to undertake or resist the test should be small, while for tests whose validity is accepted as maximal, motivation to undertake or to resist the test should be great.

The value of the competence to be assessed is assumed to interact with the degree of perceived validity of the test and the amount of change in assessed possession of the competence that is expected to result: for expected increments in competence, increases in perceived value of the competence and/or the perceived validity of the test should produce an increase in the motivation to undertake the competence testing; for expected decrements in competence, increases in perceived value of the competence and/or the perceived validity of the test should produce an increase in motivation to resist undertaking the competence testing.

The amount of information gain for an increment in competence is expected to be greatest for a test of competence that allows for a sequence of competence items starting with the easiest item, defining one's current level of competence, and gradually increasing item difficulty until the most difficult item defining the maximum level of competence. The amount of information gain for a decrement in competence is expected to be greatest for a test of competence that allows for a sequence of test items starting with the hardest item defining one's current level of competence and having a series of increasingly easier items, with the easiest item defining the minimum level of possession of the competence. These arrangements correspond to decreasing- and increasing-probability (noncontingent) paths, discussed in earlier work on achievement motivation (see chapter 2).

ASSESSMENT OF COMPETENCE VERSUS STRIVING
FOR CAREER SUCCESS AS GOALS
OF IMMEDIATE ACTIVITY

Contingent paths of a society involve the potential for both the assessment of relevant competences and the potential for career success or failure. The desire to demonstrate an increment in competence often conflicts with the desire to "stay in the ball game" to ensure progress toward career goals. If the above conception is correct, demonstrations of a substantial increment in competence can occur only for the range of tasks seen as relatively difficult for an individual, but earning the opportunity to move on is ensured only for immediate tasks that are seen as relatively easy. Thus we predict that motivation for career success for success-oriented ($M_S > M_{AF}$) individuals results in selection of relatively easy immediate tasks, with the expectation that after the individual has earned the chance to continue career striving, he or she will be faced with later challenges that provide for the chance to demonstrate an increment in competence. However, the choice of a more diagnostic test of competence too prematurely (before Ps is within the .9 to .6 range) may be less attractive than the choice of the easy immediate task, because earning the opportunity to continue may be more attractive than demonstrating an increment in competence. Thus, competence testing to increment one's perception of one's abilities may have to be separated entirely from career striving so as to continually ensure "staying in the ball game." When this occurs, the individual operates within a situation where ability is assumed constant and achievement motivation rather than competence motivation is the primary determinant of motivation for achievement. This should occur in contingent paths, where the value of the later steps in the path is seen as greater than the value of an increment in competence.

The implication of the above is that success-oriented individuals should prefer to evaluate their competences upward in decreasing-probability noncontingent-path situations, where discovery of the limits of one's increments in ability through a failure on some test of competence within the range where information about increments in competence is substantial will not also mean loss of the opportunity to pursue one's career goals.

On the other hand, the selection of immediate easy tasks for career striving might result in an immediate failure, which would not only signal loss of the opportunity to continue along the career path but also indicate a decrement in assessed competence. That is, selection of relatively easy tasks relative to one's own level of competence means that the threat of devaluation of one's competence is always present, should the unexpected failure on the presumed easy task occur. Thus, there is a double-barreled threat posed by failure in easy immediate tasks: loss of a valued competence and loss of the opportunity to try to attain one's career goals.

For individuals who have confidence in their continued upward demonstration of competence, the threat of devaluation of competence should not be present.

However, for individuals who lack confidence in their continuation of upward demonstrations of competence, and/or those who believe that they already have reached their level of "true" ability, and/or those who believe factors (such as increased age, lack of "practice," etc.) will result in loss of competences, this threat is a real one. In this case resistance to evaluation of competence might produce the choice of an increasing-probability contingent path (with a difficult immediate task), which pretty much guarantees loss of the opportunity for further career advancement, as preferable to the choice of the easy task, where a failure might signal loss of "what it takes" for career success. At least in the first instance the individual has preserved the self-image as a competent person while blaming failure on the fact that the individual (rather than others) was willing to take the difficult, risky venture.

The elaborated theory of achievement motivation predicts that motivation aroused by a long contingent path ($N = 7$ steps, for example) with $Ps = .9$ at each step along the contingent path should be greater than motivation aroused for a long contingent path ($N = 7$, for example) with decreasing-probability steps (see chapter 2). On the other hand, we expect that a decreasing-probability noncontingent path, if presented as a valid test of a valued competence, should provide far greater informational value because of the greater increment in competence expected as a result of successfully moving through the steps from the early easy ones to the more difficult intermediate ones to the later most difficult ones; but after the first success in the constant $Ps = .9$ path, no additional information concerning an increment in competence should be expected. Competence motivation predicts that individuals should prefer tests of competence constructed as decreasing-probability noncontingent paths rather than as constant-probability contingent paths with $Ps = .9$ at each step. In fact, many formal tests of ability are constructed as decreasing-probability noncontingent paths, where failure at one, two, or more successive items defines the person's level of ability. This arrangement provides the greatest potential for the diagnosis of degree of possession of the competence being assessed. On the other hand, positive motivation for career success in the contingent path is predicted to be greatest in a long contingent path was constant $Ps = .9$.

We do not see these predictions as mutually incompatible. One set applies to the evaluation of competences, or competence motivation. The other applies to the striving for career success, or achievement motivation. While it is true that individual differences in achievement-related motivation are always implicated when one actually performs on a task that can both assess competence and determine whether or not career striving can be continued, we believe that the two positions apply to conceptually different kinds of activity (competence testing vs. striving for success), and when both are aroused they will interact in the manner to be described so that their effects will depend upon the relative value given by the individual to assessment of competences (finding out about oneself) for self-esteem and the value of successful striving for attainment of future goals for self-esteem.

JOINT FUNCTIONING OF COMPETENCE MOTIVATION
AND ACHIEVEMENT MOTIVATION

For the entire range of a competence, the maximum information to be obtained is expected from a decreasing-probability noncontingent path, where tasks are perceived to be "easy" in the early steps, defining present level of ability, but are seen, right now, as of increasingly greater difficulty in later steps of the path (e.g., $Ps_1 = .9, Ps_2 = .7, Ps_3 = .5, Ps_4 = .3, Ps_5 = .1$). These represent the individual's estimates of the chances of success in meeting the requirements of good performance as the individual seees them, right now, when faced with the sequence of tasks.

For the individual who wants to test a competence, pursuit of this sequence as a noncontingent path should be expected to provide greatest information about the competence. The point at which the person fails can be expected to define the current level of competence, assuming the tasks are similar in substance and of equal perceived validity in assessing the particular competence in question. However, life striving often involves the imposition of standards of good performance that, in addition, determine whether the individual will be allowed to move on to the next step in a contingent path. According to elaborated theory, a sequence of tasks of equivalent length having $Ps = .9$ at each step should arouse greatest positive and negative achievement motivation.

How do we expect success-oriented individuals to react to the life situation where they desire to test their competence while still striving to earn the opportunity to continue to strive for long-term career success? The answer lies in the differences expected between individuals in terms of anticipated increments in a competence as a function of past experience.

Some individuals expect that they will increase their level of competence in a given area of skill. That is, when faced with the decreasing-probability path presented above, they believe that right now $Ps2 = .7$, but by the time they try, and then succeed and benefit from the experience, their Ps will be .9 rather than .7. Thus the individual's anticipated increment in ability creates a two-step path with $Ps_1 = .9$ and $Ps_2 = .9$, rather than a decreasing-probability path with $Ps_1 = .9$ and $Ps_2 = .7$. Note, however, that the absolute difficulty of the second task does not change. The second task remains one that is seen as "harder" in terms of the initial level of competence brought to the situation. Only the subjective probability of success has increased, contingent upon an increment in competence for that task. Thus, individuals expect to test their competence at a "higher level of absolute difficulty," but because of the anticipated increment in ability due to past practice and/or experience and/or success, they believe they are faced with a constant-probability contingent path of .9. Thus, both competence motivation and achievement motivation are maximized for success-oriented individuals who are faced with a decreasing-probability contingent path. The greater the anticipated increments dependent upon prior successful accomplishment, the greater the maximization of positive achievement motivation in this decreasing-Ps path; for individuals who believe successive increments to be certain, when they are faced with the competence testing defined by the decreasing-probability path, they are maximally attracted not only by competence motivation but also by achievement motivation: In absolute-Ps terms, they face the decreasing-probability path, but in subjective terms, given anticipated increments in competence, they face a constant-Ps (of .9) path of equivalent length.

COMPETENCE TESTING VERSUS EARNING
THE OPPORTUNITY TO CONTINUE

We feel that the integration of ideas about competence testing and achievement motivation move us substantially closer to a valid understanding of the determinants of motivation in skill-demanding activity and hence of motivation for achievement in life. However, we also believe that the ideas are not limited to skill-demanding activity per se, but are of much greater generality. Two sets of findings that have already been reported suggest this: (1) the fact that the elaborated theory was supported by data in a game of chance where immediate risk taking could influence the opportunity to place later bets in the game, and (2) the positive correlations obtained between self-possession, self-importance, and future-importance for the personality attribute, for example, called "popularity." These findings suggest that "guaranteeing the opportunity" to engage in later activity may be an important goal of more immediate activity, and the reason for its importance is that individuals may positively value the opportunity to strive per se. While this idea has not been developed here to any great extent, the concept of positive instrumental value may require separate conceptual treatment, independent of probabilities of success along a contingent path (see chapter 13, where this is in fact done).

12

Attribution to Success and Failure in Contingent and Noncontingent Paths

Elliot E. Entin and Norman T. Feather

A good deal of research has already examined how individuals make causal attributions for their successes and failures at tasks (Feather, 1969, 1977; Feather & Simon, 1971; Luginbuhl, Crowne, & Kahan, 1975; Simon & Feather, 1973; Weiner & Kukla, 1970; Wolosin, Sherman, & Till, 1973; Wortman, Costanzo, & Witt, 1973). Many of these studies suggest that people tend to view themselves as more personally responsible for their successes than for their failures, and to see their failures as caused by external factors (such as task difficulty or luck). As a rationale for such attributions, Miller (1976) has pointed out that, by denying responsibility for failure and taking credit for success, people can bolster and protect their egos or their self-esteem. The observed tendency for individuals to exhibit ego-enhancive behavior following success and ego-defensive behavior following failure has been referred to as the *ego-biasing* or *ego-defensive* mechanism (Larson, 1977).

Initial confidence is another variable that influences how individuals make attributions following success and failure. Feather (1969) showed that people were more likely to attribute success to their own ability when they were initially confident than when they were initially unconfident and when it could be assumed that their initial confidence was based upon their own past success at the task or similar tasks. Those individuals who experienced failure were more likely to attribute their failure to bad luck when their initial confidence was high than when their initial confidence was low. These findings were replicated by Feather and Simon (1971). Similar results were also reported when subjects' causal ascriptions for outcomes on a final examination were studied (Simon & Feather, 1973). Subjects who passed the final exam showed greater attributions to the internal factor, knowledge, when they were initially confident than when they were low in initial confidence. Those who failed to pass the final examination exhibited stronger attributions to lack of knowledge when initial confidence was low, and to bad luck when initial confidence was high. More recently, Feather (1977, p. 153) has argued that when expectancies that are grounded in considerable past experience are disconfirmed, there may be a tendency for individuals to interpret discrepant information as "particularized, variable 'noise in the system,' as exceptions to general rules, not likely to occur on a regular basis and hence insufficient to justify modification of causal schemata already established." Collectively, these contributions show the importance of an individual's confidence level to the manner in which ascriptions concerning success and failure are made.

Extending the attribution research to the study of achievement motivation, Weiner and Kukla (1970) speculated that, since a high achievement motive represents a heightened capacity to experience pride in the accomplishment of achievement-related goals, individuals in whom the achievement motive is relatively stronger than the motive to avoid failure ($M_S > M_{AF}$) might tend to appeal more to the internal attributions of ability or effort than would individuals in whom the motive to avoid failure is dominant. Failure, on the other hand, would probably be ascribed to low effort by $M_S > M_{AF}$ individuals. They further speculated that individuals in whom the motive to avoid failure is relatively stronger than the achievement motive ($M_{AF} > M_S$) have less capacity to experience pride in the attainment of achievement-related goals. Thus, $M_{AF} > M_S$ individuals would tend to attribute success to external factors, while ascribing failure to internal factors to a greater degree than $M_S > M_{AF}$ people.

Results reported by Weiner and Kukla (1970) are in partial support of these hypotheses. Individuals in whom $M_S > M_{AF}$, as assessed by Mehrabian's (1969) achievement motivation scale, were more likely to attribute success to the internal factors of ability and effort than were $M_{AF} > M_S$ individuals. There was little evidence, however, that $M_{AF} > M_S$ individuals make stronger internal attributions for failure than do $M_S > M_{AF}$ individuals. The results of a later study by Kukla (1972) were consistent with these findings. Meyer (1972), however, working with German high-school students, did find that $M_S > M_{AF}$ students ascribed success to high ability and failure to bad luck, while $M_{AF} > M_S$ students attributed success to good luck and failure to lack of ability. Further support for these latter findings was provided by Weiner, Heckhausen, Meyer, and Cook (1972).

At about the time researchers were linking achievement motivation and attribution theory, Raynor (1969, 1974a) offered an elaboration of the initial theory of achievement motivation to account for future orientation (see chapter 2). To operationalize further orientation, Raynor and Rubin (1971) introduced the concept of a contingent path. A path is said to be contingent when success is the necessary condition to proceed to the next step (task, activity, etc.) in the path and failure precludes any further activity. In contrast, a path is noncontingent when success and failure have no bearing on continuing in or leaving the path.

Raynor's elaborated theory specifies that a contingent path produces a future achievement-oriented component tendency for individuals high in Resultant Achievement Motivation (RAM; $M_S > M_{AF}$). This future-oriented tendency augments the initial achievement-oriented tendency aroused by the immediate situation, producing a larger total resultant achievement-oriented tendency to act in a contingent rather than a noncontingent path. For this reason, people high in RAM are expected to perform better in contingent than in noncontingent paths. In contrast, for individuals low in RAM ($M_{AF} > M_S$), a contingent path produces a future-oriented inhibitory tendency *not* to act. Individuals low in RAM are therefore expected to perform worse in contingent paths than in noncontingent paths, where the inhibitory tendency is lower.

A study by Raynor and Rubin (1971) supported these hypotheses. Individuals high in RAM performed more arithmetic problems correctly in a four-step contingent-path condition than in a four-step noncontingent-path condition, while individuals low in RAM showed the opposite pattern of results, performing more problems correctly in the noncontingent- than the contingent-path condition. Examining performance in the shortest possible contingent path, that of two steps, Entin and Raynor (1973) replicated the earlier findings.

The present investigation examined the attributions made to success and failure outcomes by individuals differing in achievement motivation in contingent and noncontingent paths. There are some theoretical ideas that can be appealed to in developing hypotheses about ways in which attributions may differ for high-RAM versus low-RAM individuals in contingent- versus noncontingent-path conditions. As we shall see, these approaches fall into two main classes: those that involve various forms of motivational bias consistent with self-identity, and those that consider the effects of confirming and disconfirming cognitive expectancies built on the basis of past experience. Considering the first of these two approaches, the studies of Weiner and Kukla (1970) and Meyer (1972) suggest that high-RAM individuals may employ more ego-biasing strategies than low-RAM people. In these studies high-RAM individuals consistently took internal credit for their successes. Sometimes they attributed their failures to the internal but unstable factor, lack of effort, implying that one merely had to expend the necessary effort and success would occur. In other words, they retained control over the situation. Sometimes, failure was attributed externally to task difficulty. The implication here is that since many others also failed at this task, the cause of failure was not located within themselves. In this manner, high-RAM individuals were able to protect their positive self-image or ego after both success and failure.

Low-RAM people did not do nearly as well at protecting their ego or maintaining their self-esteem. They did not always take internal credit for their successes and sometimes blamed failure on their lack of ability, a very debasing personal ascription.

It should be noted that another interpretation of these attributional differences might be that high-RAM subjects may have had relatively more successes in the past at the task they were undertaking, or at similar tasks, than the low-RAM subjects. Hence, they may have been more likely to attribute successes to ability and effort, and failures to outside factors, than the low-RAM subjects. This information-processing interpretation is a valid alternative to an interpretation that appeals to self-serving biases in attribution (Miller & Ross, 1975).

What patterns of attribution might one expect to find in relation to contingent and noncontingent path differences? One way to approach this question is in terms of self-serving biases; another way is in terms of differences in a person's past experience at the task or at similar tasks. Let us speculate first about the possibility of self-serving biases. According to Raynor's (1969, 1974a) analysis, a contingent path that draws attention to the present and future implications of task performance will be associated with intensification of both approach and inhibitory motivational forces relating to success and failure. An important reason for this intensification is that individuals have more at stake and more to lose in a contingent than in a non-contingent path. This is so because success (or failure) in a contingent path not only means gain (or loss) of immediate achievement incentives, but possible gain (or loss) of future achievement incentives as well. Such conditions might serve to intensify th ego-biasing tendencies of individuals. Thus, it might be expected that high-RAM individuals will show a stronger tendency to take internal credit for their success in a contingent- than in a noncontingent-path situation and to ascribe their success more to effort and ability in the contingent-path situation. In the case of failure in a contingent path, however, increased effort is no longer an option because the individual is no longer in the path—moving on to the next step in the path is contingent upon success, and failure terminates the performance. One might therefore expect that appeals to lack of effort, which might be found following failure in the noncontingent-path condition for the high-RAM individual, would be replaced in the contingent-path condition with ego-protective external attributions that appeal either to task difficulty or to bad luck.

For individuals low in RAM, it is assumed that tendencies not to perform an achievement task will be relatively strong, especially when this task involves a contingent path with future implications. Given these strong inhibitory forces in contingent-path situations for low-RAM individuals, it might be expected that when these low-RAM individuals succeed in contingent tasks they may tend to attribute their success externally to such factors as good luck or an easy task. Such attributions may be less likely in a noncontingent-path situation, where the inhibitory forces are not as strong. In a contingent-path situation, where inhibition is stronger, there may be a stronger tendency for low-RAM individuals to attribute their failures to such factors as lack of ability. In these ways low-RAM individuals, with a low opinion of their abilities and achievement potentialities, may protect their relatively low self-image.

These hypotheses, based upon a rudimentary analysis in terms of ego-biasing strategies, are somewhat speculative. They appeal more to motivational biases than to cognitive, informational variables. It is possible, however, to develop hypotheses from a *cognitive expectancy* viewpoint by considering the effects of an individual's past experience in contingent- and noncontingent-path situations. The evidence suggests that high-RAM individuals tend to perform better in contingent than in noncontingent task situations, whereas low-RAM individuals do better in noncontigent task situations than in task situations that have future implications. Given this difference, one might expect high-RAM individuals to have higher expectations of success in contingent task situations than low-RAM individuals—expectations that are grounded in consistent differences in past performance across contingent task situations between the two motive groups. From Feather's (1977) assumption that disconfirmation of expectancies will tend to be attributed to variable factors such as luck or other "noise in the system" when these expectancies are based upon consistent past performance across a range of tasks, it follows that success for low-RAM individuals may tend to be attributed to good luck and that failure for the high-RAM individuals may tend to be attributed to bad luck, when the task situation involves a contingent path with its future implications. The low-RAM individuals have relatively lower expectancies of success in the contingent-path condition, and success disconfirms these expectations. The high-RAM individuals have relatively higher expectancies in the contingent-path condition, and failure disconfirms these expectations.

The evidence about performance differences also suggests that low-RAM individuals may have higher expectations of success in noncontingent task situations than in contingent task situations. Again, using Feather's (1977) assumption, one might expect that low-RAM individuals may be more likely to attribute failure to bad luck in a noncontingent situation than in a contingent situation, because failure would be more likely to disconfirm their expectancies in the former situation. High-RAM individuals, on the other hand, with better performance in contingent situations, may be more likely to attribute success to good luck in noncontingent task situations than in contingent task situations, because success would be more likely to disconfirm their expectancies in the former situation. These hypotheses follow from an information-processing model that identifies disconfirmation of personally based expectancies as a basic variable influencing the tendency to make attributions to *variable* causal factors (Feather, 1977).

It should be evident, therefore, that one can develop hypotheses about causal attributions in contingent and noncontingent task situations from both motivational biasing and cognitive expectancy perspective. Let us now describe a study that provides some evidence that relates to these hypotheses.

METHOD

Subjects

All subjects were volunteers from the first-year psychology pool at Ohio University. Participation in experiments earns for the students credit points that can augment their grade. Complete data were available for 163 males.

Assessment of Motives

In group settings, all subjects completed the projective measure for the achievement motive (McClelland, Atkinson, Clark, & Lowell, 1953) and the Test Anxiety Questionnaire (TAQ) (Mandler & Sarason, 1952). Both were administered under neutral conditions and scored according to the pertinent literature concerning each (Atkinson, 1958, app. III; Mandler & Sarason, 1952). In the administration of the achievement motive measure, sentence leads were employed instead of the usual picture cues (see Entin & Raynor, 1973). Sentence leads have been shown to be equivalent to picture cues in eliciting achievement imagery (Entin, 1973). Only the first third of the TAQ, consisting of 12 items and 3 fillers, was used. It correlates between .84 and .90 with the total score (see Smith, 1964). The *n* Achievement scores were coded by one of the authors (E.E.E.) whose correlation with another expert has been established at .90.

To arrive at the Resultant Achievement Motivation Score (RAM), each motive's distribution was standardized, and then the standard score for TAQ was subtracted from the standard score for n Achievement (see Atkinson & Feather, 1966, p. 304). The resulting distribution was split about the median. Subjects in the top half were considered high in RAM ($M_S > M_{AF}$). Those in the bottom half were considered low in RAM ($M_{AF} > M_S$). The mean for the n Achievement distribution was 2.99 with a standard deviation of 3.43, and the mean for the TAQ distribution was 35.30 with a standard deviation of 8.72. The product moment correlation between n Achievement and TAQ score was .06 ($N = 163$, n.s.). This relationship was expected and is seen as consistent with the assumed independence of the two motives (see Atkinson & Feather, 1966, p. 341).

Performance Task

The task consisted of Lowell's (1952) four-letter anagrams. The anagrams were arranged 30 to the page, and each booklet contained four pages of anagrams. A blank sheet separated each test page of anagrams in the booklet. The subjects' task was to unscramble the letters of each anagram to make a meaningful English word.

Attribution Assessment

The materials devised by Feather and Simon (1971) were employed to assess causal attributions following success or failure at the task. The scales and their instructions comprised the attribution questionnaire. Subjects who experienced success at the task were directed to instructions concerning attributions for success, and they were asked to rate on each of four 10-point scales how important they thought low test difficulty, hard work, good luck, and possessed ability were as causes of their success. Those who experienced failure at the task were directed to instructions concerning attributions for failure and they were asked to rate on each of four 10-point scales how important they considered test difficulty, lack of hard work, bad luck, and lack of ability as causes of their failure. In addition, all subjects rated how satisfied they were with their performance on the test, using a 10-point scale.

Procedure

After completing the motive measures, subjects were given the test booklets and an instruction sheet containing the particular path instructions for that experimental session. The instructions were also read aloud as the subjects read silently. Instructions for the *noncontingent* path conditions were:

> The test booklet has been devised to test verbal ability. The test should represent a *moderately difficult* task. That is, a 50/50 chance of success for students of your age and ability.
> Each booklet contains four tests and each test is comprised of *30* separate anagrams or scrambled word problems. The problems on each test have been preselected to give you a 50/50 chance of solving *13* anagrams correctly in *2 minutes*. Later tests have been

adjusted for practice and learning effects to maintain this 50% level of difficulty on each of the four tests.

This estimate of your chances of success is based on a computer analysis of the performance of a large sample of students who have already taken these tests at this and other universities. Further work has confirmed the validity of the estimates. That is, approximately 50% of the respondents were able to solve *13* anagrams correctly in 2 minutes on each test.

You will also have 2 minutes to work on each test. To be considered successful you must solve *13* anagrams correctly for each test. Regardless if you succeed or fail, you will be given an opportunity to work on each of the four tests.

Those in the contingent-path condition read and heard the first three paragraphs of the noncontingent instructions. The fourth paragraph of the contingent instructions was as follows:

> You will also have 2 minutes to work on each test. The opportunity to take the next test in the series depends on how well you do on the previous test. In other words, in order to take Test 2, you must have solved 13 anagrams on Test 1 in 2 minutes. Similarly, in order to take Tests 3 and 4, you must have solved 13 anagrams on the test which came before them. If you fail to solve 13 anagrams on any test, you have failed and cannot continue on to the next test. Instead, you will remain in your seat until the end of the test period.

All subjects were then given instructions and practice on performing the anagrams. Just prior to doing the first test, all the respondents completed a mood-adjective checklist to assess achievement-related affect. This took about 5 min to complete. A reiteration of the particular induction instructions followed, and then all subjects were given 2 min to work on Test 1. Past work with this task showed that, on the average, about half the people could solve 13 problems in 2 min and, in fact, the mean number of anagrams attempted by subjects in this study was 13.80 with a standard deviation of 5.75. Also, as expected, the number of anagrams attempted was highly correlated with the number of anagrams correctly solved ($r = .93, p < .01$).

Immediately after completing Test 1, the subjects were asked to count up the number of anagrams they attempted and write that number at the bottom of the page. Subjects were told that if the number of anagrams they attempted was equal to or greater than 13 they had succeeded, and if it was less than 13 they had failed. They were then asked to turn to the attribution questionnaire and locate the appropriate instructions and scales. If they had succeeded they were to turn to the first page of the questionnaire (titled "Instructions for Students who Passed the Test"), read the instructions, and answer the four items at the bottom of the page. If they had failed they were to turn to the third page of the questionnaire (titled "Instructions for Students who Failed the Test"), read the instructions, and answer the four items at the bottom of the page. After all subjects completed the attribution questionnaire, the experiment was terminated and the students were debriefed.

Four testing situations were conducted in ABBA design, starting and ending with the noncontingent-path condition.

RESULTS

Preliminary analyses were performed to check if the testing sessions within experimental conditions were equivalent with respect to the independent and dependent variables. One-way analyses of variance were performed comparing the two testing-session means within the noncontingent-path condition for n Achievement, test anxiety, Resultant Achievement Motivation, number of anagrams attempted, number of anagrams correct, and the four attribution variables. A similar set of analyses was computed for the two testing sessions within the contingent-path condition. Seventeen of the 18 ANOVAs were nonsignificant. The only exception was a tendency for students in the second of the two testing sessions within the noncontingent-path condition to attempt more anagrams than those in the first session ($F = 3.73$, $df = 1/82$, $p < .06$). Given the overwhelming pattern of no difference, the two testing sessions within each experimental condition were considered homogeneous.

One-way ANOVAs were also performed comparing all independent variables (i.e., n Achievement score, test anxiety, and Resultant Achievement Motivation) between the noncontingent- and contingent-path experimental conditions. None of the analyses yielded statistically significant differences in means. Thus it was assumed that the students in the two experimental conditions did not differ on any of the motivational variables.

Performance Results

The elaborated theory of Raynor (1969, 1974a) predicts an interaction between Resultant Achievement Motivation and path condition. Specifically, it was hypothesized that students high in RAM could attempt and correctly solve more anagrams in the contingent- than in the noncontingent-path condition, while those low in RAM would show an opposite tendency, attempting and correctly solving more anagrams in the noncontingent- than in the contingent-path condition. Table 1 shows mean patterns in accord with these hypotheses. The ANOVAs, presented in Table 2, show significant interactions for both number of anagrams attempted ($F = 7.47$, $df = 1/159$, $p < .01$) and number of anagrams solved correctly ($F = 7.12$, $df = 1/159$, $p < .01$). There is little doubt that achievement motivation was aroused and the inductions were effective.

Table 1 Number of Anagrams Attempted and Solved Correctly as a Function of Resultant Achievement Motivation and Path

Resultant Achievement Motivation	Noncontingent path			Contingent path		
	N	Attempted	Correct	N	Attempted	Correct
High	42	10.95	9.40	39	14.62	13.05
Low	42	15.40	13.95	40	14.33	12.63

Table 2 Analysis of Variance for Number of Anagrams Attempted and Correct

| | | Attempted | | Correct | |
Source	df	Mean square	F	Mean square	F
Resultant Achievement Motivation	1	190.47	6.22*	187.38	5.30**
Paths .	1	66.30	2.16	53.22	1.50
Interaction	1	228.92	7.47**	251.78	7.12**
Error	159				

*$p < .02$.
**$p < .01$.

Attribution Results

The attribution measures were analyzed using a $2 \times 2 \times 2 \times 4$ analysis of variance design, with path (contingent, noncontingent), RAM (high, low), outcome (success, failure), and type of attribution (task difficulty, effort, luck, ability) as the four factors in the design. Type of attribution was a repeated measure (within-subject) factor. Table 3 shows the mean attributions by path, RAM, and outcome. Table 4 presents the analysis of variance. It can be seen from these tables that luck was seen as the least important cause of outcome. Effort was the most important cause, closely followed in importance by ability and task difficulty (F for within-subject main effect = 13.83, $df = 3/459$, $p < .001$). Table 4 also shows a type of attribution $\times$ outcome interaction ($F = 7.55$, $df = 3/459$, $p < .001$). The graphical

Table 3 Mean Attribution Ratings for Task Difficulty, Effort, Luck, and Ability as a Function of Resultant Achievement Motivation, Path, and Outcome

| | Attribution ratings | | | | | | | |
| Resultant Achievement Motivation and outcome | Noncontingent path | | | | Contingent path | | | |
	Task difficulty	Effort	Luck	Ability	Task difficulty	Effort	Luck	Ability
High								
Success	5.40	6.53	4.13	6.07	5.88	6.75	3.83	6.71
	(15)	(15)	(15)	(15)	(24)	(24)	(24)	(24)
Failure	4.33	4.26	3.37	3.56	4.20	3.67	4.07	3.07
	(27)	(27)	(27)	(27)	(15)	(15)	(15)	(15)
Low								
Success	5.85	6.31	3.23	6.73	5.19	7.19	4.41	5.85
	(26)	(26)	(26)	(26)	(27)	(27)	(27)	(27)
Failure	4.13	5.19	4.00	4.56	5.31	3.54	2.92	4.15
	(16)	(16)	(16)	(16)	(13)	(13)	(13)	(13)

Note. N for each condition is shown in parenthesis. The higher the rating, the more the factor was seen as a cause of outcome.

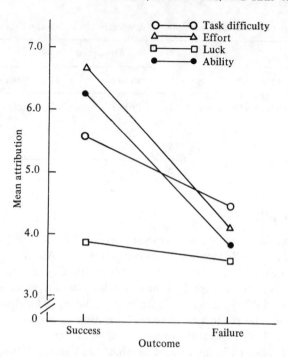

Figure 1 Mean attribution for task difficulty, effort, luck,
and ability as a function of outcome.

representation of these results in Figure 1 reveals that success tended to be attributed to the internal factors of effort and ability, whereas failure was attributed to task difficulty. These results replicate those presented by Frieze and Weiner (1971, p. 596).

Attributions made to success and failure within the noncontingent- and contingent-path conditions are shown in Figure 2. The mean attributions relating to success were about the same in both experimental conditions. Failure, however, tended to be attributed to lack of effort more in the noncontingent-path condition than in the contingent-path condition ($t = 1.66$, $df = 459$, $p < .10$), while task difficulty was seen as a more important cause of failure in the contingent-path condition than in the noncontingent-path condition ($t = 2.23$, $df = 459$, $p < .05$). It should also be noted that lack of effort was not seen as an important cause of failure in the contingent-path condition and was not appealed to more than lack of ability or bad luck.

Table 4 also shows a significant four-way interaction ($F = 3.02$, $df = 3/459$, $p < .03$). Figure 3 depicts the significant path X RAM X outcome X type of attribution interaction. It can be seen that in each path success tended to be ascribed to the internal factors of effort and ability by both motive groups. However, the attributions to failure were varied. High-RAM individuals tended to ascribe failure more to task difficulty and lack of effort than to the other factors in the noncontingent-path condition, while attributing failure more to task difficulty and bad luck than to lack of effort or lack of ability in the contingent-path condition. Individuals low in RAM saw low effort as the most important cause of failure in the noncontingent-path condition, and task difficulty as the most important cause of failure in the contingent-path condition. Furthermore, lack of effort was seen as a less important cause of failure than task difficulty or lack of ability in the contingent-path condition for low-RAM individuals. One further point to note is that high-RAM individuals saw luck as a more important cause of success than of failure in the noncontingent-path condition, but as a less important cause of success than of failure in the contingent-path condition. Individuals low in RAM showed the opposite pattern. They saw luck as a less important cause of success than of failure in the noncontingent-path condition, but as a more important cause of success than of failure in the contingent-path condition.

The four attribution variables—task difficulty, effort, luck, and ability—were each subjected to a RAM (2) × path (2) × outcome (2) ANOVA. The results of these ANOVAs are summarized in Table 5. They indicate that only the main effect of outcome yielded significant effects for task difficulty ($F = 8.73, df = 1/155$, p < .0001). In each case the mean attributions were higher in the success than in the failure conditions. Table 5 also shows a significant path × outcome interaction for effort ($F = 3.72, df = 1/153, p < .05$). Inspection of the means for effort (see Table 3) reveals that success was ascribed to effort more in the contingent- than in the noncontingent-path condition while failure was attributed to lack of effort more in the noncontingent- than in the contingent-path condition.

Table 4   Summary of Analysis of Variance of Attribution Factors

Source	df	MS	F
Between subjects			
Path (A)	1	.81	< 1
Outcome (B)	1	376.53	64.84**
RAM (C)	1	5.16	< 1
A × B	1	8.21	1.41
A × C	1	1.67	< 1
B × C	1	7.43	1.28
A × B × C	1	.80	< 1
Error between	155	5.81	
Within subjects			
Type of attribution (D)	3	82.49	13.83**
A × D	3	2.72	< 1
B × D	3	45.04	7.55**
C × D	3	2.80	< 1
A × B × D	3	7.67	1.29
A × C × D	3	1.08	< 1
B × C × D	3	2.81	< 1
A × B × C × D	3	17.98	3.02*
Error within	459	5.96	

*p < .03.
**p < .001.

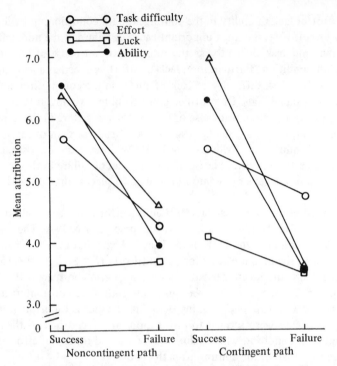

Figure 2 Mean attribution for task difficulty, effort, luck, and
ability as a function of path and outcome.

One further finding: The RAM × path × outcome interaction was significant for
luck ($F = 3.68$, $df = 1/155$, $p < .05$). Figure 4 shows that for the contingent-path
condition, subjects high in RAM made stronger attributions to bad luck when they
failed than to good luck when they succeeded, while low-RAM subjects saw good
luck as more of a cause of their success than bad luck was a cause of their failure.
In the noncontingent-path condition, the pattern of means was reversed: Subjects
high in RAM saw good luck as a more important cause of their success than bad
luck as a cause of their failure, while low-RAM subjects made stronger attributions
to bad luck when they failed than to good luck when they succeeded.

One final analysis was performed to permit comparisons with results presented
by Meyer (1972). An ability minus luck variable was derived by simply subtracting
the luck score from the ability score for each subject. Thus, the higher (more
positive) the number, the greater the attribution to ability than to luck; the lower
the number, the greater the attribution to luck than to ability. In an ANOVA involving the three factors RAM, path, and outcome, a three-way interaction was
found ($F = 4.31$, $df = 1/155$, $p < .04$). Figure 5 shows that individuals high in RAM
attributed success more to ability than luck in the contingent- than in the noncontingent-path condition, while failure was ascribed more to bad luck than low ability
in the contingent- than in noncontingent-path condition. In contrast, low-RAM subjects saw ability more as a cause of their success than good luck in the noncontin-
gent- than in the contingent-path condition, while lack of ability was seen as a more

important cause of their failure than bad luck in the contingent- than in the non-contingent-path condition.

DISCUSSION

The RAM × path interaction for the performance variables attests to the fact that the path inductions were effective and that the performance outcomes were consistent with predictions derived from the elaborated achievement motivation theory. These results bolster the general validity of Raynor's elaborated theory (1969) and validate the assumption that we are viewing attributions in aroused contingent and noncontingent achievement-oriented paths.

The general attribution results show, as expected, that people appealed more to the internal factors of ability and effort as causes of successful performance than as causes of unsuccessful performance (failure). Failure, on the other hand, tended to be ascribed externally to task difficulty. These results parallel those reported by

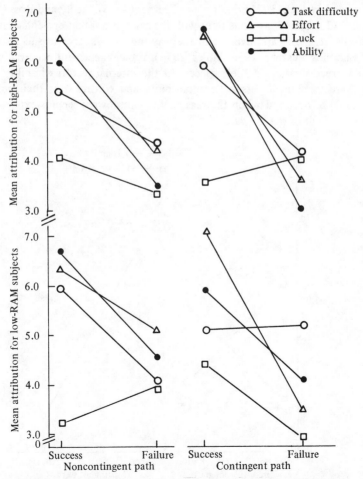

Figure 3   Mean attributions for task difficulty, effort, luck, and ability as a function of RAM, path, and outcome.

Table 5   Analyses of Variance of Attribution Scores

		F values			
Source	df	Task difficulty	Effort	Luck	Ability
Resultant achievement					
Motivation (A)	1/155	.18	.37	.27	1.60
Path (B)	1/155	.55	.60	.76	.12
Outcome (C)	1/155	8.73**	38.20**	.44	48.26**
A × B	1/155	.45	.27	.03	4.36*
A × C	1/155	.34	.06	.00	1.52
B × C	1/155	.71	3.84*	.68	.11
A × B × C	1/155	2.31	1.22	3.68*	.77

*p < .05.
**p < .01.

Frieze and Weiner (1971), Simon and Feather (1973), Sicoly and Ross (1977), and Bradley (1978) and are consistent with the assumption that ego-enhancive and ego-defensive strategies are involved in the way individuals react to success and failure (see Simon & Feather, 1973; Miller, 1976). Ego enhancement occurred when those who succeeded ascribed their success to the internal factors of ability and effort and thereby retained personal responsibility and control over their performance. Ego defense occurred when the reasons for failure were seen as externally caused and not a fault of the individual.

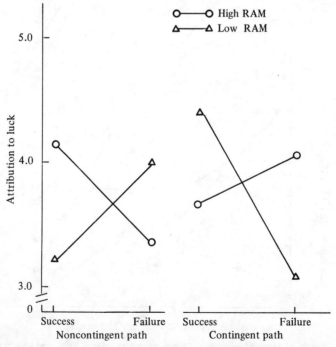

Figure 4 Attribution to luck as a function of RAM, path, and outcome.

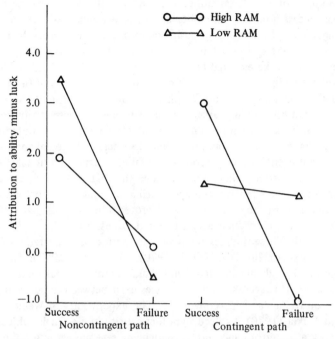

Figure 5 Attribution to ability minus luck as a function of RAM, path, and outcome.

The attribution patterns within the contingent- and noncontingent-path conditions showed that path type differentially affected failure attributions but had little effect on success attributions. In the noncontingent-path condition, subjects tended to rate lack of effort as the most important cause of failure, while in the contingent-path condition ratings tended to be highest for task difficulty as a cause of failure. It appears that the contingent-path condition, with its implication for the future, elicited greater ego-defensive attributions.

An important finding of this study, summarized in Figure 3, shows that path, RAM, outcome, and type of attribution had significant interactive effects on subjects' attribution ratings. Surprisingly, few differences appeared in the way the two different motive groups made attributions for success. Nor was there any evidence that path alone had any effect on how high- or low-RAM people ascribed success. What did appear were the differences related to the way subjects attributed causes for failure, and these differences were complex, as indicated by the significant interaction effect just noted.

In general, individuals high in RAM tended to provide higher attribution ratings to ability in the contingent- than in the noncontingent-path condition (see Figure 3). Effort was seen as a relatively important cause of success in both the contingent- and noncontingent-path conditions by the same motive group. Failure, however, was attributed equally to task difficulty and lack of effort in the noncontingent-path condition, and task difficulty and luck were rated as about equally important causes of failure in the contingent-path condition.

These results for high-RAM subjects fit nicely with the ego-biasing hypothesis. Attributing success internally to ability and/or effort enhanced the ego posture of these subjects. In the contingent-path condition, where success had additional meaning, success was attributed to the ego-enhancing factors, ability and effort. Failure tended to evoke external attributions to task difficulty and bad luck. When success was not so important and failure not so threatening to self (a situation that existed in the noncontingent-path condition), subjects high in RAM appealed to lack of effort but *not* bad luck as a cause of their failure. These attributional differences may be seen as an attempt to maintain personal control over outcomes, in the sense that a change in effort could bring about success and ego enhancement. However, in the contingent-path condition, where failure carried additional meaning and additional negative affect, there was evidence that high-RAM subjects were more likely to resort to ego-defensive strategies, such as blaming failure on bad luck.

The attributions of subjects low in RAM proved a bit more difficult to interpret. Unexpectedly, these individuals also attributed success internally, and this was true regardless of path. These findings are at variance with those reported by Weiner and Kukla (1970, experiment IV), Kukla (1970), and Meyer (1972). The results of these studies indicated that low-RAM individuals tended to make external attributions for success. However, several differences exist between the present study and the studies of Weiner and his co-workers. The experiments of Weiner and Kukla (1970) and Kukla (1970) involved hypothetical situations. Their subjects did not actually work at a performance task experiencing real success and failure. Rather, they were asked to *imagine* situations involving success and failure and to make attributions accordingly. Furthermore, both these studies and Kukla (1972) employed Mehrabian's (1969) measure of Resultant Achievement Motivation and not the traditional projective measure of need achievement (McClelland et al., 1953) and the Test Anxiety Questionnaire (Mandler & Sarason, 1952). In the Meyer (1970) study, students actually did perform a task and then made attributions about the causes of their outcomes. However, the pertinent results from Meyer's study, which led to the argument that low-RAM individuals tend to make external attributions for success, were based upon attributions made to ability and luck only. It is difficult to know how the attribution pattern would have looked if Meyer's subjects had had the opportunity to rate all four attribution factors for importance, as was the case in the present study. The results of the ability-luck analysis in the present study revealed that the pattern of attributions in the contingent-path condition matched that reported by Meyer. Success was ascribed more to ability than to good luck by high-RAM as opposed to low-RAM individuals (see Figure 5). Failure, however, was ascribed more to bad luck than to lack of ability by high-RAM than by low-RAM individuals. Results in the noncontingent path were in the opposite direction and at variance with the Meyer (1970) findings. Low-RAM individuals attributed success more to ability than to good luck, and they attributed failure more to bad luck than to lack of ability when compared with high-RAM subjects.

The results therefore suggest that low-RAM individuals tended to attribute failure more internally to lack of effort and lack of ability in the noncontingent-path condition than in the contingent-path condition. In the contingent-path condition, subjects low in RAM ascribed their failure primarily to task difficulty. The internal attribution of failure to lack of ability (observed in the noncontingent-path condition) by these low-RAM subjects is in line with the argument that low-RAM individuals have a low opinion of their abilities. It also parallels the hypothesis advanced by Weiner and Kukla (1970) and Kukla (1970) that, ". . . the individual low in resultant achievement concerns is believed to assume the blame for failure, while denying himself the luxury of personal praise for success" (Weiner and Kukla, 1970, p. 9). However, the results concerning the effort attributions are not consistent with such a hypothesis. Failure attributions to the internal unstable factor, lack of effort, implies a willingness to stay with the achievement-oriented task and strive for success, something not thought to be within the province of low-RAM individuals (see Atkinson & Feather, 1966). It is also interesting to note that attributions to lack of ability and lack of effort were more evident in the less stressful noncontingent-path condition. In the more inhibiting contingent-path condition, low-RAM individuals tended to ascribe failure externally to task difficulty—an ego-defensive posture. It might be that when a path is less inhibiting and threatening (as it is when the path is noncontingent), ego-defensive strategies are less in evidence and it is more likely that subjects will attribute failure to lack of ability and to lack of effort, thereby showing a willingness to admit their deficiencies. Furthermore, this appears to be true for individuals both high and low in RAM.

Other Results

The path X outcome results follow more or less directly from statements concerning the differences between contingent and noncontingent paths. To stay in a contingent path, one must succeed at the immediate task and continue to succeed at each succeeding step in the path. Thus, it is not surprising to find that individuals working in the contingent-path condition saw effort as a relatively important cause of their success and lack of effort as a relatively unimportant cause of their failure (see Figure 3). One may have to try harder when the opportunity to continue at the task depends on successfully meeting the criteria at each step of a contingent path. Effort should therefore be seen as a more important cause of success in this condition, and lack of effort as an unlikely cause of failure.

Why individuals who failed made stronger attributions to lack of effort in the noncontingent-path condition than in the contingent-path condition is a little more difficult to explain. One possible explanation could be that subjects in the noncontingent-path conditions argued that "whether I succeed or fail in a noncontingent path does not matter; thus I probably did not try hard and that is why I failed." This argument is consistent with the previous assumption that subjects may perceive that they have to try harder in contingent- than in noncontingent-path conditions. Effort thus becomes a more salient factor in relation to outcome.

Expectation Interpretation

The three-way interaction of RAM, path, and outcome for the luck factor may also reflect the effects of disconfirmation of expectancies of success (see earlier discussion). High-RAM subjects with relatively better past performance in contingent-path situations than low-RAM subjects may have higher expectations of success in these situations. Hence failure would be more likely to be unexpected for them and attributed to bad luck or to other particularized, variable factors (Feather, 1977). Success, on the other hand, would be relatively more unexpected for low-RAM subjects in contingent task situations than for high-RAM subjects, and so more likely to be attributed to good luck. Precisely the same argument can be applied to the results for the noncontingent task condition where low-RAM subjects may be assumed to perform relatively better and to have higher expectations of success than they would have under contingent task conditions. In this case, failure disconfirms a high expectation held by low-RAM subjects and so would be attributed to bad luck or other variable factors, while success would disconfirm a lower expectation held by high-RAM subjects and so would be attributed to good luck or other variable factors.

IV

MOTIVATION
AND AGING

In this last part we address the problem of the relationship between motivation and aging. The initial impetus for the application of the theory of motivation to issues concerning change over time came from our analysis of motivation for successive new first steps of a contingent path as a function of success (see chapter 2). A reading of Sheehy's (1974) *Passages: The Predictable Crises of Adult Life* suggested that the phenomenon she had identified concerning midcareer crises of successful individuals could be derived from the same implications of the theory used to derive the Lehman (1953) and Veroff, Atkinson, Feld, and Gurin (1960) data for creative contributions—n Achievement score as a function of age (chapter 2, Figures 14 to 16). We did not feel that Sheehy's use of Erickson's (1963) stage theory of development and change was an adequate account, using as it does fear of death, an invariant sequence of "passages" that have to be successfully resolved before the next one can be dealt with, and an inevitable shift in concern about oneself to a concern about the next generation. It seemed worthwhile to try to develop an alternative conception based on expectancy × value theory of achievement motivation, given our more limited success in dealing with motivation and aging as successful movement along a contingent life path. That effort, presented in chapter 13 as a general theory of personality functioning and change (or, described differently, a motivational theory of adult development and aging), soon went beyond existing theory in an attempt to account for both the emerging discrepancies between theory and data in research on future orientation, self-evaluation, and achievement motivation and as wide a range of phenomena as possible from a systematic point of view. The resulting confluence of several different threads of conceptual arguments, empirical findings, and suggestive new directions is reviewed in fair detail, as is the status of the resulting assumptions. Thus the background for the newer ideas can be seen as it evolved from dealings with the material presented in earlier parts of this volume.

A new direction for the theory of achievement motivation concerns our integration of it with theory concerning the self—self-identity, self-image, self-evaluation, and self-esteem. We have borrowed from and wish to acknowledge our intellectual debt to the writings of Maslow (1970) and Rogers (1959). However, we found that, in general, self-theory lacked precision, specification, and appropriate operational definitions as it existed within the "humanistic framework." Thus we have taken the liberty to redefine terms within an expectancy X value theory so that the important insights offerred by the self-theoretic approach can be integrated with the more research-oriented and empirically based conceptions that have evolved in the experimental analysis of human motivation. The integration has offered us new insights that are exciting. The newer theory not only allows us to deal with several previously unresolved issues, but opens up horizons for motivational analysis of behavior that the more limited conception could not make contact with.

Of particular note is our attempt to go beyond theory and research on achievement motivation to a general theory of personality that can be applied to any substantive area of activity. Science progresses from the specific to the general in terms of theory construction. Specific insights gained from research on achievement motivation are sufficiently well established so as to make the transition to more general concerns a reasonable and worthwhile enterprise. We are particularly encouraged by the consistency with which, for example, our conception of positive and negative psychological career striving and the Masters and Johnson (1970) understanding of human sexual functioning and dysfunction converge on fears of performance producing inhibition for action, the idea of a personal value system for unique arousal of motivation for a particular individual, and the role of evaluation of performance in change from intrinsic factors (the primary sensate focus) to difficulty and instrumental factors as a determinant of sexual functioning. There are many other instances of the convergence of our ideas with others. The most significant, we believe, concerns the work of Johnson (1973) and his colleagues concerning the understanding of the development and functioning of the psychological career commonly known as alcoholism. We make explicit use of Johnson's insights in linking the expectancy X value theory of personality and action to the psychodynamic theory of psychological defenses.

We have tried to be as precise in our assumptions as logic and the meager data that are currently available allow at the moment. However, we have avoided what we feel to be premature specification of a mathematical model in the absence of data bearing on many unresolved issues. We are particularly in need of data concerned with the predicted effects of the *retrospected past* on present self-esteem, self-identity, and motivation of immediate behavior. We do not know, for example, whether value alone, or the product of value and expectancy, influences action when maintenance of the values of past success is at stake through immediate action. Here the logic of theory is assumed, but in the absence of at least one well-controlled experimental study, we prefer to state the generalized hypothesis, which is sufficient to generate some directional hypotheses that can be tested, rather than formulate a precise model that would be based on sheer speculation. On the other hand, the mathematical equations of the elaborated theory of achievement motivation, which concern the *anticipated future*, are taken as well founded enough in previous research to be worth taking seriously as a theory about "becoming" within the context of the newer theory. Thus, in some areas we are left with less precision than we desire, but will allow criticism on this point at this stage of our knowledge rather than the criticism of premature specification and the generation of hypothesis testing that is bound to disconfirm expectations and cast doubt on the entire enterprise in an unwarranted manner. The next cycle in our work must involve the collection of empirical data guided by the general hypotheses we can now derive, and the use of those data to suggest a next stage of more formal theory construction.

The reader is presented with several descriptive chapters from which to judge the utility of our newer conception of personality functioning and change. After an experimental study in which the n Achievement score is viewed as a function of time-linked self-images (chapter 14), the theory is applied to an understanding of problems in career change and the relationship of teachers and students in the context of music-related activity (Chapter 15), to midlife transitions and career crisis in women (Chapter 16), and to identity crises and changes in motivation in the elderly (chapters 17 and 18). These attempts to use the newer ideas to reorient thinking about the problem of adult development and aging address topics that have been viewed by others. Chapter 16 places our theoretical ideas in the context of other major personality and sociological approaches to adult development and aging, as well as applying them to an understanding of a topic that has great current interest. We hope that such a contextual view will suggest new directions for empirical research that would not have been taken had we not become concerned with the problem of motivation and aging.

13

A Theory of Personality Functioning and Change

Joel O. Raynor

THEORETICAL AND EMPIRICAL BACKGROUND

The present theoretical effort is an outgrowth of earlier conceptual analyses of the role of future orientation as a determinant of achievement-related motivation (Raynor, 1969, 1974a, 1978; see chapter 2) and of the determinants of motivation for career striving (Raynor, 1974b; see chapter 2). The earlier effort—to understand the determinants of immediate achievement-oriented activity—was primarily concerned with situations where immediate success or failure is believed by the individual to determine the opportunity for subsequent striving to attain some future goal. Thus, immediate success or failure was conceived as "important" by the individual because immediate success earned the opportunity to continue and hence might lead on to future success, but immediate failure meant future failure through loss of the opportunity to continue. The conceptual analysis of such contingent-path situations led to elaboration of the basic equations of the theory of achievement motivation and provided a more general theory that now includes the earlier model as a special case of the more general one (see chapter 2). The later effort—to understand the determinants of motivation for career striving—began to focus on "important future goals" per se, (see chapters 2 and 6) as well as contingent paths that lead on to them. We introduced the consideration of the "future sense of self" or self-image (Raynor, 1974b, p. 376), which might serve as a goal of immediate activity whose attainment would indicate to the individual that "I have become who I always wanted to be."

The major impetus for the present analysis came initially from application of the equations of the more general theory of achievement motivation to contingent-path situations where a succession of immediate successes allowed continued striving for the future goal (Raynor, 1974b, pp. 382 to 384; see chapter 2) or when continued success led the individual to an increased positive evaluation of competences believed to be prerequisites for eventual career success (Raynor, 1974a, pp. 146 to 148; see chapter 11). In this way we were able to derive the effects of successive successes on motivation for (each new) subsequent activity along the career path. In fact, by using the elaborated theory of achievement motivation in conjunction with the concepts of open and closed contingent career paths, we were able to derive some rather (at the time) startling conclusions concerning the effects of success on subsequent career striving (see chapter 2 for such derivations). We discovered that motivation to achieve some (important) future goal could be expected to eventually decrease as a function of continued success if that future goal had initially been seen as the final or ultimate goal of the career path, and if no subsequent achievement goals had been added to the path as a function of earlier successes in getting closer to it. Such a closed contingent path with a final or ultimate goal was then seen as representing commonly perceived situations either for individuals who have concrete future goals that they are successfully approaching, or for individuals who now believe they are in a "dead-end career" with no prospects for subsequent advancement beyond a certain level. It became obvious that "aging" would always be positively correlated with this progression from earlier to later steps of a career path. Thus aging could be seen as a process through which the psychological effects of a series of successes (or failures) have their impact on the determinants of subsequent motivation of immediate activity, both directly as they affect the subjective probability of success for later steps of the path, and indirectly as they affect individuals' perceptions of their own competence (e.g., the extent to which individuals believe they possess the prerequisite competences for eventual success along that career path—see chapter 11). Thus the analysis of motivation and career striving laid the conceptual groundwork for extension of the theory of achievement motivation to a theory of personality functioning and change in striving for future career success. And the consideration of a "future self-image" or "future sense of self" whose attainment is contingent upon achievement of the final or ultimate goal of the career path provided the conceptual impetus for linking future goal striving to "feeling good about oneself." Thus the earlier analysis anticipated later developments to be described below.

The discovery of a positive relationship between the rated necessity of doing well now to earn the opportunity to strive for future success (future importance) and to feel good about oneself (self-importance; see chapters 10 and 11) suggested the assumption that earning the opportunity to continue was important for positive self-evaluation—because attainment of the future goal that was contingent upon immediate success is anticipated to provide positive feelings of self-worth. Findings that indicated that "important" as opposed to "unimportant" future goals were seen as of much greater motivational significance (see chapter 2) further strengthened the view that attaining some important future goal involved more than just an additional concrete achievement that one could feel good about because it was a difficult accomplishment per se, or because it meant greater financial reward, power, or security per se, although such interpretations were also possible. Rather, it also suggested and reinforced our view that "becoming a future sense of self" was also implicated in future goal striving when important future goals were involved. Feeling good about oneself would be contingent upon immediate success in earning the opportunity to continue to strive for the future goal, because attainment of the important future goal itself provided a substantial source of feeling good about oneself.

The finding of a positive interrelationship among future importance, self-importance, and the extent of perceived possession of a competence (self-possession; see chapters 10 and 11) focused attention upon the role of possession of a prerequisite competence and changes in an individual's competence judgments, as a function of continued success along the contingent career path. It now became necessary to consider the individual both *before* the results of an evaluation of prerequisite ability was known, *at the time* the individual was about to undergo test-taking behavior (which had been done by the theory of achievement motivation), and *after* the results of such an evaluation, when the individual might make inferences about how much competence was possessed in this career area by virtue of having successfully moved through a contingent gate toward the final goal of the path. It now became apparent that consideration of the resultant effects of successful striving on beliefs concerning the perceived possession of valued competences, whose possession has been validated by the process of successful movement toward the future goal, should also implicate the motivational effects of *past* success in determining motivation of immediate activity. Thus it appeared reasonable to consider, in the absence of any data bearing on the issue, that one might also be motivated to maintain past successes as a means of feeling good about oneself, or be motivated to maintain one's belief in a high level of possession of prerequisite competences (which results from past successes along the path). In fact, in an earlier study (cf. Atkinson, 1969), where retrospective reports were obtained concerning important versus unimportant past events, results suggested that past successes and failures could be conceptualized as having motivational impetus in a manner analogous to anticipated future success or failure.

While the evidence was certainly not conclusive or even strongly supportive of such a possibility, the idea that maintenance of a "past sense of self," contingent upon maintenance of the value of past successes for the continued high evaluation of prerequisite competences, led directly to consideration of the past time-linked sense of self that might provide esteem income to the individual and hence serve as a motivating influence on immediate activity. In particular, it became apparent that as an individual moved successfully through a series of contingent steps in a career path toward the final or ultimate career goal, and as the predicted decrement in (positive) motivation to attain that final goal became substantial, the individual might lose interest in attaining the future goal (future sense of self in career striving) and become increasingly more motivated to maintain past successes (past sense of self), and in that way still provide esteem income when approaching the final stages of that particular career path. This change in locus of motivation from the future to the past not only seemed plausible as a means of accounting for a wide variety of previously unrelated motivational phenomena in a variety of different contexts, but it explicitly focused attention on the need for a variable of personality organization that would go beyond the categorization of behavioral potentials (e.g., motive) or the categorization of the effects of success and/or failure on judgments about one's own abilities (e.g., competence) to one that could represent the motivational impetus to be derived from feeling good about oneself, which seemed to be contingent upon the attainment of important future goals and might very well be contingent upon the maintenance of important past goals. Thus we extended the tentative conceptual analysis of the self-image or an individual's self-concept as a future sense of self to a consideration of time-linked sense of self in general, expanded to now include the self-concept as a past sense of self and a present sense of self. We assumed that, taken together, they provide for a self-system whose collective motivational significance lies in its function as a source of esteem income based on self-identity that is tied to the outcome of action. Our conceptual effort then focused directly on the individual's self-image—its future, past, and present components—as a means of ensuring feeling good about oneself.

The concept of individual cultural value was then added as a means of differentiating between different future goals or past accomplishments, or presently possessed competences, so as to be able to determine why some might provide a valued sense of self to a greater extent than others.

We now can derive that striving to know and feel good about oneself, or self-identity as a means of positive esteem income, can be a primary goal of adult life. Use of this derivation as an underlying motivational impetus provides the basis for a theory of personality functioning and change that can integrate the study of personality and the study of motivation in a way generally analogous to that of Maslow (1954) and Rogers (1959), but using much more explicit theoretical assumptions to derive testable and disprovable hypotheses while focusing on "important life behaviors"—as well as the more general problems of self-identity, psychological morale, psychological integration, psychological health, and identity crisis. The resulting conceptual analysis can be considered both as a further extension of the theory of achievement motivation and as a general theory of personality functioning and change in its own right. It is no longer limited to occupational-educational career striving. The concept of psychological career in the newer theory represents a combination of a perceived self-image and a sequence of contingent steps prescribed by society (e.g., role) that can be applied to any substantive area. Thus the theory is assumed to be relevant to any significant source of esteem income where immediate activity can bear upon success and failure in attaining a criterion of performance that is contingently related to the opportunity to continue to see oneself in that particular way, and hence that is contingently related to the level of esteem income that can be anticipated and/or retrospected by an individual pursuing such activity. First we pursued the conceptual analysis, focusing only on outcomes contingent upon an individual's skill and/or effort in immediate activity over time as narrowly defined—as "achievement-oriented" activity. Then the theory was applied to any psychological career where competence of any kind is implicated in the outcome of action. However, we reserve for another paper the application of the present conceptual scheme to that part of the self-system that is impervious to change as a function of immediate success or failure, but rather that is assumed by the individual to consist of a pattern of enduring dispositions, traits, and/or abilities that are believed by the individual to be fixed and immutable and hence immune to feedback from immediate activity.

In subsequent sections we present the results of this conceptual effort. We do so by first presenting the assumptions of the theory, which are then applied to closed and open careers. We then derive some of the implications of the theory for these kinds of careers, and finally we apply the implications to relevant substantive issues.

ASSUMPTIONS OF A THEORY OF PERSONALITY FUNCTIONING AND CHANGE

Status of the Assumptions

The assumptions of this theory do not result from an attempt to specify the "basic," "ultimate," or "primary" causes of human behavior or to provide some underlying rationale for human existence. Instead they are "working assumptions" in that they both make sense and make predictions, or, rather, can be used to derive testable hypotheses. They have been chosen because the implications are consistent with the data we wish to account for and have led to other implications that we believe are plausible and hence worth testing. If and when data become available that are inconsistent either with the assumptions themselves or with the implications of the assumptions—and we have more confidence in the data than in the assumptions—then we shall change the theory to make its implications more consistent with the data. This has already happened in our movement from the initial theory to a more general theory of achievement motivation (part I) to this theory of personality functioning and change. We neither seek nor expect to find "prime movers" or "ultimates" among our assumptions. Nor do we wish to engage in philosophical or metatheoretical debate concerning their relation to such purported "ultimates." Our goal is to develop a theory that is closely tied to data, so that assumptions need (only) be clearly defined, embedded in theory so that they lead to unambiguous and testable hypotheses, which therefore account for the data we set out to explain, and are consistent with other data we are aware of at this time. Changes in the assumptions most certainly will (again) result when such changes are felt to lead to other implications that are more consistent with present or future data.

Value

We assume that individuals are motivated to obtain and/or maximize positive value, and to avoid and/or minimize negative value. There are two kinds of value: affective value—feeling good or bad (McClelland et al., 1953; Atkinson, 1964)—and information value—gaining or losing information (cf. Feather, 1967; Trope, 1975). There are different sources of value: intrinsic (Deci, 1974), difficulty (Atkinson, 1957), instrumental (see chapter 2), extrinsic, and cultural. It is also useful to distinguish between time-linked sources of value: the past, the present, and the future. When kind and source of value are compatible, they sum to determine total value. Kinds and sources of value can be positive or negative. The difference between total positive and total negative value determines resultant value, which for a particular kind or source may be positive or negative. When kinds and/or sources of value are incompatible, separate amounts of resultant value for each incompatible kind and/or source of value must be determined. When incompatible value is involved, by definition, attainment of value from the one prevents simultaneous attainment of value from the other.

These assumptions reflect a systematic extension and elaboration of expectancy X value theory, particularly resultant valence theory (Lewin et al., 1944), and theory of achievement motivation (Atkinson, 1964; Atkinson & Feather, 1966; Raynor, 1974a). The amount of total positive value of a source and the probability or expectancy of attaining it are assumed to combine multiplicatively to determine the strength of a tendency to think about and/or to act to attain the value, when thinking and acting are compatible. The total amount of negative value and the probability or expectancy of attaining it are assumed to combine multiplicatively to determine the strength of tendency not to think about and/or not act so as not to attain the value (Atkinson & Feather, 1966). When thinking and acting are incompatible, attainment of total resultant value through one means precludes simultaneous attainment of value through the other means (Atkinson & Birch, 1970). When acting to attain value is not (or is no longer) possible, then thinking (cognitive work) provides an alternative means of obtaining value (cf. Lewin, 1938).

The Behavioral System and the Self-System

We distinguish between the behavioral system and the self-system concerning the determinants of action. The behavioral system concerns value from thinking and acting (when they are compatible) in terms of the attractiveness or repulsiveness of past, present, and future expected outcomes of actions (valence) and the probabilities that actions will lead to or have led to those outcomes. These outcomes can have positive or negative affective value and can serve as sources of positive or negative information value. Previous expectancy X value theory of achievement motivation (see chapter 2) has been concerned with what we term here the behavioral system, with affective value, and with present (immediately expected) and future anticipated sources of value.

The self-system concerns an individual's self-identity that derives from that individual's various substantive and time-linked senses of self or self-images: Who I am in terms of my past sense of self, present sense of self, and future sense of self? Self-images can provide positive or negative esteem income (affective value) and can serve as sources of positive or negative information value (Who am I?). Affective value in the self-system refers to feeling good or bad about one's self-image(s). Information value in the self-system refers to knowing about oneself through one's substantive self-image(s). When affective and information value in the self-system are compatible and positive, individuals are simultaneously motivated to find out who they are and to feel good about themselves.

Affective and informational value can and do interact in both the self-system and the behavioral system. Knowing per se and the good or bad feelings associated with knowing can be difficult to distinguish for a particular person, either in the behavioral system or self-system. Conversely, feeling per se, and knowledge associated with feeling, can be difficult to distinguish in a particular person. Therefore, the distinction between these two sources of value is sometimes difficult to maintain. Research evidence is still unclear about many details concerning the specific nature of this interaction (sometimes referred to as cognitive versus affective). However, we believe that both sources of value are relevant for an understanding of personality functioning, and that when one or the other source is predominant, it is then useful to refer to it as the primary source of value. Motivation to find out specific information, motivation to feel good, and their corresponding negation components, are the sources of impetus to action provided in this theory.

Attractiveness and repulsiveness or valence in the behavioral system, and self-esteem, esteem income, or self-evaluation in the self-system, are different ways of viewing value. The relationship between the expectancy X value theory of thought and action as defined here and the expectancy X value theory of self-evaluation as defined here is integrated through this understanding of value.

We also distinguish between the individual's perception of value, or the internal viewpoint, and the consensual perception of value, or the external viewpoint. As psychologists we are interested in the internal viewpoint, which allows for conceptual analysis of an individual's determinants of action, self-evaluation, and changes in personality as a function of action through time. As sociologists we are interested in the external viewpoint, which allows for conceptual analysis of societal impact on an individual's actions, self-evaluations, and personality change. The present conception is believed to be equally appropriate to both the psychologist and the sociologist, the internal viewpoint and the external viewpoint. In fact, both perspectives can be used to understand the concept of psychological career, the central concept of this theory, which integrates the behavioral and self systems by linking an individual's perceptions of the opportunities for action along paths of society and an individual's self-image(s) related to that substantive area of activity—i.e., it considers social roles as opportunities for action, and self-identity as personal means for knowing and liking oneself through action in the real world.

INTRINSIC, DIFFICULTY, INSTRUMENTAL, EXTRINSIC, AND CULTURAL VALUE

Intrinsic value refers to that amount of value of an activity or outcome that is aroused by the inherent properties of that activity or outcome, for the particular individual in question. When individuals report that "I like music" or "sex makes me feel very good" or "I really hate spinach," or they act in a way consistent with these kinds of statements, the concept of intrinsic value seems appropriate, other things equal, as a conceptual means of representing this attractiveness or repulsiveness. The theory of achievement motivation has not previously employed such a concept. Intrinsic value seems to be a necessary concept in a complete theory of action, to account for the apparently inherent and acquired taste preferences that individuals and animals seem to have, and to account for the fact that some activities (like stimulation of what Freud termed the erogenous zones) are inherently pleasurable, more or less, for almost all individuals, while others, such as sticking a pin in your finger or getting an electric shock, are apparently inherently unpleasant, more or less, for almost all individuals. Note, however, that intrinsic value to the individual allows for the possibility that what is positive to some greater or lesser extent for almost all individuals might be more or less negatively valued for a particular individual.

The *difficulty* value of an outcome refers to the attractiveness or repulsiveness that derives from the individual's perceived chances of attaining that outcome. Difficulty value is similar to the concept of incentive value in the theory of achievement motivation; the easier the task, the higher the subjective probability of success and the lower the difficulty value of the outcome of that task, while the harder the task, the lower the subjective probability of success and the higher the difficulty value of the outcome of that task. However, we wish to use this concept in a more general way than as employed in the theory of achievement motivation. For example, we assume that the greater the scarcity of occurrence of certain attributes of individuals, the greater the positive or negative difficulty value they are perceived to have. We want to distinguish between the more limited use of incentive value in the theory of achievement motivation and this more general meaning in the present scheme—hence the introduction of a different term to refer to it.

Instrumental value refers to the number of opportunities for subsequent action that the attainment of an outcome, or possession of some competence, is believed to guarantee (in the future) or to have guaranteed (in the past). Future instrumental value refers to behavior in contingent paths (see chapter 2), where immediate success is believed necessary to earn the opportunity to try for some number of future successes, and immediate failure is believed to guarantee future failure through loss of the opportunity to try for future successes. Thus, the instrumental value of immediate success is greater the greater the number of steps in a path to the final goal of a contingent path. Put another way, the instrumental value of an immediate outcome varies with the length of the contingent path of which it is part. It follows that single outcomes not related to other activity outcomes usually have no future instrumental value to the individual faced with that activity. Similarly, the final or ultimate goal of a contingent path has no future instrumental value for activity in that path, since no further action is contemplated along it. It also follows that as the number of steps in a contingent path decreases as an individual moves successfully through the path, the future instrumental value of the immediate step also decreases. However, the instrumental value of a *past* success correspondingly increases as a function of success along the path when an individual perceives that some past success has guaranteed an increasingly greater number of later opportunities for success.

The fourth source of value comes from what is termed *extrinsic* value, or the "extrinsic incentives" in the previous theory of achievement motivation. These are sources of value that derive from rewards that are contingent upon goal attainment, but do not relate to the difficulty value of the task per se or to the intrinsic value of the task per se. Money, approval, power, security, etc., are common sources of extrinsic value and are assumed to function to provide positive value contingent upon immediate success when they are perceived to be appropriate and/or usual outcomes of that activity (cf. Kruglanski, Riter, Amitai, Margolin, Shabtai, and Zaksh, 1975). Extrinsic value may also be negative.

Finally, the *individual culture* value of an outcome refers to the extent to which an individual has acquired the belief that attainment of that outcome is good or bad, right or wrong, or proper or improper in the cultural context. It can also refer to how good or bad a person the attainment of that skill, outcome, or self-image is believed to make the individual. It implies a moral-evaluative source of value. The *consensual cultural* value associated with success is most often positive in our culture, and for many individuals in our culture their individual culture valuation of success is also positive. A "successful person" is believed to be a "good" person; so is an "intelligent" person. Most professional and occupational outcomes are highly positively valued along this good-bad dimension in our culture (consensual cultural value), and many individuals share that evaluation so that their individual cultural value for "doctor," "lawyer," etc., is also positive. Individual cultural value may also be negative, as might be the case for "failure" and "alcoholic." Individual cultural value was not previously represented in the expectancy X value theory of achievement motivation. It is introduced here particularly to refer to a source of esteem income that, while not uniquely tied to the self-system, is most often potently aroused when an individual is involved in pursuit of a time-linked self-image that defines "who I am." The cultural value of a self-image indicates how good or bad a person *I* am when *I* see myself in terms of that self-image. We derive that senses of self that come to be used as primary means of self-identity are those that provide substantial (cultural) value to the individual. The concept of cultural value provides an additional source of positive value that was not considered in our earlier conceptual analyses and instrumental value, on the one hand, related as they are to striving per se, and the evaluation of final or ultimate goals, on the other hand, related as they are to "important" life outcomes involving large extrinsic rewards and large cultural valuation.

THE SELF-SYSTEM

We make the distinction between the self-system and the behavioral system at the conceptual level for several reasons. First, we explicitly wish to allow for the possibility for adults, and recognize the near certainty for children, that the determinants of action need not invoke reference to self-identity, self-awareness, and/or self-image as explanatory concepts. When the behavioral system alone determines action, the self-system is irrelevant. Second, we wish to allow for predictions of the behavioral system to apply to the determinants of the behavior of animals other than humans for which at present we have no knowledge as to whether there is something analogous to "self-awareness" that might also require use of the self-system to explain its behavior. Third, for humans, the self-system can provide value without overt action.

Whether the self-system is unique to humans is an open question. We justify the use of self-awareness as the basis for a (scientific) conceptual analysis based on the simple empirical fact that most readers can verify with a minimum of effort: Many, though not all, adults, when asked the question "Who am I?" can and do give what is to them (the respondents) a meaningful answer. In addition, the answer appears meaningful to the investigator who has asked the question. Most important, the responses to the question "Who am I?" can be coded, attempts to predict the nature of these responses can be made in a scientifically justifiable manner, and attempts to predict their consequences for action can follow a scientific research paradigm.

We assume that self-identity can provide (informational and affective) value to the individual. When that value is positive, individuals are motivated to obtain and/ or maximize value from the self-system. When that value is negative, individuals are motivated to avoid and/or minimize value from the self-system. The total net value of the self-system determines whether self-identity will be a goal (net positive value) or a threat (net negative value) to a particular individual. Thus we treat the self-system as only one of two major sources of value to the individual—the other being the behavioral system. Some individuals derive little value from the self-system, so that questions concerning "who I am" have little psychological importance for them. In fact, some individuals do not know who they are in the sense that when asked the question "Who am I?" they respond "I don't know." We do not in any way imply or derive that such an answer is logically impossible, or that it is less than "adult" or "human" in its significance, or therefore assume that the person lacks other substantial sources of positive and/or negative value. Value can be obtained from the behavioral system without any need to implicate the self-system. By treating the self-system as a source of value to be distinguished from the behavioral system as a source of value, we are able to use the concept of self-image as an additional motivational variable. It serves as a "dependent" variable in that one of the major tasks of our conceptual analysis is to predict its emergence and change—what will be the substantive focus of the self-image (choice) of any individual, to what extent will it remain as a means of self-identity (persistence), and with what certainty, clarity, and intensity will it be perceived as an answer to self-identity questions (vigor)? It also serves as an "independent" variable in that another of the major tasks of the theory is to predict the functional significance of a person's self-image, or how individual differences in substantive focus and amount of value of self-images influence the direction, vigor, and persistence of action.

We treat the emergence of the self-system as an additional determinant of behavior as an empirical question. We know that at some time between early childhood and adulthood there emerges in humans the ability to respond meaningfully in one's native language to the question "Who am I?". Whether or not the self-system then becomes a significant factor in understanding and predicting adult behavior depends upon the amount of value that becomes associated with it. We end up deriving that the greater the value that can be attained by an individual from a particular self-image, the more likely that the individual will use that self-image as a means of self-identity, and that such self-identity will then influence subsequent action.

While complete definition of the self-system will depend upon its interaction with the behavioral system (see below), note that the self-concept as part of the self-system is a phenomenological concept. The existence and measurement of the self-image is, we believe, dependent upon the self-awareness, introspection, and conscious experiencing of the person possessing the self-image, or at least upon that person's being readily able to become aware of his or her answer to the question "Who am I?"

We distinguish between self-image and self-identity. We leave undefined what is meant by self-identity per se. We assume that the self-image is a consciously perceived self-identity or a self-identity that can readily come to be consciously perceived, but resist trying to define self-identity itself because of problems associated with such questions as "Who is the *real* me?" or "*Who* is it that has a particular self-image?" (the mind-body problem?) or whether self-identity has to be a consciously perceived phenomenon. When the self-image is involved in this theory, we are dealing with a phenomenological conception about the self. Consistent with our desire not to address metatheoretical questions, we leave the problem of self-identity per se as referring to the consciously perceived set of self-images of an individual, recognizing that there may be more to self-identity but it will not be dealt with within this theoretical framework.

When positive or negative value is derived from the self-system (meaning that, in part, value is derived from a self-image), we can refer to value as positive or negative self-esteem, or positive or negative esteem income.

Definition of the self-system in contrast to the behavioral system is made clearer when we assert that previous theory of achievement motivation has dealt exclusively with the behavioral system in that all the determinants of action specified by it function independently of the self-system—that is, independently of one's awareness of one's answer to the question "Who am I?" Previous theory of achievement motivation did not require explicit reference to a person's self-image as a source of arousal of achievement motivation. A major implication of the present theory is that both the behavioral system and the self-system are required conceptually to adequately account for adult human behavior, including achievement-oriented behavior, and that a theory of personality functioning will most probably refer as much to instigating force properties in the self-system as to instigating force properties in the behavioral system to provide an adequate account of adult life. Put another way, the present theory is an attempt to specify how one's awareness of oneself in terms of one's self-image(s) serves as an impetus for action, as well as an attempt to specify how this self-awareness in terms of self-image emerges from one's actions.

The Self-Image as a Source of Value.

As a rough (guess at an) empirical generalization, there are three major self-images that in Western culture generally serve as compatible sources of positive esteem income: occupational, sexual, and familial. However, there is no limit to the number or kinds of substantive self-images that may be used simultaneously by the individual as a source of positive value. Nor is it necessarily the case that all individuals utilize all three of these "major" sources, or just one or two of them. An individual need not have a self-image. An individual need not use a particular self-image as a major means of self-identity (because it does not provide sufficient positive value to do so). Nor is it true that these major self-images are always compatible rather than incompatible sources of value. But in general the substantive self-images of the occupational, sexual, and family areas of activity provide a useful framework for our later integration of the self-system and the behavioral system because opportunities for action in these three areas are commonplace. Thus the emergence of a *psychological career* by a link between a self-image and opportunities for action (a societal path) can frequently occur when sufficient positive value in these areas is available. However, it is the self-image or images (and the perceived opportunities for action) for a particular individual that are relevant for the theory (the internal viewpoint) when it is applied to prediction of the action of the individual rather than some cultural consensus or average of ratings of common self-images and/or social roles. Of course, from another perspective (the external viewpoint) we can try to make statements concerning what self-images are likely to be used by a particular individual in a particular cultural context, or by members of different social classes as a function of different available opportunities, and thus try to link the concept of self-image to that of role and position as used in the external viewpoint by the social psychologist or sociologist. Both perspectives provide a meaningful analysis. However, only the internal viewpoint provides the conceptual definition of terms of the present theory as a psychological theory of personality functioning and change. An important heuristic value of the theory is that the external and internal views of self and opportunities for action (role) can be coordinated so that a dual perspective on personality functioning in society is obtained.

Intrinsic, difficulty, instrumental, extrinsic, and cultural value can refer to either the behavioral system or the self-system. But note that the concept of cultural value (both individual and consensual) has a particularly important role in the self-system. Individual cultural value in the self-system refers to the extent to which an individual believes that a particular self-image marks that individual as a good person, or how good or bad a person one is when seeing oneself in a particular way (i.e., when using a particular self-image as a means of self-identity). That is, an individual's cultural standards can apply to a particular self-image. Thus, anticipated attainment of positive cultural value (unless otherwise noted, we mean individual cultural value) means that one sees oneself becoming a particular kind of good or better person, defined by the substantive self-image for what one is becoming; *how* good or *how much* better depends upon the amount of positive cultural value anticipated. Anticipated attainment of negative cultural value means that one sees oneself as becoming a particular kind of bad or worse person defined by the substantive self-image in question, and how bad a person depends on the amount of negative value involved. "Self-righteousness" is a term that can be used to describe the affective state associated with positive individual cultural value in the self-system. Moral anxiety or self-guilt is the term that can be used to describe the affective state associated with negative individual cultural value.[1] We do not mean to limit cultural value to the phenomenological self-image. We assert that one of the important determinants of the utilization of a particular self-image as a means of self-identity

---

[1] In Freudian terms, positive and negative individual cultural value refer to the ego ideal and the conscience, respectively, but for us, without a necessary link to sexuality, psychodynamic theory, or unconscious motivation.

is the fact that some (ready-made) self-images in society (doctor, lawyer, professor) are perceived by many individuals to offer substantial amounts of positive cultural value, while other readily available self-images offer substantial negative cultural value (alcoholic, prostitute, menial laborer). But, again, it is the amount of cultural value associated with a particular self-image for the particular person in question that is relevant. We do not claim that cultural value cannot or does not refer to non-phenomenological variables, such as unconscious factors. We merely note that for us the concept applies equally to the self-system and the behavioral system, and in fact it plays a substantial role in one's moral-evaluative views of oneself through the cultural value of one's self-images.

Time-Linked Self-Images as Sources of Value

We assume that a self-image can have a time-linked referent to self-identity. Individuals can see themselves in terms of "who I am becoming" (future sense of self) and in terms of "who I have been" (past sense of self), as well as in terms of "who I am now" (present sense of self). We therefore distinguish between the past, present, and future self-images as sources of positive or negative value. We can use the term "becoming"[2] to refer to the future self-image, and "having been" (or sometimes "has been") to the past self-image. The present self-image has two aspects, a non-contingent and a contingent aspect. The noncontingent aspect refers to the self-image of "me as I am, just because I am this way," and is often associated with an existentialist point of view. In this sense it refers to possession of attributes independently of actions and/or their outcomes. The contingent present self-image refers to those attributes of personality whose possession and/or extent of possession is believed dependent upon the outcome(s) of activity in relation to standards of performance appropriate for diagnostic evaluation of that attribute. The contingent present self-image for adults will therefore change as a function of changes in performance that are believed by the person to signal increments or decrements in degree of possession of the attribute serving as the substantive focus of the self-image (see chapter 11). Put another way, the contingent present self-image depends upon the perceived extent of possession of attributes whose degree of possession is seen as assessed by the outcomes of (either formal or informal) behavioral tests of that attribute. Particular competences and abilities that one believes oneself to possess can form the substantive focus of the present (contingent) self-image. Since we are primarily concerned with the contingent rather than the noncontingent self-image in this context, unless otherwise noted "present sense of self" refers to the present contingent self-image.

The past, present, and future self-images for a particular substantive sense of self

---

[2] I wish to thank and acknowledge my debt to Judith M. Bardwick for allowing me to read a prepublication draft of her paper "Middle Age and a Sense of Future," from which I borrowed the term "becoming" at a time when my ideas were being formulated. Professor Bardwick's conceptions and willingness to share her personal experiences provided me with a clear sense of "being on the right track" in moving from the theory of achievment motivation to this more general theory of personality functioning and change.

can serve as compatible sources of esteem income. When they do, it is assumed that positive value from these sources sums to determine the total positive value of the self-image in question. When the past, present, and future aspects of a substantive self-image provide compatible sources of negative value, total negative value is the sum of the amounts of negative value involved. The total net value for a time-linked self-image is assumed equal to the difference between compatible positive and compatible negative amounts of value.

The concept of time-linked senses of self provides an important extension of theory to incorporate the concepts of time orientation and psychological distance into the self-system. We believe that the concept of time-linked self-image is one of the most important variables for understanding adult personality functioning. It allows for the conceptual analysis of an individual's self-identity and source of motivation as time-linked variables (the past, present, and future senses of self), as well as for a conceptual analysis of an individual as that individual actually moves through time in his or her life, from either the internal or external viewpoint. In this theory, from the internal viewpoint the person's time-linked sense(s) of self combine(s) with the person's anticipated and/or retrospected activity along paths of a society, and from the external viewpoint (the observation of such movement along paths as a function of time) to provide the concept of psychological career— which is the central variable of the present theory.

INTEGRATION OF THE BEHAVIORAL
AND SELF-SYSTEMS:
THE PSYCHOLOGICAL CAREER

The term psychological career (or career, for short) is used to refer to the interaction of the behavioral system, involving a perceived path for action and anticipated or recalled movement along it, and the self-system, involving time-linked self-images. A career is both a phenomenological concept and a behavioral concept. It is the link between what a person *does* and how that person *sees* himself or herself. A career consists of time-linked senses of self that are defined by action and its outcomes. A career defines how one sees oneself in the context of one's social environment—in terms of one's future plans, one's past accomplishments or failures, and one's present competences and attributes.

If we think of the anticipated steps of a career as the opportunities for action, and if we think of the kind of person one believes one will become by successfully pursuing those steps as the future self-image (future sense of self), then we see that "psychological pursuit of a career" involves both striving to accomplish specific task goals that allow for continuation along the career path, and striving to become a particular kind of person—"I am who I am striving to become." If we think of the retrospected steps of a career as the past opportunities for action and the outcomes of those actions, and if we think of the kind of person one believes one has become as the result of those past actions, we see that "psychological maintenance of a career" involves both retrospection about past task outcomes that have allowed for continuation along the career path, and how those outcomes resulted in producing a particular self-image—"I am who I have been." And if we think of the attributes and competences whose (degree of) possession is believed to be attributable to actions and their outcomes along the path, then we see that "present psychological identity" (present sense of self) involves both evaluation of the meaning of the outcomes of action as diagnostic of possession of particular attributes, and the use of those attributes to define the kind of person one now believes one is—"I am the attributes and traits and competences I possess."

If we recall that value in the self-system is referred to as self-esteem or esteem income, we see that a psychological career—as future pursuit or "becoming," as maintenance of past outcomes or "having been," and as present characteristics or "being" —can provide three time-linked sources of positive or negative self-esteem or esteem income. Self-evaluation refers to evaluation of the amount of esteem income derived from a psychological career, or to one's view of one's own self-worth as a function of positive or negative esteem income.

We assume that the greater the positive self-esteem or esteem income of a career, the greater its psychological relevance, salience, or importance in a person's life. We assume that ratings of the importance of some past, present, or future activity or outcome for positive or negative self-evaluation (or for feeling good or bad about oneself), reflect the perceived self-esteem or esteem income of the career for which that activity or outcome provides value. This provides the link between the present conceptual analysis of personality functioning and the earlier theory and research on achievement motivation presented in this volume (see chapter 2).

Note that in the definition of psychological career given thus far, a contingent path of society is presumed to provide the behavioral opportunities for action. Non-contingent or partial contingent paths can also provide such opportunities. However, we believe that contingent paths tend to offer the greatest amounts of positive and negative value and therefore are of particular relevance for the present analysis (cf. Raynor, 1974b). Societal paths that provide substantial amounts of difficulty, instrumental, extrinsic, and cultural value tend to be paths where the self-system tends to emerge. Contingent paths of a society tend to offer such substantial amounts of positive and negative value. Thus societal contingent paths tend to emerge as those opportunities that provide individuals with psychological careers, although this need not always be so.

An individual in Western culture tends to utilize one or more self-images as a means of self-identity that provide enough positive esteem income for the individual to value himself or herself as a human being. Sources of sufficient esteem income tend to be those careers involving contingent opportunities. But since our concept of psychological career can refer to any substantive focus, unique or idiosyncratic self-images and/or opportunities for action can conceivably provide for sufficient feelings of positive self-worth (esteem income), whether they involve contingent paths and/or large *cultural* value or not. But not all possible self-images become the basis for self-identity. Our conception of career focuses on the combination of self-image and opportunity for action, on the interaction between the behavioral system and the self-system, to provide for feelings of positive self-worth. The concept of psychological career provides an integrating link between a theory of motivation and action and a theory of personality functioning and change.

Note that while the self-image or sense of self is a phenomenological concept, the idea of a psychological career need not have any phenomenological status. Thus a male need not see himself as "pursuing a career as a man" for us to utilize the concept of psychological career to understand and predict his sex-related activity. However, a male who is conceptualized as having a sexual career has to, by definition, have a self-image somehow substantively defined in terms of masculinity, and has to be engaged in activity that is perceived by him to offer sex-related value. One implication of this position is that not all humans who would be biologically classified as male are to be conceptualized as having a "masculine" career in the sexual domain. "Career" as used here is a psychological concept, not a biological or physiological concept. Nor do we expect that all males who engage in sexual activity are to be conceptualized as having a "masculine" career in the sexual domain. "Career" as used here is a psychological concept, not a social psychological or sociological concept. Individuals may fill positions in society and play roles associated with those positions, as viewed by the external observer, but they would not necessarily be conceptualized as having a psychological career defined by an image associated with a role or the activities associated with the position. In fact, we predict that for some men, sexual activity is just that—a means of obtaining positive value that does not constitute immediate activity along a career path of "masculinity." On the other hand, some men have clear-cut substantive contingent careers in the sexual domain, where sexual intercourse and related activities fulfill all the criteria of a psychological career, including providing past, present, and future senses of self that are of great value to that person in providing positive esteem income. Similarly, not all "jobs" or means of earning a living are to be conceptualized as occupational careers. And likewise, the fact that all individuals are "children" does not mean that all individuals are to be conceptualized as pursuing a career of "child" or "brother" or "sister" in the family domain, or that all married individuals pursue careers as "husbands" or "wives."

INFORMATION VALUE, INFORMATION SEEKING, AND CAREERS

The following analysis builds upon an earlier one by Feather (1967). We assume that a particular kind of information, knowledge, and/or knowing can have value, either positive or negative. The amount of value to the individual of particular information determines to what extent that individual will be motivated to acquire that information. Just as outcomes of actions are often defined in terms of some standard of performance or some level of past performance, the amount of change in amount of information often has value. The sources of value of information are the same as the sources of value of affect: intrinsic, difficulty, instrumental, extrinsic, and cultural. Each of these sources can provide positive or negative value, or both.

Individuals are assumed to be motivated to maximize positive value of information (as well as affect) and to avoid or minimize negative value of information (as well as affect). Information that has little value, positive or negative, does not arouse behavioral tendencies to seek it out or not. Information that has positive value arouses a tendency to engage in activity that is expected to lead on to that information; the greater the value, weighted by the probability of attaining it, the greater the tendency to undertake activity to attain that information. Information that has negative value arouses a tendency not to engage in activity that is expected to lead on to that information. The greater the negative value, weighted by the probability of attaining it, the greater the resistance to engaging in activity that might lead on to that information. In the behavioral system we refer to the attractiveness or repulsiveness of information or the valence of information, positive or negative.

Informational Value in the Behavioral System

Information in the behavioral system refers to the consequences of actions; or, "what is the result of what I did?" "What happens when I do this?" "If I put my hand in sand, what happens?" The information we obtain from the consequences of actions is often in terms of change in knowledge (increments and decrements). I did this before, and X happened. What will happen if I do X again? Thus, all actions can have diagnostic implications for finding out or discovering information, or for changing information, either increasing or decreasing the amount of information possessed. The amount of positive value of a particular kind or amount of information to the individual, multiplied by the subjective probability of its attainment, will determine the extent to which information value per se will arouse behavioral tendencies to acquire that information or a change in information. The amount of negative value of information, multiplied by its subjective probability of attainment, will determine the extent to which information per se will arouse behavioral resistance to those actions that are expected to result in that information. Information that has positive value arouses a tendency to acquire it. Information that has negative value arouses an inhibitory tendency not to acquire it.

Some kinds of information have positive intrinsic value, more or less, for most individuals in a given culture, whether innately so or learned. Some kinds of information have negative intrinsic value, more or less, for most individuals. However, this does not rule out the possibility that a particular kind of information might have the opposite value for a particular individual than for the great majority of individuals. The difficulty value of information refers to the difficulty of attaining that amount of information; the easier it is to attain the amount of information, the less value it has, and the more difficult it is to attain the amount of information, the greater value it has. The positive instrumental value of information refers to the number of opportunities for subsequent action that possession of a given amount or kind of information is believed to guarantee to the individual. The negative instrumental value of information refers to the number of opportunities for subsequent action that lack of possession of that particular amount of information is believed to deny. The extrinsic value of a particular kind and amount of information refers to those rewards not inherently perceived to be part of the information that are expected to be attained (or lost) upon attainment (or nonattainment) of the information. The cultural value of the information refers to the extent to which possession of the information is believed to be good or bad, proper or improper, right or wrong, or to make one a good or bad person.

Value of Information in the Self-System

Information in the self-system refers to information about self-identity; the substantive self-images of the time-linked senses of self. The answer to the question "Who am I?" is information in the self-system. The value of information in the self-system refers to the value of knowledge about oneself; the greater the value of self-knowledge, the greater the esteem income obtained from possessing that knowledge, positive or negative.

Interaction of the Behavioral and Self Systems: Value of Self-Knowledge and Information Seeking about Oneself

Information concerning self-knowledge in a psychological career concerns those actions along a path that define the substance of the time-linked self-image associated with that career. Information about the future sense of self concerns finding out about "who I am becoming" by striving to successfully attain the goals along the career path (positive future self-image) or by possible failure along the career path (negative future self-image). Information about the past self-image concerns finding out about "who I have been" through recall of past outcomes of action along the career path—where past successes yield information about positive past self-image, and past failures yield information about negative past self-image. Information about the present self-image concerns finding out about "who I am" through taking or making more or less formal or informal diagnostic tests of competences and/or attributes that are believed to be relevant to the substantive career area. By "relevant to" a career area we mean that the individual believes that these attributes and/or competences are necessary prerequisites for successful performance with regard to appropriate standards of behavior in that substantive area.

The implication of the interaction of the behavioral and self systems in a psychological career concerning information-seeking behavior is that pursuit of a career simultaneously involves, by definition, seeking positively valued information about oneself and seeking to feel good about oneself through action and its outcomes along the career path. Self-esteem or esteem income in a psychological career comes from knowing how that career defines "who I am" in terms of the kind of person the time-linked self-images of that career make me, the kind of person the behavioral outcomes of action in the career path make me, and, most important, the extent to which these behavioral outcomes validate the substantive career self-images. Informational value and affective value from both the behavioral system and the self-system are involved when an individual pursues a psychological career.

Willingness or Resistance to Undertaking a Test of Competence

The extent to which an individual is expected to seek information from a test of competence (or the evaluation of some attribute) will depend upon the total net value (positive minus negative) from both affective and informational sources of value weighted by the probability of attaining that value (see chapter 11). We generally expect that value to be greater when a test is believed to assess a competence relevant to (i.e., a necessary prerequisite for successful performance in) an individual's psychological career than when the competence either is not relevant to the career or the individual does not have a psychological career in that area for which the competence is believed relevant. If this greater value of the information to be obtained from the test is positive, we expect greater willingness on the part of the individual to seek out and/or undertake the test of competence. If this greater value is negative, we expect greater resistance on the part of the individual to undertaking the test of competence. Since the perceived validity of a diagnostic test is expected to influence the probability of attaining the value of the information sought, we expect greater willingness or resistance to undertake a test of a relevant career competence the greater the perceived validity of the diagnostic test in question (see chapter 11). Perceived validity is assumed to function by influencing the expectancy of attainment of the information.

Note that the information value of a competence or attribute is expected to involve the self-system only to the extent that that competence or attribute defines a present self-image for the individual. Self-esteem, either positive or negative, is involved in competence testing only when individuals have psychological careers for which a present self-image is defined in terms of the possession or the degree of possession of the competence believed to be assessed by the test.

Note also that we are concerned with the individual's perception of the validity of a test for a particular attribute (kind of information), rather than some external judgment about what information a particular test is supposed to yield. If we devise a test of mathematical ability, but the subject believes that the test is a valid indicator of ability to comply with an authority's instructions but an invalid measure of mathematical ability, predictions concerning arousal of tendencies to undertake the test of competence for the individual pursuing a psychological career involving "becoming a mathematician" are bound to be unsupported. There are many "informal" diagnostic tests used by individuals to obtain information bearing on validating their possession of prerequisite competences, or the degree of possession of the competence, in addition to the more "formal" ability/aptitude/trait/personality tests used by the mental tester. We assume behavior for both kinds of information-seeking to be functionally equivalent, i.e., to be determined by the same variables; positive and negative informational and affective value, and the probability of attaining that value, which is in turn influenced both by the link between the information and the individual's psychological career in that area and by the perceived validity of the test as a measure of the competence.

VALUE, ESTEEM INCOME, AND CAREERS

The concept of value, and therefore the concept of self-esteem or esteem income, is a quantitative one, involving "degrees of" from a particular source along a continuum from substantial positive through zero to substantial negative. There are important implications of this assumption for circumstances when all sources of value are compatible. The concept of value is also a qualitative one, in that different sources of value can produce different experiential phenomena for the individual. At this point we shall deal with the quantitative implication of value for the person.

By definition, any behavior engaged in by an individual serves as a source of value to that individual; behavioral tendencies to act are aroused by the expected value of an outcome and are weighted by the probability of attaining that outcome, as in any expectancy X value theory. But not all action involves the self-system. Only action that is perceived to bear on a self-image involves value as esteem income. By "bear on the self-system" we mean action perceived to be instrumental to the attainment of the positive value of a future sense of self, or perceived to be instrumental to maintenance of the positive value of a past sense of self, or perceived to be instrumental to increasing the value of the present sense of self. When such actions leads to positive value, then the individual is conceived of as increasing positive self-evaluation or total positive self-worth. The self-image in question is experienced as being more highly valued to the extent that it serves as a source of positive esteem income, and, conversely, one's perception of one's own self-worth depends upon the positive value that one is able to attain, maintain, and/or acquire. While these latter statements are a tautology, because value in the self-system and self-esteem are synonymous, the experiential phenomenon of perceiving a sense of self as valuable and therefore making one feel good about oneself for being that kind of person can be viewed as a dependent variable to be predicted as a function of the determinants of the amount of value of a self-image.

Table 1 presents, in summary form, the various dimensions and distinctions that have been made in this theory of personality functioning and change.

BECOMING, BEING, AND HAVING BEEN
ALONG A CLOSED CONTINGENT
CAREER PATH

We are now ready to apply the theory to a typical sequence of career striving. We use this as one possible application of the theory to illustrate how its assumptions lead to implications about the time orientation of the individual, one's level of esteem, possible "identity crises" that might be faced, and whether striving to attain goals through instrumental action in the real world or cognitive reorganization to defend and maintain past accomplishments will be the primary strategy for obtaining positive value about oneself.

We first introduce a means of representing the assumptions of the theory in graphic form, which may later also be used as the basis for stating the mathematical model. Figure 1 shows a "time line" that represents the person in the immediate

Table 1 Variables, Dimensions, and Distinctions of an Expectancy × Value Theory of Personality Functioning and Change.

Viewpoint	System	Motives for activity	Substantive activity	Kind of path	Time-linked value	Source of value	General kind of value	Direction of value	Substantive kind of value
External	Behavioral	Positive	Occupational	Contingent Open	Past	Outcomes of action	Affective	Positive	Intrinsic
Internal	Self	Neutral	Family	Closed	Present	Self-images	Information	Negative	Difficulty
	Psychological career	Conflicted	Sexual	Partial contingent	Future	Abilities			Instrumental
		Indifferent	Avocational	Noncontingent		Attributes			Extrinsic
		Negative	Leisure, etc.	One-step					Cultural

present at point 0, the person's anticipated future steps as positive numbers (+1, +2, +3, etc.) with the furthest anticipated future step +N as the final or ultimate step in the anticipated future, and the person's retrospected (recalled) past steps as negative numbers (-1, -2, -3, etc.), with the furthest recalled past step -N as the final or ultimate step in the retrospected past. Note that so far this time line does not refer to real events as we follow an individual from one step to another, but rather represents the individual's thoughts about (e.g., cognitive representation of) possible future steps and recalled past steps, as the individual anticipates and retrospects at point 0 in the here-and-now.

Let us assume that we are depicting a college student who, as a freshman, decides (for whatever reason) that he "wants to become a psychologist," who knows little about his own capabilities concerning the prerequisites for becoming a psychologist, but who has checked the undergraduate catalog of his university and some graduate-school brochures so that he knows the required sequence of events that must transpire to eventually earn his Ph.D. in psychology. Figure 2 depicts this student at the start of his career. Note that the anticipated steps along the path are represented as part of a closed contingent path with +N as becoming a psychologist by earning the Ph.D., and the steps to that final goal as the courses to be taken, coupled with the good grades that must be earned, to ensure continued progression through the undergraduate program, to earn a spot in a graduate program, to successfully progress through the graduate years with its contingent gates until finally the last step—planning, conducting, writing up, and finding acceptance of the doctoral dissertation. Because the student took no psychology courses in high school, and engaged in no activity contingently related to "becoming a psychologist" before enrolling in introductory psychology (the first step of the path), Figure 2 does not show any retrospected steps back into the past as the student takes the introductory course. We would describe this career as "future-oriented" and the student as "becoming." Since the student is really turned on by the prospect of "finding out what makes people tick," we assume intrinsic value to be positive. Since the student believes it is difficult to make it through all the steps to the Ph.D., the difficulty value of the future goal is relatively high. Since the student knows he must do well in introductory psychology to continue, many opportunities for future success are at stake, so the instrumental value of the first step is relatively high. Since the student believes that "it's good to be a psychologist" (psychologists are intelligent, educated, devoted helpers of their fellow humans, etc.),

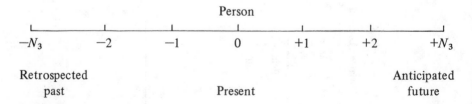

Figure 1. Time line representing the person in the immediate present, the anticipated future, and the retrospected past.

Person

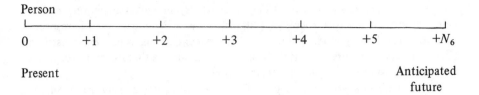

| 0 | +1 | +2 | +3 | +4 | +5 | $+N_6$ |

Present   Anticipated
                                                                               future

Figure 2 Start of career striving in a closed contingent path: "becoming."

the individual cultural value of the future goal is relatively high. And since the student believes that he can earn a good living, find security, and influence others by being a psychologist, the extrinsic value(s) of the future goal is relatively high. Thus the individual anticipates a relatively large amount of "feeling good about himself" (positive self-esteem) as he looks forward to becoming a psychologist by successfully moving through the contingent steps of this career. His sense of self is defined primarily in terms of "who he is becoming" and right now, as he anticipates his future, this makes him feel very good about himself. In other words, his present self-esteem is high because the value of his career as "becoming" is high.

Let us restrict ourselves for now to the student who successfully moves through the first several steps of this contingent career path by attaining those necessary prerequisites that allow him to psychologically accept the fact that he has met the stated requirements while at the same time allowing the external gatekeepers of the university to certify that he has met the requirements to become a "psychology major." Figure 3 depicts the student at this middle stage of career striving. Several important changes have taken place. First, the individual can now see himself *both* in terms of "becoming" and in terms of "having been." He is still striving to earn the Ph.D. by trying to do well in upper-class courses to earn the college degree to get into graduate school, to do well in graduate school, etc. At the same time, he can now look back to his past successes in negotiating the requirements to get this far along the path and "feel good about himself" as a function of the difficulty value of his past successes ("that was a tough introductory psych course—only 15 As out of 100 and I got one of them!"), the instrumental value of his past success (e.g., doing well in introductory psych earned the chance to move on, and so did doing well in statistics, and "without doing well in them, I wouldn't be where I am today"), the extrinsic value of his past successes ("being an upperclassman lets me

Person

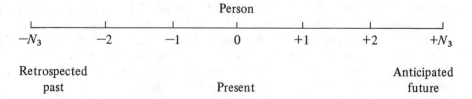

| $-N_3$ | -2 | -1 | 0 | +1 | +2 | $+N_3$ |

Retrospected   Anticipated
    past   Present   future

Figure 3. Middle of career striving in a closed contingent path: "becoming," "being," "having been."

impress the underclassmen in the Undergraduate Psychology Association), and the cultural value of his past successes ("it makes me a good person to have been a successful psychology student thus far"). His esteem income is no longer restricted to the anticipated future. He has a history of career success that, when retrospected, provides a substantial amount of esteem income.

In addition, by successfully negotiating the various gates and by attributing his success to internal factors such as high ability to do well in psychology and hard work in this area, the student has developed a much clearer present sense of self in this career owing to an increment in perceived degree of possession of those prerequisites that he believes have made success possible. The amount of esteem income that present sense of self can provide because of the increase in value produced by upward assessment of ability is increased. We refer to one's assessments of one's own ability as competence, adopting the term proposed by Moulton (1967), and can now refer to the various sources of value derived from "being"—that is, from seeing oneself as "intelligent" and "hard working" in this area. Difficulty value increases because our individual sees himself as being competent—one of the increasingly few who have progressed to this point, since only 50 of the original 100 in introductory psychology are now psychology majors; the instrumental value of "intelligence" in the area of psychology also increases because he believes that possessing this competence will allow him to successfully negotiate the later steps of the path; the extrinsic value of "being intelligent" is increased because possessing more of it allows for getting summer jobs as a research assistant with one of his instructors who was impressed with his intelligence in the course, and who asked him if he would work on his summer project at $500 per month for two months. The cultural value of "being" has increased because "an intelligent person is a good person."

We therefore see that in this arbitrary example, there are now three sources of esteem income (past, present, and future) rather than only the one (future) or possibly two (present and future) that existed at the beginning of this particular career. Other things equal, we expect an increase in total esteem income from the earliest stages of career striving. Note, however, that the increase is due primarily to an increase in esteem income due to the "present sense of self" or "being." This is because, as the past sense of self became a source of esteem income and increased in value with each successful step along the path, the future sense of self correspondingly provided less esteem income, assuming the path has remained a *closed contingent one.* (For more explicit derivations using expectancy X value for future anticipated outcomes, see the equations presented in chapter 2.) The reasons for this are important and basic to the implications of the theory. First, since the number of steps has remained anchored by the goal of "becoming a psychologist" through earning the Ph.D., and the individual has moved successfully through several steps, the instrumental value of the (next) first step along the path has decreased, because there are fewer future opportunities that the (next) immediate success can earn. That is, there are fewer steps between the individual and the final goal of the closed contingent path. In addition, the student has increased his confidence in eventual success along the path, owing to both an increase in perceived competence in this area and the fact that there are fewer contingent steps remaining, so that the difficulty value of the final goal has decreased. This means that if the cultural and extrinsic values of the final goal have not increased (let us assume that they have not, although they in fact may have), the total value of the path to the final goal, the anticipated future sense of self, has decreased, with a concomitant decrease in anticipated esteem income generated by "becoming" along this career path. In our example, the increase in esteem income produced by an increase in "having been" along this path is counterbalanced by the decrease in esteem income produced by the decrease in "becoming" along this path, although in fact it may be less than, equal to, or exceed that lost from "becoming."

Let us now follow our successful student to the end stage of career striving along this particular career path. This student has just successfully passed his oral examination and thus has "become" a psychologist by earning his Ph.D. But because this is a closed path the individual (by definition) still has not at all considered what the next step along this career path might be, if there is to be one. Figure 4 shows that there is no anticipated future, so that there is no esteem income to be derived from "becoming." On the other hand, there is a substantial past sense of self based on the entire series of successes along the path, and an increase in perceived competence concerning "having had what it takes" to have successfully negotiated the contingent path. Both the past and present senses of self can provide substantial esteem income. But note that while the student at the beginning was "becoming," at the end he is a "has been." That is, the relative impact of esteem income on the individual has shifted from future oriented to past oriented, with a continued increase in the role of the present self-image as "competent in this area" to increase (perhaps) or at least not decrease total esteem income. Note, however, that along the way the individual might have perceived a limit to his continued upward evaluation of prerequisite competences, some upper point beyond which he has not continued to upwardly evaluate his abilities, either because real-world feedback has suggested such a limitation or because he has stopped attributing his successes to his own ability and/or effort. We might expect such a limitation to occur at about the middle of career striving, although it might occur earlier or not at all. If this were the case, we would then say that the major shift that has taken place from the beginning to the end of this closed career path has been one from "becoming" to "having been."

The example presented here is an arbitrary one, but it includes what we think may represent a frequently occurring sequence, one that precedes a major career

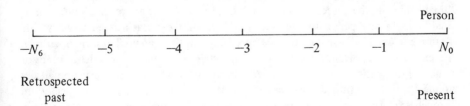

Person

$-N_6$ -5 -4 -3 -2 -1 N_0

Retrospected
   past

Present

Figure 4 End of career striving in a closed contingent path: "having been," "being."

"crisis" and one that can be reasonably used to characterize some previously observed differences as a function of aging.

The "typical" kinds of changes that this particular example illustrates may be summarized as follows: (1) a shift from "becoming" to "having been" as a function of success in a closed career path, produced by a decrease in the difficulty value of the future goal and the instrumental value of the immediate next step leading to that future goal, on the one hand, and an emerging past sense of self that forms the basis for sources of value to provide esteem income whereas at the start no such past sense of self existed for this new career path, and (2) an increase in "being" based upon upward evaluation of competences that are seen as being validated by the very successes that move the individual along the career path, up to some point, where the individual reaches some asymptotic assessment of competence.

CAREER STRIVING IN AN OPEN CONTINGENT PATH

An important distinction is made between a closed and an open career path (cf. Raynor, 1974a, 1974b). Recall that the closed path is one where the individual has a final or ultimate goal $(+N)$ whose attainment will mark the end of striving along the path because the last goal of the career is fixed at the outset and remains unchanged as a function of success in moving toward it. On the other hand, an open path is one where the individual may initially have a final or ultimate goal, but an immediate success suggests one or more new goals that add on to the end of the path so that the initial "final goal" becomes just another goal along the path whose length has now remained the same or even increased. The implications of this open path for esteem income are seen first in Figure 5a, which shows the career path in the middle stage as it would appear for a closed contingent path, and then in Figure 5b after three successes have suggested three new goals along the path $(+4, +5,$ and $+N_6)$. Note that as in the closed path (Figure 5a), both the retrospected past and the anticipated future can contribute to esteem income in the open path. But there has been no decrease in "becoming" for the open path as "having been" increases— as is the case with the closed path. In the open path the individual can build up a a source of positive esteem income as a function of past successes along the path while still retaining the initial impetus for "becoming" as a consequence of new additional goals that continually become apparent as a function of successful immediate striving, or in fact may be anticipated to appear even prior to success. In fact, so long as the path remains open—that is, so long as new goals become apparent as a function of continued immediate success—there will be no "late" or "final" stage of the career because the individual does not approach an ultimate or final goal. In an open path the final goal does not exist as a fixed target whose attainment would signal the end of "becoming" in this career. Thus the open path has extremely important implications for life striving because it provides a means of understanding the difference between individuals who remain psychologically young through continued "becoming" and those who become psychologically old through exclusive dependence upon "having been" to feel good about themselves.

The distinction between open and closed careers provides a powerful tool for the analysis of the apparently paradoxical situation where positively motivated and

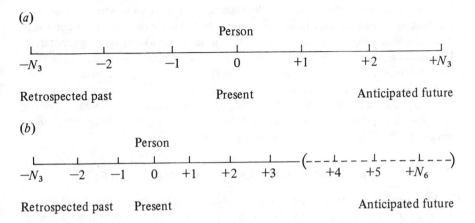

Figure 5. Middle stage of striving in (a) a closed and (b) an open contingent career path.

relatively successful individuals, who would be expected to be satisfied and "ful-filled" as a function of their success, are in fact restless, bored, uninterested, and "lost" at the pinnacle of their careers—a phenomenon that Sheehy's (1974) *Passages* identifies and that we believe to be one of the inevitable consequences of career striving along a closed as opposed to an open career path. First, esteem in-come from "becoming" is lost as a function of success in the closed career. In fact, the future sense of self is lost upon attainment of the final goal of the closed career path. The individual no longer knows "who I am becoming." This precipitates an "identity crisis" (Erikson, 1968), since the individual has previously (in this career path) seen himself or herself primarily as "becoming." We expect that the individ-ual who has been striving successfully along a closed contingent path begins to notice the loss of attractiveness of the final goal only gradually, as each success slightly diminishes its anticipated esteem income. But the impact of this loss be-comes strikingly apparent after successful attainment of the final goal itself, for now there is literally "nothing to look forward to" in the career, and while the loss of value is a gradual process, the lack of any future goal at all is seen and experienced as qualitatively different. The individual wakes up one morning to find there is no reason to continue to pursue the career. In fact, such individuals might realize that they can just as well stay in bed, retrospect about the past in the career, and assess their present competences as a function of their past success, and feel just as good about themselves as if they "go though the motions" of immediate activity, which has lost its instrumental and difficulty values for attainment of a future sense of self.

On the other hand, the individual faced with an open path never loses the anti-cipation of "becoming" because there is always a new sense of self to be attained as a function of the ever-changing (new) final goal of the career. At any given time the individual is pursuing a final goal of the career path, but this final goal continually changes. Renewed esteem income can come to be anticipated, and loss of the future sense of self avoided, while at the same time the backlog of past successes builds a source of positive "having been" and a positive sense of "being" as is the case for the closed career. If the "cake" is "becoming" and the attainment of those goals the "eating", then persons in an open career path can "have their cake and eat it, too," whereas those in a closed career path can have the cake or eat it, but not both. For in closed careers, "becoming" turns to "having been," whereas in the open path "becoming" produces "having been" while still remaining "becoming."

Note also that success in a closed path increasingly ties one to one's past as a primary means of self-identity and feeling good about oneself, whereas success in an open path provides a continued link between one's past, present, and future senses of self as the means for self-identity and esteem income.

INTERACTION OF OPEN AND CLOSED CAREERS

In the real world it is rare to find an individual whose entire life is characterized as career striving along an open path in any of the substantive (occupational, sexual, familial, etc.) self-images people usually have. More often we expect to find a path remaining open for some period of time, after which either a change in the impact of some dominant situational (path) feature of the career, such as a change in the nature of the occupation or family situation, or the impact of some internal change (often the failure to use success as a signal for continued upward evaluation of competences) produces a change in the effect of success on the perceived new opportunities for continued striving along that career path. That is, sooner or later, in the usual case, we expect open paths to become closed paths, either because the world imposes some final or ultimate goal that was not initially perceived—because the individual was too far away from that goal in the earlier stages of career striving for it to have any psychological impact, or because the individual realizes that a limit to his or her own competences in this area sets some limit on realistic prospects for continued advancement along the path—at which time the new final goal of the previously open path becomes the actual final goal of the now closed contingent path. When immediate success fails to provide for the usual new possibilities, the open path becomes closed, and a reduction in "becoming" sets in.

It is also possible that a closed path can become open. Thus, while early successes might not suggest new possibilities to add on to the path, later successes might begin to, so that the closed path becomes open. New information from external sources may also open a path. Again, the effective length of path will interact with the perception of the final or ultimate goal of the path to determine whether the path will function as open or closed at a given point in time.

The implications of the above are that the distinction between open and closed paths, while critical for an understanding of adult personality functioning, should not be taken as fixed for a given individual, since an open path can become closed and a closed path can become open. However, if and when these changes occur we can predict their effects. Such changes are believed to be critically important in adult personality functioning.

ANALYSIS OF A PARTICULAR KIND
OF MARRIAGE SITUATION AS AN EXAMPLE
OF THE APPLICATION OF THE THEORY

By now the reader has some idea of the focus and range of problems that the present theory might be addressed to. Another concrete but arbitrary example should further help in this regard. We wish to consider an instance of marriage where the partners are young and have "traditional" views of the respective roles of husband and wife at the outset of their marriage. The man conceives of himself primarily in terms of his occupational career, whereas the woman conceives of herself primarily in terms of her family career. Conceptually, this is represented as a closed contingent career path for each, and each career initially provides substantial positive esteem income. We expect that each partner will be faced with "becoming" in their respective careers. Thus both will be able to feel good about themselves by engaging in the mutually compatible activities of occupation and housewife that appear to be the traditional dichotomy for the nuclear family in mid-20th-century Western culture. The man is "becoming a success' in his occupational pursuits, while the woman is "becoming a success" in having and raising children and caring for the family. While we recognize that other simultaneous careers can also be pursued by both partners, and that identity is therefore not completely tied to the "roles" as described above, let us assume for this arbitrary example that they are the careers that provide the *greatest* source of esteem income, that these careers remain closed, and that our analysis of closed contingent careers applies equally to both partners for a period of years.

Given this specific example, we can derive that as a function of success in their respective careers, these individuals will face a "marriage crisis" as each approaches the final steps of their respective closed contingent careers. The man will no longer see himself as "becoming" in the occupational sense and will be looking for another career to provide esteem income from "becoming"—which he no longer attains through his job. The woman will no longer see herself as "becoming" in the housewife-mother sense and will be looking for another career to provide esteem income from "becoming." Both husband and wife need not face a closed career in every marriage, but in the case we are considering, while the man has perceived limits for advancement and has approached those limits, and the woman has approached her goal of getting all the children off to school (for example), they have both approached an "identity crisis" that might easily be resolved by both going their own ways in new careers that are not compatible with the original marriage "roles" they held when younger. For example, the husband might see becoming a good family man as a means of increasing esteem income, so that for him, spending increasingly greater amounts of time with his wife and family during the evenings and weekends that were previously devoted to the occupational career becomes an important issue in the marriage. On the other hand, the wife might see going back to school in the evening as the beginning of a new educational-occupational career.

While the one moves toward greater family involvement, the other moves away from it. This seems to represent a fairly typical change that more and more is a likely sequence based upon the greater limits that (present) economic conditions place on advancement for men, on the one hand, and the increased freedom that the women's movement makes apparent for women, on the other.

Notice that there are ways in which the original situation might be changed so as not to produce a set of mutually incompatible careers for husband and wife, and that the problem of individual identity crises and/or the marriage crisis is neither inevitable nor necessary at any given point. For example, the man might change jobs to one where he perceives he has greater interest in the substantive area (intrinsic value), a greater challenge (difficulty value), more opportunities for bonuses (extrinsic value), and a clearer path for advancement (instrumental value), and one where an individual does more honest work (cultural value). If he is positively motivated for this career, this change from a closed to an open occupational career path should produce a renewed source of positive esteem income in terms of a positively valued future sense of self—renewed "becoming." On the other hand, the woman might perceive dealing with her older children and their problems in contemporary America as more interesting than "diapers and lunch" (intrinsic value), dealing with issues of drug abuse and sexual growth as a challenge to be met (difficulty value), a greater opportunity for praise from her neighbors and friends for involvement in the teen-age problems of her children (extrinsic value), and a clearer path to seeing her children take successive steps away from home and become increasingly more independent adults (instrumental value), and reaffirm in her mind the value of proper help and concern by parents for their growing children (cultural value). If she is positively motivated for this career, this change from closed to open family career should also produce a renewed source of positive esteem income and sense of "becoming." While we can debate what "ought or should" happen from a sociological or political (external) viewpoint in terms of some ultimate "goods" we wish to impose on these individuals, the theory predicts that such changes will allow for continuation of the previously valued careers of these individuals, which they perceived at the outset of their marriage. Whether these individuals wish to remain within the marriage arrangement or not will be more complexly determined, particularly as regards their respective sexual careers (or lack of them), and whether they are positive or negative for that marriage. But turning the closed careers that existed at the onset of marriage into more open ones (few careers remain open for a lifetime) should increase the chances of a compatible relationship as opposed to when these careers continue to remain closed until only esteem income from "has been" and "is" remains.

Neither of the marriage partners in the above example need face an "identity crisis" (Erikson, 1968) if they are able to perceive substantial positive value from their closed careers. The man may be able to look back on a substantial record of past success in his occupational career and know and feel good about who he has been, while the woman may be able to do the same for her family career. Many individuals, however, find that the net amount of positive value is less in identifying with a past career than in pursuing a future possible career. The present theory explicitly suggests that changes in careers and "identity crises" are neither inevitable, necessarily desirable, nor to be expected in some invariant sequence (cf. Sheehy, 1974). Whether they occur, and, if so, when, depends in the present conceptual analysis on the interaction of the variables that determine the value of a psychological career to the individual in question.

MAINTAINING VERSUS ATTAINING AS TIME–LINKED ORIENTATIONS TO ESTEEM INCOME

From the present analysis we see that finding out about—and feeling good about —oneself can be an important dual goal of adult life: I *know* who I am—and I *like* who I am. Explicit in the combination of the two assumptions concerning information and affective value in the self-system is the notion that the individual consciously perceives a past, present, or future sense of self, or, at the very least, becomes aware or is made aware of time-linked sense of self—or has to become aware of it—to be conceptualized as pursuing a psychological career. We now want to make an explicit distinction between the effects of the past attributable to the automatic carry-over of unsatisfied motivation from past situations where motivation has been aroused—the concept of inertial motivation (see Atkinson & Birch, 1970, 1978)—and the esteem income and motivation of action attributable to the retrospected past, or the consciously recalled or remembered past as it relates to the self-system and past success or failure. We assume that inertial effects can influence immediate action without the mediation of the self-system, while we assume that such conscious attending to the past is the necessary ingredient for the self-system to function so that the past can influence the individual. (We assume a similar need for conscious attending for both becoming and being to influence the individual.) Thus inertial effects and retrospected effects are seen as operating independently of each other. We refer to phenomonological (consciously experienced) effects of success and failure to distinguish them from the inertial effects of success and failure.

It follows that "becoming" means a focused attention on the anticipated future, and in fact large total value associated with future goals is expected to shift the focus of the individual to the anticipated future so that the individual will be increasingly preoccupied with attaining future success and therefore with self-identity as "becoming." In the final stage of a closed-path contingent career the individual is expected to be primarily concerned with self-identity as "having been," and to an increasingly great extent as its value increases. We expect that this shift will produce an important shift in the conscious factors experienced by the individual as sustaining the career, how the individual relates to that career, and in fact on the determinants of immediate action in that career to be discussed later.

When an individual's esteem income is primarily from past success, as at the final stage of closed career striving, we expect the individual's thoughts to be primarily past oriented. We expect the individual to report that "the best part of my life (career) is in the past," if such a statement could be made without negative evaluative connotation (but see below), when faced with the late stages of closed career striving, whereas when faced with the early stages of career striving, whether open or closed, the individual should report that the "best part of my life (career) is in the future."

One who is "becoming" can continue to receive esteem income by seeing oneself as successfully moving through steps to future success, and to do so one must be primarily concerned with the task requirements for success along the path. One's goals in life within this career are those of the anticipated future, and one is dominated by thoughts of how one's present actions will translate the anticipated future into present reality.

One who "has been" successful can continue to receive esteem income by seeing oneself as having been successful in that career and, particularly, by maintaining the values of past success at levels that provide sufficient esteem income. Thus the individual is expected to be primarily concerned with the maintenance of the values of past success, such as recalling how difficult past success was, how a given success was important in earning the chance the individual is now confronted with, how much money (etc.) the past success produced, and how good that success makes the individual as a person. Note that this maintenance does not necessarily involve any action in the real world, but consists of recall and reminiscing about past success and cognitive work, thinking about the circumstances of past success and its value as now seen in the present. Failure to do this might result in the erosion of esteem income from the past. On the other hand, the cognitions involved in "becoming" consist of daydreams of future success, anticipation of how valuable that series of future successes along the anticipated career path will be, and the planning and/or doing required for immediate success. In other words, we expect the thoughts and daydreams of individuals who face early versus late steps in a closed contingent career path to be quite different in their time orientation—future oriented versus past oriented—and that their emotional outlook (affective value) should be closely tied to this cognitive outlook. When the "psychologically young as becoming" think about the future, they feel good about themselves, but when they think about the past that feeling disappears. When the "psychologically old as has been" think about the past, they feel good about themselves, but when they think about the future that feeling disappears. The psychological morale of such individuals will depend upon whether they are engaged in their usual cognitive elaboration of their stage of career striving, and it will change when they focus on a time orientation that provides a different level of esteem income.

To the extent that attaining versus maintaining involves thought exclusively, we can predict that early versus late career striving in a closed path will be dominated by thoughts of anticipated future success and what it takes to attain it, on the one hand, or by thoughts of retrospected past success and what it was like. However, in a contingent path, immediate activity is always a requirement so long as the final goal of the past has not as yet been attained. We predict that dominant thoughts, linked as we presume they are to the stage of striving, will provide the primary determinants of immediate activity—or, in the language of the dynamics of action, will provide the instigating force for action (Atkinson & Birch, 1978). That is, the stage of striving will define the purpose for which the individual engages in the immediate (next) step of the contingent career. Earlier conceptual analyses have developed how this works for "becoming," and while we shall review this below, we want first to deal with "having been," which has until now received no attention within this conceptual scheme.

MAINTAINING VERSUS ATTAINING AS DETERMINANTS OF IMMEDIATE ACTION

One of the important orientations to grow out of the extension of theory presented here is the reemphasis (cf. Lewin, 1938) on the interrelationship between *action in the real world* to attain future success, and reorganization of the cognitive field, the *maintenance of the values of past success,* as alternative means of ensuring continued esteem income. These provide for different purposes in adult life. At the beginning of career striving attainment of goals through action perceived to be instrumental to their attainment will be seen by the individual as the primary means of obtaining esteem income. And expectancy X value theory of action will predict best. At the end of career striving, with "becoming" no longer a possibility, and being limited to evaluation of abilities that cannot be further utilized because there are no future accomplishments to which they can be applied, the individual is left with retrospection about past successes and maintaining their value as the primary means of obtaining esteem income. Theories addressed to such cognitive work will predict best. In midcareer striving, anticipation of future goal attainment, retrospection about past goal attainment, and evalution of present levels of prerequisite abilities (respectively, "becoming", "having been", and "being") will all be relevant to contributing to feeling good about oneself in this career. Theory concerned with both *attaining* and *maintaining*, as well as *evaluating* competence through seeking information and making attributions to various causes of success, will all be relevant, but each will be limited in its success because all three are necessary since all three processes are expected to be occurring at once. In fact, we need theory that considers the interrelationships among orientations toward the future (attaining), the past (maintaining), and the present (evaluating), something that until now has been missing because of the failure to recognize that the dominant theories of motivation and action in psychology have dealt with different aspects of the behavioral situation. Expectancy X value theory has been concerned primarily with "becoming." Cognitive consistency theory is concerned primarily with "having been." Trait theories of personality and self-attribution theory are concerned primarily with "being."

We expect that time-linked sources of esteem income will produce quite different reactions to a situation where one is challenged either by oneself or another to justify feeling good about oneself as a function of a particular career. We expect that in the beginning of striving the individual will take the attitude that, "if I work hard to fulfill those prerequisites that will allow me to move on toward the next steps of the career path, I can justifiably feel good about myself because I will be becoming who I want to become." There is little concern with cognitive work that might involve distortion to maintain esteem income from past successes because there are none to "defend." The individual is open to information concerning "how I am doing" to meet the stated prerequisites, and is open to both positive and negative feedback that might be useful in attainment of immediate success and therefore earning the opportunity to continue to "become." However, the individual at the end of striving in a closed contingent path is predicted, in comparison to the individual at the beginning of striving in a closed contingent path, to be more motivated to use cognitive work to ensure continued positive valuation of past successes to feel good about himself or herself, and to minimize the negative value of any perceived past failures. This individual will be more likely to defend the record of past accomplishments so as to ensure that their values, which provide positive esteem income, are maintained at present value or enhanced. At this time this is the only way one can continue to feel good about oneself. There is no possibility for further accomplishment, so one believes, because all goals have been attained. Now the task is maintenance of the "historical record," the set of accomplishments, particularly if others were to attack that record. Such an attack might try to belittle the record by indicating that past successes were trivially easy (reducing difficulty value if believed by the individual under attack); that past successes had little to do with later opportunities—the person would have gotten the chance even if he or she had failed (thereby reducing instrumental value if believed); that times have changed and the current generation does not value such kinds of accomplishment (such as technological obsolescence reducing cultural value), etc. Such defensive reactions that are expected will be to protect past successes from losing their ability to provide esteem income. The primary goals are to know and to feel good about oneself, however that can be brought about. When one is constrained by events or by others to attack one's own accomplishments, a corresponding loss of esteem income from past sense of self is predicted. Generally, we predict that self-criticism will be resisted unless alternative means of feeling good and/or knowing oneself are simultaneously perceived to ensure continued positive esteem income, given devaluation of the past self-record ("has been").

As Lewin (1938) implied with regard to the issue of locomotion versus cognitive reorganization, both attaining goals that have value and maintaining the values of previously attained goals can function for the individual to provide esteem income. We explicitly predict that action will be preferred to cognitive work so long as further action is possible, so that the probability of cognitive work will be smallest in early careers, moderate in middle careers, and greatest in late careers, when these careers are perceived as closed. It follows that if a closed career becomes an open one, such cognitive work should decrease, and the decrease should be proportionate to the extent of increase in "becoming" (i.e., length of future path).

In all of the above, we assume "cognitive work" ("cognitive defensiveness") to be quite different from the automatic psychological defenses that are predicted to function to hide intense self-hatred (see below).

For individuals in the middle of careers of a closed contingent path, we expect some cognitive work, but since positive esteem income can be obtained by immediate success and the utilization of already acquired skills, we expect this to be limited. The individual can act to attain future success. Since in our society the cultural value of "becoming" is expected to be greater for the majority of individuals than that for "having been," striving to attain valued future goals is expected to provide greater esteem income than maintaining the values of past goals, holding the particular magnitudes of intrinsic, difficulty, instrumental, and extrinsic values constant. Put another way, in Western culture most individuals learn that others value more the forward-looking, open stance with its prospects for continued advancement, improvement, and success than the backward-looking, closed stance with its necessity for argumentation to defend the status quo. Various measures of openness versus closedness to new information, negative information, and use of psychological strategies of defense to distort reality should yield a consistent picture indicating greater openness for new information, negative information, and lack of defensiveness for the individual who is primarily "becoming" as described here, in comparison to the individual who is primarily "having been" as described here. Change from the end of a closed contingent path to a new contingent path, or change of a closed to an open contingent path, should produce greater openness for new information and for negative information, and less defensive reaction to maintain values of past successes.[3]

PSYCHOLOGICAL AGING AND ITS CONSEQUENCES

The concept of psychological aging is defined within the present theory in terms of the primary source of time-linked value, past, present, and/or future. It is also related to the concepts of open and closed contingent paths, and its consequences are determined by these variables in interaction with the predominant personality orientation of the individual for the psychological career in question—positively motivated, indifferent, and negatively motivated individuals.

Within the behavioral system, the concept of psychological aging refers to a shifting from the value of future anticipated outcomes as the primary source of value to the value of retrospected past and remembered outcomes as the primary sources of value. Within the self-system, psychological aging refers to a shifting

[3]The analysis presented thus far neglects the role of individual differences in motives that determine whether a given outcome of action will be perceived and/or function as offering net positive, negative, or zero value to that individual. In the preceding discussion it has been assumed that the individual referred to is positively motivated for the substantive outcome(s) in question—i.e., that the motive to appreciate and seek out that source of value is stronger than the motive to dislike and be inhibited by the prospect of seeking out that source of value—and the implications discussed thus far are explicitly limited to that individual. This corresponds to the "success-oriented individual" in the achievement domain of activity. Later sections of this chapter and material presented later (chapter 15) deal more extensively with the role of individual differences in personality (e.g., motives) that weight or color sources of value to make them net positive for one kind of individual (termed the positively motivated individual), net negative for another kind of individual (termed the negatively motivated individual and corresponding to the failure-threatened person in the achievement domain), and make them have zero net value for a third kind of individual (termed the indifferent, neutrally motivated, or indeterminately motivated individual and corresponding to those persons characterized as high or low in both the motives to achieve success and to avoid failure in the achievment domain).

from seeing oneself in terms of a future sense of self as the primary means of obtaining esteem income to seeing oneself in terms of a past self-image as the primary means of obtaining esteem income.

Psychological aging is specific to particular psychological careers. When one sees oneself in terms of distinct substantive self-images, such as occupational, sexual, and familial, and if one of these psychological careers provides a predominant amount of esteem income to one, the perception one has of oneself as aging will be substantially more pronounced than if different psychological careers provide more equal amounts of esteem income.

Psychological aging can also be conceptualized in terms of a generalized time-linked psychological career when one sees oneself primarily in terms of the nonsubstantive time-linked senses of self that are correlated with chronological aging: young person, middle-aged person, old person (i.e., senior citizen). These content-less time-linked senses of self are often used by individuals when they perceive themselves as fitting the normative age-linked categories that are used in the culture, although they need not be perceived at all by a particular individual. Particular substantive psychological careers also have normative age categories that can be used by the individual so that substantive careers can provide differential value depending upon the individual's use of these generalized time-linked senses of self. For example, the "young mother" of 14 and the "old mother" of 45 are time-linked senses of self that provide differential value not only in terms of stages of career striving (both may see themselves as "becoming"), but in terms of the value associated with the perception of a definite "normative" period for filling the role of mother in a particular culture (negative cultural value may be obtained from seeing oneself as a "too young" or a "too old" mother). From the perspective of the present theory, the value of the time-linked self-image is the critical variable, and normative age-linked expectations function through the various sources of value to influence esteem income.

It follows that psychological aging will vary greatly from individual to individual even though from the external viewpoint they appear to be faced with the same life situation. Thus, for example, as we have already seen, the perception of facing the last step of a closed contingent career produces the psychological equivalent of "old age" for that career, whereas facing the same step of an open contingent career path, other things equal, is predicted to yield a phenomenological experience more akin to "maturity," "the height of one's career," "middle age," etc. Thus the young person faced with the last step of an educational career is a psychological "has been" to the same extent as the old person who is faced with the last step of an occupational career, other things equal. It turns out that "other things" are not equal because the young person often anticipates an occupational career based upon the educational career, so that in fact the career is not perceived as "closed," but rather the educational-occupational career is seen as a continuous one where the occupational steps are anticipated to follow (contingently or not depending upon the perceptions of the individual). However, if the young person has not conceptualized what to do after graduation from high school or college, so that "graduation" is seen as the final goal of an educational career, then we predict the psychological effects of loss of esteem income from future self-image and seeing oneself in terms of "has been" rather than "becoming."

Note that the psychological effects of aging are not universally "bad" in terms of some view of psychological health or adjustment. Their consequences depend upon whether the psychological career provides predominantly positive or negative esteem income, which, other things equal, depends upon whether the individual is positively, negatively, or neutrally motivated with regard to that substantive psychological career. For example, individuals for whom the motive to achieve is relatively stronger than the motive to avoid failure might be expected to be positively motivated for an occupational or educational career, but they may be negatively motivated for a family career if, for example, their motive to avoid social rejection dominates their motive to gain social approval. We do not have empirical evidence concerning which of the social motives provide the predominant amounts of value in different substantive careers, but we can anticipate that for particular individuals the consequences of psychological aging might be quite different because for one career they might be positively motivated while for another they might be indifferent or even negatively motivated. But we can make the general prediction that, for a positively motivated career, loss of positive value through a shift from "becoming" to "having been" will produce a diminished feeling of positive self-worth, a loss of the future time-linked sense of self and the corresponding "identity-crisis," a loss of interest in activity oriented to attaining future goals, and a drop in the intensity of behavioral effort in immediate activity of that career. However, for a negatively motivated career, we predict loss of negative value through a shift from "becoming" to "having been," coupled with a net increase in self-worth and a feeling of greater net positive self-worth (through loss of negative rather than through increase of positive per se), given a history of past success. Interest and intensity of effort should increase through decrease of negative value, although phenomenologically the experience is predicted to be more like "relief" and "settling in" to a psychological career just at the time when its future-contingent steps are at an end.

A person pursuing a noncontingent psychological career is not expected to experience shifts in time-linked sources of value to nearly as great an extent as an individual pursuing a contingent psychological career, so that psychological aging is not expected to be correlated to as great an extent with the passage of time or the negotiating of successive steps in the noncontingent career as it is expected to be in the contingent career. We thus expect that the "mere passage of time" is much less important for psychological aging in a contingent career, where the effects of time-linked sources of value should be substantially greater. Time per se may be less important than what happens in time for a contingent psychological career. Individuals faced with noncontingent careers are more likely to be influenced by the normative age-linked changes in self-image that are perceived in the culture. That may or may not be "good" in terms of a view of psychological health. The young person (in age) faced with a contingent career may see himself or herself "prematurely" as old (in terms of career) and a "has been" when he or she believes that there are no more future goals to attain in a given psychological career. If the career is one that has provided substantial positive value, then self-worth is expected to diminish. Successful, highly able, positively motivated individuals thus are expected to face "premature" psychological aging in contingent careers. If the equivalent career were conceived in noncontingent terms, instrumental value at least would not be perceived to diminish, so that whatever positive value was offered by the career might not diminish until the individual begins to see himself or herself as an "older ———" rather than a "younger ———."

We do not always expect that the value of "has been" will be less than the value of "becoming." Certain individuals can obtain great positive value from conceptualizing themselves as the "experienced pro," the very successful business person, etc. It depends upon how the person's perceptions and personality combine to produce quality of value (positive or negative), quantity of value (amount), and time-linked source of value. There are no general rules that will apply for all individuals; generalizations concerning normative trends can be made from the external view only through empirical research concerning the predominant personality type, quality and quantity of value, and time-linked cultural expectations for a given group defined for purposes of societal analysis.

AGING AND CAREER STRIVING
FROM THE EXTERNAL VIEWPOINT

Of particular significance for an understanding of adult personality functioning and change in society is the correlation that might be assumed between aging and the various stages of striving outlined here. While by no means perfect, we expect some correlation between "youth" and the beginning stage of career striving, middle age and the "middle stage" of career striving, and old age and the "final stage" of career striving. We do not mean to rule out a 60-year-old facing the first step of a new career path, nor a 30-year-old faced with the last step of a closed career path. But, generally, given certain facts of life to be discussed in greater detail in later sections, we expect the usual pattern of career striving to result in such a correlation, although the variations of this pattern in fact allow us to conceptualize such phenomena as second careers, new careers, and retirement careers. This means that we can derive that young people will be characterized primarily as "becoming," whereas older people will be characterized primarily as "having been," on the average, for a given group of individuals, other things equal. This allows us to understand phenomena concerning what has been termed the "generation gap" from a new perspective, particularly why older individuals sometimes appear to younger ones to be "trying to maintain the status quo" of past successes, while the younger ones are trying to "make it" in the real world through future successes.

One factor that we have thus far neglected in our identification of "becoming" with the young or younger and "having been" with the old or older, as a rough correlation, is the fact that, as a function of age, individuals sometimes come to perceive a leveling off or even a decrement in the degree of possession of previously valued competences that, although they are still seen as prerequisites, are now also seen as skills left behind in one's youth. This perceived decrement (whether real or imagined is a separate question) in prerequisite competence has the consequence of diminishing esteem income that can come from the present sense of self, so that it often happens that as one approaches the final goal of a closed career both the future and present senses of self provide diminishing esteem income, with only the past sense of self left to provide it.

The critical assumptions of the present theory concerning age and aging can be seen from the above to be that success and failure experiences along a contingent career produce changes in various motivational variables that influence esteem income and level of motivation for activity: (1) success and failure influence perceived competence, which influences present sense of self and esteem income derived from it; (2) success and failure influence confidence, which changes the difficulty value of the future sense of self; (3) success reduces the number of steps remaining along a closed contingent path, which influences the instrumental value of the immediate next step along the path and hence esteem income from "becoming" through immediate activity; (4) success increases "has been" based on previous success, so that esteem income from the past sense of self plays an increasingly greater role; (5) effects of failure, to be discussed below.

THE EFFECTS OF FAILURE AND A REINTERPRETATION OF EGO-INVOLVEMENT

Thus far we have considered only the effects of success on functioning and change in psychological careers, particularly as success influences the time-linked sources of value in stages of striving—"becoming" versus "having been" and being. This resulted from a primary focus on contingent psychological careers, where movement through successive steps by definition requires more immediate success to earn the opportunity to do so. However, once we distinguish between success in terms of some personal criterion of action and success in terms of some moving-on criterion in a contingent path (see chapter 4), it is possible to refer to the effects of immediate failure in a contingent career path without necessarily ruling out further striving. An immediate failure that does not rule out further striving can be taken by the individual to indicate a lack of prerequisite ability, thus influencing perceived value from the present self-image due to a downward evaluation of degree of possession of a positively valued competence. Such an immediate failure can reduce the subjective probability of success for later goals along the path and thereby influence the perceived final goal of the path and/or the difficulty value of subsequent successes along that path.

Each of these possible effects of failure will have a phenomenological effect (as opposed to the effect on inertial motivation referred to earlier) that will be opposite to the phenomenological effect of success in an equivalent immediate activity of a career path. Whereas success can lead to upward evaluation of degree of possession of prerequisite ability and hence to greater positive value, failure can lead to its downward evaluation and hence to less positive value from the present self-image. Whereas an immediate success can increase the perceived length of a contingent path, or turn a closed path into an anticipated open path, failure can decrease the perceived length of the path or turn it into a closed path where previously it was perceived as an open one. And, in terms of the moving-on criterion, while immediate success guarantees continued opportunities for future striving and for becoming the person the individual is striving to be, immediate failure guarantees future failure through loss of the opportunity to continue and precipitates an "identity crisis" by guaranteeing failure to become the person the individual was striving to be. Contingent psychological careers are therefore seen as extremely important by the individual—they are highly ego involving—because immediate success allows for continued "becoming" while immediate failure guarantees a loss of future sense of self. And evaluations of prerequisite abilities that might indicate degree of possession, either sufficient to guarantee attainment of the future self-image or insufficient to guarantee loss of future self-image, are perceived as extremely important for the same reasons.

The newer definition of psychological importance and ego involvement in terms of striving in a contingent psychological career, where opportunities for action define self-identity, can also be extended to the retrospected past as well as the anticipated future and the evaluated present.

THE PROSPECT AND CONSEQUENCES OF RETIREMENT

The present conception has clear-cut implications concerning an individual's predicted reaction to the prospects and actuality of the situation commonly referred to as retirement. Psychological retirement can be conceptualized within this theory as movement beyond the final step of a psychological career, as loss of ego involvement due to no longer linking self-identity to the outcomes of action in contingent psychological careers. Defined in this way the concept may or may not correspond with the objective state of affairs that an external observer attributes to a purported retiree. An individual may no longer be enrolled in school but still conceive of himself or herself as pursuing an educational career, whereas a person still attending school may have "retired" psychologically. Psychological retirement exists when an individual perceives no additional steps to pursue in a substantive area that was previously seen as offering future possibilities for action (the behavioral system) and which previously provided a means of self-identity (the self-system). Psychological retirement is therefore not at issue when an individual gives up activity that never provided a means of self-identity. In this sense not all individuals who stop working at age 65 are to be conceptualized as faced with psychological retirement. Put another way, only when a previous psychological career existed is the possibility of psychological retirement raised with the loss of opportunity to continue along a path.

This internal view of retirement not only allows for dealing with the usual meaning of retirement, but allows for additional insights into career-related phenomena that might not previously have been seen as functionally identical to retirement. Put simply, an individual who has taken the final step of what is perceived to be a closed contingent path, and for whom no additional steps have been added to that path, is faced with "psychological retirement" and/or loss of ego involvement in that career. Whether this corresponds to the chronological age of retirement or to the external societal definition of retirement is relevant only to the extent that the perceptions that the individual has of the current situation are tied to these age- or norm-related definitions as an additional source of value. Thus the perception of one's situation has been "retired" or not is not irrelevant by any means. But the psychological consequences of having completed a closed contingent career are those that we claim are usually thought of as the consequences of retirement as externally defined. For positively motivated individuals, these include loss of self-worth, interest, and enthusiasm and a feeling of indifference and apathy in comparison to that prior to retirement. For the indifferent individual, no differences are expected after retirement. For the negatively motivated individual, retirement should increase self-worth through a loss of negative esteem income and be accompanied by relief, relaxation, and a new sense of freedom—a release from the burden of the career.

PSYCHOLOGICAL MORALE, SELF–DESTRUCTIVE BEHAVIOR, AND PSYCHOLOGICAL DEFENSES

We assume that an individual's psychological morale is synonymous with resultant value. Such phrases as "value in the self-system," "value of a self-image," "self-evaluation," "self-esteem," and/or "esteem income" refer to conscious evaluation of self-worth. We wish to make an explicit link among value, esteem income, one's perception of one's own self-worth, psychological morale, and self-destructive behavior. The conceptual term in the theory is value and its various sources. We build upon the conceptual analysis provided by Johnson (1973) in his theory of the development of chemical dependences, particularly alcoholism, to do so. Paraphrasing the Johnson theory, feeling good is operationalized in the early stages of a career (alcoholism) as "learning the mood swing," or learning that using behavior in this area (drinking) produces good feelings (e.g., the acquisition of positive affective value for outcomes of this activity). In the second stage, the individual uses the behavior (drinking) as a means of producing good feelings—use of the mood swing or psychological dependence upon the behavior (drinking) still refers to the behavioral system, although Steiner's (1971) analysis of "games that alcoholics play" notes that even in the earlier stages of alcoholism the positive self-system may also be involved—the person is "becoming" a particular kind of person who, for example, drinks to be "sociable," to be "a swinger," etc. However, in stage three, the individual attains negative cultural value and comes to anticipate more of it by violating personal standards of right and wrong behavior (negative cultural value) in continually getting drunk and then doing things that he or she would not ordinarily do when sober. This lowers the person's perception of his or her own self-worth—resultant value is less positive. We see this as now implicating the self-system; (drunk) behavior is no longer merely considered "stupid" or "bad" or "wrong" by the person—the person judges that *he or she* is stupid, a bad person, etc. The third stage is one of "harmful psychological dependence" where the individual's self-esteem is continually eroded by frequent displays of (drunken) behavior that are then later evaluated by the drinker as having violated personal standards of right and wrong (further attainment of negative cultural value). At this stage frequent attempts to stop drinking occur as the psychological career produces less total net positive value. The person first sees himself or herself as a less desirable (good) person. If sources of value other than negative cultural value remain positive and strong, after passing through a zero point, the person sees himself or herself as a more and more undesirable (bad) person. This lowering of positive self-esteem and then increase in negative self-esteem continues so long as the individual continues to drink and violate personal standards of right and wrong (behavioral system) and/or so long as the individual fails to attain/maintain/be the kind of person represented by personal positive senses of self as a drinker. When the career drinker has accumulated sufficient negative self-esteem, meaning the individual hates himself or herself, a choice point is reached, according to Johnson, where the individual either commits suicide or the automatic psychological defenses (first identified in psychoanalytic theory) are mobilized without the person's awareness, to knock out the person's perception of self-hatred (accumulated individual negative cultural value). At this point we can see for the first time the conceptual link among (1) the expectancy X value theory of action, (2) an expectancy X value theory concerning the self-system, and (3) a theory about unconscious defensive reaction to unbearable situations, namely, the person's feeling of worthlessness.

Psychological morale can be conceptualized as a direct function of positive self-evaluation, and as an inverse function of negative self-evaluation. Thus, psychological morale is high (one likes or loves oneself) when total esteem income is positive and very large. Psychological morale is low when total esteem income is negative and very large. However, there is a discontinuity where psychological defenses are mobilized to deal with intense negative self-evaluation. A different kind of motivational impetus is now assumed to be in effect. Before psychological defenses are mobilized, the individual is motivated to obtain and/or maximize positive value and to avoid or minimize negative value. After defenses are mobilized, the individual is motivated to minimize negative value only, through continued use and/or strengthening of the psychological defenses against perception of self-hate (negative affective cultural value or guilt). Now the primary goal is to minimize self-hate, and the conceptual analysis presented for "normal" adult personality functioning no longer applies. Rather, the conceptual analysis of the psychodynamic approach (Janis, 1969) is more appropriate to explain the automatic functioning of psychological defenses, coupled with the still-potent effects of (now) unconscious negative self-evaluation.

An important insight based on the Johnson (1973) approach and made part of the present theory is the continuity between motivation to obtain positive self-esteem and not to obtain negative self-esteem, which operates so long as negative self-esteem is not sufficiently strong to mobilize self-destructive behavior or the psychological defenses, and motivation to minimize negative self-esteem, which operates after negative self-esteem has become so large that it is intolerable for one to continue to see oneself in this extremely negative manner. Generally, the first time the choice point of either using psychological defenses or self-destructive behavior is reached, it seems that many (most) individuals automatically mobilize their psychological defenses without conscious awareness rather than commit suicide. Only later, when self-hatred has continued to build through continued increments in negative value, and some event occurs that provides a further increment in negative value that overwhelms the defense's ability to prevent one from seeing oneself with this much greater loathsomeness, does the probability of suicidal behavior become substantial.

At any particular time, an individual can make evaluations concerning self-worth at that time based upon the amount of esteem income provided by particular psychological careers, by other behaviors, and by reference to some generalized concept of self (see Shrauger, 1975). If we simplify for the moment by assuming that only a particular career of the individual provides esteem income, then we can utilize an adaptation of Johnson's (1973) "feeling chart" (affective value) to refer to positive value in the self-system. We represent one's judgment about one's own self-worth as a point on a line from large positive through zero through large negative. The amount of esteem income obtained from the career is assumed to move that point upward and downward as more or less positive and negative esteem income is provided through anticipation, retrospection, evaluation of the future, past, present time-linked senses of self in that career. This would correspond to a conceptualization of specific self-evaluation. On the other hand, the combined esteem income from all psychological careers of the individual would correspond to general self-evaluation, and we would now refer to total psychological morale rather than psychological morale from a particular career.

THE MOTIVATIONAL SYNDROME AND VALUE IN PSYCHOLOGICAL CAREERS

Use of the idea of a continuity of positive and negative affective value in a psychological career allows a more systematic treatment of several qualitative concepts that we have previously used to refer to different kinds of individuals in terms of motivational syndromes that develop over time: compulsive career striving, apathetic behavior, and up-tight career striving (see Raynor, 1974b). We can also include along this quantitative dimension of value or esteem income the concepts of the success-oriented personality and the more general concept of the positively motivated individual, along with the failure-threatened personality and the more general concept of the negatively motivated individual. These terms are meant to be useful, descriptive labels to demarcate different sections of the underlying quantitative dimension of value or esteem income. There are no discontinuities along the underlying quantitative dimension from very large positive value through zero value to very large negative value until, as already noted, one is assumed to occur when the automatic psychological defenses prevent the individual from perceiving large negative esteem income (self-hate) that has resulted from pursuit of a "negatively valent career," defined as one that provides resultant net value that is positive, but in doing so provides a smaller but still substantial amount of negative individual cultural value. Once the automatic psychological defenses are functioning, the individual is motivated only by the level of walled-off self-hate (unconscious affect). Motivation to reduce phenomenological positive or negative esteem income is no longer operative: the primary motivation is now unconscious, and expectancy X value theory no longer successfully predicts life behavior but rather gives way to a psychodynamic theory (cf. Janis, 1969) that conceptualizes the functional significance of psychological defenses against unconscious negative emotion.

Positively Valent Careers

When one's psychological career provides large amounts of positive esteem income and little or no negative esteem income, by definition, one highly values oneself as defined by the career self-image. One's thoughts are expected to be optimistic, and one's affective reactions positive, characterized by enthusiasm, interest, eagerness, a feeling of "aliveness." One knows who one is, one likes oneself and the world one lives in that defines one's action opportunities. The mood is upbeat; morale is high; life is a "bowl of cherries." The success-oriented individual in the achievement domain is an example of a person who is likely to develop a positively valent career in the occupational area, and one that research studies over the past two decades have given us increasingly greater knowledge about (see chapter 2 for a summary of this previous work).

We assume that for any particular kind of incentive system—be it affiliative, power, aggression, or, alternatively, occupational, sexual, or familial—that the theoretical analysis of behavior may specify, it is conceptually useful to think of individuals as simultaneously classifiable along a positive and negative dispositional dimension, and therefore along a resultant or net dispositional dimension. This resultant motive system determines value for that behavioral opportunity per se, on a continuum from positive to zero to negative. For any given behavioral opportunity we can then predict, given appropriate assessment of the resultant dispositional dimension, the extent to which a positively valent career can (potentially) emerge, given the relative amount of value that the behavioral system provides. For individuals with a net negative resultant value for the dispositional assessment, we expect little chance for a positively valent career to emerge in that activity. Rather, the individual is predicted not to engage in that activity unless constrained to do so by other sources of positive value. The negatively valent career (i.e., the failure-threatened individual who becomes an "up-tight striver") is a more likely possibility if a psychological career emerges at all. The individual with zero dispositional net value is the one most likely to be classified as an apathetic individual. If positive motivation (behavioral system) continues to increase, sufficient positive value is present to allow for self-identity through a self-image defined by the outcomes of activity in that area. If positive value still continues to grow, the effects of over-motivation on efficiency of performance (see Atkinson, 1974a, 1978), coupled with ever-increasing amounts of time spent pursuing this career to the inevitable exclusion of pursuit of other careers, creates a compulsive career striver—the success-oriented individual also high in positive extrinsic motivation. The intensity of career involvement is extremely high, as is psychological morale, and the experiential feeling approaches mania. The individual is wildly optimistic, completely self-confident, and highly self-righteous. Positive esteem income is at a maximum for a given career. If tasks along the career path become increasingly more complex, we expect the effects of immediate failure to become apparent, which will in the short run only accentuate incipient problems because positive inertial motivation (Atkinson & Birch, 1978) should only increase career involvement. But if the career involvement prevents pursuit of other neglected, the compulsive career begins to produce unanticiapted negative esteem income, not from the career itself, but because career involvement produces negative cultural value from non-career-related activities that the person believes behavioral pattern (Friedman & Rosenman, 1974) are two speicfic instances of a phenomenon that we term compulsive career striving, and Johnson's (1973) theory suggests the alcoholic career is similar.

However, as positive esteem income decreases and/or negative esteem income increases, the level of psychological morale decreases. The individual experiencing a lowering of positive esteem income becomes more indifferent to himself or herself and the world he or she lives in, less optimistic, more apathetic, less involved in the real world, more prone to "do nothing." If a self-image path or career no longer provides sufficient positive esteem income, the individual abandons that self-image as a means of self-identity, other things equal. The individual becomes less clear about "who I am." This is termed the apathetic individual. The lack of clarity concerning "who I am" produces a personality crises motivated by the need to know and/or find out "who I am" (informational value in the self-system). Introspection about the "real me," or the "essential me"—a looking inward—is the predicted consequence of this loss of positive esteem income from a previously clear-cut career that has lost its ability to provide positive esteem income. However, an apathetic individual may evolve merely from lack of positive value in the behavioral system. This will not be associated with concern about "who I am" but rather indifference to the question—"who cares who I am?"

The net lowering of positive esteem income through an increase in negative esteem income produces a quite different experiential situation. Assuming positive esteem income has remained high, we predict a greater perceived conflict, an alternation between optimism and pessimism, a greater preoccupation with a perceived negative self-image. Rather than apathy or withdrawal to introspection of the self as previously described for the apathetic individual, the conflicted individual faces continual emotional turmoil, a battle of psychological forces that is represented experientially by alternation between the positive and negative self-images that are tied to the large amounts of positive and negative esteem income experienced in this career. Vacillation between strong positive and negative emotional states, and between liking oneself and disliking oneself, are the phenomenological correlates in the self-system. However, at the behavioral level, the "do it" and "don't do it" tendencies (action and negaction) are expected to subtract so that resultant action tendency with regard to activity in the career is expected to be weak, resulting in inaction.

When negative esteem income becomes sufficiently great, particularly cultural value, but not greater than positive, we have the negatively valent career. The person's view of the self is one of self-dislike, doing things that produce negative affective and information value in the self-system. The individual starts to dwell on the negative aspects of the career, producing more negative feelings. The individual is aware of this self-dislike, is aware of the conflict between liking and disliking of self, is aware of an inability to initiate positive action, but is preoccupied by thoughts about failure, incompetence, worries about worrying, etc. The major difference between the conflicted career and the negatively valent career is that in the latter negative thoughts and feelings about the self are sufficiently strong so that they produce a preoccupation with negative self-evaluation. One cannot for long periods escape negative thoughts and feelings about oneself and one's actions in the world. This preoccupation is the sign that negative esteem income has become almost equal to positive esteem income, and that the dominant view of the self is becoming one of dislike rather than liking. This state of lowered psychological morale is not just the lowering of positive value, nor a conflict between positive and negative outlook, which alternate, but rather a domination of negative emotion and self-dislike.

SIMULTANEOUS CAREERS AND
PSYCHOLOGICAL MORALE

An individual with such a negatively valent career may have other careers that provide positive esteem income. That is, another implication of our assumption of additivity of value is that simultaneous careers, each with its own self-image and paths for action, provide amounts of esteem income that are available to the individual. Thus, a negatively motivated individual in a given occupational career may be preoccupied with dislike with regard to self and worldly prospects for career advancement per se, but when not constrained to think about this career involvement (as when at home or away from occupational cues, requirements, actions, etc.), may think about self and feel good to the extent that the familial (self-image and steps for action) career provides positive esteem income. We must distinguish between the psychological morale for a given career and the individual's total psychological morale, which is determined by the various compatible careers that the individual may pursue at a given point in time. So long as the individual is either able or allowed by circumstances to limit cues arousing the behavioral and/or self-system to mutually exclusive environments, the individual will be able to obtain positive esteem income from other simultaneously pursued careers and/or activity, despite the fact that while pursuing the negatively valent career the individual is preoccupied by self-dislike and negative emotional states, and is severely inhibited in action for that career. However, if the individual has only one negatively valent career, or has several careers, each of which is negatively valent, or the amount of negative esteem income from a given negatively valent career is so great that its magnitude when combined with esteem income from other careers produces a large net negative amount of esteem income, we can refer to the negatively valent personality.

Degree of Career Integration

Career integration refers to a particular psychological career, the extent to which one is able to obtain sufficient positive value from that career pursuit (becoming), that career maintenance (having been), and that career identification (being) so that one simultaneously sees oneself in terms of the past, present, and future senses of self (self-images) that are defined by the substantive contingent path of action of that career. Career integration is low to the extent to which one is unable to see oneself simultaneously in terms of becoming, being, and/or having been along that path because one or more of the time-linked senses of self does not provide sufficient positive esteem income. Put another way, career integration refers to the perceived time-linked continuity of the self in terms of a particular substantive contingent path of a society. One phenomenologically experiences a lack of career integration when one retrospects and/or anticipates activity that is recognized as part of the path one is pursuing (behavioral system) but is unable to obtain esteem income from such retrospection, anticipation, etc. (self-system).

Career integration is not a goal of adult life, but rather is a consequence (or not) of one's perception of the value of one's past, present, and future in providing esteem income. As the external observer, we describe such an individual as lacking in career integration when we discover that he or she is unable to obtain esteem income from one of the time-linked senses of self that are possible. By definition, younger people will tend to be lower in career integration because when they start in the first steps of a career, they lack experience that might define them in terms of a past sense of self for that career. However, there is no inevitable link between chronological age and career integration. Some younger persons might see themselves not on the first step of a career, as defined by some external observer, but in the middle steps of a career begun earlier (but not so perceived by the external observer). Thus career integration must be carefully distinguished from the internal and external viewpoints.

Personality Integration

Just as career integration refers to the ability to simultaneously see oneself in terms of the time-linked (career) senses of self, personality integration refers to the ability to simultaneously see oneself in terms of the various substantive careers offered in a particular culture. This, in turn, is dependent upon the amount of esteem income provided by various psychological careers pursued by the individual. Here again, we must be careful not to confuse the internal and external points of view. If an individual perceives being a "man," a "breadwinner," and a "father" as defining a "good person," but is unable to obtain much positive esteem income from one or more of these paths of society because they provide little or no positive value, then we expect that phenomenologically this person will experience a lack of personality integration.

PERSONALITY AS A CHANGING PHENOMENOLOGICAL CONCEPT

If the basic implications of the present theoretical conception are valid, they suggest an extremely important notion both for conceptions of personality and for views of life—and psychological health. We expect a common pattern for an individual to consist of an ever-changing, nonfixed series of self-images expressing different substantive activities currently providing positive value. Rather than describe these changes in terms of "crises" or "passages" from one state to another—as abnormal states to be gotten over—we should try to understand such changes as frequent consequences of life experiences of success and failure that often occur in pursuit of psychological careers. One derivation is that such a flux will be more common the greater the competence, confidence, positive motivation, and educational attainment of the individual, given the closed nature of the majority of societal opportunities that constitute the situational component of "occupational careers," and given the perceived limit to success that such individuals tend to construe on much of human endeavor. To understand this basic implication means that we have the choice of viewing the phenomenon in noncrisis, nonpassage terms—to view it as the changing face of adulthood that for some individuals can be expected to be as regular and inevitable as the changing of the seasons of nature.

We feel that such a view on expected change in self-identity is clearly lacking in the young, so that their surprise is great when such changes occur, and their inability to cope with the emotional experiences that accompany this change (loss of interest, indifference, loss of self-identity, and, if continued, anxiety over failure to maintain past interests, attachments and involvements) stems in large part from the misconception that things are supposed to remain fixed and constant, that "there's something wrong with me if I no longer spend 80 hours a week at my profession" (or whatever the change may be). From the experiential point of view, it seems (from anecdotal reports) that the majority of individuals are disturbed by these changes, and in fact experience them in terms of crisis. But we predict that a change in our expectations concerning "expected changes" in self-identity would remove the "crisis" atmosphere that results from the perception of such changes taking place. It is particularly important from the point of view of counseling and therapy to alert the person to the predictable and "normal" changes in self-identity that are expected as behavioral sources of value change with movement along the typical career paths of society in the occupational, family, and sexual domains of activity.

DETERMINANTS OF ACTION

Thus far we have limited our discussion primarily to sources of value in the behavioral and self systems. An expectancy $\times$ value theory of action is assumed to relate value to action. The tendency to engage in action is assumed a function of value weighted by the probability that action will lead on to or result in that value. From the internal point of view, action tendency is a function of subjective expectancy and subjective value, where motive and source of value interact to define value to the individual. Thus it follows that when both the behavioral and self systems are involved, as when (by definition) an individual pursues a psychological career, action is a function of resultant valence (behavioral system) and resultant esteem income (self-system), each weighted (multiplied) by the individual's expectancy (subjective probability) that action (overt or covert, action and thinking) will produce that amount of (positive or negative) value. When only the behavioral system is involved, action is a function only of resultant valence weighted by the subjective probability of its attainment. It follows that we expect greater impetus for action (tendency) when both the behavioral and self systems are involved. We derive that psychological careers arouse greater motivational tendencies for action (overt and covert) than activity not involved in serving as a source of self-identity.

Note again that the terms valence and esteem income do not have formal status in the theory. They are merely different descriptions of value; value in the behavioral system is referred to as valence, while value in the self-system is referred to as esteem income. A formal representation of the theory assumes that values in the behavioral and self systems sum to determine total value for a psychological career. Value in the self-system that is derived from a self-image that is not linked to opportunities for action is not expected to produce a tendency to engage in action, even though it produces an effect on psychological morale. Thus, only when the self-image and a perceived path for action interact, and therefore we say that the individual pursues a psychological career in that substantive area, do we expect self-identity to provide instigating force for action. Contemplation of "who I am" in the absence of opportunities for action to attain, maintain, or assess "who am I" in the behavioral system is not expected to produce overt instrumental activity. Arousal in the behavioral system requires perception of opportunities for action to attain value that can result from action. Thus, self-identity is linked to action only when self-images are contingent on the outcomes of action.

Toward a Model Representing the Determinants of Action

Explicit mathematical extension of the basic equations of expectancy $\times$ value theory to include both the behavioral system and the self-system, the time-linked sources of value (past, present, and future), and the different activity sources of value (intrinsic, difficulty, instrumental, extrinsic, and cultural) will not be attempted at this time. There are too many unanswered questions at present to specify an explicit formal system. Research is needed to provide the basis for assumptions concerning the determination of magnitudes of value, how certain sources of value combine with each other, and to what extent value alone versus weighted value in the self-system of a psychological career produces tendency for action. We feel that such an attempt is premature. However, there are some more general statements that can be made, to be refined as data become available that bear on them.

First, the time-linked sources of value for action can be represented as follows:

$$Tr = \sum_{n=-1}^{-N} \sum_{ijk} \sum_{n=+1}^{+N} (M_{r+} - M_{r-}) (P_{r_1} \times V_+ - P_{r_1} \times V_-).$$

Here we represent the summation of resultant weighted value $(P_{r_1} \ V_+ - P_{r_1} \ V_-)$ for a particular individual with a certain resultant motive strength for that activity $(M_{r+} - M_{r-})$, for past $(\Sigma_{n=-1}^{-N})$ steps and future $(\Sigma_{n=+1}^{+N})$ steps of a contingent path, as well as for several attributes of the individual (Σ_{ijk}) that are perceived to be evaluated by activity along the contingent path. This general statement can include both affective and information value and the five specific sources of value (intrinsic, difficulty, instrumental, extrinsic, and cultural) from both the outcome itself (behavioral system) and from the self-image defined by the outcome (self-system), if and when these are involved. Separate specification of each of these different kinds of weighted value can be accomplished using specific instances of this general equation. Thus, for example, the more general theory of achievement motivation (see chapter 2) can be seen as a specific instance of specification of tendency to act for affective value, for difficulty and instrumental value, plus extrinsic value, in the behavioral system, for future expected (internal viewpoint) steps of a contingent path, where the magnitude of difficulty and instrumental values are each assumed inversely related to the subjective probability of attaining a particular success or failure (positive or negative value) along the contingent path, and where the number of steps remaining in the path $(+N)$ also represents the relative amount of instrumental value for contingent paths with differing numbers of future anticipated steps remaining, for individuals differing in strength of achievement-related motives for skill-demanding activity (see chapter 2).

For the general model to be a predictive one, it is necessary to know the particular magnitudes of value and their subjective probability of attainment. Our experience in the area of achievement motivation points to an extremely important fact that must be taken into account in using the general model just presented. The magnitudes of many different sources of value are often determined by their subjective probability of attainment in life situations, and therefore subjective probability and value are oftentimes inversely related rather than independent of each other. This was clearly discovered in relating rankings of the prestige of an occupation to the difficulty of entering that occupation (see Atkinson, 1978b). Prestige ratings most probably represent a combination of extrinsic and cultural value, as well as difficulty value, so that, in this instance, subjective probability of success can be used to compare the relative amounts of extrinsic and cultural value that an individual might expect. Occupations that are hard to enter usually have more extrinsic and cultural value than those that are easy to get into. The general point is that we must be cautious in treating value and subjective probability as independent of each other when predicting life behavior, and particularly when dealing with behavior in a psychological career. One of the generally neglected factors in other uses of expectancy $\times$ value theory has been the failure to consider the possibility that for important human activity outside the domain of achievement motivation, value may be inversely related to probability of attainment. The best instance is that of a theoretical free-enterprise system where the increased scarcity of goods (subjective probability is low that if one tries to attain a product, one will be successful) defines their increased market value—i.e., the "law" of supply and demand. While there are many restrictions on the functioning of this "law," from both the internal and external perspectives, it is worthwhile to consider this inverse relationship (in terms of expectancy $\times$ value theory) rather than to assume that value and probability of attainment are always unrelated.

MOTIVATION DERIVED FROM THE SELF–SYSTEM

We wish to make explicit our prediction that involvement of the self-system increases aroused motivation for immediate activity. In Figure 6 we represent a series of successes for a contingent path believed faced by a student in the past and anticipated future. The basic argument is that the set of outcomes below the line for each step represent arousal for only the behavioral system, while the set of outcomes above the line represent arousal for only the self-system, and that when both are aroused they contribute greater amounts to motivation of immediate activity than when only the behavioral system is involved in arousal. For example, the goal of "becoming a doctor" is assumed to arouse greater achievement motivation than the goal of "passing the last-year medical exams" because the former involves both the behavioral and self systems while the latter involves only the behavioral system. Two students equal in all other regards would be expected to have different amounts of motivation aroused for the immediate next step of their medical-school path when one perceives of eventually "becoming a doctor" while the other is concerned with (merely) eventually passing final-year medical exams. However, it would be difficult to test this prediction in the real world of medical-school striving because we believe that the value expected in the behavioral system is so great for this kind of substantive activity that most students faced with it will have motivation aroused in both systems—i.e., most premed students pursue a psychological career in this area. That is, testing the distinction between arousal of the behavioral

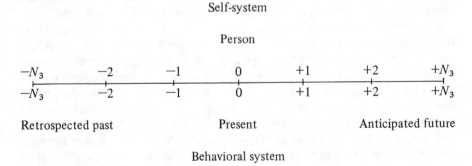

Figure 6. Representation of sources of value for arousal of past, present, and future components of motivation for immediate activity along a contingent psychological career due to value in the behavioral system and the self-system.

system alone as compared to the behavioral and self-systems interaction as in a psychological career is made more difficult by the prediction that as value in the behavioral system increases, the use of the goals of activity along the path to define "who I am" is also expected to increase. Large positive value in the behavioral system is expected to produce the emergence of the self-system for that set of opportunities for action, and these self-images then serve as additional goals of action, providing more motivational arousal than prior to their emergence. We would have to look for occupational activity involving less total value, but still enough to provide sufficient value in the behavioral system for it to serve as a means of self-identity, to then identify an individual striving to attain behavioral goals per se, and an individual striving both to attain behavioral goals and to become a particular kind of person. The same kind of distinction would apply to the value of the past, as also illustrated by the example in Figure 6.

No additional formal representation of the model seems to be needed at this time beyond that represented by the verbal distinction between the goals of "attaining a particular outcome" and "becoming a particular kind of person." Research that critically tests this implication of the theory might provide evidence that would allow for greater precision in specifying the magnitude of difference if found, as predicted, between motivation aroused by the behavioral system alone and that aroused by the interaction of behavioral and self systems, defined here as arousal by a psychological career in the substantive area of concern. At this time we want to avoid premature specification of assumptions where a firm basis in data, or a good hunch, is lacking. We believe that the model is sufficiently explicit to derive some general directional hypotheses, and to suggest research that would provide the data upon which more specific assumptions could be based.

DETERMINANTS OF ACHIEVEMENT–ORIENTED ACTION

Our prediction that immediate action in a contingent psychological career will be motivated to maintain value from both past outcomes and immediate assessment of attributes suggests a new orientation for research on achievement motivation and career striving. We predict, for example, that football players may be motivated simultaneously to *maintain* their place on the team and/or in the starting lineup (past value), to do well and make the all-star team (future value), and to assess how much skill they possess against good players (present value). The summation of expected value weighted by the probability of its attainment from retrospected past steps of a career and relevant attributes of competence (in either the behavioral or self system) is a new feature that suggests some direct follow-up research on, for example, academic motivation. We would obtain ratings of the importance of doing well in a course for (1) attaining future goals, (2) maintaining past accomplishments, and (3) assessing the possession of relevant competences. Grades would then be viewed for students high and low on each rated dimension of importance separately for success-oriented (positively motivated), failure-threatened (negatively motivated), and intermediate (neutrally motivated) motive groups. This study is a next step in our research program.

Note that predictions concerning the simultaneous effects of past, present, and future sources of motivation should be most clearly apparent for individuals neither at the beginning of a path nor at the end of a path, but rather in the middle stages of path striving. We can extend the hypotheses for this study by comparing students' performance in the same course who believe that course defines the first step, a middle step, or a last step of a contingent path. For students faced with the course as the first step, we predict that differences in future importance, that is, ratings of necessity of doing well to achieve future success, should maximally differentiate students who differ on achievement-related motive measures. For students faced with the course as a last step, differences in past importance, or ratings of the necessity of doing well to maintain past success, should maximally differentiate students who differ on achievement-related motives. Also, greater accentuation of differences in achievement-related motives is predicted when the path striving involves a psychological career so that both behavioral outcomes and self-images serve as sources of (positive and negative) value.

Note that demonstration of competence and assessment of competence are quite different (see chapter 11) in their motivational effects in that when assessment is the primary goal, information value can be expected to provide substantial sources of value (we are not sure whether this will be in addition to or instead of affective value), whereas when demonstration of competences is the primary goal, affective value can be expected to provide the substantial source of value (theory concerning seeking versus doing well on a test of competence is presented in chapter 11). Previous research on the expectancy $\times$ value theory of achievement motivation has not emphasized the information value of immediate activity, nor the distinction between the goals of assessing versus demonstrating competence.

Notice that for the negatively motivated individual (failure-threatened person in the achievement domain), the goal of maintaining past success is expected to produce greater inhibition (resistence) for immediate activity than when no such goal is involved, insofar as difficulty and instrumental value are concerned, since both are expected to be negative. However, intrinsic, extrinsic, and cultural value may be positive and substantial for this individual. Tests of the hypothesis must attempt to reduce the effects of, at least, extrinsic and cultural values. We can anticipate the same kinds of problems with regard to consistency of results for motivation to maintain past success as with motivation to achieve future success for failure-threatened individuals (see chapter 2) unless we are successful in specifying the level of value contributed by extrinsic and cultural sources.

Further extension of research on achievement motivation is implied by the use of the concept of cultural value. Generally, success from the external viewpoint is believed to have positive cultural value, while failure is believed to have negative cultural value. However, we suspect that the accentuation of achievement-related motive differences for high self-importance as opposed to low self-importance (see chapter 5) is due to a correlation between motive group and the resultant cultural value of success and failure; from the internal viewpoint, success-oriented individuals may perceive success in terms of resultant positive cultural value because they focus on the possible positive consequences of success rather than the possible negative consequences of failure, while failure-threatened individuals may perceive it in terms of resultant negative cultural value because they in fact focus on the possible negative consequences of failure rather than the possible positive consequences of success. When goal attainment is rated as important for positive self-evaluation, this may accentuate total achievement motivation, owing to the addition of resultant positive cultural value (weighted by its probability of attainment) for success-oriented individuals and owing to the addition of resultant negative cultural value (weighted by its probability of attainment) for failure-threatened individuals. Arousal in a psychological career due to the interaction of the self-image and opportunities for action should further accentuate these differences because the individual cultural values of success and failure are most often related to defining a person as good (meaning successful) or bad (meaning a failure) as a function of "important" success an failure, particularly, but not exclusively, in occupational and educational careers.

14

Time-linked Senses of Self and the n Achievement Score

Joel O. Raynor and Richard C. Teitelbaum

The present study is an attempt to determine if the *n* Achievement score obtained from Thematic Apperception Test (TAT) thought samples could be systematically influenced by differences in the time-linked sense of self described by a sentence lead used to elicit stories. Three different sentence leads were employed. One referred to a future self-image: A person is thinking about "who he or she is becoming." The person is thinking about the most important future event that defines "who he or she is becoming." A second lead referred to the present self-image: A person is thinking about "who he or she is." The person is thinking about the most important immediate/present event that defines "who he or she is." The third sentence lead referred to the past self-image: A person is thinking about "who he or she had been." The person is thinking about the most important past event that defines "who he or she has been."

The theory of personality functioning presented in Chapter 13 suggests that striving to attain a future self-image, trying to maintain a past self-image, and/or trying to evaluate oneself in terms of a present self-image are different ways for an individual to obtain esteem income. Previously, Raynor (1968a) had suggested that accentuation of characteristic effects of achievement-related motives due to differences in future orientation might be reflected in the *n* Achievement score itself, so that differences in *n* Achievement scores might reflect both concern about doing well and concern about attaining future goals, whether those future goals are achievement related or not.

In the present study we attempted to see if the *n* Achievement score would be systematically influenced by the time-linked self-image descriptions referred to above.

METHOD

Subjects.

Subjects were 38 male and 41 female undergraduates enrolled in introductory psychology at the State University of New York at Buffalo (SUNY/AB) who volunteered to participate to fulfill part of a course requirement that involved serving as a subject in psychological experiments. The subjects were tested in large group sessions in which both male and female subjects were present.

TAT

The standard procedures for obtaining stories to be scored for n Achievement were followed (Atkinson, 1958, app. III) as they have been adapted for use with sentence leads (cf. Horner, 1974; Raynor & Rubin, 1971). Subjects read the usual cover sheet describing the "sentence interpretation" task. They then looked (for 20 sec) at one of the time-linked sentence leads that appeared on the next page. They then wrote a story on the following page in response to the four sets of questions usually employed.

Stories were scored blind (by J.O.R.) as to sentence lead and sex of respondent. When a story was scored for achievement imagery (AI), the scoring subcategory of AI was noted: (1) competition with a standard of excellence CWS, (2) unique accomplishment UA, and/or (3) long-term involvement LTI. A story could be categorized in more than one subcategory if it met the criterion for each subcategory as spelled out in the n Achievement scoring manual (Atkinson, 1958, chap. 12). Raw n Achievement scores were obtained in the usual manner, as spelled out by Atkinson (1958, chap. 12). In addition, the overall distribution of n Achievement scores was broken at the obtained group median, and subjects were categorized as high and low in n Achievement. Finally, a frequency count was made of the number of times that AI stories were scored for CWS, UA, and LTI.

RESULTS

Table 1 presents the mean n Achievement scores for males and females as a function of time-linked sentence leads used to elicit stories. Note that n Achievement scores for both males and females were substantially higher for the future self-image lead than for either of the other lead conditions. For the females, there is a regular increase in n Achievement score from past to present to future lead condition. For the males, the difference is due primarily to the future-lead n Achievement score being substantially higher than the past and present lead-condition scores.

Table 2 presents the equivalent data analysis in terms of high and low groups on n Achievement. The data suggest a result similar to that obtained using mean

Table 1 Mean n Achievement Scores as a Function of Time-linked Sentence Lead and Sex

Subjects	Lead					
	Past		Present		Future	
	N	Mean	N	Mean	N	Mean
Males	13	.15	12	−.08	13	2.46
Females	12	−.33	14	.71	15	1.93

Table 2 Contingency Table Showing Subjects Scoring High and Low in *n* Achievement as a Function of Time-linked Sentence Lead and Sex

	Males*			Females**		
n Achievement	Past	Present	Future	Past	Present	Future
High	5	4	13	3	7	12
Low	8	8	0	9	7	3

*$X^2 = 14.44$, $df = 2$, $p < .001$, two-tailed test.
**$X^2 = 8.22$, $df = 2$, $p < .025$, two-tailed test.

n Achievement scores. Values of X^2 were obtained for the male and female categorical data separately (see Table 2): for men, $X^2 = 14.44$, $df = 2$, $p < .001$, two-tailed test; for women, $X^2 = 8.22$, $df = 2$, $p < .025$, two-tailed test. For both men and women significantly more subjects were categorized as high in *n* Achievement when the *n* Achievement score was obtained from the future self-image lead than when it was obtained from either the present or past self-image lead.

Table 3 shows the number of times that achievement imagery (AI) stories were scored CWS, UA, and LTI. Note that the proportion of CWS stories increases from the past (.23) to the present (.31) to the future (.46) lead condition, but that this trend does not approach statistical significance ($X^2 = 1.08$, $df = 2$, n.s.). On the other hand, the proportion of LTI stories clearly accounts for the higher *n* Achievement scores that were obtained in the future lead condition; the proportion of LTI stories is low in the past (.13) and present (.13) lead conditions, and high (.74) in the future lead condition ($X^2 = 14.04$, $df = 2$, $p < .001$, two-tailed test). The data suggest strongly that the future-oriented self-image lead produced higher *n* Achievement scores independent of reference in the story to concern over competition with standards of excellence (CWS), the generic definition of the achievement motive as inferred from the *n* Achievement score.

Table 3 Frequency with Which the Three Achievement Imagery Scoring Categories Appeared as a Function of Time-Linked Sentence

	Lead		
	Past	Present	Future
Competition with standard of excellence (CWS)	3	4	6
Unique accomplishment (UA)	0	0	2
Long-term involvement (LTI)	3	3	17

DISCUSSION

The results strongly suggest that the traditional way in which n Achievement is scored, and hence the total n Achievement score, is sensitive to motivational arousal by future-oriented self-image sentence leads. There are several possible interpretations to this finding. One is the straightforward observation that when a lead emphasizes future orientation, subjects write stories that are future oriented. True enough. But since such future-oriented stories are now scored to indicate presence of imagery reflecting the achievement motive, the data suggest that subjects who write a future-oriented story without also including imagery related to competition with a standard of excellence (CWS) may be misclassified as being strong in the achievement motive. While the elaborated theory of achievement motivation (see chapter 2) predicts an accentuation of resultant achievement motivation for future-oriented situations, such an accentuation is not necessarily indicated by a story scored LTI. "Becoming a doctor" does not necessarily indicate concern over wanting to become a *good* doctor. Other reasons for future striving may account for a subject writing an LTI story. And while the data hint that future-oriented leads about oneself also increase CWS imagery, this trend does not approach statistical significance, and there is a disproportionate increase in LTI imagery as compared to CWS imagery attributable to the future-oriented lead.

In previous research on achievement motivation the proportion of LTI stories is probably closer to 13% than to 74%. This suggests that rescoring of previous studies, omitting LTI as a category for inferring achievement imagery, would not substantially change the categorization of a subject as high or low on n Achievement, and therefore would not change substantially the relationships previously reported between n Achievement scores and other behavior. Thus the implications of the present findings would appear to be of greater conceptual than practical interest as far as research on achievement motivation is concerned.

On a more substantive level, the results raise questions concerning the role that the self-image, self-evaluation, and self-esteem have played in the traditional research on achievement motivation. Are references to the future-oriented self-system ("Who am I becoming?) a necessary condition for arousal of achievement motivation? While the present study does not address itself to this question, the clear effect on achievement arousal of the future time-linked self-image suggests that future research needs to provide an answer. Put another way, is achievement motivation necessarily linked with "becoming" that involves the self-system (see chapter 13), or can achievement motivation be aroused by immediate present or past cues with or without reference to the self-system? Raynor (see chapter 13) has suggested the possibility that expectancy $\times$ value theories of action predict only when possibilities for *future* action are possible, and that they predict best when value in the self-system is implicated. The present data are not inconsistent with such a conclusion.

It may be that the expectancy $\times$ value theory of achievement motivation is limited to the successful prediction of behavior for individuals when they are "becoming." That is, the theory may apply only to the "psychologically young" as defined here (see chapter 13), whose important life accomplishments are seen by them to lie in the future rather than in the past or the immediate present. Comparison of "psychologically old" individuals—those who believe themselves faced with the final steps of a closed achievement-oriented psychological career—and "psychologically young" individuals—those who believe themselves faced with the first steps of an equivalent career—would be of interest in this regard. It seems a fairly accurate generalization to note that the theory of achievement motivation has been primarily developed and validated based on data from relatively younger samples—primarily though not exclusively college students and younger. We have already noted that we expect some correlation (but certainly not a perfect one) between psychological age in a career and chronological age (see chapter 13). In fact, the goal-directed sequence used to conceptualize the *n* Achievement scoring system (see Atkinson, 1958, chap. 12) and expectancy $\times$ value theory of achievement motivation both presuppose a future-oriented time sequence, where the individual is striving to attain, rather than trying to maintain, an achievement-oriented goal. The fact that an "immediately expected" consequence is somewhat future oriented may be relatively unimportant in achievement arousal, reflecting the effect of the present time-linked self-image lead of the present study, in comparison to "distant-future-expected" consequences reflected in the effect of the future time-linked self-image lead of the present study. Or, in its more extreme case, will the behavior of those individuals who conceive of themselves in terms of "having been" also be adequately conceptualized, to the extent that the behavior of individuals who see themselves in terms of "becoming" apparently is?

There are two ways in which the present experimental technique can be extended to try to provide some initial answers to these questions. First, we plan to modify the self-image lead descriptions so that for one group stories are written to leads involving a "younger person" and for another group stories are written to leads involving an "older person." Also, we plan to obtain samples of individuals differing substantially in chronological age, and in terms of psychological age in their current occupational career. Comparison of the effects on the *n* Achievement score of time-linked self-image leads that differ in age specification for older and younger samples should indicate to what extent, if any, the arousal effect reported here is limited to "younger persons," as described in the lead and/or as subjects in the sample.

15

Motivational Determinants of Music-related Behavior: Psychological Careers of Student, Teacher, Performer, and Listener

Joel O. Raynor

My goal in this chapter is to provide a theoretical orientation that can be used to view some of the issues involved in trying to understand the motivational determinants of music-related behavior as a specific instance of life activity. This theory has been proposed as a theory of personality functioning and change (chapter 13). Its major assumptions include the integration of the behavioral and self-systems as sources of expected value that determine action, the use of time-linked sources of value to conceptualize the effects of the anticipated future, retrospected past, and evaluated present as sources of expected value for action, the specification of five substantive sources of value (intrinsic, difficulty, instrumental, extrinsic, and cultural), and the application of these concepts to substantive areas of activity that can provide means of self-identification and that are referred to as "psychological careers." The theory has evolved in systematic research on human motivation, particularly achievement motivation, and has been applied to the understanding of the factors involved in motivational changes over time in psychological careers—i.e., aging. The implications of these ideas have direct relevance to substantive music-

This chapter was prepared for presentation at the National Symposium on the Applications of Psychology to the Teaching and Learning of Music, sponsored by the Music Educators National Conference and the University of Michigan, Ann Arbor, July 30, 1979—the "Ann Arbor Symposium." In writing it, I have omitted most of the usual internal references for the sake of continuity of exposition for the nonpsychologist reader. However, I would like here to indicate that many of the ideas that are integrated into the theory of adult personality functioning and change that is presented have been adapted for this purpose from the work of others: information value (Feather, 1967); intrinsic value (Deci, 1973); difficulty value (Atkinson, 1957); extrinsic value (Atkinson & Feather, 1966); self-esteem (Rogers, 1959; Maslow, 1970). Other concepts, such as contingent paths, open and closed paths, instrumental value as earning the opportunity to continue, the psychological career as opportunities for self-identity, time-linked sources of value, the distinction between the self-system and behavioral system, and consideration of the stages of career striving, are based on earlier work of the author (Raynor, 1969, 1974a, 1974b, 1978). A fuller treatment of this theory and its development and implications can be found in chapter 13.

related careers—those of the music teacher, music student, music performer, and music listener.

For those who would prefer an empirical summary of research findings concerning music-related activity for which new theoretical insights might be proposed, the present chapter will be a disappointment. My defense of the strategy I have selected is basic for an understanding of what I hope to accomplish. I am not a music researcher or music educator. I do not know either literature very well. However, as a student of the psychology of motivation, involved in systematic research on "important" human behavior, and involved in attempts to build successively better theoretical understanding of such behavior, I have some confidence that individuals involved in music-related behavior share most of the properties of individuals involved in other substantive careers, so that insights concerning their behavior may be inferred from a theory built to explain research data in other areas of human activity. If I am correct, then the present effort will have been worthwhile.

We are here concerned with the molar aspects of behavior—music as an activity in a person's life. The problem of motivation, as defined by the psychologist, concerns the direction, vigor, and persistence of action and, most fundamentally, the change of activity, from one to another—or, the other side of the coin, the recurrent patterns of activity in a person's life.

MOTIVATION AND ACTION

The analysis of the motivational determinants of human activity—any human activity—is exceedingly complex. There is no "one" reason, no one cause, no one basic "why" that can account for all the phenomena that can be identified in the behavioral aspects of human activity. This is particularly so when we try to explain "important human action"—important as seen by the individual engaging in that activity. Thus many assumptions are needed to build a sufficiently complex theoretical orientation to deal with the life activity of adults engaged in, for example, the teaching of music.

However, in building the present conception I have been extremely systematic; I have started with a particular orientation, called the expectancy X value theory of action, and extended it so that the exceedingly complex analysis that is required is accomplished in terms of only two general conceptual variables—expectancy and value.

ASSUMPTIONS OF THE THEORY

An individual is assumed to be motivated to obtain and maximize positive value, and to avoid and minimize negative value. There are several different dimensions or sources of positive and negative value. We distinguish between affective and information value; among intrinsic, difficulty, instrumental, extrinsic, and cultural value; and among different time-linked sources of value: past, present, and future. We also distinguish between the external and internal points of view in analyzing sources of value, and different kinds of paths that provide sources of value, and value from the behavioral versus the self-system.

Activity as Steps in a Path

In this theory sources of value result from the outcomes of activity. A positive outcome is called a *goal*, and a negative outcome a *threat*. We conceptualize action as consisting of activity and its positive and negative outcomes; an activity and its outcomes are termed a *step*. Steps are represented in sequence to form a path. From the external view, this corresponds to a film record taken of an individual as that individual moves from one activity to another, as coded by the observer, and the outcomes of each activity, again, as coded by the observer. From the internal point of view, this corresponds to the anticipated future steps that an individual believes he or she might take (the future possible activities and their respective possible outcomes), the remembered or retrospected past (steps) activities and their respective outcomes, and the immediate present activity, and its possible outcomes, particularly as they bear on the individual's evaluation of his or her degree of possession of prerequisite abilities, attributes, and competences that are believed evaluated by the outcomes of the immediate activity (i.e., diagnostic assessment).

We conceptualize four different kinds of paths: contingent, noncontingent, partial contingent, and one-step; all but the last have both a future and a past time orientation. A future contingent path consists of a series of steps where an immediate positive outcome is believed necessary by the individual to earn the opportunity to try for additional positive outcomes along that path; a past contingent path is one where some positive outcome of past activity is believed by the individual to have led to the opportunity to try for some number of subsequent positive outcomes; for each contingent path, an immediate negative outcome is believed to lead to the loss of the opportunity to continue on along that path. A partial contingent path is one where an immediate positive outcome guarantees the opportunity to continue, but an immediate negative outcome has no bearing on future striving. A noncontingent path is one where immediate outcomes, both positive and negative, have no bearing on earning the opportunity to continue on along the path. A one-step path consists of a single activity and its positive and/or negative outcomes.

A path may be open or closed. In a closed path, the original final goal of the path remains fixed so that as the individual successively moves through the path to the final step there are fewer and fewer steps remaining as potential sources of positive and/or negative value. In an open path, the original final goal of the path is continually revised as the individual successively moves through the path so that the number of steps in the path remains the same or even increases, and therefore there is no decrease in potential sources of positive and/or negative value.

The concepts of open and closed contingent paths are crucial for the theory, for in these paths it is assumed that all future-expected steps of the path, and all past-retrospected steps of the path contribute motivation (positive and negative sources of value) sustaining the immediate activity along that path.

The Behavioral and Self Systems

We assume that each outcome of action has the potential for serving as a means of self-identity. This self-image, defined by the outcome of a past, present, or future action, can then provide its own source of positive and negative value to influence the motivation of activity. Activity and outcomes per se are referred to as the *behavioral system*, and value in the behavioral system is referred to as attractiveness (positive) and repulsiveness (negative)—corresponding to the term *valence*. Activity and outcomes that in addition define a self-image that serves as a means of self-identity are referred to as the *self-system*, and value in the self-system is referred to as positive or negative self-esteem or esteem income, as referred to self-theorists.

There are two important consequences of the emergence of the self-system in a substantive area of activity: (1) the individual's self-identity and self-worth are perceived by that individual to be evaluated by the outcomes of activity in that area, and (2) there is greater motivation (positive and/or negative) sustaining immediate activity in that area.

Immediate action is assumed to be determined by the product of each source of positive value and its expectancy or subjective probability of attainment summed over all sources of positive value, minus the product of each source of negative value and its expectancy of subjective probability of attainment. When action implicates the self-system, as when outcomes of action define "Who am I?", then net esteem income (the difference between positive and negative self-esteem) determines the individual's psychological morale for that *psychological career,* defined by the substantive activity in question, and the self-image that can be attained, assessed, and/or maintained by that action.

PSYCHOLOGICAL CAREERS

The concept of psychological career is used to relate the time-linked senses of self to action. A psychological career is conceived as a joint function of the individual's sense of self or self-image and a particular opportunity for action. In this theory, *career* is a general term that is not limited to occupational pursuits, but rather reflects any substantive self-image that is related to action opportunities that are seen as contingently related to attainment, assessment, and/or maintenance of that self-image. Thus, career is the psychological variable that links the internal view of self and the external view of role (as seen by others) so that careers are *behavioral opportunities for self-identity.*

Most individuals in our culture usually pursue at least three simultaneous senses of self-careers: in the occupational area related to earning a living, in the sexual area related to masculinity/femininity and sexual functioning, and in relation to family identity—as husband or wife and/or father or mother. In addition, leisure and avocational careers are becoming increasingly important as means of obtaining positive value.

INTRINSIC, DIFFICULTY, INSTRUMENTAL, EXTRINSIC, AND CULTURAL VALUE

Intrinsic value refers to that amount of value of an activity or outcome that is aroused by the inherent properties of that activity or outcome, for the particular individual in question. The *difficulty* value of an outcome refers to the attractiveness or repulsiveness that derives from the individual's perceived chances of attaining that outcome, or the scarcity of occurrence of certain attributes, competencies, and/or skills of individuals. *Instrumental* value refers to the number of opportunities for subsequent action that the attainment of an outcome, or possession of some competence, is believed to guarantee (in the future) or to have guaranteed (in the past). The fourth source of value comes from what is termed *extrinsic* value, or the "extrinsic incentives." These are sources of value that derive from rewards that are contingent upon goal attainment, but do not relate to the difficulty value of the task per se, or to the intrinsic value of the task per se. Finally, the *individual culture* value of an outcome refers to the extent to which an individual has acquired the belief that attainment of that outcome is good or bad, right or wrong, or proper or improper in the cultural context. It can also refer to how good or bad a person the attainment of that skill, outcome, or self-image is believed to make the individual.[1]

SOURCES OF VALUE AND THE INTERACTION OF PERSON AND SITUATION

In the above analysis it is assumed that all sources of value represent the interaction of two factors: something about the person that is brought by the person to the particular situation and that colors or weights a particular source of value, and that may be relatively stable and characteristic about that person, and something about the particular sources of value in the situation that impinges on the individuals faced with that situation and that may have similar effects on many different individuals. Thus, the notion of value as a motivational variable assumes that both individual differences in people, and differences in situations faced by people, interact to determine value to influence action.

STAGES OF CAREER STRIVING

The concept of time-linked sources of value allows us to derive significant differences in the quantity of motivation at different stages of striving along a psychological career path that is both contingent and closed. To illustrate these points, we represent the individual as a point on a time line, with the anticipated future steps of the path indicated by positive numbers, the retrospected past steps of the path indicated by negative numbers, and the present by zero (see Figure 1*a*). An individual faced with the first step of an anticipated contingent path is represented as

---

[1] See chapter 13 for a more detailed description of these sources of value.

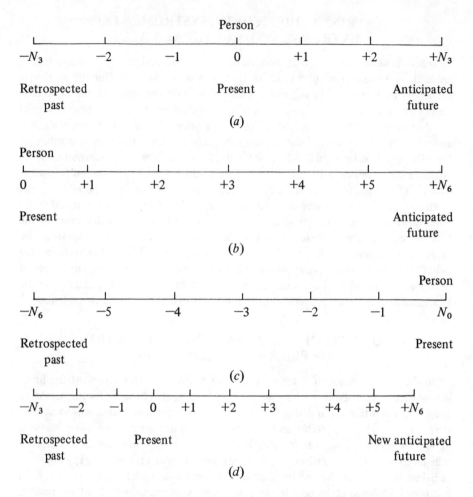

Figure 1 Various stages of striving in a closed contingent path. (*a*) Middle striving; (*b*) initial
striving (becoming); (*c*) terminal striving (having been). The middle stage of striving
in an open contingent path (*d*).

facing a series of possible sources of value in the anticipated future and in the
immediate present, but sources of value do not exist in this psychological career for
the retrospected past (see Figure 1*b*). This is the initial or early stage of career striving and is termed "becoming." If and when the individual successfully moves
through the entire series of steps of this contingent path, and the initial final or
ultimate goal has remained fixed so that the path is considered closed, the person is
represented as recalling a series of past sources of value in the retrospected past and
in the immediate future, but sources of value do not exist in this psychological
career for the anticipated future. This final or last step of career striving is termed
"having been" (see Figure 1*c*). Some intermediate point in striving along the closed

contingent path allows for the retrospected past, the anticipated future, and the immediate present to provide possible sources of value (as in Figure 1a). Thus, the attainment of goals along a contingent path inevitably produces a change in the time-linked sources of value in that career, from anticipated future, initially, to retrospected past, terminally, so long as the initial final goal of the path remains unchanged. This inevitable consequence of successful striving has important implications for understanding differences in motivation between those termed "becoming," who are considered to be "psychologically young," those who "have been" who are considered to be "psychologically old," and those who are in the middle stage of career striving. One can expect a very rough correlation between psychological age in a career and chronological age—younger people tend to be "becoming" while older people tend to be "having been"—although exceptions to this rule are to be expected and are of great interest in understanding such issues as midlife crisis, second careers, and retirement careers. That is, it is possible for a 60-year-old to face the initial stages of a psychological career and therefore to be considered "psychologically young" with reference to that career, just as it is possible for a 20-year-old to face the final stages of a career and therefore to be considered "psychologically old."

THE SELF–SYSTEM AS A SOURCE OF VALUE

In this theory we assume that an individual comes to use a particular self-image as a means of self-identity if that self-image provides substantial positive value, and such value in the self-system is called *self-esteem* or *esteem income*. Self-images can be defined in terms of the outcomes of actions, and, therefore, from the internal point of view, we see that some individuals come to see themselves in terms of time-linked senses of self that are defined by anticipated attainment of future goals, or retrospected remembering of past accomplishment, and/or assessment of possessed prerequisite competences. Thus self-identity is seen as time related in a psychological career, with the future sense of self tied to "becoming" and initial stages of striving, the past sense of self tied to "having been" and late stages of striving, and the present sense of self tied to the evaluation of prerequisite competences, skills, and abilities that are believed to have produced past success and are needed to attain future success.

The cognitive capacity to meaningfully ask the question "Who am I?" is assumed to be a necessary prerequisite for value in the self-system to emerge. In addition, an outcome of activity that defines a self-image must provide substantial value (feelings of self-worth) before such outcomes of action can serve as sources of self-identity. Taken together, these assumptions lead to the implication that the self-system may be a factor in contributing motivation sustaining immediate activity for adults but not for very young children, and that the emergence of the self-system in a substantive area of activity to define what we mean by a psychological career is an important factor in the increased motivational impetus thought to sustain "important" life behaviors. While it is possible for a very young student to see himself or herself as "becoming a musician," in general, for a very large group of grade-school children, the self-system is not a factor. Thus, there is a more limited scope for motivational determinants of action, and this is reflected in the inability to motivate children for long periods of time.

Once the self-system becomes part of striving in a given area, it is assumed that the self-images to be attained, maintained, or assessed (for the future, past, and present senses of self, respectively) can contribute value in and of themselves. "Striving to become a musician" is seen as providing sources of value in addition to the concrete goal of "striving to graduate from music school." It follows that individuals who perceive themselves faced with a contingent path linking immediate action to attainment of the concrete goal and the future self-image will be more motivated in that immediate activity than an individual merely striving to attain the concrete future goal. Thus we posit a two-step process: (1) in the first step, when a goal provides a substantial source of positive value, it becomes a source of self-identity, and (2) the source of self-identity then provides additional amounts of positive value to strive to attain it and the goal that defines the self-image. Thus when an individual is pursuing a psychological career, where by definition both the behavioral and self systems contribute value to immediate activity, we expect greater motivational effects of the anticipated future, retrospected past, and evaluated present than when only the behavioral system is aroused.

SOME GENERAL IMPLICATIONS OF THE THEORY

1. Children are less motivated than adults. Because the self-system has not as yet emerged for substantive activity in the majority of children, there is less total motivation (positive and negative) sustaining activity. This means that positively motivated children are, in general, less willing to engage in that substantive activity, they engage in it less vigorously and with less enthusiasm, and they persist for a shorter time before going on to something else, than a person for whom the self-system has emerged for that activity, and for a child who had self-identity tied to it and therefore is said to be engaged in a psychological career.

2. Younger people tend to be future oriented; older people tend to be past oriented. Because there are no past steps in the initial stages of striving, there is little or no value to be obtained from the past. Younger people tend more often to be starting out on contingent paths involving substantive activity. They are primarily oriented to obtaining positive value from long-term future goals, rather than maintaining the value of long-term past goals. On the other hand, older people are more likely to have reached the final stages of striving along a closed contingent path. They are primarily oriented to obtaining positive value from the long-term past goals, rather than attaining the values associated with long-term future goal attainment.

3. Negatively motivated individuals are, paradoxically, less inhibited, with self-identity not at stake and with value associated only with the immediate present. Because the self-system increases total motivation, and because motivational increases are negative for an individual who has the motive not to engage in the sub-

stantive activity in question stronger than the motive to engage in that activity, additional sources of motivation from the self-system tend to increase total inhibition, even if they add positive motivation as well. Thus, there is greater resistance to engaging in that activity, there is less vigorous action if the resistance is overcome and the activity is engaged in, and it is easier to interrupt the activity with attractive alternative activity. While the person is engaging in the activity, there are greater anxiety, worry, apprehension, and dread of negative consequences that might result when the self-system is aroused.

4. Open career paths arouse more motivation than closed career paths. Because new, additional sources of motivation are continually anticipated in an open contingent path, greater positive and negative motivation influence immediate activity in the open path. Difficulty and instrumental value decrease as one approaches the final goal of a closed contingent path. Because there are fewer steps, there are fewer opportunities to earn a chance to strive for, as the individual successfully moves through a contingent path. And because there are fewer "gates" to negotiate, the total probability of attaining the final goal decreases. Thus, continued success reduces both instrumental and difficulty value in a closed contingent path.

5. Identity crises are more likely when the following conditions are met: (a) One is positively motivated for the activity in question. (b) Initially, one believes oneself faced with a closed contingent path having a clear-cut final goal. (c) The path arouses the self-system, so that striving to attain the final goal involves "becoming" the kind of person defined by the self-image associated with attainment of the final goal. (d) One succeeds at each step along the contingent path so that one moves closer and closer to the final goal, until the final goal is attained. At this point one no longer knows "who one is striving to become," experienced as a loss of future sense of self and an "identity crisis." Of course, one knows "who one has been," and if one were to focus on this past identity, no crisis would be perceived, but one has always been "becoming," and the absence of "becoming" is what one sees as the loss of self-identity.

6. Identity crises are avoided and positive motivation sustained for an open contingent career, where new possibilities for future accomplishment are anticipated and/or discovered as a function of more immediate successful goal attainment. Here the individual continues to build a backlog of past sources of positive value without losing future sources of positive value. Esteem income and psychological morale, as well as enthusiasm, interest, immediate intensity, and long-term accomplishment, are expected to be greatest for positively motivated individuals faced with open contingent psychological careers, where both the behavioral and self-system continue to provide renewed sources of anticipated positive self-esteem.

IMPLICATIONS OF THE THEORY FOR
MUSIC–RELATED CAREERS

Since one of the important implications of the present theory is that different kinds of individuals will act quite differently when faced with different stages of career striving, we cannot make general statements about all musical-related careers. However, particular kinds of individual-career interactions are of great interest. We shall refer to some of these.

Of great interest because of its nonintuitiveness are positively motivated individuals who have attained their initial career goals so that they no longer perceive themselves faced with a contingent occupational and educational career path in music. They have attained positions as teachers, have been granted tenure or perceive other guaranteed job security, and have no further professional goals concerning advancement and promotion. For these individuals, in particular, sources of positive instrumental value no longer exist from the anticipated future. We strongly suspect that such an individual is going through or has already faced an identity crisis caused by the lack of motivational impetus from the future, which previously provided interest and excitement in anticipation of attaining distant future goals and a sense of self—"Who I am becoming"—but which now no longer exist because no future goals are perceived as relevant to immediate activity. These individuals experience a net drop in positive impetus for immediate activity and a net loss of esteem income when thinking about the future. They are bored, lackadaisical, and indifferent to their present teaching activity. While they still are "turned on" by the intrinsic and difficulty value of immediate activity, and can get excited and interested in such activity, the general feeling is that something that used to be there "is missing" from the activities routinely engaged in on a day-to-day basis, and both the intensity and duration of career-related activity have dropped substantially.

We believe that this is a common motivational problem faced by teachers in general, and therefore by music teachers, once they perceive that contingent future striving is ended and that future advancement is limited. However, since the intrinsic value of music-related activity is probably higher than in many other kinds of education-related activity, we suspect that the total drop in interest and enthusiasm may be much less than in other fields. This becomes an interesting question for research. Clearly, for those music educators who are able to obtain substantial intrinsic and difficulty value from their daily teaching activities, the effects of closed-path striving will be minimized and there will be less chance of apathy, indifference, and an identity crisis. But the questions must be raised: Does the environment of the music educator provide the opportunity to obtain intrinsic and difficulty value? What are the opportunities to get "turned on" by music? What are the challenges of teaching that are provided by the curriculum or the students? If the interaction with teaching is seen as now "easy as pie" so that success is virtually assured, then little difficulty value and positive motivation can be obtained from these activities. Put another way, can the teacher set personal goals of a challenging nature that will produce a source of difficulty value and therefore heighten interest and enthusiasm in immediate activity that no longer has long-term future implications for that teacher's career? If not, we find the individual confronted with a job situation where the "love of music" is the only positive feature of immediate activity, assuming the relatively small impact of extrinsic and cultural value in music education. While the reader might say, "That is great—only the relevant factor is contributing to why I do what I do," the implication is that such individuals will personally experience a drop in perceived self-worth in comparison to when they were striving to attain their professional career goals and being turned on by the challenge of teaching their students as well as by their love of music.

We do not want to judge whether it is "good" or "bad" for individuals to be motivated only by intrinsic factors associated with their professional activity. However, if we are correct in our analysis, then the effect of professional goal attainment on the individual music teacher's drop in psychological morale is one that is probably not anticipated by this person nor understood in terms of its causes, and hence when the individual is faced with it there is often the feeling of "aloneness in crisis" that compounds what is often experienced as a profound career disappointment.

For the positively motivated individual, career goals that are kept opened rather than fixed and therefore closed, and contingent steps that are imposed on career striving, are one way to provide for continued motivational impetus from "becoming." Promotions, advancements, new education for continued certification—all these newer professional hurdles—can be used to prevent this loss of positive motivation and esteem income, again provided that the individual is positively motivated with regard to the nature of the activity in question and is success-oriented in terms of achievement-related dispositions. These newer contingent steps are not perceived as "threats to job security" by these individuals, but as "opportunities for personal and professional advancement"; they are not dreaded, but eagerly anticipated. They provide a spice of forward-looking excitement and enthusiasm rather than anxiety and worry about professional failure. If we define psychological health as a maximization of positive esteem income through an integrated psychological career, then such newer hurdles serve to increase psychological health for the positively motivated individual, even if the value derives from extrinsic sources.

For readers who are positively motivated individuals, the intuitive reaction to the above will be "knowing agreement." However, for readers who are not, or who are negatively motivated individuals, the intuitive reaction will be: "But how about the job pressures that such new goals create? You suggest a new 'rat race' where competitive striving, which we thought we finally had gotten over after getting out of school, again comes back to haunt us." Of course, this is correct. Our reactions to contingent and noncontingent careers, to open and closed careers, are determined by our resultant motivational disposition, which in turn influences our experiences with the educational process, which influences our current attitudes when trying to determine educational and professional practice as "professionals." Unanimity of experience is not to be expected, and agreement based on experience is a pipe dream that will never be attained—unless individuals of like personality make up the "panel" assessing such proposed changes. The point is that as soon as suggestions for change are made, their impact on individuals who have gone through similar "systems" will differentially influence the attractiveness and repulsiveness of such changes.

The insight to be found in the above analysis is that while the positively motivated individual would welcome a renewal of career striving, the negatively motivated individual will not. For them, since sources of value other than the "love of music" are predominantly negative, their experience has been a lessening of negative motivation upon final attainment of career goals, and to reinstitute new career goals would be equivalent of reinstituting the worry, apprehension, and sometimes dread that were all too real for them during their earlier career striving. Of course, they are correct. They know what is best for themselves. They do not want these hurdles, which function as sources of inhibition of immediate activity and feelings of anxiety, worry, and negative self-esteem. These people are real; they exist; and their problem concerning future striving is no less felt than those of positively motivated individuals who lose interest and become apathetic when future career striving is no longer seen as possible.

When we turn to the impact of the retrospected past on present career behavior, we again find some important differences between positively and negatively motivated individuals. As a function of success, the impact of past outcomes along the career path increases for both individuals. There is an inevitably greater impact of the psychological past as we move from early to middle to late stages of career striving. For the positively motivated individual, retrospection about past successes provides positive esteem income and a feeling of positive self-worth and identity in terms of "that successful person I have become" and is predicted to contribute positive motivation to immediate activity whose goal is to maintain that level of past success. As the positive value of the psychological past continues to increase, the sense of self defined in terms of those past successes becomes increasingly more important to the individual. For the negatively motivated individual, retrospection about past important successes is predicted to increase worry, dread, and apprehension about *not* maintaining that level of past success, and it contributes to inhibition of immediate activity to maintain past success.

PAST VERSUS FUTURE VALUES, ATTITUDES, AND TEACHING

The analysis in this section goes beyond the theory of motivation, beyond available research findings, and beyond previous analyses of motivation and behavior within the context of this theoretical orientation. It is based on the additional assumption that "attitudes" that people have, and "attitudinal behavior" or the verbal expression of attitudes, are determined by the value of the activity/outcome step in question (cf. Peak, 1955). Thus, persons who derive positive value (esteem income) from anticipated future goal attainment along an open contingent path of their career will have a favorable attitude toward "strict standards of good performance and enforcement of prerequisites for promotion and advancement," while individuals who derive negative value (esteem income) from the anticipated future will have a negative attitude toward such practices. In fact, in one unpublished study I conducted, we found that positively motivated students favored "other-evaluation" while negatively motivated students favored "self-evaluation," and these differences were accentuated when doing well was seen as contingently related to future career success—so that the basis for this derivation is not completely lacking in empirical support. Also, the implications of this assumption concerning the determinants of attitudes are consistent with other implications of this theoretical orientation and suggest some very important insights about teachers and teacher behavior based on the notion that attitudes of teachers influence the behavior of their students.

If we assume that attitudes are verbal behaviors that express the sources of expected value referred to in the theory, then as the positively motivated individuals move from early to middle to late stages of successful career striving, they come to be more and more favorably disposed to those procedures, practices, and outcomes that they associate with their own past successes. They are more likely to verbally favor such past practices, defend their functional utility, and act to ensure that such practices are maintained for the next generation of individuals who aspire to become professional in that substantive area. So long as the individual is also obtaining anticipated value from future expected sources, the defense of past practice is shared with valuation of future practices that the individual must successfully negotiate, so that exclusive defense of the status quo is tempered by possible new (experimental) but cognitively anticipated "curriculum" or "set of opportunities" that are expected by the individual to lead to eventual future (further) career success. However, when future goals are attained, and future possibilities become past practice, the weight of favorable attitudes shifts to exclusive valuation of "the way things were for me." The implications of this analysis of attitudinal responding, coupled with the motivational analysis of career striving, offer a profound insight into the continued discrepancy between successive generations of individuals and provide a framework for understanding some of the problems that are inevitably generated between teacher and student in a given substantive area.

If the above analysis is correct, we end up deriving that "students" will value and be favorably disposed toward those practices and procedures that are seen to be consistent with attainment of maximum positive value in the anticipated future—to attainment of the student's own important positively valued future goals. Note that these practices not only have to provide the ground rules for, and ways to strive to attain, future goals, but they must maximize their positive value and minimize their negative value. On the other hand, "teachers" will value and be behaviorally disposed toward those practices and procedures that are seen to be consistent with the maintenance of maximum positive value in their retrospected past—to the maintenance of the teacher's own important positively valued past goals. (I am not saying that this should or ought to be; I am deriving an implication from a theory that will help explain what *is* often the case.)

While the above predictions are clear, they are too general if left unqualified. They refer to students as individuals in the initial stage of career striving, they refer to teachers as individuals in the final stage of career striving, and they would be appropriately modified if a student were in the late stage of career striving and a teacher in the early stage of career striving. Put another way, student becomes teacher, and a teacher can again become a student, as a function of stage of striving. Only if the correlation between teacher and late career striving represents the majority case, and that between student and early career striving does also, can we make some general statements that will apply for the majority of student-teacher attitudes.

Those who bemoan the "dead weight" of tradition in human affairs fail to recognize the inevitability of positive value and favorable attitudes that accrue to one's own successful past. To the extent that older people hold positions of power where they can influence the practices that are to be followed by the next generation, and these individuals are no longer engaged in career striving, we can predict that the attitude of "what was good for us (i.e., led to our past success, or at least we think it did, and that is what counts) is good for them." How many times do new PhDs (i.e., old students) modify the existing program they have just entered to make it fit the program they have just successfully completed? While this tendency will be prevalent once an individual goes beyond initial career stages, it will predominate once the individual has successfully completed that career. If others perceive the changes as "innovative and original," so be it; if they are seen as a perpetuation of the past, so be it. But for either judgment, the motivational impetus is, other things equal, the same.

Notice that individuals can free themselves from the effect of their past successful behavior by conceptualizing present activity as the beginning of a new psychological career. Then past activity is seen as irrelevant, and the anticipated future rather than the retrospected past will influence attitudes and behavior.

MOTIVATION AND TEACHING

Usually, when teachers talk about "motivating" students, they are referring to the question of how to motivate their students to do what they, the teacher, wants them to do. They do not consider that the scientific problem of motivation refers to the reasons why students act the way they do, or, alternatively, that it refers to the reasons why teachers act the way they do. In either case, as conceptualized here, the teacher and the student each act to maximize positive expected value and/ or positive esteem income. Neither acts to maximize the positive expected value of the other, necessarily. The teacher who wishes to create a particular kind of behavior in the student must recognize that the motivating conditions and the personality dispositions of the student interact to determine whether that act will follow—because its motivational impetus is stronger than any other act in that situation.

When we take the internal viewpoint, we see that the teacher's valuation of a particular outcome is irrelevant to the determinants of the behavior of the student. It is the student's perceived valuation of the outcomes of that action, and the probability of attainment of these outcomes, that conceptually induces motivation for action. "Reinforcement value" is a personal construct. Only if we refer to an attempt to change the magnitudes and sources of value of the student, or attempt to turn negative value for the student into positive value for the student, can we hope to induce the desired action. But change in value is a relatively long process, about which relatively little is understood, much less so than the role of value in inducing action. Thus, for the teacher to understand student behavior and provide conditions that elicit behavior from the student that is desired by the teacher, the teacher must perceive the relevant sources of value present for the student—the teacher must view the world from the internal point of view of the student. That is, the opportunities for action, their possible outcomes, and the potential for the emergence of a psychological career as (music) student must be understood by the teacher before the teacher can hope to bring about certain desired molar behavior of the student.

The critical factor that must be understood is that the values of the teacher and the values of the student have no relationship to one another. What is valued by the teacher may or may not be valued by the student. What provides positive value to the teacher may provide positive or negative value to the student. What is seen as important to the teacher may be seen as important or trivial by the student, and vice versa. To understand student behavior, we must understand the determinants of behavior as they exist for the student at that time, not as the teacher thinks they *should* or *ought* to exist, given the teacher's sources of value.

VALUES OF THE PAST VERSUS THE PRESENT FOR STUDENT–TEACHER INTERACTIONS

If teachers tend to value what they have learned in their evolving careers, particularly because of the past instrumental value of previous learning and its success in having brought them to the point of now pursuing a positively valued career, while students place little positive value on such learning because of a lack of experience with this activity outcome, then we can expect a relatively permanent discrepancy between student and teacher in their enthusiasm, interest, and willingness to work hard to deal with the particular activity in question. Whether the subject is Greek literature, the history of ancient Turkey, or the evolution of the symphonic form, we must recognize that such differences are an inevitable consequence of the differences in stages of career striving between teacher and student when the teacher, in the middle or late stages of striving, presents material that represents activity in the initial stage of student striving. Cultural values and instrumental values are usually positive and strong for the history of a field because its mastery represents past successful activity for teachers, who in the middle and late stages of their own careers assume that everyone shares their enthusiasm and appreciation of what, to students, is material devoid of positive sources of value. If teachers attempt to increase "appreciation" of such material, they must recognize that only *after* valuation has increased due to successful mastery will students' interest increase. And if they assume that exposure to that material will inevitably lead to a positive valuation of it, they fail to recognize that magnitudes of values in their own lives changed slowly, as a function of successful movement along a career path involving many years of successful striving. No wonder there is sometimes, or even often, a "communication gap" between teacher and student, a lack of mutual interest in commonly shared activity, even though the intrinsic values of the activity for the student and teacher may be equivalent and positive, and perhaps even strongly positive.

For teachers to devalue those substantive concepts of past activity along their own careers, by recognizing them as irrelevant for a current generation of students, is for these teachers to be faced with the possible loss of self-esteem and self-identity. It follows that in general teachers will act to maintain the values of their past successes, including communication of what they have successfully mastered as having great value for others; in doing so they act to preserve their own feelings of self-worth and ideas about who they are. This presents a strong resistance to attempts to substitute, modify, or share other, newer music-related activity in the curriculum.

Note that this teacher reaction is predicted only for those who have perceived that they face a closed contingent career path, and/or who have already attained the final step of their previously perceived closed contingent career path. Thus, one of the critical factors in predicting resistance to curriculum change concerns the extent to which individual teachers perceive themselves faced with an open contingent path in their careers as teachers. If opportunities for new activity are seen to be present, attaining immediate goals is seen as necessary to continue along this path, and one's future self-image is seen as tied to attainment of the future goals of that path. In this way the individual is motivated both to attain the values of future success and to maintain the values of past success, and is motivated as much with regard to the future as with regard to the past. New and innovative approaches to be mastered are seen as valuable sources of (future) positive self-esteem, so that a more balanced valuation of both past and 'on the frontier" material results.

CULTURAL VALUE AND MUSIC–RELATED ACTIVITY

There is something different, perhaps even unique, concerning "classical" music-related activity and psychological careers and self-images as opposed to other kinds of careers pursued by individuals today. This concerns the link between the differences in kinds of music and the clear-cut cultural values and self-images that these define for individuals engaged in that activity. "Classical" as opposed to jazz, pop, avant-garde, contemporary, electric, computer, 12-tone, country-and-western, etc., are but a few of the various differences that evoke widely different amounts of positive and negative cultural value for a given individual and for a group of individuals faced with any given one of these, and of the corresponding self-images that often are tied to these cultural values. Rarely is the impact of the *past,* for example, so ever-present as when one is playing or listening to music composed 150 years ago, music venerated as being the most positively valued activity—where entire systems of education are geared to the cultural transmission of the positive value of activity completed by individuals having lived 5, 10, or 20 generations ago. Rarely is there such widely disparate positive and negative cultural value anticipated concerning products of contemporary (new) music activity. The effects of these widely differing amounts of positive and negative value, which are often tied to both psychological and chronological age and aging, potentially provide the greatest single source of difference between music student and music teacher.

PERFORMANCE FROM A SCORE

Musical performance is one of the human activities where the arousal of difficulty value is an inevitable possibility. The need to reproduce the "correct notes," where there is no ambiguity as to what "correct" means, places musical performance from a score in the arena of achievement-oriented activity. The notions of good, better, and best apply automatically concerning the reproduction of the correct notes, at the minimum, and often also apply in terms of more subjective standards of "artistic performance." However, even if we leave aside the latter, we are left at the minimum with a circumstance where the music performer is confronted with the achievement-oriented activity of getting the correct notes, and the arousal of both positive and negative achievement motivation would appear to follow in ways analogous to that involving other skill-demanding activity. This has important consequences for the relationship between motivation and music performance, including the role of anxiety, so-called performance anxiety, in such situations.

Research on achievement motivation suggests that certain individuals are more predisposed than others to become excited and enthusiastic when the prospect of doing well in terms of a standard of good performance is presented to them. Such a success-oriented music student is attracted and most motivated to learn when such clear-cut standards of good performance are explicit. The command to "get the notes right" provides a challenge that is a positively valued outcome. We suppose that such students look forward to practicing and then performing when they know that they will be evaluated according to explicit standards of correct performance; that contingent-path arrangements, where they know beforehand that mastering a technique, section, or score is the necessary prerequisite for moving on to other material, further positively motivates such individuals; and that when such students see themselves as becoming musicians or good piano players this still further positively motivates those students to practice, mastery, and further accomplishment. For these students, the research evidence clearly suggests that the role of clear-cut standards, contingent-path hierarchies, and "becoming a future sense of self" all produce heightened positive involvement, excitement, and interest in the performance, and, if the tasks presented to the learner are sufficiently simple, will produce faster learning, more skillful performance, greater persistence, and greater overall accomplishment within a given time period than if no such standards, contingencies, and future self-identities were involved. An important qualification here is that the learning tasks be kept relatively simple for each step. When the tasks are made very complex, the evidence suggests that positive motivation produces what can be called "trying too hard," which interferes with recall, retention, and reproduction of the correct notes and produces a substantially lowered evaluative performance than would have been attained if less positive motivation were aroused. The prescription for maximally motivating these success-oriented students, then, is: (1) make the standards explicit, (2) set up a contingent path, (3) define the future kind of persons successful performance can make them, and then (4) keep each learning task simple. Additional theoretical variables that research has suggested will help to maximize this positive motivation include having (5) the maximum number of achievement steps in the (6) minimum time periods, and (7) having each achievement task not only simple in construction, but "easy to accomplish" within that time frame in the student's view.

Unfortunately, the research evidence suggests that all the conditions that maximally produce positive motivation for the success-oriented learner produce maximum inhibition, with the accompanying anxiety, worry, and dread, for the failure-threatened student. Thus we produce the exact opposite effects if we arrange conditions as above for the student who is predisposed to be more concerned about *failing* to get the notes right than about getting them correct. This is a negatively motivated person in the achievement domain, called the failure-threatened individual. When the prospect of success or failure to "get it right" is aroused, this person focuses (unaware and often without recognizing it) on *not failing,* rather than on succeeding. This produces resistance to engaging in such activity. For the negatively motivated student, the prospect of evaluation of performance in terms of the score—getting the correct notes—is presumed to arouse a tendency not to engage in that activity, be it practice, taking the lesson, or actual performance, and feelings of anxiety, worry, and apprehension are presumed directly proportionate to the magnitude of this behavioral resistance aroused by the prospect of failing to get it right. We presume that all individuals have some predisposition to be "turned on" by the prospect of success with its accompanying excitement and enthusiasm, and that all individuals have some predisposition to be "turned off" by the prospect of failure, with its accompanying worry and apprehension and anxiety, and that the relative strengths of these two dispositions determine the resultant disposition of the individual. The empirical evidence shows that these dispositions, as currently measured, are uncorrelated, so that there are in the general population about 25% who are clearly "success oriented," dominated by the motive to achieve relative to the motive to avoid failure, about 25% who are clearly "failure threatened," dominated by the motive to avoid failure, and a middle 50% for whom the two dispositions are about equal so that neither dominates. When the student is failure threatened, then the optimal strategy to minimize negative motivation is to minimize evaluation, eliminate contingent steps, and fail to emphasize future self-identity tied to the activity in question, and to emphasize extrinsic and cultural positive values as means of feeling good about performance.

These individual differences in relation to evaluative performance are most likely to be elicited in individual performance situations and can be counted on—when they are extreme—to produce dramatically different reactions to the individual performance situation or the face-to-face encounter between student and teacher in the "lesson-performance" situation.

The question is always asked, "Can't we turn failure-threatened students into success-oriented ones?" For extreme cases, my answer would be "no," and that it would be much better to arrange the conditions of learning to maximize the positive motivation of the success-oriented student and minimize the negative motivation of the failure-threatened student, rather than try to change personality dispositions that have taken years to develop and will take years to change, if they change at all.

Of course, the same kinds of differences in personality have influenced and continue to influence the behavior of teachers in their academic and music-related activities. Such evaluative performances (exams, recitals, etc.) have produced retrospections that could be used by teachers to identify in themselves which, if any, of these two dispositions predominates in their music-performance-related activity, as well as in their more general academic-oriented substantive work.

Practically speaking, how can these observations be translated into action by music teachers not wishing to become a psychological testing service for their students? Our research shows that affective reactions of interest, excitement, and enthusiasm on the positive side, and worry, tension, nervousness, and anxiety on the negative side, when they predominate in a particular "important" skill-demanding situation, give a very good clue as to the extreme cases of success-oriented and failure-threatened personality dispositions. Armed with this information, teachers can modify their manner of presentation of materials when one or the other reaction predominantes in the student. For example, a student who shows enthusiasm in just "puttering around" the notes, playing the melody of a song, but appears unconcerned about "whether the particular notes are correct," and whose performance therefore sounds rather terrible to the teacher's ear, who, when confronted with a demand "to get the notes right so we can move on to the next lesson," loses his or her enthusiasm and then suddenly appears quite inhibited, nervous, and anxious, should, on subsequent occasions, be treated as though getting the right notes is unimportant. This student can and does "get the notes right" eventually, but does not do nearly as well when such an explicit norm is imposed on the situation; the teacher who observes such a dramatic change should revert to the unstructured, undemanding circumstances that initially prevailed. Failure-threatened students can perform well, in fact as well or better than their success-oriented counterparts, according to our research on other skill-demanding activity, and they can learn to the same criterion in the same amount of time—but not when the same conditions of explicit evaluation are imposed on the learning or performance situation. And they pay the personal price of negative emotional reaction, and tend to drop out at the earliest possible time, if teachers continue to expose them to such evaluative standards.

It should be obvious that failure-threatened students (with regard to music-related activity) will be at a distinct disadvantage if and when public performance that demands getting the notes right becomes a requirement in their training. These are the students who experience the amount of "stage fright" that is sometimes observed in otherwise talented performers, and who literally "freeze" because of such strong inhibition. While even the most positively motivated individual becomes more nervous for an important performance than in practice (though the enthusiasm that increases more than offsets the negative reaction so that success-oriented individuals look forward to such important performances with great anticipation), the effect for the failure-threatened individual expected to give a solo performance is devastating—lapses of memory, weakness of limbs, incorrect notes, paralysis of movement. In our conception, these are not caused by being afraid, but rather both fear and poor performance result from the behavior resistance aroused by such a person's automatic predisposition to be more concerned about failure than about success. Such an extreme reaction should be a good indication for counseling against a solo performance career; group performance is probably much less inhibiting.

LISTENING TO MUSIC

Musicologist, music critic, and subscription concertgoer are several of the self-images that characterize the psychological career of "music listener." Conceptualized this way, listening to music is an activity like any other human activity. When large sources of positive motivation are aroused for it, and self-images are defined by the outcomes of the activity, then music listening becomes a psychological career, whether it be a leisure career or a professional career. More frequently, however, the self-system is not involved, since for the average music listener large extrinsic and cultural value are not seen as resulting from listening to music. The pleasure associated with listening to music for these individuals is here conceptualized as intrinsic value and, by itself, is rarely large enough to provide a valuable means of self-identity—although this certainly can be the case for a musician or conscientious concertgoer. Thus, while listening to music as background to many other activities is a very common activity, it is sustained by relatively small amounts of positive motivation. As the number and magnitude of sources of value increase, involvment in music listening is predicted to increase, so that, like other human activity, persistence of music listening is expected to be greatest for individuals positively motivated by the substantive music in question who see themselves defined in terms of the outcomes of their music-listening activity.

The imposition of standards of good, better, and best music-listening behavior, including discrmination of the instruments of the orchestra and the ability to follow polyphonic music lines, define degrees of difficulty value for the music listener. Individual cultural values concerning the kind of music that is most appreciated are sometimes exceedingly strong: One example concerns devotees of the symphony as the "best" and "highest" musical expression in Western music, who see themselves in terms of the ability to appreciate this "greatest of all" forms; for others it is "chamber music."

Note that the imposition of criteria having nothing to do with the way the notes "sound," including music structure and ensemble composition, often take on important roles in defining individual cultural value for music listening and appreciation. Often it is the case that reading the musical score and the musicologist's notes can provide almost as much positive value as the additional component of hearing the sounds produced. I think this more than anything else separates fomally trained musicians from their lay counterparts; these additional academic and intellectual criteria define additional sources of value so that, after such formal musical training, the amount of value associated with music listening tends to increase substantially. Again, I do not wish to impose my own cultural valuation upon this; I merely wish to note it, particularly in light of the fact that in such cases, "intrinsic value" plays a relatively small role in contributing value as compared to the other sources of value. I think professional musicians and musical educators, musicologists and music critics, all tend *not* to realize the relatively large contribution of sources of motivation for their music-related activities that are *not* derived from intrinsic value, but rather are derivable from their formal training and its associated sources of value for music. This tends sometimes to create a gulf between professionally trained musicians and their lay counterparts concerning "listening to music," particularly when standards of composition are relevant to the musician but not the lay listener. The two activities are experienced quite differently, if I am correct: For the professional, many sources of value are aroused, often involving self-identity, so that the intensity and positive affect of the activity of listening to music is quite substantial, while for the casual lay music listener, it is rarer for enthusiasm and interest to reach such magnitudes. I suspect that part of the goal of music educators and teachers is to impose (teach) their own sources of value on young music listeners so that they, the youngsters, will come to "better appreciate" the particular musical performance form in question. In fact, several years ago my children successfully did the same concerning my "listening to the Beatles" activity. In both instances, the activity of listening goes way beyond "listening to the notes." In different cultural contexts, the content of individual difficulty and cultural value that define good or bad music and music listeners can be expected to vary substantially without altering the definition of music activity from the listener's point of view. (Of course, the same points can and should be made concerning the music composer, since the given individual difficulty and cultural value derived from the time at which the composer happens to live are usually crucial in influencing what the composer considers to be worthwhile music to produce.)

CONCLUDING REMARKS

Motivational factors defined as the source of positive and negative value are not the only factors determinng the "worth" to the individual of an activity and its outcome; sometimes they are not even the most important factors. However, the systematic conceptualization of sources of value as presented here allows for insights into human activity in addition to, or sometimes instead of, other ways of defining worth in human activity. In particular, as emphasized in this paper, time-linked sources of value, which change as a function of stages of career striving owing to success in attaining goals, and self-linked sources of value, which define "who I am" in terms of the outcomes of activity, are useful ways to view some of the determinants and consequences of the fact that some activities are perceived by individuals engaged in them to be much more "important" than others. We believe that the greater the value involved in the outcomes of an activity, the greater its perceived importance to the actor. Thus we have the conceptual tools to understand why activity and outcome are seen as important as sources and magnitudes of value increase. My assumption has been that the importance of music-related activity to the individual can be conceptualized as being influenced by the same sources of value that influence any other human activity. If this assumption is correct, then my goal of providing some insights into the motivational determinants of music-related activity will have been attained.

16

Theories of Adult Personality Development and Socialization: Toward an Understanding of Midlife Transitions in Women

Eileen T. Brown

Nora stands in the door and says: "I don't know what will become of me. I don't know where I am going. I only know that I can no longer bother about what others say. I must find my own way." Is this not where life's possibilities lie? Not necessarily to arrive, but always to be on the way, in movement?

Liv Ullman, regarding her role as Norma in Ibsen's *The Doll's House*

Recently, the midlife period of adult personality development has become the object of serious study, but most of it has been focused on men (e.g., Brim, 1976; Levinson, 1978; Vaillant & McArthur, 1972; Gutmann, 1976). This seems odd in light of the fact that 53% of the population over 35 years old are women (U.S. Department of Labor, 1975). One possible reason may be that researchers have confused the physiological and psychological state of menopause with the more general and perhaps more rationally based construct of midlife transition. To date, only three serious researchers (Bart, Neugarten and her associates, and Lowenthal and hers) have devoted any programmatic effort to studying the psychological aspects of women at this critical juncture. An examination of these women, however, in the popular media and in whatever professional literature does exist, produces a multi-faceted and somewhat contradictory picture.

Such a woman is the depressed mother whose grown children no longer need her constant attention, who must cope with the "empty nest" (Bart, 1971, 1975). Keenly aware that her reproductive capacity is ending, she is the housewife whose chronic "problem with no name" (Friedan, 1963) has suddenly become acute. She is the heroine of a recent movie ("The Turning Point") who has reached a stage at which decisions made earlier have now become irreversible. For whatever she still hopes to accomplish, time is running out, and it is more reasonable to count time from the end of one's life than from the beginning (Neugarten, 1976). In a society with narrowly construed standards of youthful beauty, she becomes increasingly aware of gray hair, wrinkles, and sagging stomach muscles. (See Neugarten, Moore, & Lowe, 1965.) And since, in this age bracket, almost three times as many women as men are likely to be either widowed or divorced (Bell, 1970), she may be thrust precipitously onto the labor market with skills and training that are at best rusty and at worst nonexistent.

In contrast, another view, as encouraging and optimistic as the picture just painted is bleak, may emerge. At this age, we begin to see the foreshadowing of the normal androgyny of later life (Neugarten & Gutmann, 1968; Gutmann, 1975). She becomes more assertive, aggressive, and dominant. According to Kinsey, she is at her sexual peak (Kinsey, 1953). Her presence on the labor market takes its sharpest upswing, as does her re-entry into educational programs (U.S. Department of Labor, 1975; Campbell, 1973). Freed from the major responsibilities and constraints of her sex role, she can explore inner needs and new possibilities (Livson, 1976). Neugarten (1976) found that this postparental stage was associated with a higher level of life satisfaction than others. It is at this time that the predominantly professional woman may seriously reconsider other more maternal and nurturant options still open to her (Hennig & Jardim, 1977; Ginzberg & Yohalem, 1966). For many women, then, middle age may indeed be a time when "the wisdom of age and the energy and self-confidence of youth are most successfully blended" (Mayer, 1969).

It remains to ask what time frame encompasses the midlife period. Rather than emphasizing strict chronological boundaries, I prefer to focus on the phenomenological and dynamic aspects of midlife. The major concern will be that period in which a conscious choice point (either externally determined or internally derived or a combination of both) is reached; that is, a time of personal reassessment, followed by a decision that alters the future direction of one's life—a shift in career paths.

In addition, something must be said about the term "crisis" that keeps cropping up in discussions of midlife transitions. The medical, counseling, and dictionary definitions all emphasize a turning point, a critical time or occasion during which a decisive change for better or worse occurs. Gutmann's (1976) definition of crisis as "a time of both inner and outer change, during which energies tied to pre-existing structures are released, with constructive or destructive consequences, depending on the individual's personal and cultural circumstances" seems right on target. Involved may be concepts of role, status, motivation (incentive and goal systems), self-image, and social responsibility. Or it may be as relatively narrow as intermittent mood swings and isolated activities such as enrolling in a single course in a continuing education program.

A number of theoretical perspectives could be brought to bear on this broad spectrum of changes. For example, a biological approach might stress hormonal imbalance (reduced estrogen level, etc.) or other physiological phenomena such as increased blood serum uric acid, a chemical known to be positively correlated with achievement behaviors (Hyde & Rosenberg, 1976). Certainly theories of time perception, self-attribution, career development, locus of control, and decision making would be relevant.

Two bodies of theory that seem to be fundamental to the understanding of all adult personality change (as well as of any particular subset of it) are adult personality development and adult socialization. It is these that will provide the focus of our analysis.

ADULT PERSONALITY DEVELOPMENT

The various theories that have been proposed to account for adult personality development differ in their relative emphases on biological mechanisms, motivational constructs, use of psychoanalytic concepts, relative importance of experiential factors, reliance on earlier stages of the life cycle to explain happenings in later ones, and degree of adherence to a strict stage model. They vary as well in terms of their applicability to women, since many of them were developed on the generic male model. (For a more detailed analysis of the dimensions on which developmental models may differ, see Looft, 1973.)

The category schemes utilized to date to analyze this literature have been based on streams of historical development (Neugarten, 1976) or on the broad disciplines from which the ideas have been derived—e.g., biology, sociology, and psychology (Spierer, 1977)—or on the subareas within the broader fields (Emmerich, 1973). For the most part these schemes are nonintegrative and unidimensional and do not seem particularly useful in theory building.

By categorizing these theories in terms of their critical constructs, we can expand the utility of the concepts and variables within each theory, as well as build a network of underlying relationships among them. (See Cronbach & Meehl, 1955, for a further discussion of this approach to theory building.)

Examination of the seminal theoretical literature in adult personality development leads to the repeated emergence of five potentially useful key concepts: (1) homeostatic balance, (2) goal-or-task orientation, (3) commitment, (4) becoming as process, and (5) adaptation. While not logically derived from a temporal analysis of the phenomenon, these categories not only appear to partition the field descriptively but offer explanatory mechanisms as well. Only subsequent empirical elaboration will test their ultimate utility. Developmental theorists differ in their relative use of these concepts; some stress only one, while others liberally borrow from several. These relationships are illustrated in Table 1. Only those theorists whose ideas seem particularly applicable to the changes undergone by women at midlife will be discussed. A theory will be considered in the context of that construct which seems most focal to its structure and development.

It is difficult to describe women as a monolithic group. Traditionally, the primary focus and determinant for most men's lives has been occupational. Women's lives have taken on the variety of a number of different patterns, including traditional homemaking, stable conventional careers, interrupted careers, dual careers with multiple simultaneous roles, and so forth (Super, 1957; Ginzberg, 1972; Psathas, 1968; Zytowski, 1969).

The present analysis, however, will examine the "traditional" woman, the one whose major concern for the first half of her life has been home, husband, and children. Even if she has worked outside the home, her chief source of identification, the greatest input of her time, and her major sources of satisfaction have come from within it. Even if times are changing, and there are many indications that they are, current norms and expectations change slowly, and for many women the traditional model is still the reality.

Table 1   Relationship between Basic Constructs and the Theorists Who Have Utilized Them

Homeostatic balance	Goal or task orientation	Commitment	Becoming as process	Adaptation
Jung*	Levinson*	Levinson	Jung	Deutsch*
Deutsch	Buhler*	Erikson	Buhler	Gutmann
Benedek*	Frenkel-Brunswick*	Gould*	Raynor*	Thomae
Gutmann*	Kuhlen	Marcia		Havighurst
Levinson	Havighurst*	Lowenthal*		Gould
Thomae*	Erikson*	Perry*		Lowenthal*
Henry*	Peck			Vaillant*
Buhler	Marcia			Neugarten*
Kuhlen*	Gould			Erikson
Erikson	Raynor			Raynor
Lowenthal	Lowenthal			
Neugarten				

Note. An asterisk indicates that this is a focal concept for the theory.

Homeostatic Balance

Jung (1970, 1971) believed that development during adulthood was the unfolding of an original undifferentiated wholeness whose ultimate goal was the realization of full selfhood. At midlife, a merging and transvaluation of conflicting polar tendencies within the personality was likely to occur. It follows from Jung's belief in the bisexual nature of humans that, by midlife, the large store of the dominant sexual archetype has been heavily utilized, and the smaller amount of the opposite tendency can emerge, ready for expression. In the second half of life then, the female may develop her more "masculine" tough-mindedness and sharpness of mind, while the male may give vent to his more "feminine" tender feelings.

The woman, then, who has spent her early adult years in nurturing others, even at the expense of subverting her own needs, is merely following the dictates of her feminine archetype. As she turns inward at midlife, her self-survey reveals the male archetypes, largely unexplored and undeveloped. Psychic energy formerly poured into the former can now be captured and transferred to the latter, producing a rearrangement of her self-system.

Jung's concepts are intriguing and have some intuitive plausibility. The difficulty for middle-aged women, regardless of their prior career patterns, in shifting from concern with others to concern with self has been documented (Beauvoir, 1967). Nonetheless, his ideas are by and large metaphysical and incapable of proof (Glover, 1950). While they have stimulated much speculation, relatively little of it has been translated into serious experimental research.

Another theorist who proposes a male-female personality swing at midlife is Gutmann. Gutmann (1975) suggests release from the parental imperative rather than imbalances in psychic energy as the most viable explanatory mechanism. He assumes that supraindividual factors mobilized by parental bonds to our children bring out the stereotypic, traditional behaviors for which each sex has been previously socialized. Although cultural determinants may modify the basic pattern somewhat, in the first half of adult life, most females will be nurturant, passive, and expressive, while most males will be dominant, achievement oriented, and independent. In this view, differentiated sex roles are an evolutionary adaptation for the survival of the entire species, and not a social invention for the convenience of half of it.

When children grow up, however, and the concomitant responsibilities are removed, "the psychic structures predicated on the parental emergency" are to some extent dismantled "such that previously disowned behavioral and emotional potential can be lived out" (Gutmann, 1975, pp. 181 and 182). Each sex provides the context in which the other may explore those submerged facets of the personality that have been stunted and denied in the first part of the life cycle, and produce midlife changes not unlike those foreseen by Jung.

Gutmann's theory depends upon the assumption of traditional sex roles. Now that more than 50% of married women are fully employed outside the home (U.S. Department of Labor, 1975), this pattern is changing. In addition, even if early socialization practices were similar, it is unknown in childhood who will be a parent and who will not. Without the actual act of parenting and its subsequent release, the characteristic constellation of personality characteristics would not be stimulated to develop—or change—at midlife.

Although Gutman provides only partial answers, he has attempted empirical documentation (Gutman, 1976). Because he believes it is necessary to tease the effects of cultural context apart from maturational trends, much of his work is cross cultural. Using open-ended interviews and projective techniques, and studying groups as diverse as urban American and Middle Eastern Druze, he has repeatedly replicated the redistribution of masculine and feminine traits in the later years.[1]

Goal or Task Orientation

Other developmental theorists, rather than concentrating on shifting personality components, emphasize those age-related tasks that society presents to the individual throughout the life span. They vary in terms of their emphasis on particular tasks or an ultimate end point, on the specific issues to be resolved at each stage, and on the extensiveness of their theoretical underpinnings. While Buhler (1968), Frenkel-Brunswick (1968), Havighurst (1952), and Levinson (1978) represent this approach, the work of Erikson has been most influential.

For Erikson (1963), understanding personality means knowing how a series of psychosocial tasks have been handled over the life span. Psychological development proceeds by critical stages, each of which is characterized by its own conflict between bipolar dimensions. At these crucial periods, incipient growth is accompanied by a shift in instinctual energy, causing an increased vulnerability to change and supporting new and expanded ego functions (Erikson, 1968). Each ego strength

---

[1] Gutmann cites an anthropological study (Gold, 1960) in which 14 out of 26 cultures surveyed all illustrated a midlife shift to female dominance. The remainder showed no change; none had a change to greater male dominance.

arises in its time of special ascendency, until all conflicts have been resolved. Personality development follows an individual's readiness to interact with a widening radius of significant individuals and social institutions. Erikson's eight stages are summarized in Table 2. Since Erikson's stages were based primarily on the male experience, applying one age-related stage to our traditional woman produces a picture that is incomplete and unidimensional. The strengths or weaknesses established in earlier stages are built upon in later ones, and no developmental crisis is resolved forever. Therefore, it seems plausible to apply the dynamics of several prior stages to the midlife transition. For instance, in the first stage, the sense of trust emerges from the belief in the sameness and continuity of one's providers. At midlife, a woman's immediate provider, her husband, may be undergoing changes of his own that portend discontinuity. At the same time, her original providers, her parents, may also be undergoing change, so that the dependency relationship is reversed.

Successful resolution of the second stage results in the courage to choose and guide one's future. For the woman experiencing autonomy, perhaps free of contingency plans for the first time, this may be unsettling. The self-doubt that may follow is a natural consequence of actual or anticipated role change. Similarly, guilt, the negative pole of the third psychosocial crisis, may accompany the sense of exuberance that comes with the exercising of initiative and new powers. Erikson refers to the "hysterical denial" or "self-restriction" that can accompany this transition and keep the individual from living fully up to her inner capacities.

The fourth stage, with its emphasis on technology, leaves many women feeling inferior, having been socialized into believing that the mechanistic world is the

Table 2   Identity Gains in Each of Erikson's Eight Psychosocial Stages

Psychosocial Conflict	Stage of Life	Identity Gain from Successful Resolution
Trust vs. mistrust	1. Infancy	"I am what hope I have and give."
Autonomy vs. shame and doubt	2. Toddlerhood	"I am what I can will freely."
Initiative vs. guilt	3. Childhood	"I am what endeavors I plan and pursue."
Industry vs. inferiority	4. Later childhood	"I am what I can learn to make work."
Identity vs. identity confusion	5. Adolescence	"I am what has taken place which enables what is to continue to be."
Intimacy vs. isolation	6. Young adulthood	"We are what we love."
Generativity vs. stagnation	7. Midlife	"We are what we can pass on to subsequent generations."
Integrity vs. despair	8. Old age	"I am what survives of me."

Note. These phrases (with the exception of stages 3 and 7) are quoted from Erikson's (1968) discussion. For some reason, he does not offer these statements for the third and seventh stages, so I have taken the liberty of suggesting phrases that are appropriate.

proper domain of men. The technology in which she is proficient, domestic maintenance, is not really valued by society. It is no wonder that a sense of inferiority
may ensue.

The rhetoric of searching out new directions at midlife is reminiscent of an
adolescent identity crisis. A number of writers have called attention to the
similarities between these two age groups (Letchworth, 1970; Fried, 1967). Both
are undergoing increased endocrine activity, observable body change, and the re-
emergence of earlier seemingly resolved conflicts. Tottering on the brink of identity confusion, both are often beset by problems of simultaneous commitment,
abhorrence of competition, and inability to derive a sense of accomplishment from
any activity. Adolescents often take a moratorium to work out some of these
troublesome issues. Recent evidence indicates that many women do the same—using
their child-rearing years to rethink and reshape their sense of self (Daniels, 1978).

Intimacy, the strength of the sixth stage, presupposes identity. Many women,
however, postpone ego identity until they have attained intimacy—that is, until
they have found a husband with whom they can dovetail their own goals and
values. There is empirical evidence that for many college women the sequence is
indeed reversed, with intimacy followed by, not preceded by, identity (Douvan &
Adelson, 1966; Constantinople, 1969). By midlife, many women still define themselves *first* as Harry's wife or Sally's mother. How many who do choose careers do
so on the basis of what is convenient for their families? When Erikson talks of the
significant sacrifices and compromises that are necessary for the achievement of
intimacy, he ignores the fact that for years those compromises have been made
largely by women. Neither clearly sequential nor definitely commutative, the complex relationship between intimacy and identity developed on the normative male
model still needs to be unraveled.

Erikson has pointed out that mere biological generativity is insufficient to
achieve the strength of the next stage. By midlife women may see many of their
nurturant activities as trivial. In the nitty-gritty of everyday chores, they tend to
lose sight of the larger picture of contribution to future generations, and thus derive
little satisfaction from their own brand of generativity.[2]

Erikson's last stage seems premature for women who may be as young as their
mid-30's when making midcareer decisions. Yet elements of despair may be present
in the midlife depression that has been observed. When a woman sees no new viable
options and feels unprepared for anything other than what she has done before—
and that is no longer possible—she is unlikely to feel a sense of worth. She may
look at the youth-oriented culture around her and feel that she has no time left to
try out alternative roads to ego identity.

To merely examine the one stage that has been tacked on to men at midlife,
then, seems inadequate to handle the problems faced by many women. The contingencies of their lives necessitate the application of elements from other psychosocial conflicts if one is to understand more fully the turmoil they may be undergoing.

[2]In fact, Peck (1956) has expanded the developmental issues of the middle years beyond
generativity versus stagnation to include four additional dimensions.

Commitment

Commitment is defined as adherence to a particular goal or course of action in the face of potentially high costs, resulting in an observed consistency in outlook and behavior with regard to that goal or action across different situations (Becker, 1964). A number of theorists (Erikson, 1964, 1968; Levinson, 1976, 1978; Marcia, 1966; Gould, 1972) have incorporated the concept. For some (Perry, 1970), it is central. Although Perry's scheme was originally intended to study adolescents' cognitive structuring of reality and their conceptions of knowledge, it has far broader applicability. Based on intensive interviews with nearly 100 students, he developed a nine-point scale that is more easily understood by combining the stages to form three major components. Thus, the first three stages represent *dualism,* a kind of dichotomous, simplistic right versus wrong way of thinking. At this stage, individuals unquestioningly accept external givens, finding little legitimacy for conflicting viewpoints. The next major phase, *relativism,* recognizes the importance of contextual factors and the legitimacy of diversity. Empathy for others whose divergent views are now realistically perceived can be experienced. An important concomitant is an uncomfortable amount of disequilibrium as old rules of right and wrong disappear. Perry points out that people who cannot tolerate the "ambiguity of multiplicity" may regress into a dualistic orientation to the world.

In the final phase, *commitment in relativism,* one can create one's own identity in a pluralistic world. Commitment enables one to proceed meaningfully to the selection of a career, sex role, set of values, and life-style. Perry sees commitment as a dynamic process in which a balance must be maintained between flexibility and purpose, and freedom and constraint (Kroll, Kinklage, Lee, Morley, & Wilson, 1970). This scheme, which applies to many of our conceptual systems, is certainly applicable to a woman's sense of her own identity and life-style (Knefelkampf, 1976). In the early years of marriage, the woman who has chosen a traditional path may believe that hers is the right and true choice, and those who have chosen differently are blatantly wrong. This dichotomous view of the female role makes it easier to adjust to her own decision. She will selectively expose herself to the words of Marabel Morgan, Phyllis Schafly, and the like, and close her ears to the cries of the feminist movement.

Once doubts have been raised, though, a more relativistic view of one's role sets in, and a woman may recognize other diverse yet legitimate career paths. It seems reasonable to assume that this point is likely to be reached when her children no longer require her total time, or at least when she anticipates that this will soon be the case. Once having taken the responsibility for the development of her own identity in a pluralistic world, she can commit herself to a line of values and action that represents a true choice and not a foregone conclusion.

Lowenthal (1977) believes that the evolving self-concept flows as a natural consequence of commitments at various life stages. Four areas of commitment that may operate sequentially or simultaneously seem particularly important. The first, commitment to self-preservation, is the most basic and is presupposed by the other three. The second, interpersonal commitment (as with Erikson's stages), moves from the dyadic to the panhumanistic level. Sense of competence or mastery, first discussed as an important facet of human motivation by White (1966), represents Lowenthal's third area. She suggests that perceived loss of competence and control, in the work sphere for men and the family sphere for women, may be critical in the demarcation of many of life's transition points. While men tend to constrict their mastery commitments by middle age, women (reminiscent of Jung) reach out for self-assertion although they often find the opportunities lacking. The fourth area, moral commitment, is considered extensively elsewhere (Kohlberg, 1973).

A number of questions remain unanswered. It is still unclear what situational and internal cues are associated with change in the degree and nature of these commitments across the life span. Nor do we understand the adaptational consequences of their fulfillment and frustration. And the extent to which fulfillment in one area may compensate for deficits in another is unexamined. While Lowenthal sees these as potentially researchable items, she has not as yet operationalized the commitment concept sufficiently to make them practical ones.

Becoming as Process

The view that the individual is essentially a conglomeration of traits, relatively fixed in time, has pervaded much traditional research. That human beings are perhaps better conceived as a constantly changing state of becoming has been, until recently, largely the domain of the humanists (Maslow, 1970; Rogers, 1961; Ellis, 1971). Raynor's theory of motivation and aging approaches adult personality development from this perspective (see chapter 13).

Where, on the various career paths that Raynor has postulated, does the traditional woman find herself at midlife? Most of her domestic activities are like steps on a noncontingent path and have relatively low motivational value. Any occupational activity engaged in outside her home is probably a fairly low contributor to her self-esteem, as it, too, is likely to be of a noncontingent nature. If we assume that her sexual and family senses of herself are closed contingent paths, her situation at midlife becomes much clearer. Let us backtrack.

At the outset of her marital career, the anticipated future includes bright and well-behaved children, a solicitous and financially successful husband, and an attractively furnished home with all the latest conveniences. At the start, her self-esteem and motivation for striving are on the rise; her sense of becoming is high. While not always as clearly delineated as in a more formalized occupational career path, she is aware of the steps that will bring her closer to the ultimate goal. (See Figure 1, level *a*.)

As she proceeds along the path (Figure 1, level *b*), she can derive esteem income from what has been accomplished so far (steps -3 through 0), and while enjoying the fruits of her past successes can still feel good about the competence with which she copes with multiple demands. Her activities have difficulty value (other people's marriages are falling apart but hers is still intact; others' children are on drugs or dropping out of school but hers have remained on the straight and narrow path). They have instrumental value (each success of members of the family unit ensures opportunities for renewed success). They have extrinsic value (look at her new

(a)

Marriage; setting up first household.	Husband finishes school; she works to put him through.	Husband's first job; she stops working; has first child.	Husband gets raise in salary; buys new home; has second child.	Husband gets promotion; children in elementary school; refurnishes home.	Children in high school; she gets ad hoc volunteer activity.	Husband at pinnacle of career success; children leave for college.
Present						Anticipated future
0	+1	+2	+3	+4	+5	$+N_6$

(b)

			Present			Anticipated future
Retrospected past						
$-N_3$	-2	-1	0	+1	+2	$+N_3$

(c)

						Present
Retrospected past						
$-N_6$	-5	-4	-3	-2	-1	0

(d)

			Present				Return to school for refresher courses; take up new hobby with husband (e.g., golf).	Successful completion of degree program; sign up for lessons together.	New job opportunities for advancement; enter as tournament partners.
$-N_3$	-2	-1	0	+1	+2	+3	+4	+5	$+N_6$

Figure 1. Career paths in the life of a hypothetical traditional woman. (a) Start of career striving in a closed contingent path (early 20s); (b) middle of career striving in a closed contingent path (late 20s to early 30s); (c) end of career striving in a closed contingent path (late 30s to early 40s); (d) middle of striving on an open contingent path. (After Raynor's model.)

wardrobe and latest vacation), and because society is still patting her on the head, they have cultural value as well. Because of the foreseeable and attainable goals in her future, she obtains satisfaction from striving toward them. In other words, her three time-linked senses of self are operating at full steam.

As she moves toward the last steps in the path, however (a time likely to coincide with the fourth or fifth decade), the instrumental and difficulty value of her goals decrease. (See Figure 1, level *c*.) Since being "just a housewife" is now looked upon askance for a woman whose children no longer need her full attention, the cultural value is diminishing too. Sexually, she is aware of her declining attractiveness in a youth-oriented society. Having attained all original goals, she derives no esteem income from subsequent striving. Although the extrinsic value of what has been amassed may be high, it is still not sufficient to compensate for the other losses of feeling good about herself. Because she has no other readily available career path, we have the makings of a full-blown midlife crisis.

But what does it mean for the closed contingent path upon which she has been striving to become opens? The shift will not be easy—but it is possible. She can derive new sources of esteem from a redefined association with her children. She can open new spheres of shared activity and mutual interests with her husband. She can embark on a new career path that may involve returning to school, taking a new job, or throwing herself more committedly into an old one. In this manner, goals reduced in value can be replaced by new paths altogether. The extent to which esteem derived from these new paths will enhance her sense of self with regard to older paths still needs to be explored. (See Figure 1, level *d*.)

It is also possible to use cognitive means to maintain one's level of esteem. That is, a woman can continue to live through the current successes of her family, glorify her own past achievements, or take small forward leaps, become overwhelmed when the going is rough, and retreat into the rationalization that she has bitten off more than she can chew. For these women, assistance with the process of converting closed contingent paths to open ones would be an important step toward the resolution of their so-called midlife crises.

Adaptation

For any of life's important transitions, coping or adaptation is an essential facet of development. One early theorist who was particularly concerned with the psychosexual development of women from this vantage point was Helene Deutsch. She believed that the middle years present one of the most important adaptive tasks women must face. Deutsch described the menopausal era, and what has since come to be known as the "empty nest syndrome" (Bart, 1975), as a time of renewed activity in which all the forces of the ego are mobilized to overcome the "horror of the too late." Whether manifested in the emergence of long-buried artistic and intellectual urges, intensified eroticism and promiscuity, overly depressive fears of death and illness, or the immediate desire to have a "late baby," it stems from the same fundamental source (Deutsch, 1945). The energy for this activity is produced by the replaying of Oedipal themes for the third time—first in childhood, then in adolescence, and now again at menopause.

In line with her elaborate typology (Deutsch, 1945, vol. I; Williams, 1977), Deutsch hypothesized that "feminine-loving women" will make a smoother adjustment to the climacterium than any of the varieties of "masculine-aggressive ones," although all women must engage in some form of coping.[3]

Recent studies have shown, however, that neither menopause nor the empty nest is perceived to be the problem Deutsch assumed it to be (Neugarten, Wood, Kraines, & Loomis, 1968; Lowenthal & Chiriboga, 1972; Neugarten, 1978). Working with normal, rather than clinical, populations, Neugarten and her associates found that more than three-quarters of their sample viewed not having to bother with menstruation or worry about getting pregnant as a relief rather than a burden. Although there was some inconsistency in the overall responses, this was a definite trend. This part of adult female life does not seem to call forth the great adaptive powers that were once assumed, especially when they are seen as part of the normal course of development. That some of the differences with earlier researchers are attributable to a cohort effect cannot be discounted.

Neugarten has recently investigated modes and correlates of adaptation among older and middle-aged women. She considers the coping mechanisms employed more important than the particular events that elicit them (Noberini & Neugarten, 1975). Using longitudinal data from working and middle-class women, Noberini and Neugarten developed the Ego Competence Scale, an attempt to tap several aspects of coping, including the ability to weather life's expected and unexpected contingencies, the quality of interpersonal interactions, and the maintenance of sense of self. This, in conjunction with body cathexis scales, life satisfaction ratings, and incidence of symptomatology (e.g., headaches, sleeplessness), was used to measure overall adaptiveness.

It was found that high ego competence generally implied high life satisfaction, but that low ego competence was more variable in its effects. One may reason that ego competence acts as an adaptive mediating variable; then it intensifies the effect of other internal symptoms and outer events. Thus, a woman with high ego competence will cope successfully regardless of the nature of the biological and social events in her environment, while one with low levels will cope well or not depending upon whether the biological and social events in her life are stressful. The single most reliable predictor of coping skills that they uncovered was level of ego competence.

Lowenthal and her colleagues (1975) have also stressed the importance of coping mechanisms in the developmental process. In a cross-sectional survey of middle- and lower middle-class men and women, they intensively examined four transition points in the life span. Two of these (adolescents about to graduate from high school and young newlyweds) were "incremental" transitions; that is, role change involved expansion or increase in status. The other two (parents about to face the

---

[3] Deutsch exemplified this increased thrust of activity in her own midlife. She had just given birth to her only son, become actively involved with Freud, and shortly thereafter begun work on the extensive two-volume *Psychology of Women* (1945), her greatest contribution to the psychoanalytic movement. These and other aspects of her life are discussed in her recent autobiography, *Confrontations with Myself* (1973).

empty nest and imminent retirees), were "decremental," entailing constriction or decrease in status.

Interestingly, the highest risk group in terms of maladjustment was the midlife females. In spite of overt claims that they eagerly awaited the empty nest, the measures revealed a preoccupation with intrapsychic problems. These women, the most poorly adapted of the eight age-sex subgroups, had been primarily family centered in spite of the fact that a majority held full-time jobs. (For similar findings, see Lopata, 1971; Williams & Wirths, 1965; Kline, 1977.) They listed the fewest roles and exhibited the narrowest pattern of activities. They were the most likely to indicate their specific age when *not* directly asked and made the most frequent visits to physicians. They recalled the years when their children were small as best. On self-concept adjective checklists, they were the most negative group, and the self-image and goals they projected were inconsistent and highly diffuse. Predictably, they were the most likely to be lacking in hope, operationally defined as "the feeling that what is desired is also viewed as possible."

One clue to this "not very quiet desperation" of the midlife women in Lowenthal's sample comes from the finding that they were the most negative in describing their marriage relationship. This is consistent with other findings that marital dissatisfaction tends to peak in the pre-empty-nest stage (Blood & Wolfe, 1960; Burr, 1970; Rollins & Feldman, 1970).

At a time when these women are undergoing reorientation in their own goals and values, strong emotional support needed from husbands, adolescent children, and aging parents may be lacking. In fact, midlife husbands had the lowest spouse involvement scores of any group. This is particularly unfortunate, since intimate dyadic relations, according to Lowenthal, are a rich psychological resource during times of transition. At these vulnerable points, they may make the difference between successful coping and its absence. That there are different age and sex patterns of trust, support, communicativeness, and understanding creates an asynchrony in midlife couples that further reduces their adaptive potential.

Reappraisal: Key Constructs Revisited

A number of theorists, then, from a broad spectrum of viewpoints, have addressed the issues of adult personality development. An examination of Table 1 indicates that no major theorist relies exclusively on the explanatory power of only one construct. A task theorist such as Erikson, for instance, does not ignore the role of commitment or homeostatic mechanisms, nor does Lowenthal, whose main concern is adaptation, ignore balance, goal orientation, or commitment. It also appears that the major thrust of each theory falls readily under the rubric of one of these five constructs, although some appear more popular than others.

One may take the attitude of physicists who view light as corpuscular or as wavelike. They accept both hypotheses alternately, depending on the particular problem to be explained. Depending upon whether one's emphasis is on antecedent conditions, long-range dynamics, immediate motivational mechanisms, or therapeutic applications, one or more of these constructs can be chosen as the most useful.

Adult development probably does involve some sort of self-regulatory homeostatic mechanism over the long haul, and specific tasks (or goals) will no doubt have to be accomplished en route. Without an element of commitment to this accomplishment, it is not likely to be achieved. Without a specific motivational force, it is unlikely that movement toward any goal will occur. To the extent that goals, as well as the context within which they are formulated, change, and that progress toward them sometimes falls short of the mark, adaptation (a fundamental property of living systems, in any event) is essential. Are constructs other than the ones suggested here pertinent to adult personality development? Perhaps; and hopefully further research will explicate them. But at this early stage of theory building, the five that have been gleaned from the literature do seem to have heuristic value.

ADULT SOCIALIZATION THEORY

Socialization theorists do not deny the existence of maturational forces in the adult personality. From this theoretical perspective, however, changes in the life course derive from changes in a matrix of situational and environmental influences and the corresponding adjustments they induce. Transitional points and stages are built into the life cycle by the "culturally determined patterns and exigencies of social life" that a given society imposes (Schlegel, 1975). For these thinkers, including the social learning theorists, symbolic interactionists, and role theorists, personality dispositions may be defined as the sum of socialization experiences and social roles (e.g., Mead, 1934; Ahammer, 1973; Gordon, 1972; Neugarten & Datan, 1973).

Four sociological concepts appear to be particularly pertinent to the midlife passage: (1) role-related constructs; (2) social networks; (3) anticipatory socialization; and (4) asynchrony. Once again, we shall concentrate on the traditional woman, who has devoted most of her time, energy, and identity during the first half of adulthood to "kinder, küche und Kirche" (Weisstein, 1968).

Role-Related Constructs

One of the most frequently mentioned sociological phenomena regarding women in their middle years is the "empty-nest" syndrome. This is the role attrition that occurs through the shrinkage of maternal responsibilities and normative expectations, an event often associated with frustration and depression. The experience has been compared to Durkheim's *anomie,* in that the woman who has been overintegrated into society through the props of the maternal roles finds herself in a normless state, unintegrated and anomic.

Much of the research in the area has been conducted by Bart (1969, 1971, 1975). Her methods have included cross-cultural analysis of the Human Relations Area Files, epidemiological examination of the hospital records of depressed middle-aged women, and intensive interviews (including projective tests). In general, this triangulation of techniques led to the consistent result that the role loss experienced by many of these women was painful, in some cases pathologically so. That the psychological pain is a sociological phenomenon, and not merely an endocrinological by-product of menopause, is supported by her cross-cultural findings (Bart, 1969). In the five non-Western cultures studied, the position of middle-aged women actually improved. In these societies, where there were extended rather than nuclear family systems, residence patterns that kept offspring near their family of origin, and formal institutionalized grandmother and mother-in-law roles, these women actually experienced role enhancement.

More recent studies have failed to replicate the depressive symptoms of Bart's findings. Women are reporting more positive reactions to the independence of their children (Lowenthal et al., 1975; Radloff, 1975; Neugarten, 1976). For one thing, Bart chose her sample from an atypical clinical population. For another, there is evidence that she was dealing with women who were overinvolved with their role. When asked to rate the relative importance of various roles available to them, "helping my children" always topped the list, ahead of "occupational," "organizational," and "being a sexual partner to my husband" (Bart, 1969). When listing major accomplishments, it was their children's, not their own, that they mentioned. Bengston, Kasschau, and Ragan (1977) have pointed out that adjustment to role attrition is heavily influenced by the saliency of the lost role in the total spectrum of an individual's life. If we are conceived of as the sum total of our roles, the loss of a particularly prominent one creates a vacuum. Since nature abhors a vacuum, the newly created "role space" must be filled by newly emergent roles.

That the husbands of these women may still retain old expectations for them introduces the phenomenon of role conflict. It may involve intrarole conflict, in which two aspects of the same role seem to be mutually exclusive, or interrole conflict, in which there are competing demands from two separate roles held by the same individual (Brim, 1966). In the first case, a spouse may expect his wife's commitment to her new job to be minimal, while her own and her employer's expectations may be quite different. In the second, the wife may feel compelled to retain aspects of the traditional role (e.g., passive compliance, nurturance, unquestioning respect), while at the same time taking on a new occupational role that calls for assertiveness, competence, and independence. Lowenthal's (1975) research demonstrated that husbands at this stage did indeed expect continued (and even enhanced) supportiveness, companionship, and nurturance from their wives. If role conflict of either variety is extreme enough, it may lead to the suppression of achievement striving (O'Leary, 1974) or even to somatic illness (Sales, 1969).

One form of role conflict, role overload, is based on external time demands rather than on inherent contradictions in expectations (Frieze, Parsons, Johnson, Ruble, & Zellman, 1978). It is a common predicament for women who try to combine several intense role obligations simultaneously. A woman who anticipates a full-time return to the work world when her children are older may take on part-time employment or return to school for retraining while they are still at home, and thus put herself in this plight. As one harassed mother of four, who returned to get her BA at the same time she was working part-time to subsidize the cost of tuition, said, "I'm suffering from the full-nest syndrome" (personal communication).

For many women, however, the postparental years may be the first time that they have *not* been overwhelmed by role conflict and overload. Abilities and ambitions that have lain dormant now have an opportunity to emerge. Like a pressure cooker filled with high-energy steam, the emptying of the nest allows for the release of that energy.

It has been claimed that it is not role conflict that is the crux of the problem, but rather role ambivalence (Bardwick & Douvan, 1971), that is, the uncertainty as to where one really wants to end up anyway. When a woman has been socialized to be admired for a certain panoply of attributes and behaviors, she may have deep underlying ambivalences about taking on a totally new set. The fear-of-success literature provides ample evidence of this phenomenon. There may be little in her background that has taught her to cope with this new role freedom. As Bardwick and Douvan point out, "role freedom is a burden when choice is available, but criteria are unclear." For many women in midlife today, there are no clear guidelines.

Social Networks

One problem that has dominated the approach to adult development is that it zeroes in on the individual qua individual, but ignores the family unit of which he or she is an integral part. Of all the social networks in which an individual is involved in the course of a lifetime, the family is the most pervasive in its impact.

Some of this impact is due to the forces of "indirect" or "latent" socialization. That is, by merely being exposed to individuals who fill counterroles, we are indirectly socialized to the partial range of that other role (Lipman-Blumen, 1973). Thus, a woman occupying the roles of wife and mother is interacting with a whole range of male behaviors. These counterrole behaviors become incorporated in her repertoire until it is appropriate for them to emerge. It is as if she has been accumulating "idiosyncrasy credits" (Hollander's [1964] model) by conforming to society's normative expectations first. Then, when circumstances warrant it, society allows her to relax these strict sex-role controls and reveal the implicit learning that she has previously been unable to model.

Some effects of family network involvement are more direct. Due to the reciprocal nature of parent-child socialization (Brim, 1968; Ahammer, 1973), children can and do influence their parents. In an era when these offspring are receiving a better and broader education, much filters back into the family to challenge staunchly held values. A mother whose children have become the source of new and vital information and expectations regarding her, as well as themselves, will be more susceptible to change.

Another aspect of the parent-child relationship that cannot be ignored is economic. It is a truism to say that financial considerations are often decisive in a woman's choice to extend her horizons beyond her own home. When the family income falls below what has been called the "pressure line," it may be a necessity for her to supplement the family income (Gove, Grimm, Motz, & Thompson, 1973). The two times in the life course that this is likely to occur are the early stages of the marriage when the family is setting up a household, and again when the children reach adolescence. Increased costs of essentials, college tuition, and so forth, coincide with a time when most women are approaching their middle years and may motivate them to make choices they might otherwise have postponed.

Another contributor to this "family life-cycle squeeze" (Gove et al., 1973) are one's own aging parents. Apart from the profound psychological issues that come into play when parent-child dependency is reversed, parents who are ill and no longer financially secure are an economic burden as well. For the daughters of these aging parents, the burden experienced is not only monetary. Evidence indicates that older people who rely on their children turn primarily to their daughters for help in meeting their daily needs (Shanas, 1968). This new obligation (even if lovingly met) adds to the role strain of a woman who has taken on new commitments in the outside world.

The most fundamental relationship, however, to come under scrutiny during the midlife period is the dyadic social network involving the husband and wife. Much has been written about romance having gone out the window, habitual relationships, and marital boredom. Pineo (1968) has hypothesized that this disenchantment is an inevitable consequence of the passage of time and unforeseen changes in situations. Whenever a long-term commitment is made in the face of incomplete data, especially when satisfaction and "perceived fit" are maximized at the point of acceptance (likely to be the case at the outset of a marriage), there are bound to be regression effects. That is, if marital satisfaction is at a "self-contrived" peak at the time of mate selection, by midlife there will probably be a romantic regression to the mean.

In fact, those empirical studies that have explored the development of marital satisfaction have produced mixed results. Two general trends, however, are worth mentioning. First, there seems to be a gradual decline in marital happiness through the child-rearing years, reaching a trough during the children's adolescence, followed by a marked improvement during the postparental period (Brim, 1968; Deutscher, 1969; Blood & Wolfe, 1960; Rollins & Feldman, 1970; Spence & Lonner, 1971). Second, the changing pattern of marital satisfaction is not identical for males and females. Males derive greater satisfaction from marriage, and this satisfaction does not decrease in time as much as it does for their wives (Veroff & Feld, 1970; Luckey, 1961; Bernard, 1972). This may be partially due to the fact that, in a traditional marriage, more of the compromises and adjustments have been made by the woman (Troll, 1975). Women have been socialized to respond to the needs and expectations of others, rather than their own goals (Angrist & Almquist, 1975). Consequently, when a husband undergoes career-related changes, it is the wife who is more likely to adjust so as to maintain the stability of the relationship. The intimacy issue, raised before in other contexts, appears again from a sociological perspective as an important mediating variable in midlife phenomena.

Anticipatory Socialization

The anticipatory socialization that women receive for their postmaternal lives may or may not be adequate. If it is adequate, it may make them acutely aware of the negative prognosis for a healthy spouse to outlive them. The incidence of death in men, due to stress-related illness, has increased. Women are more likely to be widowed and less likely to remarry; 75% of the men over 65 are married as compared with only 47% of the women (Bengston et al., 1977). In addition, the average age of widowhood in the United States today is 56. It is highly conceivable that knowledge of these statistics could prod a homebound woman to take steps in her middle years to ensure her eventual financial and psychological independence.

In a rapidly changing and sophisticated society, however, anticipatory socialization is not always an adequate preparation for future events. Neugarten (1969) has pointed out the uncertainty and discontinuity of the issues that must be dealt with in the middle years. Previously successful role performances that were the foundation for positive self-conceptions may be less effective in new situations. Especially since age homophyly—the tendency for individuals to seek out members of the same cohort in their social interactions—is common (Neugarten & Hagestad, 1976), there is not much opportunity to communicate meaningfully with those in life stages we have not yet experienced.

It has been suggested that role discontinuity is more likely to be suffered by females than by males (Kline, 1977). Many women are processed educationally for careers and then expected to make marriage and family their chief goals. Lopata (1971) believes that inadequate anticipatory socialization is particularly endemic to the role of housewife. The socialization process is characterized as having a brief, rather compressed, "becoming" stage that peaks early; entrance, modification, and cessation are often a consequence of the activities of others rather than her own. Most of the salient career models on the horizon are successful women who have already made it. There are few transitional role models to serve as a source of encouragement and know-how to those in a state of flux. In the past, social mobility caused socialization discontinuity, since different socioeconomic strata had different sex-role norms (Emmerich, 1973). At present, the areas of mismatch between a woman's early socialization and the expectations upon her in middle adulthood are growing in frequency and intensity, even if she remains in the same stratum. A woman initially socialized to traditional activities and interpersonal behaviors may find them inappropriate in the face of new age-linked sex-role norms. It is as if these women learned to play by one set of rules and then discovered that those rules had been changed before the game was over. Today, a woman whose children are no longer small is expected to achieve in the outside world as well. Current norms of socialization are slowly changing, but because of cultural lag some of them still derive from the old model.

While some of these anticipatory inadequacies would exist even in a fairly stable society, in a society beset by future shock (Toffler, 1970), discontinuities in socialization abound. Societal expectations of what it meant to be the good husband or wife or parent or the successful careerist, or even the good human being, have changed. Time-worn values have become obsolete. The proliferation of the mass media has made available a much wider set of reference figures than most of us ever imagined. Consequently, there are few really clear conceptualizations of successful femininity (or masculinity, for that matter) in the middle years.

Asynchrony

Asynchrony has been repeatedly claimed by Neugarten to be the crucial construct in our response to life's turning points (Neugarten, 1969, 1976b; Neugarten & Datan, 1973). According to this view, it is the timing, rather than the substance of events, that is crucial. It is in the realization that one is on or off schedule for the "normal, expectable life-cycle" (Butler, 1963) that the significance of a particular transition lies. If a potentially traumatic event, such as menopause or empty nest, occurs "according to schedule," it can be anticipated, "rehearsed," and taken in stride (Neugarten, 1978; Lowenthal & Chiriboga, 1972). Conversely, significant life events that occur earlier or later than expected are stressful (Blau, 1961; Lowe, 1964; Rose, 1955).

A woman in midlife, then, who perceives that she is out of phase with other members of her cohort, will be stimulated to instigate change. If she has been primarily domestic, she will experience the malaise of getting left behind in the career socialization process.[4] By embarking on a new career 15 to 20 years after others in her age stratum, she will have difficulties in finding peer support and entering the informal social networks, often necessary for career advancement (White, 1966). In addition, because of the contracting nature of Atchley's (1975) zone of decision, there has been an attrition of openings and opportunities. Although there may be some advantages to off-time entry (Likert, 1967; Nydegger, 1973), by and large the process is a difficult one. That is one reason for the burgeoning number of programs now in existence to guide the re-entry woman (Campbell, 1973; Tittle & Denker, 1977).

Asynchrony, then, has been used primarily to refer to situations in which one is on a different timetable from other members of the cohort. But asynchrony is a multifaceted concept. It includes the discrepancy between one's original dreams and one's actual position in the real world. This is the aspiration-achievement dichotomy so often called forth as a gut issue in the male midlife crisis (Levinson, Darrow, Klein, Levinson, & McKee, 1976; Brim, 1976; Mayer, 1978). The suburban housewife who never made it to Broadway, or who quit law school, is just as likely to be dissatisfied with her lot in life as the middle manager who didn't get to be president of the company. The midlife stirrings that "it is now or never" are just as likely to activate the one as the other.

Another aspect of asynchrony is based on the fact that in any one life, there are numerous career paths. Age-related zones of decision can occur in the areas of occupation, family, voluntary associations, leisure, etc. (Atchley, 1975). These interdependent paths, which often vary in synchronization, can also stimulate action. If a man has made great strides in advancing his career, but has yet to settle down with a family, the discrepancy may remind him that at least in one area he has to catch up. If a woman is assertive and independent in her volunteer assocations, but is dependent economically because she lacks a paying job, she may take steps to eliminate that discrepancy.

---

[4] A similar process may work in reverse for the careerist, who sees that she is on a different timetable from most other women in terms of producing offspring. Of course, in this case strong biological constraints are operating as well.

Finally, asynchrony can exist within the different components of a single role (Lipman-Bluman, 1973). The various subsets of roles differ in their susceptibility to change. Overt and tangible components, such as behavior and privileges, are more vulnerable than intrinsic ones like attitudes and values. As women receive greater equity and opportunity legislatively, their own internal sense of who they are and where they should be will follow suit.

THE STATE OF THE ART

Much of what we have been discussing regarding midlife transitions in women cannot be generalized to all times and all places. If we attempt to find universal, genotypic phenomena, we are ignoring a whole host of profound and specific cohort experiences. Economic depressions, natural catastrophes, wars (which, among other things, produce changes in sex ratio), technological advances, and social and political movements all exert their effect in predictable and indeterminate ways. We need merely consider what it was like for a woman to reach middle age at the turn of the century, or during World War I, or during the great depression, or during the apathetic 1950s, or today, to become acutely aware of this.

For example, there have been demographic changes in life expectancy and the number and spacing of children (Bengsten et al., 1977; Van Dusen & Sheldon, 1976; Neugarten, 1978). Today, women are arriving at the postparental stage earlier than their mothers or grandmothers and can expect to have another 25 to 30 years of functional life after the nest is emptied. In addition, since World War II, there has been a vast expansion in industries that are service oriented rather than goods producers, and this, along with the pervasive impact of the feminist movement, has favored the employment of greater numbers of women (Van Dusen & Sheldon, 1976). It is not surprising, then, to find gradual but steady inroads being made in attitudes toward nontraditional roles for women. Generalizations drawn about midlife transitions, then, will have to remain, for the time being, cohort specific.

Even within the confines of a single cohort, however, any conclusions will have to be limited. Much of the existing literature on midlife women has a shotgun quality and zeroes in on effects and manifestations rather than underlying causes— e.g., evaluations of isolated programs to bring the traditional midlife woman back into the mainstream (Letchworth, 1970; Astin, 1976; Brooks, 1976; Nero, 1975; Klass & Redfern, 1977). With few notable exceptions (Bart, 1969, 1971, 1975; Neugarten, 1968, 1969, 1976, 1978; Lowenthal et al., 1972, 1975, 1976; Livson, 1976), as far as serious major research efforts to date are concerned, the midlife woman has been persona non grata.

The research that follows must be more broadly based, in that the male experience upon which much of the theorization has focused is not transferable in toto to most women's lives. It is fallacious to apply these findings more or less un-selectively to a much wider population (e.g., males and females). Those sex differences in personality that have been found (e.g., a gradual shift in conventionality from adolescence to adulthood, so that by midlife women report being far less conventional than men [Haan & Day, 1974]; or different patterns of intimacy and dependency in the postparental period [Lowenthal & Weiss, 1976], need to be probed more deeply.

Certainly many of the answers will lie within the two major bodies of research and theory reviewed in this chapter. Although neither of these broad theoretical perspectives was originally developed in the context of midlife transitions in women, both of them, when probed, show considerable potential for shedding additional insight on the phenomenon.

We have shown, with regard to adult personality theory, that five constructs teased from the literature are helpful in applying this vast literature to our population: (1) homeostatic balance, (2) goal (task) orientation, (3) commitment, (4) becoming as process, and (5) adaptation. In the case of socialization theory, on the other hand, four theoretical foci were useful in providing a handle: (1) role-related constructs, (2) social networks, (3) inadequate anticipatory socialization, and (4) asynchrony.

Obviously, the phenomenon of midlife transitions has more complexity than can be captured by any one perspective. It is probably not coincidental that those researchers who have been most prolific (e.g., Neugarten and Lowenthal today, and Erikson earlier) are operating very close to the interface of personality development and socialization. What may be needed is a daring effort not only to derive theory from different perspectives within each field, but between them as well.

One approach to the problem of integration might be to zero in on how our nine categories of analysis relate to each other conceptually. Are some embedded in others? Which ones are mutually exclusive? How does the cross-hatching of categories make us aware of the fact that one perspective is either inaccurate or incomplete as we try to understand a particular phenomenon? To what extent are any of the categories logically incompatible with each other?

The promise of such an approach is presented in Figure 2a. Thus we can see that both the developmental and the sociological perspectives require some sort of future-oriented process mechanism (D4 and S3). Role overload (S2) can be translated into too many simultaneous commitments (D3). Goal orientation (D2) implicitly assumes the existence of a larger social context (S2). Perhaps most exciting, Riegel's (1975) dialectic theory of development is supported by both camps.

Using a somewhat different explanatory device (Figure 2b), we can see that all nine constructs are involved in a total explanation of personality change. While they seem to operate at different levels and to serve different functions in the model, they may be flip sides of the same coin. Certainly, recurrent themes arise. From either vantage point, such concepts as self-fulfillment, adaptation, sense of timing, family relationships, intimacy, asynchrony, and the like emerge. This redundancy bodes well for paradigmatic communication.

As the data base expands and theoretical formulations become more elaborate, it may become important to specify the relative contributions of different paradigms. In the interim, open communication within and between the disciplines should be encouraged, in spite of the problems inherent in both multidisciplinary and interdisciplinary approaches. In this way we can hope to avoid the premature closure

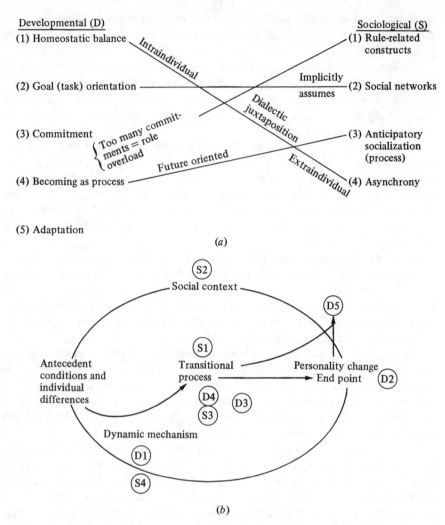

Developmental (D)

(1) Homeostatic balance

(2) Goal (task) orientation

(3) Commitment

(4) Becoming as process

(5) Adaptation

Sociological (S)

(1) Rule-related constructs

(2) Social networks

(3) Anticipatory socialization (process)

(4) Asynchrony

Intraindividual

Implicitly assumes

Dialectic juxtaposition

Too many commit-
ments = role
overload

Future oriented

Extraindividual

(a)

S2
Social context

S1
Transitional process

D5
Personality change
End point   D2

Antecedent conditions and individual differences

D4 D3
S3

Dynamic mechanism

D1

S4

(b)

Figure 2 Initial attempt at integrating concepts from personality (developmental) and socialization theories. (Modified from a schema for personality development, structure, dynamics, and change by Byrne, 1974, with permission.)

that often follows on the heels of the instant popularization of a topic that has suddenly become fashionable. Midlife crises in men have now become the butt of jokes and grist for the best-sellers list. If men make such good copy, can women and their own particular brand of midlife transition be far behind? This should not be allowed to stand in the way of serious programmatic and interdisciplinary research.

17

Applications of a Theory of Personality Functioning and Change to Three Career Identity Changes Faced by the Elderly

Hillary S. Liber

Raynor (see chapter 13) has developed a motivational theory of personality functioning and change that emphasizes the importance of open career paths for the maintenance of a positive self-image and for the accumulation of esteem income. In this chapter I shall outline the elements of the theory that are applicable to gerontology and analyze their implications for three career changes experienced by older Americans: retirement, widowhood, and parent-child role reversal.

Raynor's concept of personality is based on the interaction among self, environment, and action. According to Raynor, people are motivated to gain positive value and to avoid negative value. Different sources of value for an activity include the intrinsic value of the activity, its difficulty value, its instrumental value in offering opportunity for future action, the extrinsic rewards (value) the activity will provide, and one's view of the activity's value in one's culture (cultural value). One can find value in both affect and cognition, in self and environment, and we can analyze sources of value from the individual (internal) and consensual (external) viewpoints.

Raynor emphasizes the individual's internal view, the interaction of the behavioral and self-systems, and affective-information interaction. In other words, one is motivated to act in such a way as to feel good and not to feel bad (affective value), and an important source of good feelings is one's self-image, that is, how one sees oneself (information value). Adults are motivated both to know themselves (their self-identity) and to feel good about their self-image. Esteem income is generated by one's self-image, and people are motivated to maximize positive esteem income

Editor's note: This paper was written within the context and limitations of existing literature and research. While there is little doubt that more and better research is needed and that some "data" are wholly inadequate, the paper tries to relate that literature to the theory of personality functioning and change presented in chapter 13. While it is true that all links to the theory that are discussed here are post hoc at present, the attempt is valuable in providing concrete instances where future research can provide for predictive integration and evaluation of the construct validity of the theory in question.

and minimize negative esteem income. Generally, the clearer one's self-image, the more esteem income (positive or negative) available from it.[1]

Within the self-system, Raynor introduces the concept of time-linked senses of self. Past (having been), present (being), and future (becoming) senses of self depend on where one is in a contingent path of a psychological career. People tend to describe who they are in terms of accomplishments, attributes, and plans. In a traditional society, the past sense of self has greater positive value than in modern industrial society. Technology tends to render the past sense of self obsolete by nullifying its instrumental value. Therefore, one is a "has been" if one emphasizes one's past achievements, and one can often obtain more positive esteem income from present activities and future plans than from past accomplishments (see Footnote 1).

Raynor guesses that three major sources of esteem income are one's occupational, sexual, and family identities. These "psychological careers" combine a self-image and opportunities for action. They involve both the self-system (one's self-image) and the behavioral system (a path in society). A psychological career is the way in which one identifies oneself through action in the real world, and a contingent path is a series of action steps in which the opportunity to attempt future steps depends on success in each preceding step.

Raynor derives that for a long contingent path a first step with moderate difficulty followed by a series of easy tasks is most motivating (positive or negative) to the future-oriented individual than other types of career paths (see chapter 2). Positive motivation also depends on one's perception of one's ability. For example, a very competent person may be motivated in the beginning of a career but will lose interest quickly because difficulty value becomes insignificant—unless the career path remains open. However, many people are unsure of their competence when they begin a career, so positive motivation may increase as they develop confidence until they become moderately challenged, and then motivation due to difficulty value may decline with further increases in perceived ability (see chapter 2 for specific derivations of the effects of confidence as subjective probability of success on motivation). To maintain psychological morale, a positively valent career path must be kept open rather than closed, either by extending it to include new steps, or by developing a new career.

However, extrinsic motivation and psychological distance from the goal counteract the above motivational trends. One will continue to be positively motivated despite a drop in difficulty value if the length of path is great and the extrinsic rewards are large. Also, the time hierarchy works in opposition to the task hierarchy, in that motivation increases as one gets closer in time to the goal (Pearlson, 1979; see chapter 6).

Another crucial element of the theory is the distinction among positively motivated, negatively motivated, and indifferent individuals. In the achievement domain, Raynor and his colleagues use TAT n Achievement to measure motivation to

---

[1] References to a lecture series given by Raynor from September to December, 1978, at State University of New York at Buffalo as part of a graduate course in Theories of Personality are noted by recurring reference to this footnote.

achieve success, and the Mandler-Sarason Test Anxiety Scale to measure (negative) motivation to avoid failure (see chapter 2). Those who score high on the first and low on the second are considered to be positively motivated or success oriented, and those who score low on the first and high on the second are considered to be negatively motivated or failure threatened. Those who score high or low on both tests are indifferent behaviorally, but those who score high on both are phenomenologically conflicted individuals (see Footnote 1). Raynor (1974b) speaks of the compulsive striver as one who is highly success oriented, extrinsically motivated, and future oriented, and suffers from overmotivation (cf. Atkinson, 1974; Raynor, 1974b). The uptight striver is a person who is failure threatened but is future oriented and has strong extrinsic motivation, so that person suffers the consequences of overcoming inhibition—which are worry, dread, and apprehension—to obtain extrinsic rewards.

Atkinson cites the drop in SAT scores (as caused by overmotivation) as evidence that the success-oriented individual is the modal personality in American society today. Raynor has suggested that middle-class child-rearing practices encourage the development of strong achievement motivation and that the majority of Americans are more or less success oriented (see Footnote 1). Therefore, this chapter will emphasize the implications of Raynor's theory for the success-oriented older person, while giving less attention to the other personality types.

IMPLICATIONS FOR THE OCCUPATIONAL CAREER OF THE ELDERLY: RETIREMENT

Raynor defines psychological aging as moving toward the end of a closed contingent career path so that one must increasingly depend on one's past sense of self for positive esteem income. Retirement is usually the end of one's occupational career. Raynor predicts that the failure-threatened person will flourish in retirement, the success-oriented individual will become apathetic and may die relatively soon after retirement (unless another career is begun), and the neutrally motivated person will be unaffected by this event because this individual has always been "retired" (see Footnote 1).

Margolis and Kroes (1974) discuss the example of one man's retirement as a demonstration of how a person can be affected by the termination of a career:

> . . . The following story is about a high-powered successful business executive. This man, let's call him Mr. Winter, single-handedly ran an operation that nobody else in his company fully understood. As Mr. Winter reached his 64th birthday, a bright and talented younger man was assigned as an apprentice to learn the complex set of activities so that he could take over the operation and the old master could benefit from a well-deserved retirement. Mr. Winter objected, claiming that he did not want to retire. But the company had rules. Not long after his forced retirement, a substantial change in Mr. Winter took place. He began to withdraw from people and to lose his zest for life. Less than a year after his retirement, this once lively and productive businessman was hospitalized, diagnosed as suffering from senile psychosis . . . Mr. Winter was a vegetable.
>
> About two years after the apprentice assumed his new position . . . the young man suddenly died . . . A decision was made to approach Mr. Winter to see if he could pull

himself together enough to carry on the job and train somebody to take over . . . The idea of going back to work brought the first sparkle in Mr. Winter's eyes in two years. Within a few days, this "vegetable" was operating at full steam, interacting with people as he had years before. Again, a bright young man was called in to apprentice under the old master. When the young man was trained . . . the company once again retired Mr. Winter. Within six months, he was in the hospital, never to leave (p. 135).

We assume that Mr. Winter was a success-oriented individual, high in achievement motivation, and having a positively valued self-image identifying him in terms of his occupational career as "becoming." When it ended, he failed to develop alternative careers and apparently could not rely on his family or sexual career identities to provide sufficient positive esteem income. With no important career steps in his future, Mr. Winter had no phenomenal goal, no future sense of self to strive to attain. He considered his life to be over—and it was.

Representative Claude Pepper (1977) has used statistics about people like Mr. Winter to argue against mandatory retirement. He cites evidence from the American Medical Association, from a survey of elderly people's doctors by Sandoz Pharmaceuticals, and from National Institute of Health research. As cited by Pepper (1977), Dr. Suzanne Haynes found "greater than expected death rates in the third and fourth year after mandatory retirement," and she attributed these deaths to "the general disenchantment" caused by "inadequate pensions, loss of friends, and loss of an occupation."

However, not all the research data support this position. Bischof (1976) states that, although some adults die shortly after retirement, there is some evidence that those who do were in poor health prior to retirement. Although retirement, adjustment, physical health, and mortality are interrelated, it is difficult to prove causation and/or specify which comes first. Bischof (1976) believes that adjustment to retirement involves more than physical health: it involves self-image, personality, success in achieving life goals, planning ahead, attitudes of one's spouse and other family members, financial status, and whether retirement was voluntary or compulsory. He points out that professional people, particularly academic professionals, adjust well to retirement, and he attributes their success to their ability to remain involved in their careers through research, publication, and lecturing. In terms of Raynor's theory, they are able to keep their career paths open, and although their greatest accomplishments are probably in the past, they still have a series of future career steps that combine to provide positive esteem income.

In the Cornell Study of Occupational Retirement, Streib and Schneider (1971) found that retirement did not have the negative results that role theorists predict. They suggest this is an example of differential disengagement in which one retires in one sphere but not in all areas of life (i.e., one career path ends but other paths still offer future steps to pursue). According to Raynor's theory, this is one possible explanation of successful retirement, but it is not the only one.

The personal meaning of work undoubtedly has an effect on one's adaptation to retirement. That is, if one is success-oriented in one's occupational career, retirement from it can be terminal—not all individuals look forward to the end of work. Morse and Weiss (1962) interviewed 401 working men, asking them if they would continue to work if they no longer had the financial need to do so, and found that 80% of them, and 66% of those 55 to 64 years old, would want to keep working. They gave the following reasons: to keep occupied (32%), to keep healthy (10%), for enjoyment (9%), to avoid going crazy (14%), and to avoid idleness (10%). When asked what they would miss most if they retired, over two-fifths feared loss to their well-being, and one-third mentioned the social aspects of working. According to these data, work may involve more than an occupational identity for most people and may involve several careers, so when people positively motivated for an occupational career retire, they must find ways to create future steps in a number of different career paths to ensure amounts of positive esteem income equivalent to those previously obtained from work.

As shown in Table 1, Shanas, Townsend, Wedderburn, Friis, Mohaj, and Stehower (1968) found that retirees had concerns similar to those of workers about losses in retirement, although in different proportions. Moreover, in real life (as opposed to Morse and Weiss's hypothetical case), retirement poses financial difficulties, especially for middle-class workers who are accustomed to a higher standard of living than the poor but have been unable to save for its continuation as upperclass workers have. Financial burdens cause changes in other career identities and close off a number of potential alternative paths. Also, it is important to note that in the United States only a small minority did not miss work at all.

However, not all retirees are positively motivated with regard to their occupational career. As Atchley (1974) notes, "many people are never highly workoriented and thus they may provide a model for others concerning what it would be like to derive life satisfaction from leisure." These people are either failure threatened or apathetic individuals, or uptight career strivers, and they are expected by Raynor to adjust well to retirement.

There is some evidence that achievement motivation declines in the later years. Results from a national survey (Veroff, Atkinson, Feld, and Gurin, 1960) recently presented by Atkinson (1977) show first an increase and then a decrease in the n Achievement score and in creative contributions as a function of age (see also chapter 2). Davis (cited in Elias, Elias, and Elias, 1977) found that success caused older men (ages 66 to 85) to drop their aspiration level, and Streib (1976) discovered that retirees place less emphasis on their children's upward mobility than do employed persons. Atchley (1971b) sent retired teachers and phone-company

Table 1   Major Item Missed in Retirement, Men Aged 65 and Over

Item	Denmark	Britain	United States
Nothing	48%	56%	9%
People at work	8	10	16
Feeling useful	5	5	8
Things happening around one	5	–	3
Work itself	18	4	18
Money	14	24	45
Other	1	–	1

employees a work-commitment questionnaire and found that although a small minority are work oriented even in retirement, most retirees exhibit a low degree of work orientation. Still, one must question if the decline in achievement motivation is a function of aging per se, or a method of adjustment to retirement. This would be difficult to ascertain, as many success-oriented older people would avoid retirement, and those low in work orientation would dominate in the sample.

Another factor influencing adjustment to retirement is future orientation. Kastenbaum and Durkee (1964), using the Important Years Question, found that the percentage of people naming at least one important year in the future declines after 40, until none is mentioned after age 54. Kastenbaum believes that failure to anticipate one's later years causes one to ram into old age with shock. Its implications are even greater, according to Raynor. When one abandons "becoming," one eventually loses value from "being" due to obsolescence of skills, and depends totally on "having been," something not highly valued in technological societies and therefore producing little positive esteem income. Spence (as cited by Elias et al., 1977) has also demonstrated a decline in future orientation and an increase in disengagement after age 75, and suggests that the model of successful aging is the composed planner, one who is satisfied with one's lifestyle yet continues to make future commitments and plans. Thus, although decline in future orientation may be adaptive for some people, those who are most successful in aging are future oriented.

Clearly, success-oriented retirees require a psychological career in which they can continue "becoming." One way to do this is to emphasize one's other career identities. Individuals who have spent much of their life striving in their occupational careers now have time to devote to their family careers and to their relationships with their spouses. Both Atchley (1971a) and Streib (1976) stress that few people base their identity on a single role, so that for most individuals, retirement causes a modification of a continuing identity, rather than an identity crisis.

Another way to continue becoming is to work part-time or to work in other branches of one's occupation. Thus, a research scientist or academician might continue to publish or help edit others' work, and those retiring from public life could give public lectures or write their memoirs.

Other individuals begin alternative careers upon their retirement. Some are occupation oriented: for example, retired businesspeople and professionals become academicians, teaching courses in their field at local colleges and universities, or open small businesses that reflect prior avocational interests. Other alternative careers involve leisure activities without financial remuneration.

Many social scientists question if esteem income can be provided by leisure pursuits. Rosow (1969) estimates by extrapolation from his biased sample that loss of status is three times as great for elderly people who take total retirement than it is for older persons who are able to continue working at least part-time, and he predicts the gap will widen in the future. He explains that status depends more on income and occupation than on the amount of leisure time one has, that approved leisure in our society is voluntary and a reward for one's current productivity, and that old people's leisure therefore confers no status.

Rosow's argument is largely based on Miller's (1968) identity-crisis theory. He hypothesizes that retirement indicates failure in one's occupation and implies inability to perform in other areas, that leisure roles are not legitimate in our society, and that the only kinds of leisure which provide identity and esteem income are work substitutes that create something or earn money. He suggests that hobbies that earn money, volunteer work, and, to a lesser extent, further education can be rationalized, and that it is important to use existing valued roles in society rather than create new ones for old people, or these new roles will quickly lose their value.

However, Peppers (1976), in his analysis of types of leisure among retirees, found that Life Satisfacton Index A scores were higher for retirees who increased the number of leisure activities than for those whose activity levels remained constant or declined after retirement. He also found that social and/or physical leisure, as opposed to isolated and/or sedentary activities, had a positive effect on life satisfaction. Thus, Peppers showed that, for some people at least, a leisure career can be an alternative source of esteem income. His data also show that people maintain identity continuity by pursuing the same kinds of leisure as retirees as they did prior to retirement.

Maddox (1968) also discusses the importance of developing a network of satisfying relationships and activities before retirement, a network that can carry over into the later years. He believes all people, not just the elderly, need education to develop social and personal resources appropriate to the leisure role, because work has become meaningless for many people and occupational careers are increasingly disorderly, and because leisure is coming to denote status.

Atchley (1971) offers a third argument disputing identity-crisis theory, and he calls his position *identity continuity*. The Scripps Foundation Studies in Retirement, which he conducted with Cottrell, demonstrated that work-oriented people could adapt well to careers of leisure activity. He believes that individuals will continue to see themselves as whatever their occupational identity was before retirement, and that other nonoccupational roles help bridge the transition period. Furthermore, he found that one can find esteem income in leisure pursuits if one has enough money, if one's peers accept one's leisure, and if one can see usefulness in the activity. Thus, for some people, leisure can be an esteem-producing alternative career.

Raynor emphasizes the importance of individual differences in personality and the internal view, as well as situational factors, in predicting behavior. This emphasis is quite clear in the patterns of adjustment to retirement identified by Reichard, Livson, and Peterson (1968). Although their sample was small and limited, and their list of patterns does not cover all possible outcomes, their outline indicates several examples of the interaction between person and environment. They found three successful patterns of adjustment and two unsuccessful ones. The "mature men" moved into old age easily and had satisfactory relationships and activities. We presume that these were the success-oriented individuals who continued part-time in their occupational careers or found alternative ones. The "rocking-chair men" welcomed passivity. We presume that they were failure-threatened people, possibly uptight strivers, who appreciated the decline in demands upon them. The "armored men" warded off their dread of physical decline by keeping active. We presume that they were the successful compulsive strivers. In contrast to these adjusted groups, the two poorly adjusted patterns showed failure to achieve their goals, but the "angry men" blamed others, and the "self-haters" blamed themselves. The angry men may have been apathetic, conflicted, or failure-threatened men who were external in locus of control, while the self-haters were more likely to have been internally controlled compulsive strivers or success-oriented individuals who did not succeed. (See chapter 13 for a discussion within the context of Raynor's theory of the development of self-hate and defenses against it that may follow.)

From the above discussion it is clear that there are numerous ways of coping with retirement. For failure-threatened individuals, retirement is a relief. Success-oriented individuals emphasize other career identities, develop future steps in their current occupational path, or choose new careers to substitute for the terminated career. Apathetic individuals continue as they had been doing before retirement, and there is some evidence that becoming apathetic by losing one's orientation to success and/or to the future is one mode of adaptation to retirement. People who have not succeeded in past careers have the most difficult adjustment because they can derive little positive esteem income from having been and are unlikely to derive any from becoming. These varying patterns of adjustment demonstrate that both "activity" and "disengagement" theories, and both "identity continuity" and "identity crisis" theories, can be applicable. According to Raynor, adjustment to retirement depends on one's personality, one's perceived opportunities for action, and one's perception of self-images that are related to action outcomes in this environment. Each of these other theories appears limited in dealing with only one aspect of the person-situation-self interaction.

IMPLICATIONS FOR THE FAMILY AND
SEXUAL CAREERS OF THE ELDERLY: WIDOWHOOD

Just as retirement signals a major change in one's occupational career, widowhood represents a crisis in one's family and sexual careers. For many women who never had a worker role, for those of both sexes who no longer have an occupational career because they have retired, and for elderly people whose family career is restricted to the marital relationship owing to separation from children and other relatives, the marital role has central importance in their self-identity, and its termination through widowhood will result in multiple losses of esteem income. Furthermore, in contrast to retirement, which is usually expected at a certain age or may not happen at all, few people anticipate and plan for widowhood as they might for retirement. In fact, Caine (1974) offers herself as an example of those who fail to take advantage of the forewarning of imminent widowhood during a spouse's terminal illness, who refuse to face the reality that widowhood is inevitable, and who avoid planning for the day when they will be alone.

The first body of research bearing on widowhood as a career crisis is the bereavement literature. Lindemann (1944) is often cited as the pioneer in the study of bereavement. In his 1944 study of those bereaved by the Cocoanut Grove fire in Boston, he found that the symptomatology of acute grief includes somatic distress, preoccupation with the image of the deceased, guilt, hostile reactions, loss of patterns of conduct, and the appearance of traits of the deceased in the bereaved's behavior. Whereas in normal grief, grief work can be resolved within 6 weeks, morbid grief involves either a delayed reaction that surfaces up to years later or distorted reactions including overactivity, identification, medical disease, altered social relationships, furious hostility, schizophrenic behavior, lasting loss of patterns of conduct, self-punitive detrimental behavior, and agitated depression.

Marris (1958) conducted unstructured interviews with 72 London working-class widows in the mid-1950s. He concluded that emotional reactions to bereavement (expressions of grief and adherence to mourning customs), social relationships (where help is obtained, family ties, and attitudes toward remarriage), and practical problems (reduced income and inadequate social insurance benefits) interact to determine the outcome of the crisis. He found that mourning takes 2 years or more, and that widowhood impoverishes one's social life. Although independence is the best adjustment, it implies a loss of status and esteem income owing to reduced financial income and increased loneliness.

Criticizing Lindemann (1944) for biasing his sample with psychoneurotics, and Marris (1958) for using a retrospective approach, Clayton, Desmaris, and Winokur (1968) interviewed relatives of deceased hospital patients to compile a profile of normal bereavement. They found that only depressed mood, sleep disturbance, and crying were symptomatic of over half their sample, although difficulty concentrating, loss of interest in TV and news, and anorexia were frequent in less than half the group. They also indicate that only 4% were worse at their 2- to 4-month follow-up, compared to 81% who were better, although this is only a measure of improvement and not adjustment.

Parkes (1972) conducted four studies of typical as well as abnormal grief in widowhood. He found that the normal response includes realization of loss(es), alarm reaction, searching for the lost object(s), anger, guilt, loss of self, and gaining a new identity, while atypical grief involves either prolonged grief or a delayed reaction of the sort mentioned by Lindemann. However, unlike Lindemann (1944) and Clayton et al. (1968), Parkes (1972) found that grief work takes longer than a few weeks or months, and in fact grief generally lasts beyond the first year.

Lopata (1973) has done extensive research on the postbereavement problems of American widowhood. She found that most widows live alone, and they prefer to do so, enjoying their independence and freedom, although they list loneliness as their greatest problem. They experience loneliness for the person, for the love object, for the receipt of love, for companionship, for another's presence, for sharing of the work load, for previous life style, and for previous higher status (Lopata, 1970). Thus, widowhood involves losses of esteem income from many different sources in the past, present, and future, and therefore it constitutes a crisis as defined by Raynor (see Footnote 1). Furthermore, loneliness is compounded by changes in other social relationships because the widow had been occupied with her husband during his illness, because friends don't want to be involved in grief work and mourning owing to their own fear of death, because social relationships may have depended on friends' ties to the spouse, and because Americans socialize in couples so the widow is a "fifth wheel." Widows also may be getting negative esteem income from other roles, such as being female in a male-dominated society, being old in a youth-oriented culture, and being poor or a member of a minority group (Lopata, 1971). Widowhood itself is a very vague role in America, so identity reconstruction is quite difficult, and many widows face great obstacles in finding new ways to gain positive esteem income.

Kastenbaum (1969) predicts that bereavement in later life is even more difficult than for the young. The older person is likely to have already experienced multiple losses and may be apprehensive about imminent losses of ailing friends and relatives. Because of one death following another in quick succession, the older person may never be able to complete the grief work for each loss. Moreover, the elderly experience many other losses, including the retirement losses discussed above, changes in environment, and losses of physical health and personal abilities. Kastenbaum (1969) speaks of a "bereavement overload" that can cause physical deterioration, suicidal attempts, neglecting one's own care, and increased irritability and bitterness. This type of process would seem to follow from Raynor's theory of career termination, in that the future-oriented individual sees no reason to live when cut off from any positive esteem income in the future, while facing much potential negative income (see chapter 13 for further discussion of negative self-esteem and self-destructive behavior).

However, Heyman and Giantruco (1973) hypothesized that old people respond to a spouse's death with emotional stability, support from a stable social network of family and friends, and few life changes. In a pilot study, they found that the elderly bereaved had little or no health deterioration, only a small decline in work, usefulness, and total attitude scores, and support from continued home occupancy, personal networks, and religious faith. The researchers believe that the elderly are prepared for bereavement and have come to accept a placid disengaged social role. This study, of course, is only a beginning, and more comprehensive research should be done comparing matched old and young widows and widowers.

Many researchers have tried to identify factors that determine the outcome of conjugal bereavement. Parkes (1972) speaks of antecedent, concurrent, and subsequent determinants of abnormal grief (i.e., those linked to past, present, and future senses of self). Unfortunately, research data on the directions of these various correlations is often conflicting. Parkes's (1973) antecedent factors include previous losses, mental illnesses, and life crises, poor or ambivalent relationship with the spouse, and sudden death of spouse. Carey (1977) found that happiness in marriage was not significantly related to adjustment to widowhood in his sample, but did concur with Parkes that ability to engage in anticipatory grief did aid adjustment, especially for females, and especially for those who had had unhappy marriages. However, Gerber, Hannon, Battin, and Arkin (1975) found that elderly people whose spouses died from chronic illnesses, especially lengthy illnesses lasting more than 6 months, had more medical problems after their spouse's death than did those whose spouses died of acute illness. This effect was greater for males than for females. Maddison (1968) also found that overt neurosis, pathological marital relationship, disturbed relationship with one's mother, and a protracted dying period all were correlated with poor outcome. All these antecedent factors involve the amount of past successes from which one can derive esteem income during the bereavement.

Parkes's (1972) concurrent determinants are sex, age, socioeconomic status, nationality, religion, cultural expressions of grief, and ability to express feelings. Carey (1977) found that, along with forewarning of death, sex was the greatest predictor of outcome, with widowers better adjusted than widows. More education, higher income, and greater age also correlated positively with adjustment. Atchley (1975) used data from his retirement studies discussed above to design a model of the impact of widowhood. In his model, widowhood, sex, and social class interact to define income adequacy, which in turn affects car driving and social participation, which ultimately determines amount of loneliness and anxiety. Maddison (1968) also found young age and suppression of affect negatively correlated with adjustment. These concurrent factors involve the competences available in one's present sense of self to be utilized in surviving the crisis and in developing a new self-identity.

Subsequent factors in adjustment, according to Parkes (1972), include the degree of social support or isolation, the other stresses in the widow's life, and the options available to her. Maddison (1968) agrees with Parkes that pathological reaction in another family member, multiple crises, and problems with the husband's family were determinants of bad outcome in his sample. Furthermore, bad-outcome widows perceived the environment to be lacking the types of support they needed (active encouragement to express affect and to discuss the past), whereas good-outcome subjects preferred permissive support and were satisfied with their environments. Also, Arling (1976) found that, among elderly widows, availability of neighbors and friends significantly contributed to morale, much more than availability of contact with family members. These subsequent factors involve alternative sources of esteem income one can rely upon to substitute for the losses caused by widowhood.

The final area of bereavement literature bearing on this topic is that which examines methods of coping with the crisis and adjusting to widowhood. Caine (1974, 1978), who has popularized the topic of widowhood by recounting her personal experiences, stresses the importance of preparedness. She urges women to learn about grief and widowhood before it happens, because statistically it most likely will; to prepare for their role as "head of household" by having regular "contingency days" with their spouses to discuss financial matters, and to prepare for life alone by having an identity independent from that as "Mr. X's wife." Thus, it is important for one to be sure that there are options available. Caine also advises the widowed to be honest and open in expressing their feelings. She suggests talking with family and friends, especially children, writing down thoughts one has difficulty discussing, seeing a professional counselor experienced in bereavement counseling if necessary, trusting other women and relying on them for emotional support, and finding the cure for loneliness by discovering one's inner "hidden self." This corresponds with Raynor's concept of "need to know" (information value in the self-system). Even if it will result in negative *affective* esteem income, one needs to understand what one has been and what one is (information value), before deciding what one will become.

One way to learn about oneself and one's role as widow is through widow-to-widow interaction, either through self-help groups such as the 3-month crisis intervention "classes" run by nurses Miles and Hays (1975) or through one-to-one mutual help as in Silverman's (1975) Widow-to-Widow program. Those who advocate this type of assistance for the bereaved emphasize that widowhood is a "normal" life problem, not a deviant pathology, that it does not necessarily require professional intervention, and that experienced widows can help each other by providing models for the newly bereaved, as well as by offering concrete suggestions for identity reconstruction. This is in accord with Raynor's treatment of widowhood as just another of many changes in psychological careers within one's lifetime (see Footnote 1).

Numerous bereavement counselors and advisors urge the recently bereaved to wait, sit tight, and make as few changes as possible following their spouse's death. Caine (1978), for example, explains the rationale using a stress model. She says that each change in one's life involves a specified number of stress points, and if one's total stress score is too high to tolerate, mental illness will result. Widowhood itself causes a number of inevitable changes and stresses, so the newly bereaved should not voluntarily make additional changes. The advice against unnecessary change is considered in Raynor's theory, but is explained by the need to maintain the positive value of one's past and present senses of self to as great an extent as possible in the face of a major career identity crisis due to an uncertain future sense of self.

The most important set of solutions to this crisis involve future orientation. Caine reminds widows to have regular personal contingency days, during which they examine their options and plan for their future. (She also urges them to take stock of their achievements, thus building upon the esteem income from a positive past sense of self.) Steps in future planning move from keeping busy to emphasizing other available roles (careers) to developing new ones.

Champagne (1964), in her handbook for living without a husband, lists the following avenues for keeping busy: social activities, work, children, clubs, politics, travel, church, and hobbies. Kutscher (1969) suggests reading, music, art, theater, movies, radio, TV, sports, travel, crafts, and hobbies, and he stresses the importance of moving from spectator to participant as one leaves grief behind and regains pleasure in living. Caine (1974, 1978) urges widows to consider whatever organizational help is available where they live; to improve their appearance through exercise, a new hairdo and new clothes, yoga and meditation, and good nutrition; to find ways to get out of the house, away from the family and its demands; to avoid being lured by television because it encourages escapism; and especially to plan to keep busy on holidays, weekends, and vacations, as these are vulnerable times. Thus, a first step in recovering from the abrupt termination of a career is to involve oneself in a variety of activities to avail oneself of opportunities to find alternative careers.

Another way to become involved is through previously neglected roles. Old friends, ignored children, and hobbies and clubs one never had time for before are all avenues to recovery. When one's life revolves around the career of spouse, one tends to neglect, ignore, or do without certain roles or activities that do not involve or interest the spouse. These roles become opportunities for career development when the spouse is no longer there. Also, some widows turn to the role of parent or grandparent and devote to that career energy that had previously been used in the marital career.

The third avenue of involvement is the development of new careers, especially occupational ones. For some widows, this is not a matter of choice but of necessity, but Caine suggests that all unemployed widows should find a job, even an unpaid one, to form an identity separate from that of spouse or widow. However, Lopata (1970) indicates that the ability to develop new relations in widowhood is restricted to the middle and upper classes.

All suggestions made thus far deal with widowhood as a multifaceted career crisis. However, Raynor emphasizes marriage also as a sexual career, as do Peterson and Payne (1975). As Peterson and Payne point out, every person needs intimate relationships, but single adults over 55 have few opportunities for such relations, because of the radical disproportion between men and women in that age bracket, because American society is couple- and marriage-oriented, and because popular opinion does not accept the findings of the Kinsey studies on the sexual interest and activity of the elderly. Even if remarriage is an option for older widows and widowers, elderly couples are better off financially if they remain single, because those who marry can expect to lose $70 to $200 in social security and supplemental income payments.

Peterson and Payne (1975) suggest that the single elder consider sociologist Bernard's (1972) five alternatives to marriage as applied to senior adults. The swinging model refers to unrelated seniors on fixed incomes living independently but within the subculture of the retired. The cocktail-lounge model is a semiserious, semistable, enduring relationship and often involves a male (or female) whose spouse is seriously incapacitated but who doesn't wish to terminate the marriage. The campus model involves living together either before or instead of marriage. It is on the increase among senior citizens, possibly because of social security and pension laws. The hippie model, or polygamy, gives women the chance to remarry, offers a meaningful family group, and enhances health by improving diet, providing home health care, arranging for housework, reducing depression, and solving sexual problems. The one-sex community model includes those interested in nonsexual companionship as well as those who seek homosexual experiences. Finally, Peterson and Payne (1975) point out that nursing-home residents also need privacy and opportunities for intimate sexual behavior.

Sexual interest typically disappears in early bereavement but generally returns, according to Caine. She tells widows not to feel guilty about feeling sexually aroused and for wanting to masturbate and engage in intercourse, but she cautions them about becoming involved in relationships they are not yet ready to handle, about being lured by men taking advantage of their vulnerability, and about jumping into remarriage as an escape from having to honestly reconstruct their lives. Although society allows the industrious widow to compensate for many of the career changes caused by widowhood, it permits few, if any, alternatives to ending one's sexual career, an option that is hardly desirable. Sexual interest continues in old age, and the possibility of future sexual activity is necessary for a person to derive positive esteem income from this second of the three major career identities.

IMPLICATIONS FOR THE FAMILY CAREER
OF THE ELDERLY: PARENT–CHILD ROLE REVERSAL

The career changes dealt with thus far have been multifaceted, with ramifications for more than one career. However, as has been shown, the endpoints they signal are reversible, and the resourceful senior adult can continue "becoming" after resolving the crisis or crises at hand. In contrast, the parent-child role reversal of the later years is usually a permanent termination of a lengthy career, and there can be no future steps in the career path. Therefore, adaptation to this change depends almost entirely on one's past sense of self.

It is important to note that, while dependence is not a problem faced by the majority of the elderly at any given time, it is one that all older persons will probably face unless they die before deteriorating physically and/or mentally to that level. For many years, the parent is the strong and independent protector of the weak, dependent child, but over time first the child becomes independent and then the parent loses strength, until finally the two have permanently exchanged roles. According to Silverstone and Hyman (1976), although some parents gladly abdicate the leadership position to their capable and willing child(ren), others refuse to relinquish their nominal power, while still others find their children incapable or unwilling to take the role, or at least resentful of having to do so. Although most older Americans prefer that the government, rather than their children, provide for their food, shelter, medical care, and income, a public orientation toward youth means that our communities provide for our elders in a meager, piecemeal fashion. And even though most elderly parents prefer not to impose upon their children, few of them plan for the day when they cannot care for themselves, so eventually they do come to depend on their children, often when their children have their own family demands and financial problems, or are far away geographically and/or emotionally (Silverstone and Hyman, 1976).

Recently, the issue of parent-child role reversal has been popularized by trade books on the subject (cf. Silverstone, Hyman, Otten, and Shaller, 1976). However, most publications on the topic deal with the problem from the perspective of the child rather than from the view of the aging person. Although the children of aging parents face great difficulties, and although Silverstone and Hyman (1976) devote many pages of their book to consideration of the older person's feelings (preparation that is similar to preretirement programs), effort must also be devoted to preparation of the elderly for loss of independence. This is especially important for families in which the older generation was a unifying force and that may fall apart as the parent becomes unable to fulfill the bridging role. Families may emerge from the crisis of dependency strengthened by the resolution process, or they may dissolve in civil war (cf. Silverstone and Hyman, 1976). For this crisis in aging, much more than for the two previously discussed, it is critical to have family involvement in decision making, with honesty and openness about facts and feelings.

Smith (1965) has reviewed the literature on the relationship between the aged and their adult children. He maintains that, despite the sacrosanct independence of the conjugal family, married children are obliged to continue close relationships with their parents. Social pressures induce adult children to provide needed services for their elderly parents, including physical care, shelter, housework, and sharing of leisure time. The child's sense of duty and attitudes toward financial aid vary with sex (higher for daughters), birth order (higher for first-born), childhood experiences (and resultant adult relationships with parents and siblings), and socioeconomic status. However, the older person values care and affectional support by children more highly than material or financial assistance.

Smith (1965) also reports that the emotional adjustment of both parties depends on the consistency between performance in, and expectations for, the relationship. In smaller communities, norms for interaction are more clear-cut and better understood, thus aiding adjustment. Also, the parent-child interaction is more satisfying when the residence of the older person is a matter of choice rather than necessity. Smith (1965) points out that, as the aged become more dependent, this reversal of parent-child roles causes role conflicts and personal problems for both parent and child. Smith's findings indicate the importance of planning for dependence before it happens, so that what results is a matter of choice and is well understood and accepted by all involved parties. As Silverstone and Hyman (1976) suggest, the second major responsibility for children of aging parents who can manage for themselves (after encouraging and emotionally supporting their chosen lifestyle) is helping them plan for the time when they cannot manage.

Thus, the major solution to this career change appears to be foresight—for two reasons. First, if older persons have not planned for what will happen to them (i.e., planned to remain in their own homes with community support services, move in with a certain child, move to a congregant living situation with other seniors, or select a specific nursing home), others will make the decision for them once they become dependent, and they may not like the choice. Second, once a career is terminated (in this case, the career of parent), the only way it provides esteem income is through one's past sense of self, and one can only obtain positive feelings about a career if one has been successful in it. Therefore, it is important to satisfy one's expectations of oneself as a parent, and to resolve problems arising in the parent-child relationship(s) as the career evolves, before the career terminates in one's dependency on one's child or children.

Furthermore, once the career terminates, the older person must be willing to cooperate with his or her children, helping them to assume their new roles successfully. Silverstone and Hyman (1976) refer to "the games old people play"—manipulation of their children, denial of infirmities, exaggeration of infirmities, self-belittlement, and bribing with inheritance promises. These games may be solutions to the immediate problem, but in the long run all they do is postpone the admission of and adjustment to the end of the parenting career. There are better ways to adjust. For example, when moving to a nursing home or any higher level of care than one has been accustomed to, it helps for the elderly persons to arrange the details of the move themselves, to take along some of their possessions and to arrange for the disposal or distribution of the remainder, to be patient and give themselves time to adjust to the new surroundings, to stay informed of and involved in family and community happenings while still living their own life in the new home, and to agree to further changes that are in their best interest. There is, therefore, a give and take in this role reversal. The elderly parent should be encouraged to maintain his or her personality and identity but should remain flexible, allowing new relationships and roles to evolve, and not expecting others (i.e., family or staff) to relinquish their identities either.

SOME CONCLUDING REMARKS

Silverstone and Hyman (1976) define the aging process as a series of losses. There is a decline in physical health: losses in appearance, sensation, mobility, and ability to heal and recover. There is a loss of social contacts, through illness and death of friends and relatives and through changes in neighborhood and community environments. There is the the loss of the familiar roles of parent, breadwinner, spouse, householder, and homemaker. There is usually a loss of financial security, which affects one's ability to deal with other losses. And all these losses contribute to a loss of independence and power, losses that are perhaps the greatest blow to self-esteem. Finally, there may be loss of mental stability, due either to a pathological disturbance or as a "normal" adaptive reaction to the other losses.

This chapter has dealt with three common losses of aging—loss of occupation, loss of spouse, and loss of parenting role, but any of the other losses mentioned above may constitute a career crisis. It depends on whether or not the contingent path can be reopened, whether the person is positively, negatively, or neutrally motivated for the outcome of the career, whether or not the person can find value in past successes, and what competences are available in the present sense of self to cope with the loss (see Footnote 1). As Bischof (1976) summarizes, successful adjustment to aging involves a past history of successes (past sense of self), having an active life-style, having money, and being useful and needed (present sense of self) and composed planning, the making of future commitments, and the maintenance of flexibility (future sense of self).

In most career crises the problem is a change in the present or future sense of self, so one must depend on esteem income from the past sense of self while building a new future career path and sense of self. Eventually, as one ages, one reaches the point where there can be no future sense of self, or at least not in a particular career identity. Then one must depend totally on past successes in that career. Therefore, Raynor discusses the importance of "banking esteem income," that is, saving mementos, scrapbooks, trophies, and the like, so that one has a "treasury" of positive feelings stored up from the past for the times when one is not earning any in the present. Also, most people tend to enhance their past by remembering successes and suppressing failures (Raynor calls this cognitive enhancement), even if it requires "reorganization of the cognitive field," a form of rationalization that is not influenced by unconscious factors but rather is analogous to a cognitive strategy (see Footnote 1).

Although esteem income is available from what one "has been," I believe that it should only be used as a last resort, because greater positive value can be obtained from present and future senses of self. Except for uptight and compulsive career strivers, the prescription for old age, in my opinion, is to recommit oneself to "becoming." Various alternatives have been discussed, including paid work for those with financial problems, volunteer work for those without financial difficulties, gradual or flexible retirement, the role of citizen, club membership, friendship relations, religious activity, active leisure pursuits, the student role, and family relationships. Resourceful senior adults plan new careers in which they continue becoming and from which they derive positive esteem income. However, as Clague (1971) point out, inadequacy of social security and pension benefits hampers the resourcefulness of even the most imaginative golden ager. Therefore, seniors' groups must advocate not only for preretirement training programs and postretirement career opportunities, but also for adequate economic assistance to enable them to utilize the esteem-producing options listed throughout this chapter.

In Raynor's theory of motivation and career striving, the losses of aging represent final steps in closed contingent paths, so as one path closes, the older person must turn to other career paths for positive esteem income. Eventually, one runs out of alternative careers and must come to grips with one's own finitude. Munnicks (1966) hypothesizes that, once the aging individual reaches a final point of view, he or she begins to disengage in preparation for death.

One of the great debates of gerontology concerns the applicability of activity theory versus disengagement theory. From Raynor, we learn that this depends on individual differences as well as situational factors. As long as the success-oriented person has possible future career steps, activity theory applies. But for the failure-threatened, the conflicted individual, or the success-oriented person whose past failures are so great that they prevent becoming, disengagement is the proper adaptation to aging. Just as there are different ways to grow up, there are different ways of growing old, and the mode of aging chosen by an individual will depend on the interaction between one's personality, one's environment, and one's perception of self-identity that is tied to the outcomes of action in that environment.

18

Changes in Motivation in the Elderly Person

Robin J. Ridley

The changes that distinguish the elderly person are both physical and mental. Most research has indicated that these changes are usually in the form of a decline or a deterioration of some kind. But, as the research on sexual functioning has pointed out (Verwoent, Pfeiffer, & Wang, 1969), this decline may be occasioned more by social pressures than physical circumstances. The older person is expected to decline, to move away from life, to retire. A study of motivation may reveal those factors that pressure the elderly to change, since most psychogenic changes involve fluctuations in motivation.

But how does the elderly person fit into the complex concept of motivation elaborated by Atkinson (1958), Atkinson and Feather (1966), and Atkinson and Raynor (1974)? Most researchers find that the elderly subject poses special problems for research in motivation. Unlike persons at the beginning or middle of their lives, the elderly find that many career roles are closed to them, and their time orientation is often limited to the past or present.

How does the theory of achievement motivation explain the motivation and behavior of the elderly person? The most recent reformulation of the theory (chapter 13) assumes that adult motivation is related to four factors: psychological career, time orientation, sources of value, and motivational tendency. A person's motivational tendency is determined in part by the positive and negative motives for the particular activity in question. A person can range from positively motivated through neutral to negatively motivated. A positively motivated person is enthusiastic in striving to attain positive value, while a negatively motivated individual suffers great anxiety in overcoming inhibition aroused to avoid incurring negative value.

The psychological career refers to a person's self-image and the opportunities for action available to that person. Psychological careers fall into three basic types: occupation (or what is generally regarded as a career), sexual (being able to enact the characteristics of one's sex), and family (playing out one's part in the family structure), although any substantive career is possible.

Time orientation refers to time-linked sources of value in a career. These range from future orientation (value from working toward a future goal) through present (value from evaluating one's attributes) to past (value from past success or failure).

Finally, value refers to the positive or negative outcomes that result from success or failure in a career. There are five sources of value: *extrinsic* value (including material rewards), *intrinsic* value (determined by the task itself), *cultural* value (meeting a culturally defined standard), *instrumental* value (earning an opportunity for future action), and *difficulty* value (succeeding against low odds of success).

PSYCHOLOGICAL CAREERS

Not everyone is involved with pursuing all three types of psychological careers. Many persons in their twenties are concerned with establishing a profession and starting families (Baltes & Goulet, 1971; Baltes & Schaie, 1970). In midlife, individuals may choose to sit back and consolidate the success they have gained in their profession, or they may change professions altogether. Interest in family and sexual careers may also go through changes (Block, 1971; Erikson, 1959; Sheehy, 1974; Williams & Wirths, 1965). The elderly person is severely restricted. Until very recently, mandatory retirement was the rule. But many persons, whether from desire or social pressure, still retire from an occupation without replacing it with an alternative occupation. The picture of the retired person leaving work behind and receding from life is an accepted one (Cumming & Henry, 1961; Harris, 1975).

In the nuclear family, children have often moved away, and the elderly person is usually cut off from family (Brody, 1966; Johnson, 1978; Miller & Swanson, 1958; Townsend, 1957; Troll, 1971). In addition, spouses and relatives of the same generation may have died, making family roles vague and sometimes unsatisfying (Johnson & Bursk, 1977; Lopata, 1973; Sussman, 1976).

Many men believe that virility will fail. Many women fear that menopause marks the end of their sexual life. In connection with the fear that sexuality *will* end (Atchley, 1975; Block, 1973; Hartley, 1964) is the belief that it *should* end.

How does the elderly person adjust to these changes? Research appears to indicate that the life of leisure will satisfy the elderly person only as a temporary measure. Soon the elderly person is unable or unwilling to return to his or her former career, and yet cannot find a new fulfilling career to substitute. In this dilemma, the elderly person will begin to retreat from life, and will experience boredom and a sense of worthlessness and despair. It is at this point that an elderly person will remain in bed all day, waiting to die (Baltes & Zerbe, 1976; Butler, 1968; Dohrenwend & Dohrenwend, 1974; Gubrium, 1970; Holsti, 1971; Maddox, 1963; Spence, Cohen, & Kowalski, 1975).

For good adaptation to later life, elderly persons must either maintain their old careers or change them. Maintenance of a career occurs when one is devoted to upholding the value of a past career and the identity that the career gave one. For example, consider a former nurse.[1] Although he is no longer able to do his job, and

---

[1] The case studies presented in this paper are based on client work I conducted while working at a senior citizens' center. Over a period of about 6 months, I visited 10 clients in the capacity of a "friendly visitor." In this job I visited the client's home once a week for an hour; some three or four times and others about fifteen times. These examples are attempts to explain behavior as I saw it in terms of Raynor's theory of personality functioning and change (see chapter 13). The interpretations are subjective and have not been verified by others. The purpose of this chapter is to present anecdotal examples of the theory to show how it might be applied to real-life situations. I have disguised the clients' identities to maintain their privacy.

loopholes unknown to many workers within the social welfare system. But others may be indifferent. It is even possible that high extrinsic value in the past may have a negative motivational effect—the comparison of past income and status with present circumstances can easily be depressing (Wolf & Teleen, 1976).

Past positive instrumental value is a difficult concept to define—"What success in the past allowed you to reach your present position?" In my experience, even persons asked about past professional careers find it hard to name events that have past positive instrumental value. (Interestingly enough, I have found more people who could relate events of negative past instrumental value. I heard several instances where past *failure* had led to a person's present position: "The only reason I am in Buffalo is because the other 15 schools turned me down, and I had no choice but to come here.") In my experience, lack of past instrumental value occurs in connection with family and sexual careers as well as professional careers. Careers such as housewife and mother (careers that many elderly persons have been involved with at one time or another) do not include events that can be seen as having instrumental value. They are probably noncontingent career paths. Consider the example of the housewife: What would constitute a successful event to move ahead in her career? Marriage? Having a home to take care of? (See chapter 16 for further discussion of this point.)

Difficulty value appears to have great salience. Many persons have had some experience in which they feel they overcame a great obstacle or performed a difficult task. These experiences range from the man who managed a hospital ward during an influenza epidemic to a woman who defied social conventions to wear pants and work in a gas station in the early 1920s. Contrary to some results of traditional stress research, weathering a number of difficult events is not always adverse to psychological well-being, and it may be beneficial, owing to its past difficulty value (Dohrerwend, 1974).

Cultural value has great importance for past careers (Stenback, 1973). Many elderly persons will extol the virtues of the past: the stricter morality, obedience to conventions, people were friendlier and worked harder, etc. Many older people also apply cultural value to their present lives: "The world may not be as moral (as good, as nice) as when I was young, but I at least still live by that standard." In a way, the elderly may be the group most closely tied to cultural values. Cultural values are set down by traditions—traditions and values that were transmitted by older generations to younger ones.

Cultural value helps to motivate many elderly persons. It is not acceptable to buckle under. So one finds instances such as the woman who, despite being severely depressed after a bout with illness, would almost literally force herself to get up in the morning, get dressed, eat, clean her house, and go through the motions of everyday life. And she did all this despite her expressed opinion that she had no reason to go on living. Another man, disabled, took great pride in his ability to care for himself and to need a minimum of outside help. Cultural value appears to bolster independence and self-reliance (Shanas et al., 1968), and to maintain personality integrity in the absence of close personal contacts.

Intrinsic value is especially important for those persons who do not have a specific future path. Interest or enjoyment must be aroused by the career for the person involved in a present or past orientation, and who is not interested in pursuing some as yet unattained goal. A person who has turned to photography as a hobby following retirement may devote himself or herself to the new career. The person is not interested in photography as a money-making profession, or in competition, or in meeting a criterion of excellence, but works at photography because it is enjoyable. The photographer forms an interesting contrast with the carpenter discussed above. The carpenter would not become as discouraged about his career if he were receiving intrinsic value from it.

MOTIVATIONAL TENDENCIES

The negatively motivated person may have fewer problems in old age than the positively motivated individual. Since the prospect of a future career is no longer a salient issue for many, the negatively motivated person is freed from a major motivational block—fear of future failure—and will therefore adjust quite easily to old age and retirement. One man, a retired farmer, seems to illustrate the retired negatively motivated person. This man had been a hard worker all his life, from childhood to late life. He suffered a stroke in his late sixties. He was told by his doctor that in the future he would have to cut back severely on his farm work. His family expected that he would have problems adjusting to inactivity. But, on the contrary, his adjustment was quite easy. He plowed up his strawberry patch and replanted it with irises, which he loved and which required little care. He spent a lot of time mowing the lawn. His procedure was to mow a strip of grass, rest and enjoy the fresh air, and then mow another strip. Retirement seemed to free him so that he could do the things that gave him intrinsic value.

However, the positively motivated individual is used to moving toward a future goal and, indeed, is highly motivated by such a prospect. When the future begins to shrink as one approaches old age positively motivated individuals may have serious problems. They may totally retreat from any action when becoming is no longer possible. It is in these cases that formerly ambitious and forward-moving persons will suddenly and totally retreat from life—by staying in bed all day or refusing to leave the house, for example. These are the persons who need a future orientation to live and who, once they have a future path, will function happily.

DIRECTIONS FOR RESEARCH

One major problem in gerontological research has been that, until very recently, research was based on assumptions that are now being questioned. For example, Birren (1973) pointed out that stress research usually considers the impact of "negative" events, with events defined as positive or negative by the researcher. Birren found that not all so-called negative events were always considered negative by the elderly persons who experienced the event. Many stated that they found such an event stimulating, a challenge they enjoyed meeting (an example of difficulty value). Additionally, Butler (1977) and Maas and Kuypers (1974) published findings that indicated that the elderly are more dynamic, are more diverse, have a strong will to live and enjoy living, and find old age a time of fulfillment (cf. Erikson, 1968).

Research in motivation among the elderly should carefully and accurately examine the processes of the elderly, and not the researchers' expectations and preconceptions. At the same time, the theory used to guide these observations seems a useful one that merits further consideration and application, as well as more critical evaluation than is possible through the anecdotal material presented here.

References

Ahammer, I. M. Social-learning theory as a framework for the study of adult personality development. In P. B. Baltes & K. W. Schaie (Eds.), *Life-span developmental psychology: Personality and socialization.* New York: Academic Press, 1973.

Angrist, S., & Almquist, E. *Careers and contingencies: How college women juggle with gender.* New York: Dunellen, 1975.

Arling, G. The elderly widow and her family, neighbors, and friends. *Journal of Marriage and the Family,* 1976, *38,* 775–758.

Astin, H. S. Continuing education and the development of adult women. *Counseling Psychologist,* 1976, *6,* 55–60.

Atchley, R. C. Retirement and leisure participation: Continuity or crisis? *The Gerontologist,* 1971, *11,* 13–17. (a)

Atchley, R. C. Retirement and work orientation. *The Gerontologist,* 1971, *11,* 29–32. (b)

Atchley, R. C. Dimensions of widowhood in later life. *The Gerontologist,* 1975, *15,* 176–178.

Atchley, R. C. The life course, age-grading, and age-linked demands for decision making. In N. Datan & L. H. Ginsberg (Eds.), *Life-span developmental psychology: Normative life crises.* New York: Academic Press, 1975.

Atkinson, J. W. *Studies in projective measurement of achievement motivation.* Unpublished doctoral dissertation, University of Michigan, 1950.

Atkinson, J. W. The achievement motive and recall of interrupted and completed tasks. *Journal of Experimental Psychology,* 1953, *46,* 381–390. Also in D. C. McClelland (Ed.), *Studies in motivation.* New York: Appleton-Century-Crofts, 1955.

Atkinson, J. W. Motivational determinants of risk-taking behavior. *Psychological Review,* 1957, *64,* 359–372.

Atkinson, J. W. (Ed.). *Motives in fantasy, action, and society.* Princeton: Van Nostrand, 1958.

Atkinson, J. W. *An introduction to motivation.* Princeton: Van Nostrand, 1964.

Atkinson, J. W. An approach to the study of subjective aspects of achievement motivation. In J. Nuttin (Ed.), *Motives and consciousness in man. Proceedings of 18th International Congress in Psychology.* Symposium 13, Moscow, 1966.

Atkinson, J. W. *Strength of motivation and efficiency of performance: An old unresolved problem.* Paper presented at the meeting of the American Psychological Association, Washington, D.C., September 1967.

Atkinson, J. W. *Measuring achievement-related motives.* Unpublished final report, NSF Project. GS-1399, University of Michigan, 1969.

Atkinson, J. W. Motivation for achievement. In T. Blass (Ed.), *Personality variables in social behavior.* Hillsdale, N.J.: Lawrence Erlbaum Associates, 1977.

Atkinson, J. W. Strength of motivation and efficiency of performance. In J. W. Atkinson & J. O. Raynor (Eds.), *Personality, motivation, and achievement.* Washington, D.C.: Hemisphere, 1978. (a)

Atkinson, J. W. The mainsprings of achievement-oriented activity. In J. W. Atkinson & J. O. Raynor (Eds.), *Personality, motivation, and achievement.* Washington, D.C.: Hemisphere, 1978. (b)

Atkinson, J. W., Bastian, J. R., Earl, R. W., & Litwin, G. H. The achievement motive, goal setting, and probability preferences. *Journal of Abnormal and Social Psychology,* 1960, *60,* 27–36.

Atkinson, J. W., & Birch, D. *The dynamics of action.* New York: Wiley, 1970.

Atkinson, J. W., & Birch, D. The dynamics of achievement-oriented activity. In J. W. Atkinson

& J. O. Raynor (Eds.), *Personality, motivation, and achievement.* Washington, D.C.: Hemisphere, 1978. (a)

Atkinson, J. W., & Birch, D. *Introduction to motivation* (2nd ed.). New York: Van Nostrand. 1978.(b)

Atkinson, J. W., & Feather, N. T. (Eds.). *A theory of achievement motivation.* New York: Wiley, 1966.

Atkinson, J. W., Lens, W., & O'Malley, P. M. Motivation and ability: Interactive psychological determinants of intellective performance, educational achievement, and each other. In W. H. Sewell, R. M. Hauser, & D. L. Featherman (Eds.), *Schooling and achievement in American society.* New York: Academic Press, 1976.

Atkinson, J. W., & Litwin, G. H. Achievement motive and test anxiety conceived as motive to approach success and motive to avoid failure. *Journal of Abnormal and Social Psychology,* 1960, *60,* 52–63.

Atkinson, J. W., & O'Connor, P. A. Neglected factors in studies of achievement-oriented performance: Social approval as an incentive and performance decrement. In J. W. Atkinson & N. T. Feather (Eds.), *A theory of achievement motivation.* New York: Wiley, 1966.

Atkinson, J. W., & Raphelson, A. C. Individual differences in motivation and behavior in particular situations. *Journal of Personality,* 1956, *24,* 349–363.

Atkinson, J. W., & Raynor, J. O. (Eds.). *Motivation and achievement.* Washington, D.C.: Hemisphere, 1974.

Atkinson, J. W., & Raynor, J. O. (Eds.). *Personality, motivation, and achievement.* Washington, D.C.: Hemisphere, 1978.

Atkinson, J.W., & Reitman, W. R. Performance as a function of motive strength and expectancy of goal attainment. *Journal of Abnormal and Social Psychology,* 1956, *53,* 361–366. Also in J. W. Atkinson (Ed.), *Motives in fantasy, action, and society.* Princeton: Van Nostrand, 1958.

Bachman, J. B., Kahn, R. L., Mednick, M. T., Davidson, T. N., & Johnson, L. D. *Youth in transition* (Vol. 1): *Blueprint for a longitudinal study of adolescent boys.* Ann Arbor, Mich.: Survey Research Center, Institute for Social Research, 1967.

Backman, C. W., & Secord, P. F. The self and role selection. In C. Gordon & K. J. Gergen (Eds.), *The self in social interaction* (Vol. 1). New York: Wiley, 1968.

Baltes, M., & Zerber, M. Independence training in nursing home residents. *Gerontologist,* 1976, *16,* 428–432.

Baltes, P. Prototypical paradigms and questions in life-span research on development and aging. *Gerontologist,* 1973, *12,* 458–467.

Baltes, P., & Goulet, L. Exploration of developmental variables by manipulation of age differences in behavior. *Human Development,* 1971, *14,* 149–170.

Baltes, P., & Schaie, K. (Eds.). *Life-span developmental psychology: Personality and socialization.* New York: Academic Press, 1973.

Bardwick, J. M., & Douvan, E. Ambivalence: The socialization of women. In V. Gornick & B. K. Moran (Eds.), *Women in sexist society: Studies in power and powerlessness.* New York: Basic Books, 1971.

Barr, A. J., Goobnight, J. H., Sall, J. P., & Helwig, J. T. *Statistical analysis system.* P.O. Box 10522, Raleigh, N.C., 1976.

Bart, P. Why women's status changes in middle-age: The turns of the social ferris wheel. *Sociological Symposium,* Fall, 1969 (3), 1–18.

Bart, P. In V. Gornick & B. K. Moran (Eds.), *Women in sexist society: Studies in power and powerlessness.* New York: Basic Books, 1971. (a)

Bart, B. Depression in middle-aged women. In V. Gornick & B. K. Moran (Eds.), *Women in sexist society: Studies in power and powerlessness.* New York: Basic Books, 1971. (b)

Bart P. Middle age: Planned obsolescence. In E. Zuckerman (Ed.), *Women and men: Roles, attitudes and power relationships.* New York: Radcliffe Club of New York, 1975.

Beauvoir, S. *The woman destroyed.* New York: Putnam, 1967.

Becker, H. Personal change in adult life. *Sociometry,* 1964, *27* (1), 40–53.

Bell, I. P. The double standard of aging. *Transaction,* November/December 1970, *8,* 75–80.

Benedek, T. *Psychosexual functions in women.* New York: Ronald Press, 1952.

Benedek, T. Parenthood as a developmental phase. *Journal of the American Psychoanalytic Association,* 1959, *7,* 389–417.

Bengston, V. L. *The social psychology of aging.* Indianapolis: Bobbs-Merrill, 1973.

Bengston, V., Kasschau, P., & Ragan, P. The impact of social structure on aging individuals. In J. Berren & K. W. Schaie (Eds.), *Handbook of the psychology of aging.* New York: Van Nostrand Reinhold, 1977.

Bernard, J. *The future of marriage.* New York: Bantam Books, 1972.

Birreń, J. The experience of aging. In R. Davis & M. Neiswender (Eds.), *Aging: Prospects and issues.* Los Angeles: University of Southern California, 1973.

Bischof, L. J. *Adult psychology.* New York: Harper and Row, 1976.

Blau, Z. Structural constraints on friendships in old age. *American Sociological Review,* 1961, *26,* 429–439.

Block, J. *Lives through time.* Berkeley, Calif.: Bancroft Books, 1971.

Block, J. Conceptions of sex roles. *American Psychologist,* 1973, *28,* 512–526.

Blood, R. O., Jr., & Wolfe, D. M. *Husbands and wives: The dynamics of married living.* New York: Free Press, 1960.

Botwinick, J. *Aging and behavior.* New York: Springer, 1973.

Bradley, G. W. Self-serving biases in the attribution process: A reexamination of the fact or fiction question. *Journal of Personality and Social Psychology,* 1978, *36,* 56–71.

Brecher, P. J. *Examination of achievement-oriented performance decrement in contingent pathways.* Unpublished master's thesis, Ohio University, 1972.

Brecher, P. J. *The effect of extrinsic incentives on achievement-oriented performance in contingent paths.* Unpublished doctoral dissertation, Ohio University, 1975.

Brim, O. G. Socialization through the life cycle. In O. G. Brim & S. Wheeler (Eds.), *Socialization after childhood.* New York: Wiley, 1966.

Brim, O. G. Adult socialization. In J. A. Clausen (Ed.), *Socialization and society.* Boston: Little, Brown, 1968.

Brim, O. G. Theories of the male mid-life crisis. *The Counseling Psychologist,* 1976, *6* (1), 2–9.

Brody, E. The aging family. *Gerontologist,* 1966, *6,* 201–206.

Brooks, L. Supermoms shift gears: Reentry women. *The Counseling Psychologist,* 1976, *6,* 33–37.

Brown, M. A. *A set of eight parallel forms of the digit symbol test.* Unpublished set of tests, University of Waterloo, Ontario, Canada, 1969.

Brown, M. Determinants of persistence and initiation of achievement-related activities. In J. W. Atkinson & J. O. Raynor (Eds.), *Motivation and achievement.* Washington, D.C.: Hemisphere, 1974.

Buhler, C. The developmental structure of goal setting in group and individual studies. In C. Buhler & F. Massarik (Eds.), *The course of human life.* New York: Springer, 1968.

Burr, W. R. Satisfaction with various aspects of marriage over the life cycle: A random middle class sample. *Journal of Marriage and the Family,* 1970, *32,* 29–37.

Butler, R. N. The life review: An interpretation of reminiscence in the aged. *Psychiatry,* February 1963, *26,* 65–76.

Butler, R. Toward a psychiatry of the life cycle: Implications of socio-psychological studies of the aging process for the psycho-therapeutic situation. *Psychiatric Research Reports,* 1968, *23,* 233–248.

Butler, R. *Aging and mental health.* St. Louis: Mosby, 1977.

Byrne, D. *An introduction to personality.* Englewood Cliffs, N.J.: Prentice-Hall, 1974.

Byrne, D., & Lamberth, J. The effect of erotic stimuli on sex arousal, evaluative responses, and subsequent behavior. *Technical reports of the Commission on Obscenity and Pornography* (Vol. 8). Washington, D.C.: U.S. Government Printing Office, 1971.

Caine, L. *Widow.* New York: Morrow, 1974.

Caine, L. *Lifelines.* Garden City, N.Y.: Doubleday, 1978.

Campbell, J. W. Women dropping back in: Educational innovation in the sixties. In A. S. Rossi & A. Calderwood (Eds.), *Academic Women on the move.* New York: Russell Sage Foundation, 1973.

Carey, R. G. The widowed: A year later. *Journal of Counseling Psychology,* 1977, *24,* 125–131.

Champagne, M. *Facing life alone: What widows and divorcees should know.* New York: Bobbs-Merrill, 1964.

Clayton, P., Desmaris, L., & Winokur, G. A study of normal bereavement. *American Journal of Psychiatry,* 1968, *125,* 64–74.

Constantinople, A. An Eriksonian measure of personality development in college students. *Developmental Psychology,* 1969, *1,* 357–372.

Cronbach, L. J., & Meehl, P. E. Construct validity in psychological tests. *Psychological Bulletin,* 1955, *52,* 281–302.

Cumming, E., & Henry, W. *Growing old.* New York: Basic Books, 1961.

Daniels, P. *Family/career transitions in women's lives.* Paper presented at the meeting of the American Psychological Association, Toronto, Canada, August 1978.

DeCharms, R. *Personal causation.* New York: Academic Press, 1968.

Deci, E. L. *Intrinsic motivation.* New York: Plenum Press, 1974.

Deutsch, H. *The psychology of women.* New York: Grune and Stratton, 1945.

Deutscher, I. From parental to post-parental life: Exploring shifting expectations. *Sociological Symposium,* Fall, 1969, *3,* 61–73.

Dohrenwend, B., & Dohrenwend, P. *Stressful life events: Their nature and effects.* New York: Wiley, 1974.

Douvan, E., & Adelson, J. *The adolescent experience.* New York: Wiley, 1966.

Elias, M. F., Elias, P. K., & Elias, J. W. *Basic processes in adult developmental psychology.* St. Louis: Mosby, 1977.

Ellis, A. *Growth thru reason: Verbatim cases in rational emotive therapy.* Palo Alto, Calif.: Science and Behavior Books, 1971.

Emmerich, W. Socialization and sex-role development. In P. B. Boltes, & K. W. Schaie (Eds.), *Life-span developmental psychology: Personality and socialization.* New York: Academic Press, 1973.

English, L. D. *The effect of achievement motivation and self perceptions on performance efficiency.* Unpublished master's thesis, State University of New York at Buffalo, 1974.

Entin, E. E. *The relationship between the theory of achievement motivation and performance on a simple and a complex task.* Unpublished doctoral dissertation, University of Michigan, 1968.

Entin, E. E. Comparison of *n* achievement scores elicited from pictures and sentence cues. *Perceptual and Motor Skills,* 1973, *36,* 959–963.

Entin, E. E., & Freedman, M. *Validation of presence-absence and abbreviated scoring procedures for* n *Achievement.* Unpublished manuscript, Ohio University, 1978.

Entin, E. E., & Raynor, J. O. Effects of contingent future orientation and achievement motivation on performance in two kinds of task. *Journal of Experimental Research in Personality,* 1973, *6,* 134–320.

Erikson, E. *Identity and the life cycle.* New York: International University Press, 1959.

Erikson, E. *Childhood and society* (2nd ed.). New York: Norton, 1964.

Erikson, E. H. *Identity, youth and crisis.* New York: Norton, 1968.

Feather, N. T. The relationship of persistence at a task to expectation of success and achievement related motives. *Journal of Abnormal and Social Psychology,* 1961, *63,* 552–561.

Feather, N. T. Persistence at a difficult task with alternative task of intermediate difficulty. *Journal of Abnormal and Social Psychology,* 1963, *66,* 604–609.

Feather, N. T. An expectancy-value model of information-seeking behavior. *Psychological Review,* 1967, *74,* 342–360.

Feather, N. T. Attribution of responsibility and valence of success and failure in relation to initial confidence and task performance. *Journal of Personality and Social Psychology,* 1969, *13,* 129–144.

Feather, N. T. Causal attributions for male and female success and failure at occupations differing in perceived status and sex-linked appropriateness. *Australian Journal of Psychology,* 1977, *29,* 151–165.

Feather, N. T., & Simon, J. G. Attribution of responsibility and valence of outcome in relation to initial confidence and success and failure of self and others. *Journal of Personality and Social Psychology,* 1971, *18,* 173–188.

Festinger, L. A theoretical interpretation of shifts in level of aspiration. *Psychological Review,* 1942, *49,* 235–250.

Festinger, L. A theory of social comparison processes. *Human Relations,* 1954, *7,* 117–140.

Finn, J. D. *NYBMUL.* State University of New York at Buffalo Computing Center, 1969.

French, E. G., & Thomas, F. H. The relation of achievement motivation to problem-solving effectiveness. *Journal of Abnormal and Social Psychology,* 1958, *56,* 46–48.

Frenkel-Brunswick, E. Adjustments and reorientation in the course of the life span. In B. Neugarten (Ed.), *Middle age and aging.* Chicago: University of Chicago Press, 1968.

Fried, B. *The middle-age crisis.* New York: Harper and Row, 1967.

Friedan, B. *The feminine mystique.* New York: Norton, 1963.

Friedman, M., & Rosenman, R. H. *Type A behavior and your heart.* New York: Knopf, 1974.

Frieze, I., Parsons, J., Johnson, P., Ruble, D., & Zellman, G. *Women and sex roles, a social psychological perspective.* New York: Norton, 1978.

Frieze, I., & Weiner, B. Cue utilization and attributional judgments of success and failure. *Journal of Personality,* 1971, *39,* 591–605.

Gazzo, B. *The effects of achievement motivation, self-future orientation, and competent versus nurturant role descriptions on interest and expectancy of success in a tutorial program.* Unpublished honors thesis, State University of New York at Buffalo, 1974.

Gerber, I. R., Hannon, R. N., Battin, Ḍ., & Arkin, A. Anticipatory grief and aged widows and widowers. *Journal of Gerontology,* 1975, *30,* 225–229.

Ginzberg, E. Toward a theory of occupational choice: A restatement. *Vocational Guidance Quarterly,* 1972, *20,* 169–176.

Ginzberg, E., & Yohalem, A. *Educated American women: Self-portraits.* New York: Columbia University Press, 1966.

Gjesme, T. Goal distance in time and its effect on the relations between achievement motives and performance. *Journal of Research in Personality,* 1974, *8,* 161–171.

Gjesme, T., & Nygard, R. *Achievement-related motives: Theoretical considerations and construction of a measuring instrument.* Unpublished report, University of Oslo, 1970.

Glixman, A. F. Recall of completed and incompleted activities under varying degrees of stress. *Journal of Experimental Psychology,* 1949, *39,* 281–295.

Glover, E. *Freud or Jung.* New York: Norton, 1950.

Gold, S. Cross-cultural comparisons of role change with aging. *Student Journal of Human Development* (Committee on Human Development), University of Chicago, 1960, *1,* 11–15.

Goodman, L. A. Simple methods for analyzing three-factor interactions in contingency tables. *Journal of the American Statistical Association,* 1964, *59,* 319–352.

Gordon, C. Role and value development across the life cycle. In J. A. Jackson (Ed.), *Sociological studies IV: Role.* London: Cambridge University Press, 1972.

Gould, R. The phases of adult life: A study in developmental psychology. *American Journal of Psychiatry,* 1972, *129,* 521–531.

Goulet, L., & Baltes, P. *Life-span developmental psychology: Research and theory.* New York: Academic Press, 1970.

Gove, W. R., Grimm, J. W., Motz, S.C., & Thompson, J. D. The family life cycle: Internal dynamics and social consequences. *Sociology and Social Research,* 1973, *57,* 182–195.

Gubrium, J. Environmental effects on morale in old age and resources of health and solvency. *Gerontologist,* 1970, *10,* 294–297.

Gutmann, D. L. Parenthood: Key to the comparative psychology of the life cycle? In N. Daton & L. Ginsberg (Eds.), *Life-span developmental psychology: Normative life crises.* New York: Academic Press, 1975.

Gutmann, D. Individual adaptation in the middle years, developmental issues in the masculine mid-life crisis. *Journal of Geriatric Psychiatry*, 1976, *9*, 41–59.

Gutmann, D. Life events and decision making by older adults. *Gerontologist*, 1978, *18* (5), 462–467.

Haan, N., & Day, D. A longitudinal study of change and sameness in personality development: Adolescence to later adulthood. *International Journal of Aging and Human Development*, 1974, *5*, 11–39.

Harrington, M. *The other America*. New York: Macmillan, 1969.

Harris, L., and Associates. *The myth and reality of aging in America* (poll). Washington, D.C.: National Council on the Aging, 1975.

Hartley, R. A developmental view of female sex-role definition and identification. *Merrill-Palmer Quarterly*, 1964, *10*, 3–16.

Havighurst, R. *Developmental tasks and education*. New York: McKay, 1952.

Havighurst, R. Successful aging. In R. Williams, C. Tibbits, & W. Donahue (Eds.), *Processes of aging*. New York: Atherton Press, 1963.

Hays, J. R. Memory, goals, and problem solving. In B. Kleinmuntz (Ed.), *Problem solving: Research, method and theory*. New York: Wiley, 1966.

Hennig, M., & Jardim, A. *The Managerial Woman*. Garden City, N.Y.: Anchor Press/Doubleday, 1977.

Heyman, D. K., & Giantruco, D. T. Long term adaptation by the elderly to bereavement. *Journal of Gerontology*, 1973, *28*, 359–362.

Holland, J. G., & Skinner, B. F. *The analysis of behavior*. New York: McGraw-Hill, 1961.

Hollander, E. P. *Leaders, groups and influence*. New York: Oxford University Press, 1964.

Holsti, O. Crisis, stress and decision making. *Social Science Journal*, 1971, *23*, 53–57.

Horner, M. *Sex differences in achievement motivation and performance in competitive and non-competitive situations*. Unpublished doctoral dissertation, University of Michigan, 1968.

Horner, M. Performance of men in noncompetitive and interpersonal competitive achievement-oriented situations. In J. W. Atkinson & J. O. Raynor (Eds.), *Motivation and achievement*. Washington, D.C.: Hemisphere, 1974.

Humphrey, M. M. *The effects of future orientation and achievement motivation upon acquisition and performance*. Unpublished master's thesis, Ohio University, 1973.

Hyde, J., & Rosenberg, B. G. *Half the human experience, The psychology of women*. Lexington, Mass.: Heath, 1976.

Isaacson, R. L., & Raynor, J. O. *Achievement-related motivation and perceived instrumentality of grades to future career success*. Unpublished paper, University of Michigan, 1966.

Janis, I. L. (Ed.) *Personality: Dynamics, development and assessment*. New York: Harcourt, Brace, and World, 1969.

Johnson, E. "Good" relationships between older mothers and their daughters: A causal model. *Gerontologist*, 1978, *18* (3), 301–306.

Johnson, E., & Bursk, B. Relationships between the elderly and their adult children. *Gerontologist*, 1977, *17*, 90–96.

Johnson, V. E. *I'll quit tomorrow*. New York: Harper and Row, 1973.

Jung, C. G. *The development of personality* (Vol. 17 of the *Collected Works*). Princeton, N.J.: Princeton University Press, 1970.

Jung, C. The stages of life (R. F. C. Hull, trans.). In J. Campbell, *The Portable Jung*. New York: Viking, 1971.

Kastenbaum, R. Death and bereavement in later life. In A. H. Kutscher (Ed.), *Death and bereavement*. Springfield, Ill.: Thomas, 1969.

Kastenbaum, R., & Durkee, N. Young people view old age. In R. Kastenbaum (Ed.), *New thoughts on old age*. New York: Springer, 1964.

Kinsey, A. C., Pomeroy, W. B., Martin, C. E., & Gebhard, P. H. *Sexual behavior in the human female*. Philadelphia: Saunders, 1953.

Klass, S., & Redfern, M. A social work response to the middle aged housewife. *Social Casework*, 1977, *58*, 100–110.

Kline, C. The socialization process in women. In H. Peters & J. Hansen (Eds.), *Vocational guidance and career development* (3rd ed.). New York: Macmillan, 1977.

Knefelkamp, L., Widick, C., & Stroad, B. Cognitive-developmental theory: A guide to counseling women. *The Counseling Psychologist,* 1976, *6,* 15-19.

Kohlberg, L. Stages and aging in moral development: Some speculations. *Gerontologist,* 1973, *13,* 497-502.

Kroll, A., Kinklage, L., Lee, J., Morley, E., & Wilson, E. *Career development: Growth and crisis.* New York: Wiley, 1970.

Kruglanski, A. W., Riter, A., Amitai, A., Margolin, B., Shabtai, L., & Zaksh, D. Can money enhance intrinsic motivation?: A test of the content-consequence hypothesis. *Journal of Personality and Social Psychology,* 1975, *31,* 744-750.

Kuhlen, R. Developmental changes in motivation during the adult years. In B. L. Neugarten (Ed.), *Middle age and aging.* Chicago: University of Chicago Press, 1968.

Kukla, A. *Cognitive determinants of achieving behavior.* Unpublished doctoral dissertation, University of California at Los Angeles, 1970.

Kukla, A. Cognitive determinants of achieving behavior. *Journal of Personality and Social Psychology,* 1972, *21,* 166-174.

Kutner, B., Fanshal, D., Togo, A., & Langner, T. *500 over 60: A community survey on aging.* New York: Russell Sage, 1956.

Kutscher, A. H. *Death and bereavement.* Springfield, Ill.: Thomas, 1969.

Larson, J. R. Evidence for a self-serving bias in the attribution of causality. *Journal of Personality,* 1977, *45,* 430-441.

Lehman, H. C. *Age and achievement.* Princeton, N.J.: Princeton University Press, 1953.

LeShan, E. *The wonderful crisis of middle age: Some personal reflections.* New York: McKay, 1973.

Letchworth, G. E. Women who return to college: An identity-integrity approach. *Journal of College Student Personnel,* 1970, *11,* 103-106.

Levine, A. Women at work in America: History, status, and prospects. In H. R. Kaplan (Ed.), *American minorities and economic opportunity.* Itasca, Ill.: Peacock, 1977.

Levinson, D. *The seasons of a man's life.* New York: Knopf, 1978.

Levinson, D., Darrow, C., Klein, E., Levinson, M., & McKee, B. Periods in the adult development of men: Ages 18 to 45. *The Counseling Psychologist,* 1976, *6* (1), 21-25.

Lewin, K. *Conceptual representation and measurement of psychological forces.* Durham, N.C.: Duke University Press, 1938.

Lewin, K. Defining the "field at a given time." *Psychological Review,* 1943, *50,* 292-310.

Lewin, K., Dembo, T., Festinger, L., & Sears, P. S. Level of aspiration. In J. McV. Hunt (Ed.), *Personality and the behavior disorders* (Vol. 1). New York: Ronald Press, 1944.

Lewis, H. G., & Franklin, M. An experimental study of the role of the ego in work. II. The significance of task-orientation in work. *Journal of Experimental Psychology,* 1944, *34,* 195-215.

Likert, J. (Ed.). *Conversations with returning women students.* Ann Arbor, Mich.: Ann Arbor Center for Continuing Education of Women, University of Michigan, 1967.

Lindemann, E. Symptomatology and management of acute grief. *American Journal of Psychiatry,* 1944, *101,* 141-148.

Linton, R. *The cultural background of personality.* New York: Appleton-Century-Crofts, 1945.

Lionells, M., & Mann, C. *Patterns of mid-life in transition.* New York: William Alanson White Institute, 1974.

Lipman-Blumen, J. Role de-differentiation as a system response to crisis: Occupational and political roles of women. *Sociological Inquiry,* 1973, *43,* 105-129.

Lipman-Blumen, J., & Leavitt, H. Vicarious and direct achievement patterns in adulthood. *The Counseling Psychologist,* 1976, *6,* 26-32.

Livson, F. Patterns of personality development in middle-aged women: A longitudinal study. *International Journal of Aging and Human Development,* 1976, *7,* 107-115.

Looft, W. R. Socialization and personality throughout the life-span: An examination of contemporary psychological approaches. In P. B. Boltes & K. W. Schaie (Eds.), *Life-span developmental psychology: Personality and socialization.* New York: Academic Press, 1973.

Lopata, H. Z. Loneliness: Forms and components. *Social Problems,* 1970, *17,* 248–262.

Lopata, H. Z. *Occupation: Housewife.* New York: Oxford University Press, 1971. (a)

Lopata, H. Z. Widows as a minority group: Part II. *The Gerontologist,* 1971, *11,* 67–77. (b)

Lopata, H. Z. Living through widowhood. *Psychology Today,* 1973, *7,* 87–92.

Lowe, J. *A study of the psychological and social impact of age-expectations on an age-graded career–the army officer.* Unpublished paper on file, Committee on Human Development, University of Chicago, 1964.

Lowell, E. L. The effect of need for achievement on learning and speed of performance. *Journal of Psychology,* 1952, *33,* 31–40.

Lowenthal, M. F. Sociopsychological theory of change. In J. Birren & K. W. Schaie (Eds.), *The handbook of the psychology of aging.* New York: Van Nostrand-Reinhold, 1977.

Lowenthal, M. F., & Chiriboga, D. Transition to the empty nest. *Archives of General Psychiatry,* 26, January 1972.

Lowenthal, M. F., Majda, T., Chiriboga, D., & associates. *Four stages of life: A comparative study of women and men facing transitions.* San Francisco: Jossey-Bass, 1975.

Lowenthal, M. F., & Robinson, B. Social networks and isolation. In R. H. Binstock & E. Shanas (Eds.), *Handbook of aging and the social sciences.* New York: Van Nostrand-Reinhold, 1976.

Lowenthal, M. F., & Weiss, L. Intimacy and crises in adulthood. *Counseling Psychologist,* 1976, *6,* 10–15.

Luckey, E. Perceptual congruence of self and family concepts as related to marital interaction. *Sociometry,* 1961, *24,* 234–250.

Luginbuhl, J. E. R., Crowne, D. H., & Kahan, J. P. Causal attributions for success and failure. *Journal of Personality and Social Psychology,* 1975, *31,* 86–93.

Maas, H., & Kuypers, J. *From 30 to 70.* San Francisco: Jossey-Bass, 1974.

Maddison, D. The relevance of conjugal bereavement for preventive psychiatry. *British Journal of Medical Psychology,* 1968, *41,* 223–233.

Maddox, G. Activity and morale: A longitudinal study of selected elderly subjects. *Social Forces,* 1963, *42,* 195–204.

Maddox, G. L. Retirement as a social event in the U.S. In B. L. Neugarten (Ed.), *Middle age and aging.* Chicago: University of Chicago Press, 1968.

Mandler, G., & Sarason, S. B. A study of anxiety and learning. *Journal of Abnormal and Social Psychology,* 1952, *47,* 166–173.

Marcia, J. E. Development and validations of ego-identity status. *Journal of Personality and Social Psychology,* 1966, *4,* 132–141.

Margolis, B. L., & Kroes, W. H. Work and the health of man. In J. O'Toole (Ed.), *Work and the quality of life.* Cambridge, Mass.: MIT Press, 1974.

Marris, P. *Widows and their families.* London: Routledge & Kegan Paul, 1958.

Marrow, A. J. Goal tensions and recall. Part 2. *Journal of General Psychology,* 1938, *19,* 37–64.

Martel, M. Age-sex roles in American magazine fiction. In B. Neugarten (Ed.), *Middle age and aging.* Chicago: University of Chicago Press, 1968.

Maslow, A. H. *Motivation and personality* (2nd ed.). New York: Harper and Row, 1970.

Masters, W. H., & Johnson, V. E. *Human sexual inadequacy.* Boston: Little, Brown, 1970.

Mayer, N. *The male mid-life crisis: Fresh starts after 40.* Garden City, N.Y.: Doubleday, 1978.

Mayer, T. Middle age and occupational processes: An empirical essay. *Sociological Symposium,* No. 3, Fall 1969, 89–106.

McClelland, D. C. *The achieving society.* Princeton: Van Nostrand, 1961.

McClelland, D. C., Atkinson, J. W., Clark, R. A., & Lowell, E. L. *The achievement motive.* New York: Appleton-Century-Crofts, 1953. Reissued with a new preface by J. W. Atkinson, New York: Irvington (Halstead Press/Wiley), 1976.

McClelland, D. C., Atkinson, J. W., Clark, R. A., & Lowell, E. L. A scoring manual for the achievement motive. In J. W. Atkinson (Ed.), *Motives in fantasy, action, and society.* Princeton: Van Nostrand, 1958.

McClelland, D. C., Clark, R. A., Roby, T. B., & Atkinson, J. W. The projective expression of needs. IV. The effect of the need for achievement on thematic apperception. *Journal of Experimental Psychology*, 1949, *39*, 242–255.

Mead, G. H. *Mind, self and society*. Chicago: University of Chicago Press, 1934.

Mehrabian, A. Male and female scales of tendency to achieve. *Educational and Psychological Measurement*, 1968, *28*, 493–502.

Mehrabian, A. Measures of achieving tendency. *Educational and Psychological Measurement*, 1969, *29*, 445–451.

Mehrabian, A. Male and female scales of tendency to achieve. *Educational and Psychological Measurement*, 1969, *29*, 445–451.

Meichenbaum, D. H. Cognitive modification of test anxious college students. *Journal of Consulting and Clinical Psychology*, 1972, *3*, 370–380.

Meyer, W. V. Selbstverantwortlichkeit and leistungs motivation. In B. Weiner (Ed.), *Theories of motivation*. Chicago: Markham, 1972.

Miles, H. S., & Hays, D. R. Widowhood. *American Journal of Nursing*, 1975, *75*, 280–282.

Miller, D., & Swanson, S. *The changing American parent*. New York: Wiley, 1958.

Miller, D. T. Ego involvement and attributions for success and failure. *Journal of Personality and Social Psychology*, 1976, *34*, 901–906.

Miller, D. T., & Ross, M. Self-serving biases in the attribution of causality: Fact or fiction? *Psychological Bulletin*, 1975, *82*, 213–225.

Miller, N. E. Experimental studies of conflict. In J. McV. Hunt (Ed.), *Personality and the behavior disorders* (Vol. 1). New York: Ronald Press, 1944.

Miller, S. J. The social dilemma of the aging leisure participant. In B. L. Neugarten (Ed.), *Middle age and aging*. Chicago: University of Chicago Press, 1968.

Miller, S., & Schooler, K. In D. Kent et al. (Eds.), *Research, planning and action for the elderly*. New York: Behavior Publications, 1972.

Mitchell, J. S. *Relationships between achievement motivation, contingent future orientation, and subjective probability of success*. Unpublished honors paper, Department of Psychology, State University of New York at Buffalo, 1974.

Morse, N. C., & Weiss, R. S. The function and meaning of work and the job. In S. Nosow & W. H. Form (Eds.), *Man, work and society*. New York: Basic Books, 1962.

Moulton, R. W. Motivational implications of individual differences in competence. Paper presented at the meeting of the American Psychological Association, Washington, D.C., September 1967. Also in J. W. Atkinson and J. O Raynor (Eds.), *Motivation and achievement*. Washington, D.C.: Hemisphere, 1974.

Munnicks, J. M. A. *Old age and finitude*. New York: Karger, 1966.

Nero, S. *Exploratory study of sociological and psychological impacts of mid-career changes for females*. Final report, ERIC (ED 120567), 1975.

Neugarten, B. L. The awareness of middle age. In B. L. Neugarten (Ed.), *Middle age and aging*. Chicago: University of Chicago Press, 1968.

Neugarten, B. L. Continuities and discontinuities of psychological issues into adult life. *Human Development*, 1969, *12*, 121–130.

Neugarten, B. Personality and aging. In J. E. Birren & K. W. Schaie (Eds.), *Handbook of the psychology of aging*. New York: Van Nostrand-Reinhold, 1976. (a)

Neugarten, B. L. Adaptation and the life cycle. *The Counseling Psychologist*, 1976, *6*, 16–20. (b)

Neugarten, B. L. Unpublished manuscript, 1978.

Neugarten, B. L., & Datan, N. Sociological perspectives on the life cycle. In P. B. Boltes & K. W. Schaie (Eds.), *Life-span developmental psychology: Personality and socializaton*. New York: Academic Press, 1973.

Neugarten, B. L., & Gutmann, D. Age-sex roles and personality in middle age: A thematic apperception study. In B. L. Neugarten (Ed.), *Middle age and aging*. Chicago: University of Chicago Press, 1968.

Neugarten, B. L., & Hagestad, G. Age and the life course. In R. Binstock & E. Shanas (Eds.), *Handbook of aging and the social sciences*. New York: Van Nostrand-Reinhold, 1976.

Neugarten, B. L., Moore, J., & Lowe, J. Age norms, age constraints, and adult socialization. *American Journal of Sociology,* 1965, *70,* 710–717.

Neugarten, B. L., Wood, V., Kraines, R. J., & Loomis, B. Women's attitudes toward the menopause. In B. L. Neugarten (Ed.), *Middle age and aging: A reader in social psychology.* Chicago: University of Chicago Press, 1968.

Noberini, M., & Neugarten, B. L. *A follow-up study of adaptation in middle-aged women.* Paper presented at the Annual Meeting of the Gerontological Society, Louisville, 1975.

Nydegger, C. *Late and early fathers.* Paper presented at the Annual Meeting of the Gerontological Society, Miami Beach, 1973.

Oates, W. *Confessions of a workaholic.* New York: World, 1971.

O'Leary, V. E. Some attitudinal barriers to occupational aspirations in women. *Psychological Bulletin,* 1974, *81,* 809–826.

Otten, J., & Shelley, F. D. *When your parents grow old.* New York: Signet, 1976.

Parkes, C. *Bereavement—Studies of grief in adult life.* New York: International Universities Press, 1972.

Peak, H. Attitude and motivation. In M. R. Jones (Ed.), *Nebraska symposium on motivation.* Lincoln, Nebr.: University of Nebraska Press, 1955.

Pearlson, H. B. *Future plans of college men: A motivational analysis.* Unpublished masters paper, State University of New York at Buffalo, 1972.

Pearlson, H. B. *The effects of two types of time perspective on the arousal of achievement-related affect.* Unpublished paper, State University of New York at Buffalo, 1975.

Pearlson, H. B. *Effects of temporal distance from a goal and numbers of tasks required for goal attainment on achievement-related behavior.* Unpublished doctoral dissertation, State University of New York at Buffalo, 1979.

Peck, R. Psychological development in the second half of life. In J. Anderson (Ed.), *Psychological aspects of aging* (Conference on Planning Research, 1955). Washington, D.C.: American Psychological Association, 1956.

Pepper, C. We shouldn't have to retire at 65. *Parade Magazine,* September 4, 1977.

Peppers, L. G. Patterns of leisure and adjustment to retirement. *The Gerontologist,* 1976, *16,* 441–446.

Perry, W., Jr. *Intellectual and ethical development in the college years.* New York: Holt, Rinehart, and Winston, 1970.

Peterson, J. A., & Payne, B. *Love in the later years.* New York: Association Press, 1975.

Pineo, P. Disenchantment in the latter years of marriage. In B. Neugarten (Ed.), *Middle age and aging.* Chicago: University of Chicago Press, 1968.

Psathas, G. Toward a theory of occupational career choice for women. *Sociology and Social Research,* 1968, *52,* 253–268.

Radloff, L. Sex differences in depression: The effects of occupation and marital status. *Sex Roles,* 1975, *1,* 249–265.

Raynor, J. O. *The relationship between distant future goals and achievement motivation.* Unpublished doctoral dissertation, University of Michigan, 1968.

Raynor, J. O. *Achievement motivation, grades, and instrumentality.* Paper presented at the meeting of the American Psychological Association, San Francisco, September 1968.

Raynor, J. O. Future orientation and motivation of immediate activity: An elaboration of the theory of achievement motivation. *Psychological Review,* 1969, *76,* 606–610.

Raynor, J. O. Relationships between achievement-related motives, future orientation, and academic performance. *Journal of Personality and Social Psychology,* 1970, *15,* 28–33.

Raynor, J. O. Future orientation in the study of achievement motivation. In J. W. Atkinson & J. O. Raynor (Eds.), *Motivation and achievement.* Washington, D.C.: Hemisphere, 1974. (a)

Raynor, J. O. Motivation and career striving. In J. W. Atkinson & J. O. Raynor (Eds.), *Motivation and achievement.* Washington, D.C.: Hemisphere, 1974. (b)

Raynor, J. O. *The engagement of achievement-related motives: Achievement arousal versus contingent future orientation.* Paper presented at the meeting of the American Psychological Association, New Orleans, September 1974. (c)

Raynor, J. O. Future orientation in the study of achievement motivation. In J. W. Atkinson and J. O. Raynor (Eds.), *Personality, motivation, and achievement*. Washington, D.C.: Hemisphere, 1978. (a)

Raynor, J. O. Lecture series for Psychology 610, Theories of Personality, State University of New York at Buffalo, September to December 1978. (b)

Raynor, J. O., Atkinson, J. W., & Brown, M. Subjective aspects of achievement motivation immediately before an examination. In J. W. Atkinson & J. O. Raynor (Eds.), *Motivation and achievement*. Washington, D.C.: Hemisphere, 1974.

Raynor, J. O., Entin, E. E., & Raynor, D. *Effects of n Achievement, test anxiety, and length of contingent path on performance of grade school children*. Unpublished paper, State University of New York at Buffalo, 1972.

Raynor, J. O., & Harris, V. A. *Performance in decreasing and increasing probability contingent paths*. Unpublished data, 1973.

Raynor, J. O., & Rubin, I. S. Effects of achievement motivation and future orientation on level of performance. *Journal of Personality and Social Psychology*, 1971, *17*, 36–41.

Raynor, J. O., & Smith, C. P. Achievement-related motives and risk-taking in games of skill and chance. *Journal of Personality*, 1966, *34*, 176–198.

Raynor, J. O., & Sorrentino, R. M. *Effects of achievement motivation and task difficulty on immediate performance in contingent paths*. Unpublished paper, State University of New York at Buffalo, 1972.

Reichard, S., Livson, F., & Peterson, P. G. Adjustment to retirement. In B. L. Neugarten (Ed.), *Middle age and aging*. Chicago: University of Chicago Press, 1968.

Riegel, K. F. Age life crises: Toward a dialectic theory of development. In N. Datan & L. H. Ginsberg (Eds.), *Life-span developmental psychology: Normative life crises*. New York: Academic Press, 1975.

Riley, M., & Foner, A. *Aging and society*. New York: Russell Sage, 1968.

Rogers, C. *On becoming a person*. Boston: Houghton Mifflin, 1961.

Rogers, C. R. A theory of therapy, personality and interpersonal relationships, as developed in the client-centered framework. In S. Koch (Ed.), *Psychology: A study of a science* (Vol. 3). New York: McGraw-Hill, 1959.

Rollins, B. C., & Feldman, H. Marital satisfaction over the family life cycle. *Journal of Marriage and the Family*, 1970, *32*, 20–29.

Rose, A. Factors associated with the life satisfaction of middle-class, middle-aged persons. *Marriage and Family Living*, 1955, *17*, 15–19.

Rose, A. A social-psychological theory of neurosis. In A. Rose (Ed.), *Human behavior and social processes*. Boston: Houghton Mifflin, 1962.

Rosen, B. The achievement syndrome. *American Sociological Review*, 1955, *21*, 203–211.

Rosenthal, G. *Separation of success from moving on in a contingent path and its effect on choice of goal for achievement-oriented subjects*. Unpublished master's thesis, Ohio University, 1974.

Rosow, I. Retirement, leisure and social status. In *Proceedings of Seminars, 1965–1969, Center for the Study of Aging and Human Development*. Durham, N.C.: Duke University Press, 1969.

Rozensweig, S. Experimental study of repression with specific reference to need-persistive and ego-defensive reactions to frustration. *Journal of Experimental Psychology*, 1943, *32*, 64–74.

Sales, S. Organizational role as a risk factor in coronary disease. *Administrative Science Quarterly*, 1969, *14*, 325–336.

Sandler, J. A test of the significance of the difference between the means of correlated measures, based on a simplification of student *t*. *British Journal of Psychology*, 1955, *46*, 225–226.

Sarason, S. B., Davidson, K. S., Lighthall, F. F., Waite, R. R., & Ruebush, B. K. *Anxiety in elementary school children*. New York: Wiley, 1960.

Sarason, S. B., Sarason, E. K., & Cowden, P. Aging and the nature of work. *American Psychologist*, 1975, *30*, 584–592.

Schlegel, A. Situational stress: A Hopi example. In N. Datan & L. H. Ginsberg (Eds.), *Life-span developmental psychology: Normative life crises.* New York: Academic Press, 1975.

Schulz, J. The economics of aging. Belmont, Calif.: Wadsworth, 1976.

Shanas, E. The family and social class. In E. Shanas, P. Townsend, D. Wedderburn, H. Friis, P. Milbaj, & J. Stehower, *Old people in three industrial societies.* New York: Atherton Press, 1968.

Shanas, E., Townsend, P., Wedderburn, D., Friis, H., Mohaj, P., & Stehower, J. *Old people in three industrial societies.* New York: Atherton Press, 1968.

Sheehy, G. *Passages: Predictable crises of adult life.* New York: Dutton, 1974.

Shrable, K., & Sassenmath, J. M. The effects of achievement motivation and test anxiety on performance on programmed instruction. *American Educational Research Journal*, 1970, *7*, 209–219.

Shrauger, J. S. Responses to evaluation as a function of initial self-perceptions. *Psychological Bulletin*, 1975, *82*, 581–596.

Sicoly, F., & Ross, M. Facilitation of ego-biased attributions by means of self-serving observer feedback. *Journal of Personality and Social Psychology*, 1977, *35*, 734–741.

Silverman, P., & Cooperband, A. On widowhood: Mutual help and the elderly widow. *Journal of Geriatric Psychiatry*, 1975, *8*, 9–27.

Silverstone, B., & Hyman, H. K. *You and your aging parent.* New York: Pantheon, 1976.

Simon, J. G., & Feather, N. T. Causal attributions for success and failure at university examinations. *Journal of Educational Psychology*, 1973, *64*, 46–56.

Smith, C. P. *Situational determinants of the expression of achievement motivation in thematic apperception.* Unpublished doctoral dissertation, University of Michigan, 1961.

Smith, C. P. Achievement-related motives and goal setting under different conditions. *Journal of Personality*, 1963, *31*, 124–140.

Smith, C. P. Relationship between achievement-related motives and intelligence, performance level, and persistence. *Journal of Abnormal and Social Psychology*, 1964, *68*, 523–532.

Smith, C. P. The influence of testing conditions and need for achievement scores and their relationship to performance scores. In J. W. Atkinson & N. T. Feather (Eds.), *A theory of achievement motivation.* New York: Wiley, 1966.

Smith, C. P., & Feld, S. How to learn the method of content analysis for n Achievement, n Affiliation, and n Power. In J. W. Atkinson (Ed.), *Motives in fantasy, action, and society.* Princeton: Van Nostrand, 1958.

Smith, H. E. Family interaction patterns of the aged: A review. In A. Rose & W. A. Peterson (Eds.), *Older people and their social world.* Philadelphia: Davis, 1965.

Sorrentino, R. M. *An extension of theory of achievement motivation to the study of emergent leadership.* Unpublished doctoral dissertation, State University of New York at Buffalo, 1971.

Sorrentino, R. M. An extension of theory of achievement motivation to the study of emergent leadership. *Journal of Personality and Social Psychology*, 1973, *26*, 356–368.

Sorrentino, R. M. Extending theory of achievement motivation to the study of group processes. In J. W. Atkinson & J. O Raynor (Eds.), *Motivation and achievement.* Washington, D.C.: Hemisphere, 1974.

Sorrentino, R. M., Short, J. C., & Raynor, J. O. *Uncertainty motivation: Implications for a general theory of human motivation.* Unpublished manuscript, 1979.

Spence, D., & Lonner, T. The "empty nest": A transition within motherhood. *The Family Coordinator*, 1971, *20*, 369–375.

Spence, D., Cohen, S., & Kowalski, C. Mental health, age and community living. *Gerontologist*, 1975, *15*, 77–82.

Spence, K. W., Farber, L. E., & McFann, H. H. The relation of anxiety (drive) level to performance in competitional and noncompetitional paired-associates learning. *Journal of Experimental Psychology*, 1956, *52*, 296–305.

Spierer, H. *Major transitions in the human life cycle, a summary of a conference on the signifi-*

cance of the biomedical and the social sciences in understanding the aging process. New York: Academy for Educational Development, 1977.

Steiner, C. *Games alcoholics play: The analysis of life scripts.* New York: Globe Press, 1971.

Stenback, A. Research in geriatric psychiatry and the care of the aged. *Comprehensive Psychiatry,* 1973, *14* (2), 9–15.

Streib, G. F. Social stratification and aging. In R. H. Binstock & E. Shanas (Eds.), *Handbook of aging and the social sciences.* New York: Van Nostrand-Reinhold, 1976.

Streib, G. F., & Schneider, C. J. *Retirement in American society.* Ithaca, N.Y.: Cornell University Press, 1971.

Super, D. E. *The psychology of careers.* New York: Harper and Row, 1957.

Sussman, M. The family life of old people In R. Binstock & E. Shanas (Eds.), *Handbook of aging and the social sciences.* New York: Van Nostrand-Reinhold, 1976.

Tittle, C. K., & Denker, E. Re-entry women: A selective review of the educational process, career choice, and interest measurement. *Review of Educational Research,* Fall 1977, *47,* 531–584.

Toffler, A. *Future shock.* New York: Random House,1970.

Townsend, P. *The family life of old people.* London: Routledge and Paul Kegan, 1957.

Troll, L. The family of later life: A decade review. *Marriage and Family Living,* 1971, *33,* 263–290.

Troll, L. E. *Early and middle adulthood: The best is yet to be—maybe.* Monterey: Brooks/Cole, 1975.

Trope, Y. Seeking information about one's own ability as a determinant of choice among tasks. *Journal of Personality and Social Psychology,* 1975, *32,* 1004–1013.

Trope, Y., & Brickman, P. Difficulty and diagnosticity as determinants of choice among tasks. *Journal of Personality and Social Psychology,* 1975, *31,* 918–925.

Tulving, E. Intratrial and intertrial retention: Notes towards a theory of free recall verbal learning. *Psychological Review,* 1964, *71,* 219–237.

Ullman, L. *Changing,* New York: Knopf, 1977.

U.S. Department of Labor, Employment Standards Administration, *1975 Handbook on women workers,* Bulletin 297, 1975.

Vaillant, G. E., & McArthur, C. C. Natural history of male psychologic health: 1. The adult life cycle from 18–50. *Seminars in Psychiatry,* 1972, *4,* 415–427.

Van Dusen, R., & Sheldon, E. B. The changing status of American women: A life cycle perspective. *The American Psychologist,* 1976, *31,* 106–116.

Veroff, J., Atkinson, J. W., Feld, S., & Gurin, G. The use of thematic apperception to assess motivation in a nationwide interview study. *Psychological Monographs,* 1960, *74* (12, Whole No. 499). Also in J. W. Atkinson & J. O. Raynor (Eds.), *Motivation and achievement.* Washington, D.C.: Hemisphere, 1974.

Veroff, J., & Feld, S. *Marriage and work in America.* New York: Van Nostrand-Reinhold, 1970.

Verwoerdt, A., Pfeiffer, E., & Wang, H. Sexual behavior in senescence. *Geriatrics,* 1969, *24,* 137–154.

Walker, S., & Teleen, S. Psychological and social correlates of life satisfaction as a function of residential constraints. *Journal of Gerontology,* 1976, *31,* 89–98.

Wechsler, D. *The measurement and appraisal of adult intelligence* (4th ed.). Baltimore: Williams and Williams, 1958.

Weinberg, W. T. *Perceived instrumentality as a determinant of achievement-related performance for groups of athletes and nonathletes.* Unpublished doctoral dissertation, University of Maryland, 1975.

Weiner, B. The effects of unsatisfied achievement motivation on persistence and subsequent performance. *Journal of Personality,* 1965, *33,* 428–442. Also in J. W. Atkinson & J. O. Raynor (Eds.), *Motivation and achievement.* Washington, D.C.: Hemisphere, 1974.

Weiner, B. Role of success and failure in the learning of easy and complex tasks. *Journal of Personality and Social Psychology,* 1966, *3,* 339–344.

Weiner, B. Implications of the current theory of achievement motivation for research and performance in the classroom. *Psychology in the Schools,* 1967, *4,* 164-171.

Weiner, B. *Theories of motivation.* Chicago: Rand-McNally, 1972.

Weiner, B. *Achievement motivation and attribution theory.* Morristown, N.J.: General Learning Press, 1974.

Weiner, B., Frieze, I., Kukla, A., Reed, L., Rest, S., & Rosenbaum, R. M. *Perceiving the causes of success and failure.* New York: General Learning Press, 1971.

Weiner, B., & Kukla, A. An attributional analysis of achievement motivation. *Journal of Personality and Social Psychology,* 1970, *15,* 1-20.

Weiner, B., Heckhausen, H., Meyer, W., & Cook, R. E. Causal ascriptions and achievement behavior: Conceptual analysis of effort and reanalysis of locus of control. *Journal of Personality and Social Psychology,* 1972, *21,* 239-248.

Weisstein, N. *"Kinder, kuche, kirche" as scientific law. Psychology constructs the female.* Boston: New England Free Press, 1968.

Weitzenkorn, S. D. An adjusted measure of achievement motivation for males and females and effects of future orientation on level of performance. *Journal of Research in Personality,* 1974, *8,* 361-377.

Wendt, H. W. Motivation, effort, and performance. In D. C. McClelland (Ed.), *Studies in motivation.* New York: Appleton-Century-Crofts, 1955.

White, R. *Lives in progress* (2nd ed.). New York: Holt, Rinehart and Winston, 1966.

Williams, J. *Psychology of women: Behavior in a biosocial context.* New York: Norton, 1977.

Williams, R. H., & Wirths, C. G. *Lives through the years.* New York: Atherton, 1965.

Winer, B. J. *Statistical principles in experimental design.* New York: McGraw-Hill, 1962.

Winterbottom, M. The relation of childhood training in independence to achievement motivation. In J. W. Atkinson (Ed.), *Motives in fantasy, action, and society.* Princeton: Van Nostrand, 1958.

Wolk, S., & Teleen, S. Psychological and sociological correlates of life satisfaction as a function of resident constraint. *Journal of Gerontology,* 1976, *31,* 89-98.

Wolosin, R. J., Sherman, S. J., & Till, A. Effects of cooperation and competition on responsibility attribution after success and failure. *Journal of Experimental Social Psychology,* 1973, *9,* 220-235.

Woodruff, D. S., & Birren, J. E. Age changes and cohort differences in personality. *Developmental Psychology,* 1972, *6,* 252-259.

Wortman, C. B., Costanzo, P. R., & Witt, T. R. Effect of anticipated performance on the attribution of causality to self and others. *Journal of Personality and Social Psychology,* 1973, *27,* 372-381.

Zajonc, R. B. Social facilitation. *Science,* 1965, *149,* 269-274.

Zeigarnik, B. Uber das Behalten von erledigten und unerledigten Handlungen. *Psychologisches Forschung,* 1927, *9,* 1-85.

Zytowski, D. G. Toward a theory of career development for women. *Personnel and Guidance Journal,* 1969, *47,* 660-664.

Author Index

Subject Index